Communications in Computer and Information Science   508

T0220840

More information about this series at http://www.springer.com/series/7899

Guadalupe Ortiz · Cuong Tran (Eds.)

Advances in Service-Oriented and Cloud Computing

Workshops of ESOCC 2014
Manchester, UK, September 2–4, 2014
Revised Selected Papers

 Springer

Editors
Guadalupe Ortiz
University of Cádiz
Puerto Real
Spain

Cuong Tran
The University of Manchester
Manchester
UK

ISSN 1865-0929   ISSN 1865-0937   (electronic)
Communications in Computer and Information Science
ISBN 978-3-319-14885-4   ISBN 978-3-319-14886-1   (eBook)
DOI 10.1007/978-3-319-14886-1

Library of Congress Control Number: 2015932139

Springer Cham Heidelberg New York Dordrecht London

Printed on acid-free paper

Springer International Publishing AG Switzerland is part of Springer Science+Business Media (www.springer.com)

Preface

This volume contains the technical papers presented in the four high-quality workshops associated with ESOCC 2014 (European Conference on Service-Oriented and Cloud Computing, held in Manchester, UK, on September 2–4, 2014), focusing on specific topics in domains related to service-oriented and cloud computing: 4th International Workshop on Adaptive Services for the Future Internet (WAS4FI 2014), 2nd International Workshop on Cloud for IoT (CLIoT 2014), 2nd International Workshop on Cloud Service Brokerage (CSB 2014), and Seamless Adaptive Multi-cloud Management of Service-based Applications (SeaCloudS Workshop). There were a total of 39 submissions, from which 22 papers were accepted giving an acceptance rate of 56 %. The review and selection process was performed rigorously, with each paper being reviewed by at least three Program Committee (PC) members. Here, a brief description of each workshop is given.

WAS4FI aims to address different aspects of adaptive Future Internet applications, emphasizing the importance of governing the convergence of contents, services, things, and networks in order to achieve building platforms for efficiency, scalability, security, and flexible adaptation. The Future Internet has emerged as a new initiative to pave a novel infrastructure linked to objects (things) of the real world to meet the changing global needs of business and society. It offers Internet users a standardized, secure, efficient, and trustable environment, which allows open and distributed access to global networks, services, and information. To be consistently adopted, the Future Internet will be enabled through standards-based notations for messaging, semantics, process, and state, enabling distributed systems and entities to be described in a scalable and flexible robust dynamic environment. Future Internet applications will have to support the interoperability between many diverse stakeholders by governing the convergence and life cycle of Internet of Contents (IoC), Services (IoS), Things (IoT), and Networks (IoN). These applications should handle dynamic and continuous change and they should also bear in mind that the Future Internet should provide a better experience for the user journey, with personalized and context-aware contents, adapted to their preferences, and where users also play an active part in creating or sharing services. The first part of this volume comprises all the technical papers of WAS4FI 2014.

CLIoT focuses on the limits and advantages of existing cloud solutions for IoT, proposing original and innovative contributions for enhancing real-world resources over cloud environments. The Internet of Things (IoT) aims to represent the physical world through uniquely identifiable and interconnected objects (things), allowing interactions or generating events about them. Thus, information travels along heterogeneous systems, such as routers, databases, information systems, and the Internet. In turn, this leads to the generation and movement of enormous amounts of data which have to be stored, processed, and presented in a seamless, efficient, and easily interpretable form. In this regard, cloud computing represents a very flexible technology, able to offer theoretically unlimited computing and storage capabilities, and efficient communication services for transferring terabyte flows between data centers. All these features make cloud computing a promising choice for supporting IoT services: the cloud allows to access IoT-based resources and capabilities, to process and manage IoT environments and to deliver on-demand utility IoT services such as sensing/actuation as a service. CLIoT also enjoyed an additional keynote talk by Orazio Tomarchio (University of Catania) entitled "A semantic framework for matching business requirements in cloud markets." The second part of this volume comprises all the technical papers of CLIoT 2014.

CSB looks to a future in which a multi-cloud ecosystem exists, within which many cloud providers and consumers interact to create, discover, negotiate, and use software services. Supporting this ecosystem are cloud brokers, whose role is to bring together providers and consumers, by offering service portals with added value for all parties. A central feature of the brokers, role will be to assist with software service generation (from abstract models to platform-specific deployments), multi-cloud translation (model-driven adaptation and deployment of services), and assure quality control (governance; functional testing and monitoring), service continuity (failure prevention and recovery; service substitution), and market competition (arbitrage; service optimization; service customization). To promote the creation of this kind of ecosystem, it is necessary to develop common standards, methods, and mechanisms that will operate across a wide variety of platforms and infrastructure, and across disparate service protocols, which currently include: WSDL/SOAP-based services, RESTful services, and Rich Client/AJAX applications. The third part of this volume comprises all the technical papers of CSB 2014.

The objective of the SeaCloudS workshop is to discuss problems, solutions, and perspectives of the ongoing research activities aimed at enabling an efficient and adaptive management of service-based applications across multiple clouds. Deploying and managing in an efficient and adaptive way complex service-based applications across multiple heterogeneous clouds is one of the problems that has emerged with the cloud revolution. The current lack of universally accepted standards supporting cloud interoperability is severely affecting the portability of cloud-based applications across different platforms. SeaClouds also enjoyed an invited talk by Alex Heneveld (Cloudsoft) entitled "Going to CAMP via Apache Brooklyn," a round table on multi-cloud interoperability, and a session devoted to presentations of ongoing EU research projects. The fourth part of this volume comprises all the technical papers of Sea-CloudS workshop.

The program also included the shared opening keynote by Simon Moser (IBM) entitled "From TOSCA landscapes to the Foundry - A walkthrough."

Special thanks go to the workshop organizers, as well as to the authors, keynote speakers, and participants. We also want to thank the main conference organizers for their support all along the process.

November 2014   Guadalupe Ortiz
                                                                 Cuong Tran

Organization

ESOCC 2014 was organized by the School of Computer Science of The University of Manchester (UK).

Contents

CSB 2014

SeaCloudS 2014

WAS4FI 2014

4th International Workshop on Adaptive Services for the Future Internet (WAS4FI 2014): Preface

Javier Cubo[1]($\boxtimes$), Juan Boubeta-Puig[2], Howard Foster[3], Winfried Lamersdorf[4], and Nadia Gámez[1]

[1] University of Málaga, Málaga, Spain
cubo@lcc.uma.es
[2] University of Cádiz, Cádiz, Spain
[3] City University London, London, UK
[4] University of Hamburg, Hamburg, Germany

The Future Internet has emerged as a new initiative to pave a novel infrastructure linked to objects (things) of the real world to meet the changing global needs of business and society. It offers internet users a standardized, secure, efficient and trustable environment, which allows open and distributed access to global networks, services and information. There is a need for both researchers and practitioners to develop platforms made up of adaptive Future Internet applications. In this sense, the emergence and consolidation of Service-Oriented Architectures (SOA), Cloud Computing and Wireless Sensor Networks (WSN) give benefits, such as flexibility, scalability, security, interoperability, and adaptability, for building these applications.

WAS4FI encourages a multidisciplinary perspective and welcomes papers that address challenges of Future Internet applications. Participation of researchers and practitioners from academia and industry are encouraged in order to promote cross-community interactions and thus avoiding disconnection between these groups. As the proud organising committee and chairs of the 4th International Workshop on Adaptive Services for the Future Internet, we would like to take this opportunity to welcome you to WAS4FI 2014.

In this fourth edition, WAS4FI again aims to bring together the community at ESOCC and addresses different aspects of adaptive Future Internet applications, emphasizing the importance of governing the convergence of contents, services, things and networks in order to achieve building platforms for efficiency, scalability, security and flexible adaptation. In this workshop, we cover the foundations of the aforementioned technologies as well as new emerging proposals for their potential in Future Internet services. To promote collaboration, WAS4FI has a highly interactive format with short technical sessions complemented by discussions on Adaptive Services in the Future Internet Applications.

The broad scope of WAS4FI is reflected in the wide range of topics covered by the 12 submissions that we received. Of these, with the 23 members of the WAS4FI Program Committee from both academic and industrial research

G. Ortiz and C. Tran (Eds.): ESOCC 2014, CCIS 508, pp. 3–5, 2015.
DOI: 10.1007/978-3-319-14886-1_1

labs, we selected 6 research papers. These papers are grouped into two sessions, representing two key themes of Adaptive Services for the Future Internet. The two session themes are:

1. Service Matching, Elastic Scalability and SLA
2. Service Network and Business Processes

We hope that this workshop will be an enjoyable and productive opportunity for you to meet and discuss various adaptive services and future internet issues with your counterparts from other countries and other industrial segments.

We would like to thank all the people who contributed to make this workshop a reality, including the WAS4FI Program Committee, the ESOCC 2014 Workshop Chairs Guadalupe Ortiz and Cuong Tran and all the presenters, authors and participants. Again welcome to WAS4FI, and enjoy your time here.

Javier
Juan
Howard
Winfried
Nadia
WAS4FI 2014 Chairs

Organization

Organizing Committee

Javier Cubo, University of Málaga, Spain
Juan Boubeta-Puig, University of Cádiz, Spain
Howard Foster, City University London, United Kingdom
Winfried Lamersdorf, University of Hamburg, Germany
Nadia Gámez, University of Málaga, Spain

Programme Committee

Marco Aiello, University of Groningen, The Netherlands
Vasilios Andrikopoulos, University of Stuttgart, Germany
Antonio Brogi, University of Pisa, Italy
Florian Daniel, University of Trento, Italy
Valeria de Castro, Universidad Rey Juan Carlos, Spain
Gregorio Díaz, Universidad de Castilla La Mancha, Spain
Schahram Dustdar, Vienna University of Technology, Austria
Nadia Gámez, University of Málaga, Spain
Laura González, Universidad de la República, Uruguay
Alberto Lluch Lafuente, Technical University of Denmark, Denmark
Tiziana Margaria, University of Potsdam, Germany

Massimo Mecella, Univ. Roma La Sapienza, Italy
Raffaela Mirandola, Politecnico di Milano, Italy
Claus Pahl, Dublin City University, Ireland
Ernesto Pimentel, University of Málaga, Spain
Pascal Poizat, Universitél Paris Ouest, France
Franco Raimondi, Middlesex University, United Kingdom
Gustavo Rossi, Universidad Nacional de La Plata, Argentina
Romain Rouvoy, University of Lille 1, France
Antonio Ruiz-Cortés, University of Sevilla, Spain
Quanzheng Sheng, The University of Adelaide, Australia
Massimo Tivoli, University of L'Aquila, Italy
Gianluigi Zavattaro, University of Bologna, Italy

Matching of Incomplete Service Specifications Exemplified by Privacy Policy Matching

Marie Christin Platenius[1]([✉]), Svetlana Arifulina[2], Ronald Petrlic[2],
and Wilhelm Schäfer[1]

[1] Heinz Nixdorf Institute, Paderborn, Germany
{m.platenius,wilhelm}@upb.de
[2] Department of Computer Science, University of Paderborn, Paderborn, Germany
{s.arifulina,ronald.petrlic}@upb.de

Abstract. Service matching approaches determine to what extent a provided service matches a requester's requirements. This process is based on service specifications describing functional (e.g., signatures) as well as non-functional properties (e.g., privacy policies). However, we cannot expect service specifications to be complete as providers do not want to share all details of their services' implementation. Moreover, creating complete specifications requires much effort. In this paper, we propose a novel service matching approach taking into account a service's signatures and privacy policies. In particular, our approach applies fuzzy matching techniques that are able to deal with incomplete service specifications. As a benefit, decision-making based on matching results is improved and service matching becomes better applicable in practice.

Keywords: Service discovery · Service matching · Fuzzy matching · Fuzziness · Uncertainty · Privacy policy matching

1 Introduction

Nowadays, service providers provide software components in the form of services in service markets. In order to buy and use those services, service requesters have to discover services that fit their requirements. For this reason, service brokers apply *service matching* approaches that determine to what extent a provided service's specification matches a requester's requirements [11]. Service matching is the most accurate if many different properties of a service are considered [6]. This means, not only functional properties including structural and behavioral information should be described and matched but also several non-functional properties. For example, in this paper, we focus on service specifications including signatures and privacy policies.

Current service matching approaches come with the problem that they assume specifications to be complete with all considered service properties specified in

---

This work was supported by the German Research Foundation (DFG) within the Collaborative Research Center "On-The-Fly Computing" (CRC 901).

G. Ortiz and C. Tran (Eds.): ESOCC 2014, CCIS 508, pp. 6–17, 2015.
DOI: 10.1007/978-3-319-14886-1_2

detail. However, in the real world, we cannot expect service specifications to be perfect or complete for several reasons [12]. One of the reasons is that providers often do not know all information about their services. For example, quality properties (e.g., response time) are hard to judge if they depend on third-party servers. In addition, providers may not want to share everything in order to protect business interests. Furthermore, creating detailed and machine-readable specifications costs much effort. Especially if they are not used to it, it is hard to convince people to work on such specifications. Current matching approaches are not able to deal with such incomplete specifications and return false matching results in the presence of incompleteness. This leads to requesters rejecting actually fitting services or accepting unfitting services without knowing that the matching result is uncertain.

We propose a novel service matching approach that extends traditional signature and privacy policy matching by applying fuzzy matching techniques. In particular, our approach is able to deal with incomplete service specifications as it reflects the grade of incompleteness in a *fuzziness score*. The contribution of this paper is twofold: On the one hand, it provides an improved approach for service brokers that allows better decision-making during service selection. On the other hand, it represents a first step to bring service matching into practice, coping with real world assumptions like incomplete specifications.

The remainder of this paper is structured as follows. In Sects. 2 and 3, we describe the service specifications for signatures and privacy policies and how they are matched as a foundation. Section 4 motivates fuzzy matching and explains how we cope with it. Section 5 describes a concrete application of fuzzy matching to privacy policies. In Sect. 6, we briefly summarize related work and we conclude the paper in Sect. 7.

2   Service and Request Specification

As a running example, we consider a market where service providers offer different software services for university management. In order to find a suitable service, a service requester specifies her requirements, e.g., the requirements for a service that prints out an overview of grades. Such a request has to be matched to the specifications of the available provided services.

We specify services using our Service Specification Language (SSL) [14] because it has been optimized for efficient and accurate matching of comprehensive service specifications. It describes different service properties including structural information, behavioral information, and non-functional properties of a service. In this paper, we only focus on two aspects: signatures and privacy.

A signature describes the inputs and outputs of a service's operation. For example, the signature presented in the middle part of Fig. 1 describes the operation `printOverview` of the provided service `OverviewOfGradesPrinter` with two input parameters (`grades` of type `List` and `id` of type `ID`) and one output parameter (`diagram` of type `Diagram`). All data types used in the signature are defined by ontological concepts that represent knowledge of different domains

Provided Service: OverviewOfGradesPrinter

Signature:
printOverview(List grades, ID id) : Diagram diagram

Privacy Policies:

Parameter	Purpose	Delegation Depth	Retention Period	Visibility	Location Limit
grades	Visualization	0	12		Germany
id	Visualization	0	12		Germany
diagram	Visualization	0	0		Germany

Provided Service: Visuals4Grades

Signature:
printGrades(List grades,ID id):Diagram diagram

Privacy Policies:

Param.	Purpose	Del. Depth	Ret. Period	Vis.	Location Limit
grades	Visualization	0	?		Germany
id	Visualization	0	?		Germany
diagram	Visualization	0	?		Germany

Request

Signature:
printOverview(List studentGrades, UniversityID studentID, MailAddress address) : Graph overview

Privacy Requirements:

Parameter	Purpose	Delegation Depth	Retention Period	Visibility	Location Limit	Sensitivity
studentGrades	Visualization	*	0		Europe	Very High
studentID	Visualization	0	12		Europe	High
address	Contact	1	12	Notification Services	Europe	Medium
overview	Visualization	0	0		Europe	Very High

Fig. 1. Example ontologies, a specification of a provided service, and a request

including concepts and relations between these concepts. For example, the upper part of Fig. 1 depicts extracts of ontologies for the domains of visualization, contact, university, and locations.

Our privacy specifications are based on an integration of several existing languages. Most parts follow the principles of the privacy policy model by Costante et al. [4,5] including further elements from the approaches presented by Kapitsaki [8] and Tbahriti et al. [16]. We adapted, united, and extended these approaches and integrated them into SSL. In particular, we connected the privacy specification to the above described signature specification.

The middle part of Fig. 1 depicts the privacy specification of OverviewOf-GradesPrinter in a tabular notation. Each row in this table represents a privacy policy. Each privacy policy refers to a parameter from the service's signature and specifies what kind of usage regarding the data corresponding to this parameter is permitted. In our example specifications, every parameter of the signature is covered: the two input parameters grades und id and the output parameter diagram. The columns represent the different restrictions that can be specified for a policy:

Purpose defines the reason for the collection of the corresponding data and its usage [4]. For example, the policies for all depicted parameters are related to the purpose of Visualization. All other kinds of usage of grades, id, and diagram are not allowed for OverviewOfGradesPrinter. All terms used as purpose have to be defined in an ontology. A parameter may also appear in several policies with different purposes.

Delegation Depth refers to the amount of levels (i.e., services) a parameter may be forwarded to. This becomes relevant if a service is used as part of a composition. The privacy policy for OverviewOfGradesPrinter is very strict with respect to delegation as it allows no delegation of the given data at all. The default range for delegation depth is [0,10] [4]. Additionally, the values undefined and infinity are supported.

Retention Period defines for how long (here: how many months) the service will store given data. The more privacy-critical a parameter is, the more critical it is to store it. However, storage may be necessary in order to perform certain purposes. For example, for hotel reservation services, much data has to be stored for billing purposes. In our example, the OverviewOfGradesPrinter stores the grades as well as the id for 12 months. This is due to the provided functionality to create visualizations of comparisons of the grades of different terms. For retention period, we support values in [0,100] as well as undefined and infinity.

Visibility allows providers to restrict a policy to a set of service providers, service categories, or even specific services. For example, one can allow certain data to be visible only to services provided by Google, only to notification services, or only to the Google Alert Service.

Location Limit restricts privacy policies with respect to a location. For example, for the OverviewOfGradesPrinter, the provided data may only be processed in Germany. This also holds for delegated data. The location limit field can contain one or more terms defined in an underlying ontology of locations. Thus, the granularity of values (e.g., cities vs. countries vs. continents) depends on the ontology used.

We consider specifications that specify all properties listed above as complete. If any property is not specified, a specification is *incomplete*. For example, the provider of the second service in Fig. 1, Visuals4Grades, did not provide any information about retention periods.

A requester specifies her privacy requirements with the same concepts (see lower part of Fig. 1). In addition, she specifies a column *Sensitivity*. Thereby, the requester can define the importance of each requirement. She can choose between "very low", "low", "medium", "high", "very high", and "mandatory".

Please note that Fig. 1 only shows extracts of the complete specifications that can contain much more information, e.g., more detailed information about the service's behavior.

3   Service Matching

In order to decide to what extent provided services satisfy a given request and to find out which one fits best, the services' specifications are matched to the request. Matching is performed using a stepwise matching process. In general, our matching process includes comparisons of structural requirements, behavioral requirements, and requirements for different non-functional properties [12]. In this paper, we focus on two steps of the matching process: Signature Matching and Privacy Matching. The lower part of Fig. 1 illustrates an exemplary specification of the request from our running example. In the following, we explain how this request is matched to the provided specification of OverviewOfGradesPrinter.

3.1 Ontological Signature Matching

Our signature matching approach follows the principles of established signature and semantic matching approaches [9, 10, 15]. In addition, our matcher is configurable and can take into account different parts of a signature, e.g., operation names, parameter types, parameter names, optional parameters, and exceptions. In this paper, we focus on signature matching based on parameter types.

The parameters are matched based on the rules for contravariance and covariance. This means, two signatures match if (a) the set of input parameters of the provided service's signature is a subset of the input parameters of the requested service's signature and (b) the set of output parameters of the requested service's signature is a subset of the output parameters of the provided service's signature. To achieve this, the signature matcher compares all parameter types of the two signatures pairwise, applying bipartite graph matching. Each data type pair is matched based on the referenced ontologies. Two parameter types match if (a) the input parameter type in the requested service's signature is either equivalent or more specific (i.e., a subclass) than the corresponding input parameter type in the provided service's signature and (b) the output parameter type of the provided service's signature is either equivalent or more specific than the output parameter type in the requested service's signature. For example, in the ontologies depicted in Fig. 1, the concept UniversityID is more specific than the concept ID and Graph is equivalent to Diagram. For our running example, this means, the matcher determines the following matching pairs:

- requester's input studentGrades and provider's input grades
- requester's input studentID and provider's input id
- requester's output overview and provider's output diagram

As all output parameters of the requester signature found a match and all input parameters of the provider signature found a match, the two signatures match 100 %. This result, including the determined parameter pairs, is an input to the subsequent privacy matching step.

3.2 Privacy Policy Matching

The privacy policies of a provided service match the privacy requirements of a request if the provided policies are more strict than the requested ones. For this purpose, the matching algorithm iterates over the requirements (rows) of

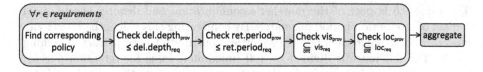

Fig. 2. Privacy matching algorithm

the requester's specification and checks all the columns as depicted in Fig. 2:
(1.) Find a corresponding policy in the provider's specification based on the
parameter pairs created during signature matching and the specified purposes.
(2.) Match delegation depth and (3.) retention period: both checks succeed if the
provider's value is lower or equal than the requester's value. (4.) Match visibility
and (5.) location limits: both succeed if the provider's values are a subset of the
requester's values, using an ontology to find relations between values. At the
end, the final matching result is aggregated taking into account the requester's
sensitivity specifications; the final result is a value between 0 (does not match
at all) and 1 (matches perfectly).

For our running example, these five steps work as follows:

(1.) Based on the preceding signature matching and an ontology-based matching of the purposes, we know that the studentGrades policy of the request corresponds to the grades policy of the provider's specification. Furthermore, the
studentID policy of the request corresponds to the id policy of the provider's
specification and the overview policy corresponds to the diagram policy. As the
parameter address has not been assigned during signature matching, there has to
be no corresponding policy for the requester's address requirement. As a consequence, this requirement is ignored as always holds: since address is not taken
as an input, its privacy requirements cannot be violated. (2.) In our example,
all requirements match with respect to delegation depth as the provider's specification is very strict in this context $(0 \leq *, 0 \leq 0, 0 \leq 0)$. (3.) Retention
period matches for studentID $(12 \leq 12)$ and for overview $(0 \leq 0)$. However,
for studentGrades, the requester's retention period is stricter $(12 \geq 0)$. This
is considered a mismatch. (4.) The visibility restrictions match if the visibility
restrictions of the provider are a subset of the allowed visibilities of the requester.
For our running example, this is the case for the three policies to be considered.
(5.) Furthermore, these policies also match regarding the location limit because
the locations specified in the provider's policies are part of the locations specified
by the requester $(Germany \leq Europe)$. This relation is defined in the underlying
ontology (see upper part of Fig. 1).

Due to the retention period mismatch in one of the policies, the final result
for our example must be less than 1. The concrete value is calculated as follows: Each policy starts with a result of 1. This result is reduced with each
mismatch depending on the difference. For example, because of the retention
period mismatch above, we calculate the result for the studentGrades pol-
icy as follows: $result_{policy} = 1 - min(1, 0.5 + ((providerRetentionPeriod - requesterRetentionPeriod)/100)) = 1 - min(1, 0.5 + ((12 - 0)/100)) = 0.38$.

The value 0.5 is part of the matcher's configuration and denotes the minimal impact of a retention period mismatch. By configuring this value, the broker can customize how much each of the properties contribute to the privacy matching result. The difference is divided by 100 (maximum value for retention period) for normalization. The results for the policies are aggregated to a final result for the whole privacy aspect. For this, we use a weighted average about the results of each policy multiplied with a multiplier corresponding to its sensitivity level. The higher the sensitivity level, the larger is the multiplier ("very low" $= 0.2$, "low" $= 0.4$, "medium" $= 0.6$, "high" $= 0.8$, "very high" $= 1$). For policies with the sensitivity "mandatory", any kind of mismatch results in a matching result of 0. According to these values, for our example, we have the following aggregation function: $finalresult = (result_{studentGrades} \cdot 1 + result_{studentID} \cdot 0.8 + result_{overview} \cdot 1)/(1 + 0.8 + 1) = 0.78$. In addition to the final, numerical matching result, the requester can be provided with a detailed log about the matching process including a list of all mismatches.

4   Fuzziness in Service Matching

Current service matching approaches work fine if we count on several assumptions including that the providers share all information about their services and specify them in detail. As discussed in Sect. 1, there are several reasons for doubting this. However, when dropping these assumptions, uncertainty or *fuzziness* can be induced in service matching. Induced fuzziness leads to the fact that current matching approaches potentially deliver false results or even cannot be applied at all. In our earlier work, we describe different fuzziness sources [12,13]. In this paper, we focus on *provider-induced fuzziness*, i.e., the case of incomplete specifications.

Coping with fuzziness in service matching leads to the problem that we require some kind of measurement in order to enable assessing the risk for fuzziness of a matching result. As an example, consider Fig. 1. With current matching approaches, both services, OverviewOfGradesPrinter and Visuals4Grades, would receive a very similar matching result considering the depicted request because in both cases, retention periods do not match. However, in the first case, we are certain that there is a mismatch, while, in the second case, we are uncertain, and the service could potentially match completely. For a requester, the second service would be a better choice as it matches at least as good as the other one, but, probably, even better. Because of such uncertainties, we propose that matchers should not only determine and output the matching result but also a *fuzziness score* reflecting the confidence a requester can have regarding the delivered matching result.

There are some requirements such fuzziness scores should satisfy:

– Normalization: For the requester, it should always be clear whether a returned fuzziness score is low or high. This means, the maximum possible fuzziness score and the minimum possible fuzziness score should be known.

- Comparability: Fuzziness scores calculated for different services need to be comparable. For example, if the requester chooses between two services based on matching results of $m_{serviceA} = 90\%$ and $m_{serviceB} = 95\%$ and fuzziness scores of $f_{serviceA} = 10\%$ and $f_{serviceB} = 50\%$, it should make sense to choose $serviceA$ because its matching result is very close to the best available matching result while it is the less fuzzy one.
- Severity: The severity of fuzziness should be reflected in the fuzziness score. For example, if fuzziness occurs in a part of the specification that is irrelevant for the matching result, it should be ignored.

Our idea is to let each matching step return one fuzziness score and to aggregate these at the end to get a final fuzziness score. Thereby, the fuzziness measurements can leverage the specifics of each matching step best in order to fulfill the mentioned requirements, as we will show in the next section.

5 Fuzzy Matching of Incomplete Privacy Policies

In the example of privacy, a provider has to provide policies by law. However, this still does not mean that she also provides a formal representation as required for matching and that this representation includes all properties used during the matching process. In this section, we apply the fuzzy matching concepts introduced in Sect. 4 to privacy matching based on incomplete specifications.

5.1 Considering Incompleteness During Matching

In the presence of incomplete specifications, the matching approach has two possibilities to take into account missing values. (1) The optimistic case is to consider all missing information on the provider side as the most strict case, e.g., retention period $= 0$. This potentially increases the number of false positives. This means, the matcher returns a high matching result although, in reality, the service does not match. (2) The pessimistic case is to substitute missing information with the least strict case, e.g., retention period $= *$. This can lead to false negatives because, in uncertain cases, the matcher might return low matching results although, in reality, the service would be a good match. The choice whether to use a pessimistic or an optimistic approach depends on the broker's strategy and the risk affinity of the requesters.

5.2 Measuring Fuzziness Scores

There are different ways to measure incompleteness in privacy policies such that the returned fuzziness score satisfies the requirements mentioned above. In this paper, we describe one selected algorithm. The algorithm takes the mapping of requirements to corresponding provided policies, as determined during signature matching, as an input. It builds upon the privacy matching algorithm as it iterates through the specified concepts in similar ways.

For each requirement, the algorithm checks, whether one of the requested properties is not specified at the provider's side. In general, the more values are missing at the provider's side, the higher is the fuzziness score. If nothing is missing, the fuzziness score is 0. If everything is missing (the provider didn't specify privacy policies at all), the fuzziness score is 1.

The fuzziness score for privacy matching is an aggregation of fuzziness scores for the different policies. A policy's score grows with respect to (a) the requester's sensitivity for this policy and (b) the weight assigned according to the severity of the provider's restrictions. The rationale for taking sensitivity into account is as follows: if a policy cannot be checked due to incompleteness and the requester's sensitivity regarding this policy is very high, the fuzziness is critical; if his sensitivity for this policy is rather low, fuzziness is less critical. The rationale for taking the severity into account is as follows: if a requester allows an infinite delegation depth (or retention period) for a certain policy, it does not matter if the provider's delegation depth for this policy is not specified; but if a requester is very strict and specified an allowed delegation depth of 0, fuzziness induced by the missing provider's delegation depth is much more critical.

As an example, consider the specification of Visuals4Grades and the request depicted in Fig. 1. Note that the provider did not specify any retention periods. The fuzziness score of the grades policy will be calculated as follows: $f_{grades} = 1 \cdot 1 = 1$, with the first 1 being a constant assigned to the requester's sensitivity value "very high" (see Sect. 3.2) of the corresponding studentGrades policy and the second 1 being a constant corresponding to the minimum value 0 that the requester specified for retention period. Accordingly, the fuzziness score of the id policy will be calculated as follows: $f_{id} = 0.8 \cdot 0.8 = 0.64$, with 0.8 being the constant assigned to the sensitivity "high" and 0.8 being a constant corresponding to a medium low value 12 the requester specified for retention period in this policy. As a result, the fuzziness value for the grades policy is lower because the requester required a very strict policy for grades, while she specified a less strict policy with respect to retention period for id.

As we see in this example, the requirements *Severity* as well as *Comparability* are satisfied. As a foundation for *Comparability* and with all fuzziness values determined by this approach being normalized to a value between 0 and 1, the requirement *Normalization* is satisfied as well.

5.3   Case Study

We implemented our specification and matching approaches including the presented algorithm to measure incompleteness within an Eclipse-based tool-suite. Using this implementation, we evaluated the concepts presented in this paper together with privacy experts from the CRC 901 "On-The-Fly Computing" [17]. Our evaluation question was: how well do the results returned by our approach support a requester in deciding for a service. For this, we performed our fuzzy privacy matching approach on 21 pairs of example specifications and requests from the university management domain. For all these pairs, we first determined the matching results manually by expert knowledge, based on complete specifications. After that, we ran our approach on incomplete versions of these specifications. After that, the experts' matching results based on full knowledge were compared to the results the matcher determined for the incomplete specifications. Thereby, we could determine correct matches (calculated matching result was equal to the expert's result, i.e., a true positive or a true negative) as well as mismatches (calculated matching result was not equal to the expert's result, i.e., a false positive or a false negative). Precision turned out to be 0.714 and recall was 1. Furthermore, we measured fuzziness scores and compared them to the matching results. The case study's results showed that the fuzziness scores for true positives and true negatives were rather low while the results for false positives and false negatives were comparatively high in 95 % of all cases. Based on a selection strategy that does not select services with a high (>0.5) fuzziness score, true positives have been reduced. Accordingly, the precision has been increased to 0.857. This result suggests to answer the evaluation question with "yes" as the determined fuzziness scores can contribute to an improved decision-making. In the future, we plan to evaluate our approach more extensively, taking into account more examples and more evaluation questions.

6   Related Work

Many approaches about service matching have already been published. The novelty of our approach is the combination of privacy matching and ontological signature matching considering fuzzy techniques to handle incomplete specifications. Thus, approaches considered related to our work are, on the one hand, privacy matching approaches, and, on the other hand, matching approaches that are able to handle incomplete service specifications.

There are many privacy matching approaches. The approach closest to our approach is the approach presented by Costante et al. [4,5], which is also a foundation for our work. For example, the concepts of purpose, delegation depth, retention period, visibility, and sensitivity are based on their work. However, we added our own notions of ontology references and the connections to signatures and signature matching. In addition, their approach focuses on service composition, while we only focus on matching and provide additional concepts of fuzzy matching. Costante's original approach does not deal with incomplete specifications. The same differences hold for the works of Kapitsaki [8] and Tbahriti [16]. Further similar approaches are semantic matching approaches for WS-Policy specifications [3,18]. Although these specifications describe rather security-related properties [18] or other quality properties [3] instead of privacy, the presented matching approaches are based on ontologies, as well. However, these approaches do not address the challenge of matching incomplete specifications and quantifying fuzziness occurring during fuzzy matching.

The challenge of matching incomplete service specifications has not been focussed in literature up to now. In our earlier work [13], we surveyed fuzzy matching approaches in general and came to the conclusion that the quantification of fuzziness, especially in the presence of incomplete specifications, is still an open issue. There are some approaches that consider incomplete knowledge at the provider's side, e.g., [1] or [19], however, they do not quantify and return this incompleteness. Instead, the matching result is "adulterated" and does not provide the requester with information about uncertainty or its severity. Furthermore, these approaches deal with rather simple specifications without considering different characteristics of quality properties like our privacy specification does. Other approaches deal with incomplete specifications by trying to extract them either from a service's implementation or from other parts from the specification. For example, StrawBerry synthesizes protocols [2]. This is no substitute for measuring and returning fuzziness scores and it probably does not work for all kinds of service properties, but it could reduce the induced fuzziness. Thus, it would be interesting to combine such approaches with ours. Similarly, component adaption approaches (e.g., [7]) could be used to enforce requested properties, e.g., delegation depth, in case of uncertainty.

To conclude, although there are many service matching approaches that can be used for privacy policy matching and service matching in general, the challenge of matching incomplete specifications and reflecting incompleteness is the matching result is new.

7   Conclusions

In this paper, we propose a service matching approach for combined signatures and privacy policies matching using fuzzy matching techniques. In particular, in addition to returning matching results, our approach measures and returns fuzziness score representing the degree of fuzziness induced by incomplete service specifications. This fuzziness score reflects the extent and criticality of the occurring fuzziness and, thereby, improves the service requester's decision-making. In general, the benefit is a novel service matching approach doing first steps to make service matching applicable in practice by reducing the assumptions existing service matching approaches make.

In the future, we want to learn more about how to improve our fuzzy matching concepts by applying them to other service aspects. For example, incompleteness at the provider side could occur if the service's reputation is matched: If a service is new in the market, then there are only few or no ratings.

Acknowledgments. We would like to thank Shafi Vijapurwala for contributing to our algorithm for measuring incompleteness in privacy specifications.

References

1. Bacciu, D., Buscemi, M., Mkrtchyan, L.: Adaptive fuzzy-valued service selection, pp. 2467–2471. ACM (2010)
2. Bertolino, A., Inverardi, P., Pelliccione, P., Tivoli, M.: Automatic synthesis of behavior protocols for composable web-services. In: Proceedings of the the 7th Joint Meeting of the European Software Engineering Conference and the ACM SIGSOFT Symposium on the Foundations of Software Engineering. ACM (2009)

3. Chaari, S., Badr, Y., Biennier, F.: Enhancing web service selection by QoS-based ontology and WS-policy. In: Proceedings of the 2008 ACM Symposium on Applied Computing, pp. 2426–2431. ACM (2008)
4. Constante, E., Paci, F., Zannone, N.: Privacy-aware web service composition and ranking. In: IEEE 20th International Conference on Web Services (ICWS), pp. 131–138. IEEE (2013)
5. Costante, E., Paci, F., Zannone, N.: Privacy-aware web service composition and ranking. Int. J. Web Serv. Res. (IJWSR) **10**(3), 1–23 (2013)
6. Cubo, J., Pimentel, E.: On the service discovery using context-awareness, semantic matching and behavioural compatibility. In: IEEE 15th International Conference on Computational Science and Engineering. IEEE (2012)
7. Gay, R., Mantel, H., Sprick, B.: Service automata. In: Barthe, G., Datta, A., Etalle, S. (eds.) FAST 2011. LNCS, vol. 7140, pp. 148–163. Springer, Heidelberg (2012)
8. Kapitsaki, G.M.: Reflecting user privacy preferences in context-aware web services. In: IEEE 20th International Conference on Web Services (ICWS). IEEE (2013)
9. Klusch, M., Kapahnke, P.: The iSeM matchmaker: A flexible approach for adaptive hybrid semantic service selection. J. Web Semant. Sci. Serv. Agents World Wide Web **15**, 1–14 (2012)
10. Moser, O., Rosenberg, F., Dustdar, S.: Domain-specific service selection for composite services. Trans. Softw. Eng. **38**(4), 828–843 (2012)
11. Papazoglou, M.P., Van Den Heuvel, W.-J.: Service oriented architectures: approaches, technologies and research issues. VLDB J. **16**, 389–415 (2007)
12. Platenius, M.C.: Fuzzy service matching in on-the-fly computing. In: Proceedings of the 9th Joint Meeting of the European Software Engineering Conference and the ACM SIGSOFT Symposium on the Foundations of Software Engineering (2013)
13. Platenius, M.C., von Detten, M., Becker, S., Schäfer, W., Engels, G.: A survey of fuzzy service matching approaches in the context of on-the-fly computing. In: Proceedings of the 16th International ACM Sigsoft Symposium on Component-Based Software Engineering (2013)
14. SSE Development Team. Service Specification Environment - Website. http://goo.gl/E7QjPN. Last Access May 2014
15. Stroulia, E., Wang, Y.: Structural and semantic matching for assessing web-service similarity. Int. J. Coop. Inf. Syst. **14**(04), 407–437 (2005)
16. Tbahriti, S.-E., Medjahed, B., Ghedira, C., Benslimane, D., Mrissa, M.: Respecting privacy in web service composition. In: 2013 IEEE 20th International Conference on Web Services (ICWS), pp. 139–146. IEEE (2013)
17. University of Paderborn. Collaborative Research Center "On-the-Fly Computing" (CRC 901). http://sfb901.uni-paderborn.de. Last Access Apr 2014
18. Verma, K., Akkiraju, R., Goodwin, R.: Semantic matching of web service policies. In: Proceedings of the Second Workshop on SDWP, pp. 79–90 (2005)
19. Wang, P.: QoS-aware web services selection with intuitionistic fuzzy set under consumer's vague perception. Expert Syst. Appl. **36**(3), 4460–4466 (2009)

Implementing Elastic Capacity in a Service-Oriented PaaS

Alberto Zuccato[(✉)] and Tullio Vardanega

Department of Mathematics, University of Padova, Padova, Italy
{azuccato,tullio.vardanega}@math.unipd.it

Abstract. In their quest for elastic capacity that balances resource lease at the infrastructure level with quality of service at the top, SaaS providers have a hard time at mapping application requirements onto infrastructure performance indicators. The role of a pure service-oriented platform layer to that regard has not been completely investigated and still less exploited. In this paper we illustrate a case study in which we enabled elastic scalability within an existing SOA cloud platform prototype: PaaSSOA. The latter integration and its subsequent tests allowed us to demonstrate the potential benefits arising from exploiting SOA and PaaS capabilities together, especially to release SaaS providers from the burden of reserving infrastructure capacity to met SLAs and of managing web application.

Keywords: Service oriented architecture · Cloud computing · Platform as a service · Elastic scalability · Service level agreement · Inference engine

1   Introduction

With the advent of cloud computing, more and more companies are migrating to the cloud model to reduce the cost of possession and management related to hardware infrastructure, software OSs, development platform, and line-of-business software. As a consequence of this shift of mentality, providers offering cloud services strive to streamline and optimize the use of their resources in order to enforce quality of service stipulated with users, and increase their profit.

Especially important for independent SaaS providers, those who typically offer web applications as a service and whose offering is not part of a vertical solution, is to reduce costs by optimizing the use of their infrastructure resources. The infrastructure resources, whether on-premise or acquired as a cloud service (IaaS), are needed by the SaaS provider to sustain the (unpredictable) load determined by users of the web applications. However, the provider would like to avoid over-provisioning resources so as to take advantage of the infrastructure in the most cost-effective way (e.g. by enabling Elastic Scalability).

In order to maximise its economic margin, the SaaS provider must strike a dynamic compromise between the service-level agreement (SLA) attached to the customer request profile and the infrastructure provisioning cost. The SaaS

© Springer International Publishing Switzerland 2015
G. Ortiz and C. Tran (Eds.): ESOCC 2014, CCIS 508, pp. 18–30, 2015.
DOI: 10.1007/978-3-319-14886-1_3

provider must enforce the SLA maintaining the appropriate QoS as stipulated in the service contract, which obviously disallows or penalizes under-provisioning. On the flip side, the SaaS provider must also avoid over-provisioning infrastructure, so as to keep financial reward. In practice, the quantity of infrastructure resources allocated by the SaaS provider at a given moment has to be enough to not infringe the SLA, but not too excessive to incur over-provisioning.

In this paper we focus on the role that can be played by a pure service-oriented cloud platform layer in implementing the elastic scalability sought by the SaaS provider. In the platform layer in fact the provisioning responsibilities that complicate the life of the SaaS provider can be better apportioned.

This paper is organized as follows. Section 2 presents a background on some terminology used and on the specific SOA-based PaaS prototype improved during this research. In Sect. 3 we provide an overview of the existing work on cloud platform that provides similar ideas but different approaches. Section 4 describes the high-level architecture of PaaSSOA more specifically with regard to the resource model, then continues by presenting the integration of the Elastic Scheduler into the existing framework. In Sect. 5 we describe the inner details of the Elastic Scheduler. In particular, we explain how events are gathered from PaaSSOA runtime and processed by the Inference Engine. Section 6 explains the test of the Elastic Scheduler. At first we introduce the Simulation Toolkit that has been implemented to overcome hurdles in the test of the Elastic Scheduler, then we explain how the test of elastic scalability had been accomplished using the toolkit. Section 7 contains the conclusions and the future perspectives in the context of the PaaSSOA framework.

2   Background

The cloud SPI stack is the cloud provision/business model applied to Infrastructure, Platform and Software concepts, which determines the three cloud layers: Software-as-a-Service (SaaS), Platform-as-a-Service (PaaS), and Infrastructure-as-a-Service (IaaS), hence the acronym SPI.

Below we describe briefly these three layers. The IaaS (Infrastructure as a Service) is the lowest layer, it provides raw resources (CPU, RAM, storage, network) as a commodity in form of Virtual Machines and is intended for system administrators. The PaaS (Platform as a Service) is the intermediate layer, it provides operating systems, compilers, interpreters, databases, middleware and standardized software platforms as a service mainly intended for developers. This layer builds on the raw computing power provided by the bottom layer. Lastly, the SaaS (Software as a Service) is the upper layer, it provides specialized web applications as a service to suit the needs of the most disparate categories of users. The SaaS level exploits the abstraction provided by the bottom layer because code at this level may needs many software frameworks in order to run.

Service Orientation has been rejuvenated by the advent of Cloud Computing and may play an important role in its very foundation. The service-orientation paradigm supplies the SaaS provider with the necessary support for the implementation of interoperable services which can be flexibly distributed and scaled as needed [1]. The SOA concept allows Cloud providers to adapt more quickly to the challenges of business [2]. On the other hand, cloud computing is about providing ease of access to and usage of services [3].

We note in passing that the architecture of applications specifically designed to run "in the cloud" should adhere to the principles of SOA. As reported by the author of the book [4], application designed for horizontal scaling - which increases overall application capacity by adding entire nodes - have nodes allocated to specific functions. Often enough in fact, when a traditional client/server application is brought to the Cloud "as-is", its architectural limits become evident because the application wastes a lot more resources to scale owing to need to monolithically replicate component parts that have no real need [5]. In the latter case, the SaaS providers get very little benefit, if at all, from such a coarse-grained implementation of elastic scalability.

According to the National Institute of Standards and Technology (NIST) definition [6], Cloud Computing exhibits five characteristics: on-demand self-service, broad network access, resource pooling, rapid elasticity, measured service.

Our research focuses on Rapid elasticity, or equivalently, Elastic Scalability, which allows the cloud provider to dynamically adapt service capacity according to the use profile determined by customers. In this paper, our aim is to explore the interplay between two axes (Cloud Computing and Service-Orientation) to prove that a service-oriented PaaS layer can exhibit useful and powerful potential for providing elastic capacity to SaaS providers.

As a side note, Jolie is a service-oriented language based on Java, it is built on a strong mathematical foundation (SOCK [7]) and provides an intuitive and easy to use C-like syntax to deal with the implementation of architectures made of services. The definition of the Jolie language [8] provided the foundation for a variety of projects, including PaaSSOA [9].

The primary purpose of the PaaSSOA project was to explore the role of the cloud platform layer. An important postulate to that project was the vision that deploying SOA principles could greatly facilitate build an open cloud platform. PaaSOA is in fact a cloud platform prototype built entirely using Jolie service-oriented language. Jolie is the first general-purpose service-oriented programming language based on Java which facilitates the development of modular, heterogeneous, distributed, and concurrent applications.

What the original authors of PaaSSOA [9] have proposed is a prototype framework to control the deployment and the execution of Jolie services, where the latter are the building blocks of cloud applications. Although the idea of a PaaSSOA seems promising, it lacked the elastic scalability characteristic needed to demonstrate its usefulness as a cloud platform layer.

In the work described in this paper, we approach the provision of that capability in PaaSSOA by implementing a simple threshold logic able to dynamically change the number of instances of selected services according the use profile of each of them, with the intent of preserving the attached SLA and of minimizing the extent of incurred over-provisioning. The SLA represents a threshold for the latency of a Jolie service. Elastic capacity is expressed in SLA parameters fixed at the SaaS level, and reasoned about and acted up at platform level.

In keeping with the SOA principles, PaaSSOA conceives all its modules as services so it was natural to contain the elastic capability into a new PaaSSOA core service called Elastic Scheduler. For the task of monitoring the conformity of services to their SLA we leveraged the Drools inference engine since it allowed implementing the new PaaSSOA core service more logically and with less effort than with the traditional imperative approach. Drools is written in Java and allowed us to exploit the embedding mechanism of Jolie to build a service which wraps the Drools engine Java instance.

The test of the elastic capability in PaaSSOA proved to be more problematic and has been conducted using a purpose-built test simulator. The test regarded two simplified scenarios: in the first, the Elastic Scheduler detects the SLA violation whenever a service exceeds the response time threshold, therefore, it reacts by adding one instance of that service in order to increase the overall service's capacity. In the second scenario the Elastic Scheduler detects the opportunity for optimization each time the volume of requests to a service is low too to justify the execution of all the instances, therefore, it reacts by removing under-utilized service instances in order to prevent waste of resources.

By these tests we wanted to demonstrate the potential benefit deriving from the adoption of a cloud platform which can offer elastic capacity to SaaS providers. Attaining elastic capability would help SaaS providers face the intrinsic difficulty in mapping high-level application requirements to low-level infrastructure requirements (e.g. in the form of VM instance definitions and quantity).

3   Related Work

The PaaSSOA [9] approach is quite unique as it uses a specific service-oriented technology that is Jolie. However, other works have been made in similar areas, in the following we present some of them.

In [10] the author presents a modeling technique to generate accurate model of service level. Only hypervisor counters are used as input to train models and predict application response times, hence SLA violations. The author followed a similar idea because understood the SLA as the latency of the application, thus creating a high-level requirement for the allocation of VMs. At the same time this work is very different from us as SOA and PaaS are not mentioned.

The choice of Drools over other approaches to implement elastic scalability in PaaSSOA is no coincidence, but based on the autonomic services researches conducted in [11]. In fact, the problem of verifying whether a system conforms to a set of requirements is very common. The declarative-based rules support provided by the Drools inference engine has allowed us to cohesively specify "What to do and when" and not "How to do" separately from deciding when, for a definitely easier solution.

The SOA concept is transversal to the theme of cloud platforms, and it seems that topics such as heterogeneity and portability are most debated [12]. In [13], for example, the authors propose a PaaS layer which encapsulates services in so-called micro-containers which are then independently executed by the deployment of resources supplied by the IaaS. Another work that focuses on micro-containers for hosting service-based applications on the Cloud is [14]. One important difference however is that the authors of the previous works solely focus on compatibility and portability rather than on resource optimization.

Lastly, in [15], the authors present a service oriented architecture for Cloud Computing which they call SOCCA but they do not consider the possibility that service performance may be controlled and optimized directly from the PaaS layer.

4   The PaaSSOA Framework

At the present state of the art, the community is still far from having a solid understanding of the PaaS architecture and from a standard definition of the interaction protocols between the SPI stack layers. The PaaSSOA project may help investigate the principal constituents of an open PaaS framework, capable of federating multiple IaaS and of offering elastic capacity to SaaS [16].

PaaSSOA is an evolving work that aims at establishing a proof-of-concept model, equipped with a prototype, for facilitating the development and the standardization of PaaS frameworks by capturing the main functions which characterize the Cloud from the PaaS perspective and the interactions the PaaS has to have with the two adjacent levels in the Cloud SPI stack [9]. The latest snapshot of the PaaSSOA code is available for inspection at [17].

4.1   Resource Model

The resource model of PaaSSOA provides base abstractions for Jolie services at two levels: the virtualization layer, and the SOABoot services, as illustrated by Fig. 1. The former is provided by the IaaS, expressed in capabilities for deploying and executing Virtual Machine (VM) images. The latter is the container service of PaaSSOA, one for each VM, which offers basic functionalities to the SaaS provider for managing the installation, starting it up, shutting it down, and removing specific Jolie services inside that VM.

PaaSSOA can manage two types of resources: SOABoot containers and Jolie services which represent building blocks of SaaS applications. The latter are deployed and executed in PaaSSOA and located within SOABoot services. In this scenario, the SaaS provider deploys services into the available SOABoots, if needed new VMs can be requested from the IaaS in order to increase the available capacity or can be released with the aim to optimize the current resources usage. As illustrated by Fig. 1, a SOABoot service gives access to the virtualized environment.

4.2   The New Elastic Scheduler Service

We integrated the Elastic Scheduler as a core service in PaaSSOA assigning a dual responsibility: monitoring and action. The former consists in keeping statistics about deployed services and SOABoot services. The latter provides Elastic

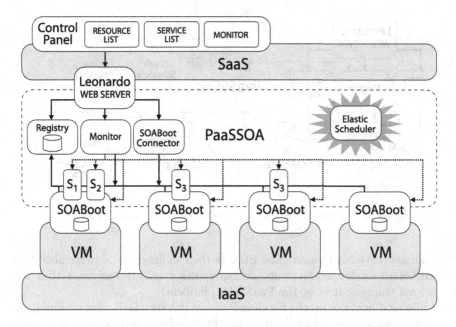

Fig. 1. PaaSSOA's overall architecture and resource model.

Scalability of deployed services ensuring that SLAs associated with deployed Jolie services are always met.

We recall that the SLA represents a threshold value for the latency of a (deployed) service so Elastic capacity is expressed in SLA parameters fixed at the SaaS level, and reasoned about and acted up at PaaS level. When a service is overloaded due to a high volume of requests, its response time might exceed the SLA threshold. At that point, the Elastic Scheduler intervenes by increasing the availability of the relevant service (e.g. by replication) until the response time measured at the SaaS level come back below the set threshold. Conversely, when the volume of requests decreases below a certain amount, the Elastic Scheduler reduces the footprint costs borne by the SaaS in using resources from the Infrastructure (e.g., by termination of service's instances), thus capping the risk of over-provisioning.

To fully integrate the Elastic Scheduler service in PaaSSOA, some changes to the initial framework were required, which is useful to recall as they may teach something to the reader. The first set of modifications has been made to the monitoring mechanism, to extract and send events from service monitors to the Elastic Scheduler in the exact moment they are generated, that is, in accord with a Push Monitoring architecture model. The previous approach, in contrast, extracted events through polling.

The second set of modifications concerned the PaaSSOA Control Panel Web GUI, which is built with Google Web Toolkit (GWT). The Control Panel had been modified by implementing the input fields needed to insert the service's

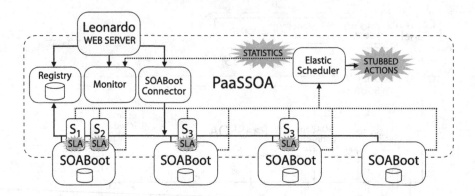

Fig. 2. Integration of the Elastic Scheduler service within PaaSSOA.

SLA latency threshold value. The SLA is then defined for a particular Jolie service before service deployment and represents a quality assurance that will be ensured transparently by the PaaSSOA platform.

While modifications on the Services Panel of the Web GUI were minimal, the Monitor Panel had been heavily reworked by enabling the reception of services statistics from the Elastic Scheduler. Statistics are calculated by the Elastic Scheduler thanks to its Drools embedded service from the raw events received by running Jolie services. As an integral part of the Monitor Panel layout design, each service statistics section provides a chart which represents the activity of the service, also called the use profile. Figure 2 shows the final high-level PaaSSOA design resulting from the integration of the new Elastic Scheduler service.

5   Elastic Scalability with Drools Inference Engine

The events processing was defined using the Drools [18] rule-based declarative approach. Since we hold the knowledge which regards the state of monitored services inside the inference engine using POJO, we need to convert the raw Jolie events coming from services monitors to Java objects events before inserting them into the inference engine. Then the act itself of injecting events into the engine causes a forward-chaining inference process due to pattern matching of the conditional part of declarative rules. In turn, specific semantic code blocks inside the rules are executed, possibly modifying the knowledge. We can summarize this process saying that the Elastic Scheduler always reaches a conclusion (e.g. replicate service to enforce the SLA) according to its input data and its knowledge through a chain of rules activations which translates in actions.

Basically, the Drools inference engine receives raw events coming from monitored services, processes them updating its internal knowledge (POJO holding the statistics of monitored services), then logs and removes raw event from its working memory. The knowledge that we extract from raw events serves for a dual purpose: the first is to keep track of the status and to maintain statistics of services executing in PaaSSOA, the second is to allow for a comparison of their current status in respect to their SLAs. We designed the Elastic Scheduler to spot SLA violations and opportunity for optimization during runtime thus stubbing the actions aimed to adapt of the number of service's instances according to the volume of requests (Fig. 2).

The rules we defined for the aggregation of raw events exploit a simple principle. Since for each operation requested by a consumer service to a Jolie monitored provider service, four events are generated by the provider service in response to the execution of the operation (SessionStarted, OperationStarted, OperationEnded, SessionEnded), we have the corresponding four events inserted in the inference engine at different times.

Essentially, we defined some rules to match the end event with the correspondent start event (i.e. relative to the same service, the same operation, and the same request). Within the rule matching that state, we put code to process the attributes of the events (e.g. obtaining the duration of the operation from the difference of the two events timestamps attributes), and to update the POJO object which holds the statistics of the service. Then a new point will be available in the Monitor Panel to the service's instance use profile chart. Additional rules take care of stubbing the replication of Jolie services instances which present SLA violation and stubbing the removal of under-utilized Jolie services instances.

6 Experimental Evaluation

In essence, the goal that we have achieved in PaaSSOA is represented by the elastic adaptation of services capacity. The capacity is changed dynamically by the Elastic Scheduler through the replication and the removal of VMs (SOABoots) and Jolie services instances (i.e. horizontal scalability), in this way it becomes possible to scale, enforce the services SLAs, and optimize the costs arising from the use of the infrastructure.

It worth noting that the actions triggered by the Drools declarative rules with the aim to vary the number of running service's instances are only stubbed, this means that such actions work only in the context of our purpose-built Simulation Toolkit. In fact, the PaaSSOA framework, being a prototype, does not yet implement the necessary functionalities to ensure services replication and services migration. Moreover, the interface toward the IaaS was not yet implemented at the time of this writing.

To quantitatively assess the goodness of our approach we conceptually divided the experimental evaluation in two consecutive phases: in the first phase we proved the effectiveness of upward scalability which allows us to cope with a peak of requests which overloaded some service causing SLA violation. Instead, in the second phase we prove the effectiveness of downward scalability which reduces the number of service's instances in execution in order to prevent under-utilization, without affecting the quality of service.

In the first case the Elastic Scheduler detects the SLA violation whenever a service exceeds the response time threshold, therefore, it reacts by adding one

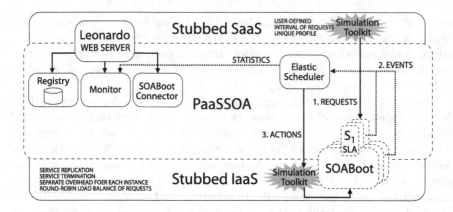

Fig. 3. Architecture for the test of the Elastic Scheduler.

instance of that service in order to increase the overall service's capacity thus allowing the response times of subsequent requests to return within the SLA limit. In the second scenario the Elastic Scheduler detects the opportunity for optimization each time the volume of requests to a service is low too to justify the execution of all the instances (i.e. the same work can be done by fewer service's instances without exceeding the SLA), therefore, it reacts by removing under-utilized service instances in order to eliminate unnecessary costs due to the use of infrastructure resources.

6.1 Simulation Toolkit

The features needed for services replication and services migration are not yet implemented in PaaSSOA so a real test would have led to an unnecessary complication as it would have prevented us from testing the results of the actions performed by the Elastic Scheduler. In this sense, our purpose-built Test Toolkit helped testing the Elastic Scheduler with less effort, to cause the actions we created and inserted the events directly in the Drools engine without the need deploy any service.

As shown in Fig. 3, we decoupled the test of the Elastic Scheduler service from the deployment mechanism of PaaSSOA thus to achieve the of actions directly on the Toolkit. This approach has allowed us to model the service's use profile directly from the Toolkit by controlling the creation of events. Events are created and inserted in Drools coherently (e.g. attributes values, time of insertion) with the purpose to simulate the service and the operations served by it as if it had been a real monitored service.

For our purposes, it was sufficient to represent the use profile by means of sequential operations so we have adopted a very simple approach where we added also a little bit of randomization to get a more realistic simulation. The Toolkit's core is constituted by a loop in which every iteration mimics a request to one operation of the simulated service. We have modeled the use profile using four parameters: the base duration of a simulated operation, the maximum delay of the simulated operation, the base duration between two consecutive simulated operations, and the maximum delay between two consecutive simulated operations. At each iteration the first two parameters are combined to form the duration of the served operation (operation-duration) while the conjunction of the remaining two parameters produces the elapsed time between the start of two consecutive operations (time-between-requests).

Whereas we want to increase the operation-duration value until a SLA violation is produced, we don't want to do it directly because otherwise we lose the relation between the volume (i.e. frequency) of operations and the overhead of the VM environment where the service is executing (which led to the service's delay). In practice, we implemented an overhead parameter to simulate the service's overload by simply changing the overall operations frequency. Note the overhead value is summed to newly generated operation-duration (accumulated) only in case the time-between-requests value is below 1000 ms. On the other hand we concurrently decrease the overhead value by a fixed quantity every second so, in a sense, we set the capacity of the service to perform work (the overhead is always ≥ 0).

The Toolkit, when the number of service's instances is greater than one, takes care of simulating one operation for each of the currently available service's instances (round-robin load balancing) and keeps separate overhead values to simulate the service's instances load independently from one another as if they were on separate SOABoots, or VMs.

6.2 Upward Scalability

We started the test of upward scalability by simulating a single instance of a service (SOABoot1/TestService1) and causing the SLA violation by increasing the frequency of requests. When the amount of requests exceeds the capacity of the instance, the instance begins to accumulate delay. If the capacity is exceeded for a sufficiently long span of time, the response time of the instance increases to such an extent as to go beyond the service's SLA causing the Elastic Scheduler to detect the SLA violation. The Elastic Scheduler then reacts by starting an additional service instance through the Simulation Toolkit (using replication) thereby addressing the present lack of capacity.

We have also simulated a fixed artificial delay (30 s in the experimental setting) to represent the entry into operation of the new instance. During this period of time the addInstance action will be disabled as to prevent further invocations, the action will be re-enabled only after some time the new instance is ready. As illustrated by Fig. 4, we can see the result of the service replication on the duration of the operations, so the ability of the Elastic Scheduler to add service instances in order to keep the service's response time within the SLA threshold.

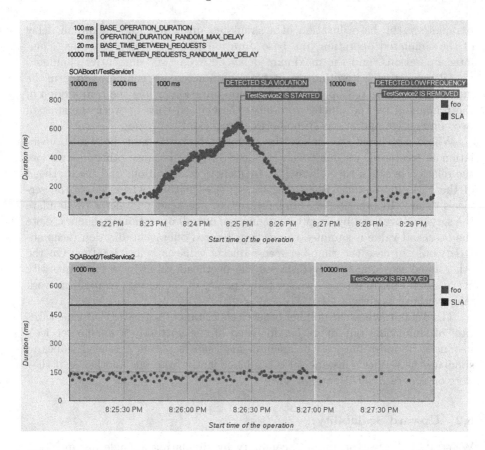

Fig. 4. Experimental evaluation of elastic scalability using the Simulation Toolkit.

6.3   Downward Scalability

After the test of upward scalability we needed to experiment with downward scalability. The second phase of test was merely a continuation of the previous scenario, so we resumed from the point where we have left.

The experiments were conducted by decreasing the frequency of operations in the use profile. Therefore, when the Elastic Scheduler detects that the frequency of operations on a particular instance has fallen below the limit of 30 operation per minute, triggers the removeInstance operation on the Toolkit with the aim to reduce the number of instances. The effect of the instance removal is that the Toolkit's main loop has fewer instances on which to simulate operations, so the frequency of operations simulated on the remaining instance increases. Also in this case, we add a delay to simulate the entry into effect of the reduction of capacity.

We see that as long as the capacity reduction does not affect the durations of operations we are freeing unused capacity. In this way we can see the ability of the Elastic Scheduler at adapting the service's instances according to the work-load in order to use only the resources needed. Therefore, the Elastic Scheduler ensure downward scalability to avoid under-provisioning and to minimize the cost of allocated infrastructure resources. However, there is potential deception involving such a reactive approach in that thrashing of services resources may occur.

7   Conclusion

In conclusion, the integration of the Drools engine allowed us to put reason-ing capacity into PaaSSOA. In a sense, we can see and analogy between the cloud platform layer and a "cloud operating system" since it efficiently mediates requirements across adjacent layers and ensures the adaptation of the number of services instances to match the application use's profile. The results confirmed that the PaaS is the right place where to encapsulate the complexity of resources management, in fact, a cloud platform can raise many management burden to SaaS providers, allowing them to optimize the usage of infrastructure without impacting the architecture of the application thus providing valuable support to increase agility and financial rewards.

However, in the light of the experimental evaluation, we still need to con-sider the cost of resources under provision to the application and the logic of replication and migration of services between the available SOABoots, joined to the acquisition and the release of VMs from the infrastructure level. This is mainly due to the lack, in PaaSSOA, of a connector to the lower level and of the functionalities which ensure migration and replication of Jolie services.

The future work on PaaSSOA will regard the development of suitable con-nections toward both public and private IaaS clouds. While for public cloud a solution on the top of AWS is under study, for the private cloud there is not yet any consolidated feature. However, we plan in the future to leverage the wide-spread hypervisors API and Infrastructure Management Tools to improve our SOA-based PaaS solution.

References

1. Buyya, R.: Market-oriented cloud computing: vision, hype, and reality of delivering computing as the 5th utility. In: CCGRID 2009–9th IEEE/ACM International Symposium on Cluster Computing and the Grid, p. 1. IEEE (2009)
2. Josuttis, N.M.: SOA in Practice. The Art of Distributed System Design. O'Reilly Media, Sebastopol (2007)
3. How SOA can ease your move to cloud computing. http://www-01.ibm.com/software/solutions/soa/newsletter/nov09/article_soaandcloud.html
4. Wilder, B.: Cloud Architecture Patterns. Develop Cloud-Native Applications. O'Reilly Media, Sebastopol (2012)
5. Cacco, F.: GeoServer nel Cloud. Un Caso di Studio sulle Modifiche Architetturali nel Passaggio a Piattaforme Cloud. Master thesis, University of Padova (2013)

6. The NIST Definition of Cloud Computing. http://csrc.nist.gov/publications/nistpubs/800-145/SP800-145.pdf

7. Guidi, C., Lucchi, R., Gorrieri, R., Busi, N., Zavattaro, G.: SOCK: a calculus for service oriented computing. In: Dan, A., Lamersdorf, W. (eds.) ICSOC 2006. LNCS, vol. 4294, pp. 327–338. Springer, Heidelberg (2006)

8. Montesi, F., Guidi, C., Zavattaro, G.: Service-oriented programming with Jolie. In: Bouguettaya, A., Sheng, Q.Z., Daniel, F. (eds.) Web Services Foundations, pp. 81–107. Springer, New York (2014)

9. Guidi, C., Anedda, P., Vardanega, T.: PaaSSOA: an open PaaS architecture for service oriented applications. In: CLOSER 2012 - Proceedings of the 2nd International Conference on Cloud Computing and Services Science, pp. 279–282. ScitePress (2012)

10. Chan, L.L.: Modeling Virtualized Application Performance from Hypervisor Counters. Master thesis, Massachussets Institue of Technology (2011)

11. Bragaglia, S.: Monitoring Complex Processes to Verify System Conformance. Ph.D. thesis, University of Bologna (2013)

12. Moreno-Vozmediano, R., Montero, R.S., Llorente, I.M.: IaaS cloud architecture: from virtualized datacenters to federated cloud infrastructures. Computer **45**, 65–72 (2012)

13. Yangui, S., Tata, S.: PaaS elements for hosting service-based applications. In: CLOSER 2012 - Proceedings of the 2nd International Conference on Cloud Computing and Services Science, pp. 279–282. SciTePress (2012)

14. Omezzine, A., Yangui, S., Bellamine, N., Tata, S.: Mobile service micro-containers for cloud environments. In: WETICE 2012 - Proceedings of the 2012 IEEE 21st International Workshop on Enabling Technologies: Infrastructure for Collaborative Enterprises, pp. 154–160. IEEE Computer Society (2012)

15. Tsai, W., Sun, X., Balasooriya, J.: Service-oriented cloud computing architecture. In: ITNG - 7th International Conference on Information Technology: New Generations, pp. 684–689. IEEE Computer Society (2010)

16. Guidi, C., Anedda, P., Vardanega, T.: Towards a new PaaS architecture generation. In: CLOSER 2012 - Proceedings of the 2nd International Conference on Cloud Computing and Services Science, pp. 279–282. SciTePress (2012)

17. jSOA. http://sourceforge.net/projects/jsoa/

18. JBoss Drools Documentation. http://drools.jboss.org/documentation

Towards Compensable SLAs

Carlos Müller[✉], Antonio Manuel Gutierrez, Manuel Resinas,
Pablo Fernandez, and Antonio Ruiz-Cortés

University of Sevilla, Seville, Spain
cmuller@us.es

Abstract. Service Level Agreements (SLA) describe the rights and
obligations of parties involved (typically the service consumer and the
service provider); amongst other information they could include the definition of compensations: penalties and/or rewards depending on the
level of service provided. We coin the concept of Compensable SLAs to
such that include compensation information inside. In such a context, in
spite of important steps towards the automation of the management of
SLAs have been given, the expression of compensations remains as an
important challenge to be addressed. In this paper we aim to provide
a characterization model to create Compensable SLAs; specifically, the
main contributions include: (i) the conceptualization of the Compensation Function to express consistently penalties and rewards. (ii) a model
for Compensable SLAs as a set of guarantees that associate Service Level
Objectives with Compensation Functions. We provide some properties
and aspects that have been used to analyse two real-world SLAs.

1 Introduction

The shift from product to services (software provided, human provided, or
hybrids) in the industry is a general trend for developed countries. In such a
context this evolution implies the creation of a network of dependable organizations that exchange services and, as a consequence, there is a craving for guarantees that support a reliable service consumption. In this challenge, Service
Level Agreements (SLA) represents a first-class citizen to describe the rights
and obligations of both service consumer and provider.

SLA-driven systems may be established with SLAs as pivotal element to
define a set of Service Level Objectives (SLO) that should be enforced by one
party (the guarantor) to another party (the beneficiary). In most cases the former
correspond to the service provider, and the latter to the service consumer. Such
information included in the SLAs may be the basis for the decision making
of involved parties in SLA-driven systems along service lifecycle. In this sense,
some SLAs may include a set of compensations that represent the consequences
of underfullfiling (penalties) or overfullfiling (rewards) the SLOs. We coin the

This work was partially supported by the European Commission (FEDER), the
Spanish and the Andalusian R&D&I programmes (grants P12-TIC-1867, TIN2012-
32273, TIC-5906 and IPT-2013-0890-3).

G. Ortiz and C. Tran (Eds.): ESOCC 2014, CCIS 508, pp. 31–38, 2015.
DOI: 10.1007/978-3-319-14886-1_4

concept of Compensable SLAs referring to such SLAs that include at least a compensation action, either a penalty or a reward.

The expression of different kinds of compensations and the checking of some desiderable properties that compensations may fulfill, are still challenging tasks. In addition, the automated extraction of information from such compensations would bring important benefits for service consumers and providers in SLA-driven systems in general and in compensable SLAs in particular: (i) on the one hand, providers could automate the optimization of the provision of services based on the compensations involved, and (ii) service consumer could automate the analysis of guarantees in the SLA to understand its risk.

In this paper we go into details about the concept of Compensable SLAs by providing an appropriate specification model for compensation actions, either penalties or rewards. This model incorporates a catalog of properties that can be easily checked. The main element of our proposal is a compensation function inspired in a penalty function provided by Leitner et al. [4], but extended to support the rewards. Our proposal has been validated in two real world SLAs.

2   Motivating Scenarios

SLAs are widely used in the industry in situations where consumers and providers need or desire to explicitly express certain guarantees over the service transaction. These guarantees are typically tied to certain consequences in terms of penalties and rewards depending whether the guarantee is unfulfilled or overfulfilled; we commonly refer to these consequences as compensations.

In this section we motivate the need for formal compensable agreements with two real world scenarios that include both human-driven services and computing services. In both cases, there is a strong need to express compensations related to the guarantees defined.

GNWT Scenario. The Government of the Northwest Territories (GNWT) of Canada outsources the IT support. Specifically, the demanded services include issues related to: reporting, user support, problem correction, application enhancement, process and application improvement, and other services. They provide a template for establishing an SLA with an external vendor providing the mentioned kind of IT support with the desired service levels and compensations. Four examples of terms with compensations have been extracted from its SLA template[1] and they are depicted in Fig. 1.

AWS EC2 Scenario. Amazon Web Services (AWS) is a service catalogue that has boosted the idea of cloud computing in the industry; amongst them, the Elastic Computing Cloud (EC2) represents a widely used Infrastructure as a Service providing a set of virtualized resources that can be consumed and paid on an on-demand basis.

The aim of this service is to provide an escalable infrastructure to organizations that have variable needs or they need to grow seamlessly without the

---

[1] Available at http://www.fin.gov.nt.ca/ocio/sim/sdlc/3/resources/sla.htm.

Type	Measurement	Penalty
Quarterly Status Report	Delivered at quarterly intervals and not less than five business days before scheduled review meeting	5% of monthly invoice

Sample 1 (page 5 of the template)

Severity Code	Initial Response	Estimation Response	Subsequent Responses	Resolution
1	15 minutes	2 hours	Every 30 min.	4 hours

Type	Measurement	Reward	Penalty
Severity 1 Resolution	All Severity 1 problems are resolved in less than 2 hours.	10% of monthly fees	NA
	One or more Severity 1 problems are resolved in over 4 hours.	NA	10% of monthly fees

Sample 2 (page 7 of the template)

Type	Measurement	Reward	Penalty
Maximum Problem Aging	No problem is older than 60 days.	5% of monthly fees	NA

Sample 3 (page 8 of the template)

Type	Measurement	Reward*	Penalty
Project Delivery	Total elapsed days until delivery is more than 20% greater than planned.	NA	10% of the amount invoiced for the project.
	Total elapsed days until delivery is 20% less than planned.	5% of the amount invoiced for the project.	NA

Sample 4 (page 9 of the template)

Fig. 1. Compensations actions extracted from the SLA of GNWT

investment for an internal data center. In this context, the reliability of a virtualized infrastructure represents a key point for customers (i.e. IaaS consumers) in order to choose a service like AWS EC2.

As a consequence, Amazon has explicitly published an SLA for EC2[2] that is based on the idea of Monthly Uptime Percentage (MUP); this element, characterizes a guarantee over the availability of the virtual resources requested. Specifically, in case the MUP drops below 99.95 percent and in case the MUP drops below 99 percent. In this scenario, the actual compensation is defined as a 10 and 30 percent of discount in the next billing cycle a.k.a Service Credit Percentage (SCP), respectively.

3 Compensable SLAs

In this section we identify the concept of Compensation Function as the key element to express both, the penalties and rewards in a consistent structure that allows a formal definition of compensable SLAs.

A compensation function represents the relation between the level of fulfillment of a guarantee and the possible compensations for the involved parties in the service consumption (the service consumer and the provider). Complementary, in the context of a guarantee two roles can be played: the guarantor and the beneficiary; in most cases, these roles are respectively covered by consumer

---

[2] Available at http://aws.amazon.com/es/ec2/sla/.

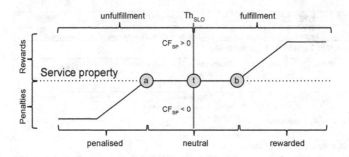

Fig. 2. A generic example of compensation function

and provider. However, there could exist scenarios where service consumers act as guarantor developing some sort of guarantee to the provider and vice versa.

A compensation function for a given service property sp, denoted by CF_{SP}, is a function from SP to $\mathbb{R}$, where SP denotes the set of all possible values of the service property ($SP = \{v_1, ..., v_n\}$). Thus, each v_i maps to a given compensation value and we identify a partition in three sets for the service properties values: Rewarded values that are positive values (e.g. $v_i \mapsto 7$) and represent situations where the beneficiary must compensate the guarantor ($CF_{SP}(v_i) > 0$); Penalised values that are negative values (e.g. $v_i \mapsto -7$) and represent situations where the guarantor must compensate the beneficiary ($CF_{SP}(v_i) < 0$); and Neutral values (e.g. $v_i \mapsto 0$) which represent the lack of compensation ($CF_{SP}(v_i) = 0$).

Figure 2 shows a generic example of an increasing compensation function. This kind of increasing function would model the compensation for service properties such as the MUP in which the higher values the more interesting for beneficiary. On the contrary, decreasing compensation functions would model the compensation of service properties such as the resolution hours in which the lesser values the more interesting for beneficiary. In this sense, to denote that a value v_1 for a service property is less interesting for the beneficiary than other value v_2 by $v_1 \preceq v_2$. Since omission means a lack of compensation in natural language, when there is not explicit definition of a penalty or a reward, we consider $CF_{SP}(v_i) = 0$. Figures 3 shows the different compensation functions from the GNWT scenario. In the Figure, while a dark point denotes the inclusion of the value in the interval, gray points means the value exclusion.

In order to analyse and characterize the possible compensation functions, we identify the following list of interesting properties:

Property P_1 ***(Consistent)*** Let CF_{SP} a compensation function, it is said to be consistent if the compensation for a lesser degree of fulfillment of service property is lesser or equal than the compensation for a greater degree of fullfillment of such property. This property assures the monotonicity of compensation functions. Samples 1 and 2 of Fig. 3 depict a decreasing and an increasing consistent compensation function, respectively.

$$\text{consistent}(CF_{SP}) \iff \forall v_1, v_2 \in SP \cdot v_1 \preceq v_2 \Rightarrow CF_{SP}(v_1) \leq CF_{SP}(v_2)$$

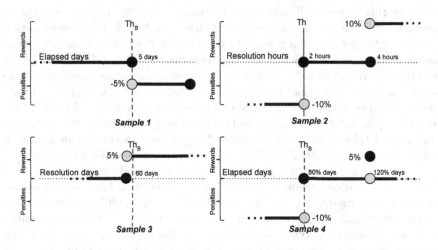

Fig. 3. Samples from GNWT SLA

Property P_2 *(Saturated)* Let CF_{SP} a compensation function, it is said to be saturated if there exist a minimum (v_{min}) and a maximun value (v_{max}) for the service property, that delimit the higher compensation, either penalty or reward.The compensation functions of Fig. 3 are all saturated.

$$saturated(CF_{SP}) \iff \forall v_i \in SP, \exists v_{max}, v_{min} \in SP.$$
$$CF_{SP}(v_i) \le CF_{SP}(v_{max}) \land CF_{SP}(v_i) \ge CF_{SP}(v_{min})$$

Property P_3 *(Valid)* Let CF_{SP} a compensation function, it is said to be valid if it is consistent and saturated. We consider this because of the following two aspects that, in our opinion a compensation function should assure: (1) on the one hand, consistency assures that the compensation for a more interesting service property value for the beneficiary has more reward or less penalty than a less interesting service property value; (2) on the other hand, saturability assures that penalties and rewards are bounded. Samples 1–3 of Fig. 3 are valid compensation functions, but sample 4 is not valid due to a lack of consistency because the service property value 120 % has more reward than higher values.

$$valid(CF_{SP}) \iff consistent(CF_{SP}) \land saturated(CF_{SP})$$

The formalization of Service Level Agreements (SLA) have been a research topic during last decade. Amongst other results, WS-Agreement [1] currently represents the most prominent specification for formal agreements for both academia and industry. This specification formalizes the SLA as a set of terms for describing the service and the associated guarantees. Specifically, a guarantee term, (guarantees from now on) is defined around the idea of a Service Level Objective (SLO) that should be guaranteed (by the guarantor) to the'beneficiary (e.g. *Response Time < 100* ms or *Monthly Uptime Percentage ≥ 99.95 %*) Complementary, this specification also includes a placeholder to express penalties and rewards that can be extended with domain-specific languages [6,7].

Taking this conceptualization as a starting point, we coin the concept of Compensable SLAs referring to such SLAs that include at least a compensation action, either a penalty or a reward to be considered when at least one of the comprised guarantees is underfulfilled or overfulfilled, respectively. Thus, at least one of the guarantees included within a compensable SLA is composed of an SLO and a compensation function that defines the penalties and rewards derived from underfullfilling or overfullfilling the SLO. For instance, Sample 2 of GNWT scenario (Fig. 1) includes the SLO in the first table and the compensation function in the second table. The other Samples of Fig. 1 just provide a compensation function but not the SLO. Figure 2 shows a typical compensation function that depicts the relationships between the fulfillment regions delimited by the SLO and the compensation regions defined by the compensation function. Moreover, as shown in this figure, it is important to highlight that fulfillment regions are not necessary coupled with compensation regions; specifically, figure exemplifies a case having neutral service properties values between a and b without any compensation: service properties values between t and b are unfulfilled but not penalized, and similarly service properties values between a and t are fulfilled but not rewarded. In addition, figure shows how threshold Th_{SLO} delimits the fulfillment from the unfulfillment values.

Figure 3 presents our modeling of guarantees identified in the GNWT scenario. Each example, corresponds with a guarantee showing the specific compensation function (as a black line) along with the Th_{SLO} (as a solid vertical line) derived from the SLO; in case there is no SLO explicit, we have inferred a threshold (Th_G or Th_B) depending on whether the SLA was specified by the guarantor (AWS EC2 scenario) or the beneficiary (GNWT and Telecomm. SLA scenarios); these inferred thresholds are depicted as discontinuous lines.

In a guarantee with both, an SLO and a compensation function, we must study the coherence between them. Then we identify the following preconditions that could be checked by an automated tool to assure the validity of guarantees in compensable SLAs: (i) The compensation function should be valid (i.e. Satisfy P_3) (ii) SLO definition must imply a partition of two sets (fulfilled and unfulfilled) in the service property domain (iii) Fulfillment set of values defined by SLO should be coherent with compensation function model: Th should be such fulfilled value that is less interesting for the beneficiary ($Th \preceq v_i, \forall v_i \in SP \cdot CF_{SP}(v_i) \geq 0$) (iv) SLO must define at least a neutral service property value without compensation.

3.1 Analysis of Real Compensable SLAs and Related Work

Table 1 presents a comparative study of the properties fulfilled by the compensations found in both, the real world SLAs of Sect. 2, and examples found in relevant research papers that include the idea of SLAs with penalties and/or rewards. Regarding the properties fulfilled by the compensations of the real word SLAs, we highlight that GNWT Sample 4 of Fig. 3 depicts an inconsistent compensation function; this may represent a mistake in the SLA derived from the usage of natural language.

Table 1. Comparative study of the properties fulfilled by the examples found.

		P_1	P_2	P_3
GNWT Sample 1		✓	✓	✓
GNWT Sample 2		✓	✓	✓
GNWT Sample 3		✓	✓	✓
GNWT Sample 4		✗	✓	✗
AWS EC2 Sample		✓	✓	✓
Letiner et al. [5]	TimeToOffer<=2 (Pag.2)	✓	✓	✓
	OrderFulfillment<=5 (Pag.2)	✓	✓	✓
	ProcessLeadTime<=6 (Pag.2)	✓	✓	✓
	CostCompliance<=5 (Pag.2)	✓	✓	✓
Leitner et al. [4]	SLA Cost = Penalties (Pag.3)	✓	✓	✓
Buco et al. [2]	Penalties (Pag.12)	✓	✓	✓
	Penalties & Reward (Pag.18)	✗	✗	✗
Grabarnik et al. [3]	Penalties & Reward (Pag.7)	✓	✓	✓
Rana et al. [6]	ExecutionTime (Pages 6-7)	✓	✗	✗

With regards to the examples found in the related work, it is remarkable that the proposal of Leitner et al. in [5] formalizes the problem of finding the optimal set of adaptations, which minimizes the total costs arising from SLA violations and the adaptations to prevent them. In this work, a model for penalty functions is presented; this formalization has been the starting point of our motivational scenario description presented in Sect. 2 and consequently, our approach represents an extension to this model in order to develop a complete formalization for Compensable Guarantees and SLAs. Based on our model, we have studied 4 examples (page 2) included presented in [5] relating to the cost of violations of one service property, namely: time to offer, order fulfillment time, process lead time, and cost compliance. In [4] the same authors present an approach for optimally scheduling incoming requests to virtual computing resources in the cloud, so that the sum of payments for resources and loss incurred by SLA violations is minimized. The studied example (page 3) includes a linear penalty function with two point of discontinuities. The example relates the penalty with a service property representing the duration of requests to virtual computing resources in the cloud. Other examples taken from relevant related works are the following: Buco et al. propose in [2] an SLA management system, called SAM that provides penalties in a Service Level Management process. In the first studied example (page 12) the compensation function relates some penalties with a service property denoting the alert time for SLA managers. In the second example some penalties and rewards are specified depending on the service level fulfillment of the SLAs; these last examples define overlapping values for the rewards (i.e. same value can have different compensations) and therefore, the compensation function cannot be defined. Grabarnik et al. propose in [3] a model that can be used to reduce total service costs of IT service providers using alternative delivery teams and external service providers. The studied example (page 7) includes penalties and rewards for a service property that represents the process execution time. Rana et al. identifies in [8] how SLOs may be impacted by the choice of specific penalty clauses. From such a work we have studied an example (pages 6–7) that relates the penalty of different levels of service execution time. It is important to note that the compensation function does not meet the saturation property and therefore it does not fulfill the validity property.

4 Conclusions

In this paper we characterise the concept of Compensable SLA, that include a definition of guarantees with penalties and rewards for involved parties the Service Level Objective (SLO) is underfulfilled or overfulfilled. We motivate our proposal upon the study of two real world SLAs over human-driven or computing services, and define a model to formally express Compensable SLAs by conceptualizing the Compensation Function as the appropriate artifact to consistently combine penalties and rewards in the context of an SLO. In order to support the modelling and analysis of Compensable Functions and SLAs, we define several properties and aspects about the compensation functions and SLOs of guarantees. This list of properties is used to develop a comparative study over several samples taken from the real SLAs joint with a set of samples found in related work from the literature.

References

1. Andrieux, A., et al.: Web Services Agreement Specification (WS-Agreement) Version 1.1 draft 20, September 2006
2. Buco, M.J., et al.: Utility computing sla management based upon business objectives. IBM Syst. J. **43**(1), 159–178 (2004)
3. Grabarnik, G., et al.: Management of service process qos in a service provider-service supplier environment. In: The 9th IEEE International Conference on Enterprise Computing, E-Commerce, and E-Services (CEC/EEE), pp. 543–550, July 2007
4. Leitner, P., et al.: Cost-efficient and application sla-aware client side request scheduling in an infrastructure-as-a-service cloud. In: 2012 IEEE 5th International Conference on Cloud Computing (CLOUD), pp. 213–220, June 2012
5. Leitner, P., et al.: Cost-based optimization of service compositions. IEEE Trans. Serv. Comput. **6**(2), 239–251 (2013)
6. Müller, C., et al.: Automated analysis of conflicts in ws-agreement. IEEE Trans. Serv. Comput. **7**(4), 530–544 (2014)
7. Müller, C., et al.: Comprehensive explanation of SLA violations at runtime. IEEE Trans. Serv. Comput. **7**(2), 168–183 (2014)
8. Rana, O.F., et al.: Managing violations in service level agreements. In: Grid Middleware and Services Chapter Title - Managing Violations in Service Level Agreements, pp. 349–358 (2008)

Service Network Modeling: A Generic Approach

Aneta Kabzeva[✉], Joachim Götze, and Paul Müller

Integrated Communication Systems Lab (ICSY), University of Kaiserslautern,
Kaiserslautern, Germany
{kabzeva,j_goetze,pmueller}@informatik.uni-kl.de

Abstract. With the broad adoption of service-orientation for the realization of business applications and their provisioning and usage over open cloud infrastructures, the topology of the resulting service networks is becoming extremely complex. Due to the composition of services for value-added business capabilities and the reusability of a service in multiple compositions, the execution of one service often depends on other services and changes in its provisioning can affect the health of large parts of the service network. The lack of insight on the relationships between the network components makes the management of the service network's health and change impact hard and error prone tasks. This paper proposes a service network modeling approach for capturing the topology of a service network at design time. The model is used to validate the health of the service network to ensure the operability of its services. At run time the model can be applied for analyzing the effects of evolutionary events such as service modification or withdrawal. Our major contributions are a generic and adaptable modeling structure and a classification of service network entities and relationships. The applicability of our approach is demonstrated on an example service network scenario.

Keywords: Service network · Service network model · Adaptability · Service network health analysis

1 Introduction

With the adoption of service-orientation as paradigm for the development of business applications and the introduction of cloud infrastructures, the organization of today's IT landscapes is changing. Organizations are focusing on their core competency. Supporting non-core functionality is consumed on demand as third-party services in the cloud [16]. The resulting sophisticated relations between services of different vendors and consumers connect the IT landscape in a complex value co-creation service network [15].

Since the structure of a network always affects its functionality [23], the modeling of service networks as an instrument for understanding the complex interactions between the actors and the resources in a service network is an emerging research field in service science [22]. Based on a comprehensive service

© Springer International Publishing Switzerland 2015
G. Ortiz and C. Tran (Eds.): ESOCC 2014, CCIS 508, pp. 39–50, 2015.
DOI: 10.1007/978-3-319-14886-1_5

network model capturing the relationships between the service network components, analysis approaches can be used to study and optimize the value creation in the underlying service network [6]. However, due to the maturity level of the modeled service network and the different perspectives of the heterogeneous network actors, the scope of the entities relevant for a service network model can differ. The semantic of the relationships between the entities can also differ widely according to the role and the analysis needs of the actor [14].

To provide a model able to support these different service networks and the needs of the various stakeholder roles, the underlying modeling approach needs to (i) be *adaptable* to the heterogeneous modeling concepts for service network components, (ii) be *applicable* for diverse analysis scenarios, while (iii) providing a *uniform* representation of the core modeling concepts. Hence, while allowing to capture private and public service networks with all relevant entities and multiple relationships with different semantics between them, the approach should be able to present different aspects of the model for each network and each stakeholder to address their different requirements and expectations.

The DAME solution proposed in this paper is a metamodel approach for graph-based network models comprised of entities and relationships of customizable types and extensible set of properties. This abstraction provides flexible adaptation of the models and their applicability for heterogeneous networks.

The remainder of the paper is structured as follows: Sect. 2 introduces a motivation scenario for our approach. Related work on service network modeling is addressed in Sect. 3. The modular structure of our approach is described in Sect. 4. Following this structure, Sect. 5 presents a classification of service network entities and relationships identified as initial preset for modeling service networks. The applicability of the approach for impact analysis based on the selected scenario are discussed in Sect. 6. A summary and an outlook to future work in Sect. 7 conclude the paper.

2   Motivation Scenario

The following scenario presents a simplified service network. It presumes a platform-as-a-service (PaaS) cloud infrastructure where actors (A) interested in a collaboration can publish or consume services (S). Figure 1 shows a segment of the network with the interactions of three actors: the private person *John Doe* interested in a *Credit Card Payment* capability (P), which is provided by the *Credit Card Management* service of *Smart Billing Ltd.*, and *Safe Shopping Inc.* providing a *Shipping Management* and *Product Order Management* services on the platform. Safe Shopping Inc. acts further as a consumer within the service network, since it uses its own Product Order Management service for the realization of its *Product Delivery* capability. The Product Order Management service on its side is a value-added service combining the functionality of the Credit Card Management service and the Shipping management service to check the validity of a card before shipping the goods listed in an order.

In this scenario a number of properties of the network participants and a variety of relationships between them can be observed. Information on properties like

Fig. 1. A service network involving multiple services

the different roles of the actors or the complexity of the provided services is valuable for estimating the productivity of the service network. Together with the non-functional ownership of processes or services we observe functional dependencies on existing services for providing the operability of a composite service, or resource dependencies between the participants in a composition (e.g., Shipping Management awaits an acknowledgment on the validity of a credit card from Credit Card Management to start processing). Already in this small scenario one can see that making the existing relationships explicitly visible will ease the analysis on the service network's health and the management of evolutionary changes. The information could be applied for estimating the area of effect of the different participants and for the identification of hot spots within the topology.

3   Related Work

Numerous research works are focusing on the definition of service network models covering a wide scope of application scenarios. Some of them apply the models for value flow calculation [2,11], others for the derivation of possible service compositions [5], or providing an overview on business relationships [8]. Cause-effect correlations analysis and service market share [7], service performance tracing [24], and documentation of collaborations for risk-aware management [15,20] are also considered as motivation for the design of service network models. Depending on the application domain for a model, the scope of the considered model components and the nature of the relationships between them vary greatly.

The value-based model in [2] remains completely on the business entities level of service networks, modeling services, knowledge,and intangible value exchange between organizations. Business tasks are added to the business entities level in the models in [8,11]. The relationships in [11] remain on the value flow level, while [8] focuses on the ownership of offerings and requests, and the provisioning relations between them.

The model in [7] is based on rich relationships with multiple properties referred to as multi-layer relationships. A multi-layer relationship connects only services and is defined along six dimensions: role, level, involvement, comparison, association, and causality. Dependencies between services are also the focus of the model in [20]. Here however, the service level agreements of a service are separately modeled and build their own dependency topology.

The approach in [5] proposes a formalism for modeling service networks as demand-driven, ad-hoc interplay of providers and their services. Each model targets the satisfaction of one complex service request and describes all feasible combinations of services that may satisfy the request. The best alternative can be selected by calculating the minimal costs noted on the relationship edges. The scope of our work is different, in that we support the modeling of existing relationships rather than possible ones. Existing collaboration relationships and competition relationships between services are considered in [15]. Provisioning and consumption relationships to the business entities are also defined as part of the approach. However, compared to our approach no possibility for adaptation or weighting of the relationships is considered. The modeling concept in [24] is the only one considering all three abstraction levels of service networks including the business entities, the process, and the service level. However, the approach does not specify concrete relationships between the layer participants. The information on customer involvement, participant interaction, granularity, human operation involvement, software service involvement, and dependency are modeled as part of a service-centered assessment.

4   Generic Modeling Approach for Service Networks

The foundation of the DAME service network management approach is the conceptual service network model. A service network model comprises a number of different entities and relationships between them. A conceptual model defines the types of entities and the types of relationships between them that have to be captured to provide an efficient support for service network analysis. A formal representation of the conceptual service network model can be used then to derive processes for model retrieval, validation, and scoping, and to develop a framework implementing these processes.

The modeling language is defined according to the metamodeling principles of linguistic and ontological metamodeling [4]. As illustrated in Fig. 2, it comprises three ontological metalayers (Oi) which avail themselves of the linguistic constructs (Lj) of XML and XML Schema: the metamodel layer O2 defines the language for the specification of service network models; the model layer O1 defines the specification concepts for service network models conform to the language from the upper layer; the instances layer O0 contains concrete models of service networks using the concepts from the upper layer.

Inspired by [1], the DAME conceptual model consists of two modules – the *DAME Schema* and the *DAME Preset* (cf. Fig. 2). The *Service Network Metamodel* of the schema provides the basic language elements for the description of service network models. The *Model Base* of the schema defines the representation of the elements needed for the specification of a service network model conform to the metamodel. The *Core Concepts* of the preset contribute to the representation, capturing, and analysis of service network models through the

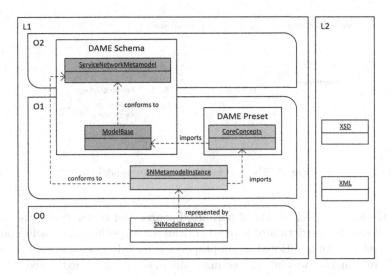

Fig. 2. An overview of the model components

definition of entities and relationships identified as reasonable for the structuring of service network models, their extraction from established entity modeling notations and analysis functions respectively.

Via the modular structure of the approach the uniformity and adaptability properties of the solution are supported. Providing generic metaconcepts for the service network structures, the schema facilitates the dynamic addition of new types of entities and relationships, while the definition of universal and necessary concepts for modeling relationship information in the preset allows for uniform representation. Addressing the required applicability property for the solution, a subset of the core concepts relevant for the needs of the modeled environment can be selected.

4.1   Service Network Metamodel

The Service Network Metamodel defines the language elements for specifying service network models (cf. Fig. 3). The root element SNModelDefinition describes the data types available for the description of a service network model.

An *Artifact Type* is a generalization for the types of entities and relationships comprising the service network model. Each artifact type is identifiable by a unique name. It should be well-chosen and describe the nature and the purpose of the artifact in the network.

An *Entity Type* is a specialization of artifact type comprising entities with common properties. The definition for entity types is kept generic. It does not require any mandatory information on the properties of an entity type.

A *Relationship Type* is correspondingly a specialized artifact type for the description of relations with common properties. Each relationship type connects a source entity type with a target entity type. With the provisioning of

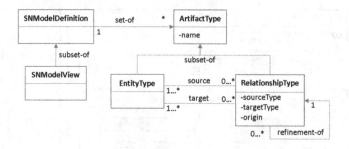

Fig. 3. The Service Network Metamodel

attributes for the specification of permitted source and target types, the meta-model allows the restriction of allowed entities for a specific relationship on the model level O1. An additional origin property is included to indicate if the relationship information was introduced manually in the model or extracted through automated processing of artifact descriptions.

Additionally, the metamodel introduces the concept of views. A view is a specification of a service network model definition with a restricted subset of entity types and relationship types, allowing a simplified representation of a model for specific analysis purposes [9].

4.2 Model Base

This part of the model instantiates the Service Network Metamodel and defines the structure of the elements in a service network model. Figure 4 provides an overview on the elements.

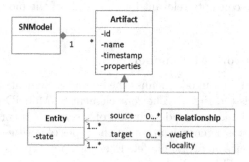

Fig. 4. The model base

An *Artifact* is an abstract element representing the common features of entities and relationships in the model. Additionally to its unique *id* within the model and a *name*, each artifact should save a *timestamp* indicating the insertion of the artifact into the service network model in order to be able to trace the evolution of the network over time. The *properties* attribute provides an extensible storage structure for artifact-specific properties.

An *Entity* is an instantiation of an entity type used to represent the different members of a service network. The generic representation of an entity inherits all properties of an artifact. Entity-specific fragments can be included in the description via the properties attribute. Additionally, an entity entry is defined by its *state* providing information on the operability of the entity, which depends on the validity of its interconnection within the network.

A *Relationship* is an instantiation of a relationship type used to represent relations between entities. It references the unique identifiers of the two entities which it connects. Additionally to the properties inherited from artifact, a relationship is specified by two additional attributes. The *weight* attribute allows the specification of the occurrence frequency of links that can be caused by the reusabillity of resources in a service network [10]. Considering the third-party consumption of resources as one of the main characteristics of service networks [17], the value of the *locality* attribute is applied as indicator for relationships crossing domain or even network borders.

4.3 Core Concepts

The preset part of the model comprises an initial information model for the uniform representation of service network models, extraction concepts for their capturing from established modeling languages in the context of service orientation, and analysis concepts providing help functions for the calculation of diverse service network health factors. The structure of the initial information model is discussed in the next section. The initial extraction concepts for BPMN, BPEL, and WSDL and the analysis functions considering the segmentation of the model in different views on the network level and single actor level are work in progress and not part of this paper.

5   Core Representation Concepts

The information model defined by the DAME preset comprises three types of entities and eight types of relationships. The selection of the entity types mirrors the socio-technical character of service networks [17]. The process of emergence of service networks from the composition of third-party services and the risks involved have served as inspiration for the relationship type identification.

Entity Types. With the erosion of the people/system boundary and the new paradigms for simultaneous acquisition and operation of a services [17], the development, operation, and evolution of service network are a cooperative initiative of multiple actors. Thus, the set of entities carving the landscape has to include not only the services responsible for the automation of capabilities, but also the human actors and the processes defining the requirements on services and inducing their collaboration [21]. Therefore, the preset defines an initial set $\mathcal{E}$ of entity types including *actors, processes*, and *services*.

An *actor* $\mathcal{A}$ indicates a physical entity supporting the evolution of a service network through the provisioning and/or consumption of resources. Thus, each network actor should own at least one process or provide at least one service. Each actor is characterized with two properties. The *role* property is used to specify if an actor participates in the network as a provider, a consumer, or both. A *type* property can be specified to indicate the nature of the actor [8], i.e., a private human or a business organization.

A *process* $\mathcal{P}$ is a sequence of activities performed together to realize a business capability [3]. Thus, a process entity represents the non-executable description of a business capability. Each process belongs to exactly one actor. One or more services are responsible for the realization of a process, and thus define the need for consumption of services and their interlinking into a network. Additionally to its operability *state* inherited from the model schema, a process entity is characterized with two additional properties. Its *version* indicates variations of the same capability. *Type* is used to specify the complexity of the process, i.e., *atomic* or *composite*.

A *service* $\mathcal{S}$ is a technical entity enabling the access to one or more capabilities [18]. A service consists of a service description and an execution component provided by an actor. The service description provides an interface in the form of available operations and contract specification needed for the usage of a service. The service logic implemented by the execution component is a black box for the service network.

A service entity is characterized with five properties. The *state, version*, and *type* attributes correspond to the ones defined for process entities. A *lifecycleStage* attribute allows the specification of the development stage of the service, e.g., initiation, design, testing. An *access* property indicates the target audience of a service [13]. A differentiation between domain-internal and domain-external services with respect to access [19] allows for better estimation of the QoS requirements and customization effort on a service.

Relationship Types. Considering the variety of entity types involved in the evolution of service networks, the model can be separated in different abstraction levels. Therefore, relationships can be differentiated into *vertical* relationship connecting entities from different type, and *horizontal* relationships connecting entities from the same type.

The vertical relationships are further classified into realization, ownership, and consumption relationships. *Realization* relationships $\mathcal{R}_r$ indicate the refinement of a source entity by the target entity. The source has to fulfill at least one requirement of the target. This relationship provides the basis for expressing the interconnection between the business level and IT level of the service network.

An *ownership* relationship $\mathcal{R}_o$ is used to express the responsibility of a source entity for the target entity. This type of relationship connects the social level of the service network with the resources of business and IT level. Thus, the source of an ownership relation is always an actors. The set of target entity types includes the set of processes and services. One actor can own multiple processes and services. Each process and service interconnected in a service network belongs exactly to one actor. This actor is responsible for the provisioning of their specified quality.

A *consumption* relationship $\mathcal{R}_u$ expresses the usage of resources within the network. It does not specify how the source makes use of the target but specifies that the target is of interest for the source. This relationship connects the social network layer with the technical services layer. The information is deduced from the realization relationships of the actor's processes. Each actor can consume multiple services. The more of the actor's processes are realized by a service, the higher the weight of the consumption relationship for the actor.

The horizontal relationships in a service network can be further separated into equivalence and associative relationships. Equivalence relationships connect similar entities as competition or evolution parties. A *competition* relationship $\mathcal{R}_c$ connects entities providing the same communication interface, i.e. services providing the same functionality. The actors owning competing services are correspondingly also competitors. A service can have multiple competitors, but not every service has a competitor, e.g., services providing niche functionality. The strength of a competition relationship between actors providing competing services depends on the number of the competing service pairs they own. Although possible in case of intra-domain redundancies, a competition relationship between services of the same provider will not lead to an actor competition relationship.

An *evolution* relationship $\mathcal{R}_e$ indicates that a source entity is a descendant from the target entity. Thus, it connects two versions of the same entity with a modified interface existing at the same time in the service network. Multiple versions of a process or a service may be present within the network with slightly different scope of the provided capabilities or quality. Yet, an evolution relationship is allowed only between resources provided by the same actor.

Associative relationships include dependency relations between entities from the same type. These are divided into cooperation, flow, and resource relationships. A *cooperation* relationship $\mathcal{R}_v$ expresses the collaboration of entities to provide a more complex capability. The result of a collaboration is a value-added entity combining the capabilities of existing entities. The composition of entities in a complex value-added entity can take place on the process level and on the service level. A composite entity can combine multiple existing entities. A cooperation relationship is included from the composite entity to each of its sub-entities. Via deduction from the cooperation between entities from different providers, cooperation relationships can be included on the social level of the model between all actors participating in the provisioning of the value-added entity.

A *flow* relationship $\mathcal{R}_f$ expresses a temporal dependency from the source entity regarding the provisioning of the target entity. Flow relationships occur between entities participating in the composition of a value-added entity and represent the control flow defined by the value-added entity. Thus, a flow relation connects either process or service entities. The wight of the relationship between two entities increases with the number of value-added entities defining the same control flow between both entities.

A *resource* relationship $\mathcal{R}_d$ expresses a data dependency from the source entity regarding the execution of the target entity. Resource relationships occur also between the participants of a composition and represent the exchange of data objects provided by the source and further processed by the target. The weight of the relationship relates to the number of objects exchanged between the connected entities.

6   Application of the Model for Impact Analysis Support

To validate the usefulness of the model a demonstration of its applicability for impact analysis support is considered. Impact analysis in general is the assessment process of the possible consequences of pursuing a course of action[1]. In the context of service-based applications, impact analysis is focused on determining the scope of modifications needed on the different modeling layers of the application to accomplish a change [12]. Impact analysis for service networks broadens the scope of the process to consider the consequences of a change across all applications referencing the resource under modification.

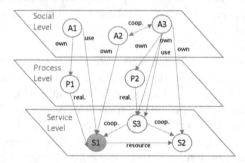

Fig. 5. An exemplary service network model

The **objective** of the impact analysis process is to determine the interconnectivity of a certain entity within the service network. This is important for identifying hot spots within the service network, i.e., entities that will immensely influence the health of the network in case of modification. In order to determine these entities all incoming and outgoing relationships to all entities have to be considered.

The **problem** of identifying the critical entities in a complex service network landscape is twofold. First, since services do not know for which capabilities they

---

[1] http://www.businessdictionary.com/definition/impact-analysis.html.

are applied in the network. Second, neither services nor processes know in what value-added entities they are composed. This knowledge is only implicitly available in the descriptions of the more complex entities, which also know only their direct successors.

A **solution** for the problem is provided by the capturing and analysis of an integrated service network model following the approach proposed in this paper. Figure 5 shows an example service network model for the motivation scenario from Sect. 2. Analyzing the number and nature of the incoming and outgoing relationships for all eight entities, we identify S1 as the entity with the greatest impact in the network. Following its cooperation and resource relationships on the service level we see that S1 will affect the operability of all other services within the network. Also both processes on the process level will be influenced by a change of S1: P1 via its direct realization relationship to S1 and P2 via its relationship to S3, which is in the impact set of S1.

7   Conclusion and Future Work

The explicit availability of information on the relationships between the artifacts in a service network is important for analyzing the operability state of the service network and for the estimating the impact of changes that can occur during the evolution of the network. As illustrated in this paper, relationships can be observed vertically between the social, process, and services abstraction layers of the service network model, as well as horizontally between entities of the same type. Moreover, relationships can be of different types.

With the purpose to provide a definition of an extensible and uniform service model, this paper proposed a meta-model based modeling approach providing a generic language schema and a preset of entities and relationships following that schema. The applicability of the resulting model is demonstrated for the discovery of critical entities in an impact analysis scenario.

As part of our future work we plan the evaluation of the model with more complex service networks. Additionally, we will provide a set of analysis functions as part of our core concepts preset providing useful calculations on the basis of the initial information model presented here.

References

1. Adersberger, J.: Modellbasierte Extraktion, Repräsentation und Analyse von Treceability-Informationen. Herbert Utz Verlag (2013)
2. Allee, V.: Reconfiguring the value network. J. Bus. Strategy **21**(4), 36–39 (2000)
3. Alonso, G., Casati, F., Kuno, H., Machiraju, V.: Web Services: Concepts, Architectures and Applications. Springer, Heidelberg (2004). ISBN 3-540-44008-9
4. Atkinson, C., Kuhne, T.: Model-driven development: a metamodeling foundation. IEEE Softw. **20**(5), 36–41 (2003)
5. Blau, B., Kramer, J., Conte, T., Van Dinther, C.: Service value networks. In: IEEE Conference on Commerce and Enterprise Computing 2009. CEC 2009, pp. 194–201. IEEE (2009)

6. Cardoso, J., Miller, J.A., Bowman, C., Haas, C., Sheth, A.P., Miller, T.W.: Open service network analysis. In: 1st International IFIP Working Conference on Value-Driven Social, pp. 81–88 (2011)
7. Cardoso, J., Pedrinaci, C., De Leenheer, P.: Open semantic service networks: modeling and analysis. In: e Cunha, J.F., Snene, M., Nóvoa, H. (eds.) IESS 2013. LNBIP, vol. 143, pp. 141–154. Springer, Heidelberg (2013)
8. Danylevych, O., Karastoyanova, D., Leymann, F.: Service networks modelling: an SOA & BPM standpoint. J. Univers. Comput. Sci. (J.UCS) **16**(13), 1668–1693 (2010)
9. Danylevych, O., Leymann, F., Nikolaou, C.: A framework of views on service networks models. In: Barjis, J., Eldabi, T., Gupta, A. (eds.) EOMAS 2011. LNBIP, vol. 88, pp. 21–34. Springer, Heidelberg (2011)
10. Erl, T.: SOA Principles of Service Design. Prentice Hall PTR, Upper Saddle River (2007)
11. Gordijn, J., Akkermans, H., Van Vliet, J.: Designing and evaluating e-business models. IEEE Intell. Syst. **16**(4), 11–17 (2001)
12. Hirzalla, M., Zisman, A., Cleland-Huang, J.: Using traceability to support soa impact analysis. In: IEEE World Congress on Services, pp. 145–152. IEEE (2011)
13. Josuttis, N.: SOA in Practice. O'reilly, Sebastopol (2007)
14. Kabzeva, A., Götze, J., Müller, P.: Service network modeling approaches: overview, classification, and analysis. In: Proceedings of the 40th Euromicro SEAA Conference, Verona (2014)
15. Liu, Y., Fan, Y., Huang, K.: Service ecosystem evolution and controlling: a research framework for the effects of dynamic services. In: Proceedings of the International Conference on Service Sciences (2013)
16. Motahari-Nezhad, H.R., Stephenson, B., Singhal, S.: Outsourcing business to cloud computing services: opportunities and challenges. HP Laboratories, HPL-2009-23 (2009). www.hpl.hp.com/techreports/2009/HPL-2009-23.html
17. Northrop, L., Feiler, P., Gabriel, R.P., Goodenough, J., Linger, R., Longstaff, T., Kazman, R., Klein, M., Schmidt, D., Sullivan, K., et al.: Ultra-Large-Scale Systems: The Software Challenge of the Future (2006)
18. OASIS: Reference model for service oriented architecture 1.0, October 2006
19. Repp, N., Schulte, S., Eckert, J., Berbner, R., Steinmetz, R.: Service-inventur: Aufnahme und bewertung eines services-bestands. In: MDD, SOA und IT-Management (MSI 2007) Workshop, Oldenburg, April 2007. p. 13. GITO mbH Verlag (2007)
20. Schulz, F., Caton, S., Michalk, W., Haas, C., Momm, C., Hedwig, M., McCallister, M., Rolli, D.: Integrated modeling of technical and business aspects in service networks. Integration of Practice-Oriented Knowledge Technology: Trends and Prospectives, pp. 119–128. Springer, Heidelberg (2013)
21. Sommerville, I., Cliff, D., Calinescu, R., Keen, J., Kelly, T., Kwiatkowska, M., Mcdermid, J., Paige, R.: Large-scale complex it systems. Commun. ACM **55**(7), 71–77 (2012)
22. Spohrer, J., Maglio, P.P.: Service science: toward a smarter planet. In: Karwowski, W., Salvendy, G. (eds.) Introduction to Service Engineering, pp. 1–30. Wiley, Hoboken (2010)
23. Strogatz, S.H.: Exploring complex networks. Nature **410**(6825), 268–276 (2001)
24. Wang, Y., Taher, Y., van den Heuvel, W.J.: Towards smart service networks: an interdisciplinary service assessment metrics. In: Enterprise Distributed Object Computing Conference Workshops (EDOCW), pp. 94–103. IEEE (2012)

Context-Aware Decentralization Approach for Adaptive BPEL Process in Cloud

Molka Rekik[1]([✉]), Khouloud Boukadi[1], and Hanene Ben-Abdallah[2]

[1] Mir@cl Laboratory, Sfax University, Sfax, Tunisia
molka.rekik@gmail.com
[2] King Abdulaziz University, Jeddah, KSA

Abstract. When outsourcing BPEL process in the Cloud, the decentralization of its execution can resolve any QoS degradation inherent to the centralized execution. Each task within the BPEL process can be executed on a virtual machine (VM) then all tasks are orchestrated together to respect the business process logic constraint represented through the tasks' dependencies and communication requirements. The BPEL process decentralization must account for a set of contextual information such as the dynamic availability of the Cloud provider's resources and the customer QoS preferences. So, in this paper, we present a decentralization approach which accounts for several essential factors that best represent the context of the BPEL process when it is outsourced into the Cloud in order to dynamically adapts its initial configuration.

Keywords: BPEL process · Outsourcing · Cloud · Decentralization · Context · Dynamic · Adaptation · Configuration

1 Introduction

Motivated by a better business agility, a higher competitive progress and a reduced cost, enterprises have been taking advantage of Business Processes Outsourcing (BPO). With the emergence of Cloud models, enterprises have the possibility to use services to further reduce costs through improved resources utilization, reduced infrastructure cost, and faster deployment of their business processes. In this paper, we investigate how these new delivery models affect the BPO. BPEL is the *de facto* standard for executing an SOA-based business process which is a series of related tasks implemented by a set of web services performed together to produce a defined set of results. When these web services are centrally executed, a single BPEL engine is responsible for coordinating the execution of the components, which may create a bottleneck and degrade the QoS of the business processes. When the business process is deployed in the Cloud, decentralization of its execution can resolve these problems. Indeed, each task can be executed on a Cloud resource (*e.g.*, a VM which has a BPEL engine). Then, all tasks are orchestrated to respect the business process logic. Besides the business logic constraint represented through the tasks' dependencies and communication requirements, such decentralization approach must account for a set

© Springer International Publishing Switzerland 2015
G. Ortiz and C. Tran (Eds.): ESOCC 2014, CCIS 508, pp. 51–62, 2015.
DOI: 10.1007/978-3-319-14886-1_6

of contextual information such as the dynamic availability of the Cloud provider's resources and the customer QoS preferences *e.g.*, execution time and cost. BPEL process decentralization in the Cloud is considered as an NP-hard problem due to, first, the huge number of resources. Second, to the satisfy multiple criteria at the same time (*e.g.*, minimizing the execution time, minimizing the execution cost, maximizing the resources utilization). This problem can be further classified into a multi-objective optimization problem which must find the best resources allocation tasks. Our literature review shows that many efficient algorithms were already proposed such as those in [1,6]. In these approaches, each task allocated to a given cloud resource is assumed to execute successfully until its termination. However, during the BPEL process execution, a Cloud resource may fail or become overloaded and, consequently, it would not execute the scheduled task under the predefined QoS constraints (*i.e.*, the initial BPEL configuration (the task-resource allocation) becomes inappropriate). To account for the highly sensitive of the BPEL process to its environmental context (like the unavailability of computing resources, the variation of user demand, etc.), we propose an innovative context-based approach for decentralizing BPEL processes. For this, we proceed by identifying the most relevant contextual information when outsourcing a BPEL process into the Cloud. This latter interprets the context, which is considered as its building block, in order to trigger the on-demand resource provisioning and adapt the initial BPEL process configuration. We propose an algorithms which select the suitable resource (VM) from a set of available ones in such a way that the contextual constraints remain satisfied. To examine the advantages of our proposition, we extended the popular CloudSim simulator in order to implement and evaluate our scheduling approach.

The remainder of this paper is organized as follows: related work is reviewed in Sect. 2. Section 3 presents the relevant contextual information which affects the outsourcing of BPEL process into the Cloud. Section 4 describes our context-aware decentralization approach for adaptive BPEL processes in the Cloud; in addition, it defines the multi-objective optimization problem. In Sect. 5, we discuss how we extended CloudSim to implement and present a preliminary evaluation of our approach. Finally, Sect. 6 summarizes the presented work and outlines areas of future work.

2   Related Works

The BPEL process decentralization problem was widely studied in the Grid environment. In [2], the authors describe an approach for the optimized execution of computational tasks. They define an optimization algorithm that supports the dynamic deployment of software components on-demand, in order to fulfill user requirements *e.g.*, the total workflow execution time. This work is similar to ours in that it choose dynamically the optimal decentralization plan at run-time based on monitored information (monitors the execution time). However, in our approach, we also generate optimum decentralization with respect to a cost constraint. Moreover, unlike our approach, this Grid-based approach is not suitable for the Cloud which differs from Grids in terms of their huge number of resources that need to be configured. In the Cloud, the problem is studied as a resource scheduling problem. The approach proposed in [1] assigns Cloud resources to distribute workflow tasks while minimizing the overall execution time and cost incurred from using Cloud resources. They define three complementary bi-criteria approaches. In the aggregation approach, the bi-criteria problem is transformed into a mono-criterion problem. The Pareto approach is applied when no criterion is dominant, and the ϵ approach is applied when a criterion is more important than the other. Similar to Bessai's work, in our approach, we offer a time-based and a cost-based BPEL decentralization algorithms. However, to reduce the complexity of the scheduling problem, our approach allows the user to define weights for both criteria (time and cost) in such a way that the problem becomes a mono-criteria problem. A second distinction of our approach from [1] is the dynamic reconfiguration: [1] schedules statically tasks to Cloud resources with no consideration of the resource capacities variations. It does not consider the degradations of the resource capacities during the workflow execution. Among those approaches that account for the dynamic variation of the resource capacities, [7] propose an adaptive resource allocation mechanism for task execution which increases the utilization of providers' resources. This approach takes in consideration only the resources context, that is the workloads degradation of resources. This is justified by the fact that this approach seeks only to maximize the utilization of Cloud resources. In contrast, our approach aims to satisfy both Cloud providers and users by trying to maximize resource utilization and minimize execution cost and time. Moreover, this work is not suitable for BPEL processes: In fact, it considers a single application while our approach takes into account the business process logic modeled via the composition of inter-related tasks.

3   Context Categorization for Adaptive BPEL Processes in the Cloud

The categorization of context is an important stage for BPEL process decentralization in the Cloud. In our work, we divide context into three sub-contexts: task-related, resource-related and user-related.

3.1   Task-Related Context

A task is a work unit that constitutes, with other tasks, a business process. Based on our previous work [3], we define the task context by its functional and non-functional context. Just, to mention that the functional context is mainly used in the outsourcing decision phase. We refer the reader to our previous work in this field [10] but it is out of the scope of this paper. The non-functional context captures a set of parameters that specify the quality of a service required to maintain a good performance of the task, usually known as QoS. QoS encompasses several quality parameters that characterize a task in a cloud computing environment such as: execution time (the time spent by the VM executing the task); transfer time (the time to transfer data between tasks); communication time (the time to migrate data from a Virtual Machine to another); execution cost (the cost for executing a task on a VM); and communication cost (the cost to migrate data from a VM to another over the network).

3.2 Resource-Related Context

In an IaaS Cloud environment, a resource is a virtual machine (VM) acting as a orchestration engine capable of executing the BPEL code. In this work, we consider that each VM is used to execute one task of the BPEL process. To run a task, each VM requires its components: CPU, memory, storage and/or bandwidth which interconnects it to other VMs. Because a VM's context is mainly related to the availability of these components, the resource-related context is explicitly defined by Cloud providers. Generally this information models the competitive advantage that Cloud providers may have over one another. In this work, we look for optimizing the resources utilization. Note that resource-related context often evolves during a task execution. For example, the resource workload, which is measured by the resource utilization rate (UR), changes dynamically influencing the entire business process. Note also that the resource-related context interferes with the task-related context. For example, given that the resource is overloaded (UR $\simeq 100\,\%$) or underloaded (UR $\simeq 0\,\%$), the task execution cost increases and the task execution time becomes slower.

3.3 User-Related Context

The user-related context represents available information characterizing a given user. For example, a user profile might represent a set of information of the characteristics of the clients or their preferences such as preferred Cloud provider location, preferred pricing mode, as well as QoS priorities when outsourcing the BPEL process (e.g., reduce the BPEL execution time, minimize the BPEL execution cost, guarantee the process reliability, etc.). In this paper, we account for different user preferences by weighting the scheduling criteria according to the user requirements. For example, if the user assumes that having a minimum execution time is of high priority, then the business process scheduler should consider the time criterion and focus on minimizing the execution, transfer and communication times.

4 Decentralizing Adaptive BPEL Process in the Cloud

4.1 Decentralization Problem Definition

We should mention in the beginning that BPEL process decentralization problem in the Cloud is in reality a scheduling problem. In this work, we focus only on the sequential BPEL process which is represented by a directed acyclic graph where

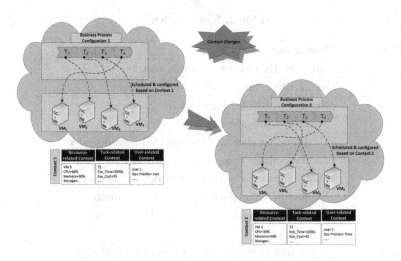

Fig. 1. Context-aware BPEL process decentralization approach

the nodes are the tasks and the edges are the dependencies between tasks. We consider an initial BPEL process configuration running on an IT infrastructure adapted for a particular context. We assume that each VM is correctly configured to execute one task (i.e., the VM must include a BPEL engine). During the BPEL process execution, the context can change frequently and consequently affect the initial BPEL configuration. So, we must adapt the initial configuration and propose a reconfiguration that considers the new contextual information (Fig. 1). We introduce, in the Table 1, the notations used during our work.

The execution cost is given by the multiplication of the execution time and the resource utilization cost:

$$EC(t, v, r) = ET(t, v, r) * UC(v, r) \tag{1}$$

The communication time is given by dividing the task data amount by the bandwidth capacity while the communication cost is computed by multiplying the communication time by the network utilization cost:

$$CT(t(v, r), t(v', r)) = data(t(v, v'))/Bw(v, v') \tag{2}$$

$$CC(t(v, r), t(v', r)) = UC(v, v') * CT(t(v, r), t(v', r)) \tag{3}$$

The BPEL configuration initial cost is defined as the sum of the execution costs of all its tasks, given by:

$$C0 = \sum_{i=1}^{n} \sum_{j=1}^{m} EC(ti, v, rj) \tag{4}$$

Table 1. Key notations

Notation	Description
C0	Initial BPEL process execution cost($)
T0	Initial BPEL process execution time(Sec)
n	Number of BPEL process tasks
p	Number of providers
Thr	Maximum number of VMs provided by a provider
Tc	Total execution time, constraint defined by user(Sec)
Cc	Total execution cost, constraint defined by user($)
Nb	Number of VMs allocated for a configuration
UC(v,r)	Usage cost of resource r on the VM v per time unit ($/Sec)
UC(v,v')	Usage cost of the network connecting v and v' per time unit ($/Sec)
ET(t,v,r)	Execution time of task t on resource r of the VM v (Sec)
EC(t,v,r)	Execution cost of task t on resource r of the VM v ($)
TT(t(v,r),t'(v,r))	Data transfer time from task t to task t' executed on the resource r of the VM v(Sec)
data(t(v,v'))	Data amount of task t transferred from the VM v to VM v'(Mb)
CC(t(v,r),t(v',r))	Communication cost between the two VMs v and v'($)
CT(t(v,r),t(v',r))	Communication cost between the two VMs v and v'(Sec)
Bw(v,v')	Capacity of the bandwidth connecting v and v'(Mb/Sec)
C	Total BPEL process execution cost($)
T	Total BPEL process execution time (Sec)

The BPEL configuration initial time is the total of tasks execution time including the data transfer time between each task and its predecessors (Pred), calculated by:

$$T0 = \sum_{i=1}^{n}\{\sum_{j=1}^{m} ET(ti, v, rj) + \sum_{p \in Pred} TT(ti(v,r), tp(v,r))\} \qquad (5)$$

After the adaptation, the execution cost of the BPEL reconfiguration includes the tasks execution costs and the data communication cost between VMs due to the utilization of the network in order to migrate the task between VMs, given by:

$$C = C0 + CC(t(v,r), t(v',r)) + EC(t, v', r) \qquad (6)$$

The execution time of the BPEL reconfiguration includes the tasks execution times and the data communication time between VMs, given by:

$$T = T0 + CT(t(v,r), t(v',r)) + ET(t, v', r) \qquad (7)$$

The BPEL execution cost must respect the cost constraint defined by the user:

$$C < Cc \tag{8}$$

The BPEL execution time must respect the time constraint defined by the user:

$$T < Tc \tag{9}$$

Our context-based decentralization approach is in fact a multi-objective optimization approach that aims to ensure the user QoS priorities. The objective functions (Eqs. 10 and 11) consist of discovering a VM v such as it minimizes, respectively, the execution cost and time. The objectives functions (Eqs. 12 and 13) consist of discovering a VM v such as it minimizes, respectively, the communication cost and time. Finally, the objective function (Eq. 14) consists of discovering a VM v such as it minimizes the transfer time.

$$\min_{v}(ET(t, v, r)) \tag{10}$$

$$\min_{v}(EC(t, v, r)) \tag{11}$$

$$\min_{v}(CT(t(v, r), t(v', r))) \tag{12}$$

$$\min_{v}(CC(t(v, r), t(v', r))) \tag{13}$$

$$\min_{v}(TT(t(v, r), t'(v, r))) \tag{14}$$

4.2 Adaptive BPEL Process Decentralization Algorithms

We propose two decentralization algorithms for adaptive BPEL process according to the user QoS priority. The first re-plans Cloud resources to tasks while minimizing the execution time and maximizing the use of these resources in the case that the user accords the high priority to the time criterion. The second algorithm re-schedules tasks to resources while reducing the execution cost and maximizing the use of resources if the cost criterion has the highest priority. In our proposed algorithms, we monitor the number and the utilization rates of VMs, we re-evaluate the execution times and costs of the tasks (i.e. when the execution time/cost surpasses the user constraint, we identify the problem source (CPU, RAM or bandwidth overloaded)) and we propose to migrate tasks. We denote the initial configuration by a tuple Config0=<Ti, vj, R, C0, T0> which specifies that the task Ti is executed on the set of resources R of the VM vj with a cost C0 and a time T0 and each reconfiguration is denoted by a tuple Config=<Ti, vj, R, C, T> which signifies that the task Ti is executed on the set of resources R of the VM vj with a cost C and a time T. Let w_t be the weight associated to the time criterion and w_c be the weight associated to the cost criterion. In the following, we present our time-based decentralization algorithm for adaptive BPEL process configuration (Algorithm 1). Our cost-based decentralization algorithm performed in this phase has been formalized in our site [9], but is omitted here due to space limitations.

Next, we present how to select the suitable VM (v') from a set of available ones.

Input: Config0=<Ti,Vj,R,C0,T0>
Output: Config=<Ti,Vj,R,C,T>
Functions:
LoadBalancing(VM v, VM v')//use Round-Robin to load balance the workload
of the resources v et v' while migrating the task from v to v'
createVM(VM v')//create a new VM v'
Equation6(c) return C//calculate the cost C by using E6
Equation7(t) return T//calculate the time T by using E7

if $wt > wc$ then
    receive the task-related context of Ti;
    //the time of the task Ti surpasses the time constraint
    if $T0 > Tc$ then
        monitor UR(r) of R on each allocated VM;
        if $UR(r)=100\%$ of the VM v then
            search and select v' with UR(r)=0 % such as minimizing ET, CT
            and TT by using E10, E12, E14;
            if *exists v'* then
                LoadBalancing(v, v');//migrate Ti from v to v'
                Equation6(C0);
                Equation7(T0);
                update tasks dependencies;
            end
        else if $Nb < \sum Thr$ then
            //all VMs are busy and the sum of thresholds is not reached
            createVM(v');
            Nb++;
            LoadBalancing(v, v');
            Equation6(C0);
            Equation7(T0);
            update tasks dependencies;
        end
        else
            search and select v' with (UR=%0) in cloud federation such as
            minimizing ET, CT and TT by using E10, E12, E14;
            LoadBalancing(v, v');
            Equation6(C0);
            Equation7(T0);
        end
        end
    end
end

Algorithm 1. Time-based decentralizing Algorithm for Adaptive BPEL
Process Configuration

4.3   VM Selection Approach

Solving a Multi-Objective Optimization (MOO) problem is a hard mission
because it is an exponential problem. Both, the Pareto approach proposes a

set of optimal solutions (set of no-dominate points) for MOO problems and the weighted sum method provides a single solution point that reflects preferences presumably incorporated in the selection of a single set of weights [8]. The idea of the weighted sum method is to convert the MOO into a single objective optimization problem. In our work, we adopt the weighted sum approach to solve our problem in selecting one suitable resource (VM) from multiple ones taken of different providers. While taking into account the user QoS priority, the optimization problem will be more refined. If the user gives a high priority to the time criterion, then the objective function $F(x)$ aims to minimize the execution and communication times:

$$F_t(x) = [objective1(x); objective2(x)] \ where:$$
$$objective1(x) = ET(t, v, x) \ and \ objective2(x) = CT(t(v, r), t(v', r)) \quad (15)$$

On the other hand, if the user gives a high priority to the cost criterion, then the $F(x)$ should minimize the execution and communication costs:

$$F_c(x) = [objective1(x); objective2(x)] \ where:$$
$$objective1(x) = EC(t, v, x) \ and \ objective2(x) = CC(t(v, r), t(v', r)) \quad (16)$$

Hence, our utility function is defined as the weighted sum of cost and time, and it is represented as the following scalar optimization problem:

$$U = \min(w_t * F_t(x) + w_c * F_c(x)) \quad (17)$$

where:

$$0 < w_t, w_c < 1 \quad (18)$$

$$w_t + w_c = 1 \quad (19)$$

5 Validation and Evaluation

To validate and evaluate our work, we use the CloudSim toolkit [4] which is an extensible simulator for cloud computing environments. It is an open source simulator, based on Java language and it allows the easy modeling of virtualized environments, supporting on-demand resource provisioning, and their management. For modeling workflow applications with communicating tasks, we use the simulation framework *NetworkCloudSim* defined by Garg et al. in [5]. We extend the **NetworkDatacenterBroker** in order to define our **ContextAwareBroker**. We present in the listing 1.1 a part of our broker's code where we take into account:

1. The dependencies and the communications between cloudlets (the tasks are defined as cloudlets in the CloudSim simulator).
2. The Pareto distribution to distribute cloudlets to VMs according to Pareto approach (line 11).

3. The monitoring of the resource-related context to trigger the adaptation (lines 5–7).
4. The migration of cloudlet between two VMs (line 15).

Listing 1.1. ContextAwareBroker

```
1   public class ContextAwareBroker
2   {...
3    protected void updateVmProcessing (int VmId)
4    {double time = 0, UR = 0, sumThr = 0;
5     for (ResCloudlet rcl : getCloudletExecList ())
6     {UR += rcl . getCloudlet (). getUtilizationOfCpu (time);
7     if (UR==100)//reschedule the application on VMs
8     {for (AppCloudlet app : this . getAppCloudletList ())
9      {List<Integer> vmids = new ArrayList<Integer >();
10     int numVms = linkDC . getVmList (). size ();
11     ParetoDistr pareto = new ParetoDistr (2, 5);
12     for (int i=0; i<app.numbervm; i++)
13      {int vmid = (int) getVmList ().get(i).getId ();
14      if (!vmids.isEmpty())
15      {migrateCloudlet (getVmList ().get(i));
16       app.createCloudletList (vmids);}
17      else
18       ...
19       }}}}}
```

In the following, we illustrate our **ContextAwareBroker** with a simple example. Let's consider that:

1. The Datacenter characteristics are: 2048 MB RAM, 1 TB of storage (data base), 1 CPU and 1 bandwidth of 10 KB of capacity, the cost of using the CPU, RAM, data base and bandwith are, respectively, 3, 0.05, 0.001 and 1 $.
2. An initial BPEL process configuration which assigns the task T1 to the VM V0, the task T2 to V2 and the task T3 to V1. This Initial configuration is based on the Context0 defined in the Table 2.
3. A change affects the resource-related context. So, the resource becomes overloaded (its CPU utilization rate is equal to 100 %). The Table 2 presents the contextual information of the initial BP configuration (Context0) and the contextual information after this supposed change (Context1).
4. An adaptation action consists of migrating cloudlet from the overloaded VM V2 to another which minimizes the time. So, our **ContextAwareBroker** redistributes tasks to VMs while respecting, on the one hand, the dependencies between them and on the other hand, the new context. The BPEL reconfiguration assigns the task T1 to the VM V1 where it is executed with 2000 s time, the task T2 to the VM V0 where it achieves 4000 s execution time and the task T3 to the VM V0 with 8000 s execution time (Fig. 2(b)).

To evaluate our approach, we consider a process with 10 tasks. Its execution requires 10 VMs which are hosted in a datacenter including three hosts.

Table 2. An example of context change

	Context0	Context1
Task-related Context	T1(2000 s,3\$), T2(8000 s,3\$), T3(12000 s,3\$)	T1(2000 s,3\$), **T2(12000 s,5\$)** T3(12000 s,3\$)
Resource-related Context	V0(UR(CPU,RAM,BW) = 40 %), V1(UR(CPU,RAM,BW) = 50 %) V2(UR(CPU) = 80 %, UR(RAM,BW) = 70 %)	V0(UR(CPU,RAM,BW) = 40 %) V1(UR(CPU,RAM,BW) = 50 %) **V2(UR(CPU) = 100 %** UR(RAM,BW) = 80 %)
User-related Context	Wt = 0,6, Wc = 0,4	Wt = 0,6, Wc = 0,4

The Fig. 2(a) depicts the VMs' performances. So, with our time-based decentralizing algorithm, we can migrate the cloudlets from the VMs overloaded (VM1, VM6, VM8) to others underloaded (VM2, VM4, VM7). In this way, we get an optimal solution that minimizes the tasks' execution time comparing with the one obtained by using the time-shared scheduler proposed by the CloudSim (Fig. 2(b)). By applying this scheduler, which implements First Come First Served Policy (FCFS) for allocating tasks to VMs, the execution time of each running task decreases if the number of submitted tasks increases. Hence, with the time-shared scheduler the workflow execution terminates in 66000 s when by using our algorithm it ends in 58000 s.

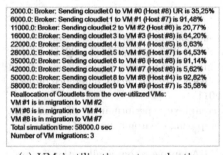
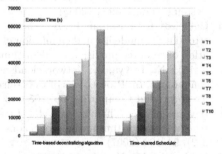

(a) VMs' utilization rate evaluation   (b) Execution time evaluation

Fig. 2. Time-based decentralizing algorithm evaluation

6 Summary and Future Work

In this paper, we presented a context-based BPEL decentralization approach to adapt the initial BPEL configuration affected by a fluctuation of workloads or a violation of the execution time/cost requested by user. So, the reconfiguration for executing the BPEL process must consider the new context information and maximize the user satisfaction, business benefits and resources usage. We defined a context categorization and a set of contextual events that affect a BPEL configuration in the Cloud. Then, we proposed two decentralization algorithms in order to propose a BPEL reconfiguration that fits the new context. According to the user QoS priority, the first decentralization algorithm is time-based while the second is a cost-based decentralization algorithm. Finally, we illustrated the efficiency of our approach through a simulation based on the extended CloudSim toolkit.

As a future work, we plan to improve the context categorization for BPEL processes in the Cloud in order to consider other criteria such as delay and energy. In addition, we plan to improve the proposed algorithms to include workflow patterns such as parallel and conditional task compositions which influence the computation of the execution time and cost.

References

1. Bessai, K., Youcef, S., Oulamara, A., Godart, C., Nurcan, S.: Bi-criteria workflow tasks allocation and scheduling in cloud computing environments. In: Proceedings of the IEEE Fifth International Conference on Cloud Computing, pp. 638–645 (2012)
2. Binder, W., Constantinescu, I., Faltings, B., Heterd, N.: Optimized, decentralized workflow execution in grid environments. Multiagent Grid Syst. **3**(3), 259–279 (2007)
3. Boukadi, K., Chaabane, A., Vincent, L.: A framework for context-aware business processes modelling. In: International Conference on Industrial Engineering and Systems Management (2009)
4. Calheiros, R.N., Ranjan, R., Beloglazov, A., De Rose, C.A.F., Buyya, R.: Cloudsim: a toolkit for modeling and simulation of cloud computing environments and evaluation of resource provisioning algorithms. Softw. Pract. Exp. **41**(1), 23–50 (2011)
5. Garg, S.K., Buyya, R.: Networkcloudsim: modelling parallel applications in cloud simulations. In: Proceedings of the Fourth IEEE International Conference on Utility and Cloud Computing, pp. 105–113 (2011)
6. Ilavarasan, E., Thambidurai, P.: Low complexity performance effective task scheduling algorithm for heterogeneous computing environments. J. Comput. Sci. **3**(2), 94–103 (2007)
7. Li, J., Qiu, M., Niu, J., Chen, Y., Ming, Z.: Adaptive resource allocation for preemptable jobs in cloud systems. In: ISDA, pp. 31–36 (2010)
8. Marler, R.T., Arora, J.S.: The weighted sum method for multi-objective optimization: new insights. Struct. Multi. Optim. **41**(6), 853–862 (2010)
9. Rekik, M.: https://sites.google.com/site/molkarekiklaadhar/contextawarebroker
10. Rekik, M., Boukadi, K., Ben Abdallah, H.: A decision method for business process outsourcing based on enterprise context. In: Workshops on Enabling Technologies: Infrastructure for Collaborative Enterprises, pp. 324–329 (2013)

Assisting Business Process Outsourcing to the Cloud

Mouna Rekik[1]([✉]), Khouloud Boukadi[1], and Hanene Ben-Abdallah[2]

[1] Mir@cl Laboratory, Univeristy of Sfax, Sfax, Tunisia
rekik.mona@yahoo.fr, Khouloud.Boukadi@fsegs.rnu.tn
[2] King Abdulaziz University, Jeddah, Saudi Arabia
hbenabdallah@kau.edu.sa

Abstract. The business/IT alignment is an important concept as it creates a coherence between business goals and vision and the IT strategies and decisions. The adoption of cloud computing is one of the IT strategies that is increasingly being considered by several enterprises. When enterprises focalize on the business process outsourcing to the cloud, many issues should be tackled such as its suitability as an environment for running the business process, the selection of parts of business process to be outsourced, and the depiction of the most suitable cloud providers for its execution. This papers major contribution is a decision method framework presenting guidelines to support decision makers aiming to outsource their SOA-based business process to the cloud. The framework assists experts in the fastidious task of analyzing and resolving the BPO problem and its relevance to enterprises context. Its top-down characteristic allows for the study of the enterprise business needs, lacks, and perspectives and the depiction of the implied IT resources creating thus a harmonious correspondence between the two levels which is very demanded in enterprises to guarantee their persistence in the economic markets.

Keywords: Decision method · Cloud computing · IT/business level · Business process outsourcing · Enterprise context

1 Introduction

Enterprises are facing an enormous number of challenges in sustaining their position in the currently high competitive economic environment. To guarantee their success, various considerations should be regarded within the enterprise beginning from building solid strategies related to both IT and business levels. In this context, business/IT alignment is an important concept as it creates a coherence between business goals and vision and the IT strategies and decisions. The adoption of cloud computing is one of the IT strategies that is increasingly being considered by several enterprises. Cloud computing is currently exploited by many start-ups due to its multiple benefits including scalability, cost-effectiveness, freeing adopters from hardware and software investment [1]. Despite these benefits,

© Springer International Publishing Switzerland 2015
G. Ortiz and C. Tran (Eds.): ESOCC 2014, CCIS 508, pp. 63–70, 2015.
DOI: 10.1007/978-3-319-14886-1_7

uncertainties and conflicts may prevent experts from exploiting this new IT environment. Indeed, portrayed benefits and disadvantages vary from one enterprises point of view to another because each enterprise has its own context, goals and architecture. This variation may render opportunities offered by cloud computing for one enterprise considered as drawbacks for others. For instance, platform services (Paas) delivered by a cloud may be opportune to a specific enterprise due to the flexibility of their developed software but may not be suitable for another due to the legacy nature of their owns. When enterprises focalize on the business process outsourcing (BPO) to the cloud and more precisely SOA-based business processes, many issues should be tackled such as its suitability as an environment for running the business process, the selection of parts of the business process to be outsourced, and the depiction of most suitable cloud providers for its execution. This papers major contribution is the decision method presenting guidelines to support decision makers aiming to outsource their business process to the cloud. It is a representation of the decision toolkit components that cover all important aspects in the enterprise starting from the business to the IT levels. This allows experts to understand the enterprises context, the cloud adoption challenges, and the real requirements of the enterprise. Moreover, it assists them in the BPO to the cloud decision by: the depiction of implied business processes that need to enhance its performance, the study of the influential factors of the performance, the identification of services to be outsourced and finally the proposition of cloud providers list using previous studies as input. The sequel of the paper is as follows: Sect. 2 overviews works related to cloud adoption for enterprises. Section 3 presents the decision method. Finally, Sect. 4 summarizes the presented work and highlights its future directions.

2   Related Work

Studying and analysis of business data and requirements is knowing an important interest from researchers. The aim is to assist business experts in the fastidious task of interpreting the business evolution of their enterprises. Reference [14] presents a modeling approach to facilitate the interpretation and consultation of business data of enterprise such as goals, strategies, and processes. Besides the modeling of business concerns, assessing the continuous improvement of business process performance is tackled by [15] which is done based on execution measurement model comprising a set of execution measure. The solution proposed for the improvement doesn't tackle the BPO to the cloud, which may be an interesting opportunity for the enhancement of business processes. In the same context, [14] proposed a formal analysis of execution of organizational scenarios. Few works focused on the evaluation and assessment of cloud adoption suitability for BPO. The evaluation of cloud adoption suitability have other concerns in literature. Khajeh-Housseini et al. proposed a cloud computing adoption toolkit [2] where many considerations can be examined like the technology suitability, cost and energy consumption analysis and the stakeholder impact analysis. In their study, Trigueros-Preciado et al. [3] identified different barriers and effects of the adoption of cloud computing. They define barriers that may prohibit enterprises from adopting cloud as the doubt about security, availability and quality of service, data lock-in and the control loss of data. Besides, the authors define opportunities like cost reduction, access to IT better resources, cloud properties like scalability, flexibility and accessibility and finally the possibility to focus on core business. Another work is proposed in [4] which highlights some of the unseen technical hurdles faced by small and medium-sized enterprise (SME) in selecting and identifying software-as-a-service offerings. This work was undertaken through an analysis of providers considered by businesses, the businesses sought, and an ethnographic observation of a service selection. The results are used to propose indicative success dimensions for cloud service selection and a need for more detailed research to support SME in service selection.

Overall, the reported researches focalize on IT needs within the enterprise that can affect the decision of adopting the cloud computing. They try to assist decision makers in the assessment of the suitability of cloud computing adoption. However, very little number of researches propose the study of the business needs and requirements of enterprises. The ignorance of this important aspect creates a gap between the business and IT levels within the enterprise leading to misappropriate decisions. We believe that the elaboration of the business plans and vision is the most important phase prior to any decision related to the IT architecture of the enterprise such as the adoption of cloud computing. Finally, to the best of our knowledge, there is no approach that tackled the assessment of the cloud as an alternative environment of SOA-based business process execution when a degradation of performance is detected.

3   The Proposed Approach

This section presents an overview about how to decide about the suitability of the BPO to the cloud. It describes the tools needed for the decision method which will be a relevant toolkit support for experts to assist them from business to IT levels. We begin by defining the input of the method, tools used in each step, and finally the output of the decision method. Figure 1 presents the framework of our decision method.

3.1   The Input of the Decision Method: The Enterprise Context

We provide our decision method with the possibility to introduce relevant data reflecting the situation and needs of any enterprise. For more flexibility, and to make the decision adaptable to the variation of enterprise context, our decision of BPO to the cloud is context-aware. The enterprise context covers the organizational context, the enterprise architecture, and the SWOT analysis for the cloud adoption. The organizational context presents a view about the enterprise actual status as the cost of running business processes, the resources implied, their security features, etc. We elaborated the depicted organizational context in our previous work [5]. In addition to the organizational context, the enterprise

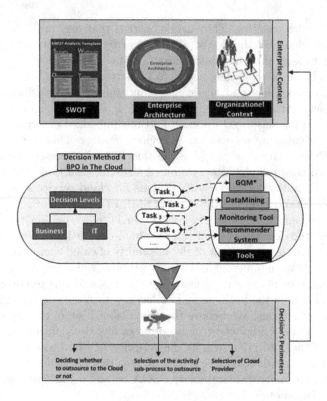

Fig. 1. The decision method framework

context contains the enterprise architecture. The MIT Center for Information Systems Research (MIT CISR) in 2007 defined enterprise architecture as: *EA is the organizing logic for business processes and IT infrastructure reflecting the integration and standardization requirements of the companies operating model.* The enterprise architecture will be an important element in our decision method to realize the business process cartography and depict running business processes within the enterprise. The SWOT analysis referring (strength, weakness, opportunities and threats) is an analysis tool used to elaborate development strategies. It is important for any decision/strategy taken within an enterprise to be aware about external and internal factors. The SWOT analysis referring (strength, weakness, opportunities and threats) is an analysis tool used to elaborate development strategies [8]. These are the three essential components consisting the enterprise context considered as input of our decision method. Details of the decision method are presented in the next section.

3.2   Our Decision Method

The enterprise context we use as input for our decision method allows firstly to the depiction of the most important business processes running or need to be implemented within the enterprise. To ensure the achievement of the enterprise business goals and vision, monitoring the performance of running SOA-based business processes is essential. The monitoring phase requires the depiction of metrics to be monitored insured by the use of the goal-question-metric approach (GQM) [7]. To be more convenient with our purpose, we adapted this approach so it lists both IT and business metrics called process performance indicators [11–13]. The former step presents the input for the recommender system which is a valuable mean to guide experts for the adoption of suitable cloud providers able to enhance the performance of business processes. In this paper we will focus only on identifying candidate business processes to be outsourced by the elaboration of different steps depicted previously. As previously mentioned, the enterprise context considered as input for our decision method allows for the elaboration of a deep analysis of the enterprise business needs vision, and requirements. Considering an example of an European bank, experts define vision behind adopting cloud computing as: being the bank leader in Europe. For the realization of this vision, different strategic goals are defined such as:

- SG1: Have good relation with clients
- SG2: Be present in all Europe countries

The business process cartography is a mean for experts to depict business processes running within the enterprise. For illustration purpose, we only consider one essential business process: The real estate credit request.

Assess Business Process Performance. After the enumeration of essential business processes two different alternatives can be followed:

- If the business process is running within the enterprise, experts need to monitor their performance and assess whether they attain their related business goals. The monitoring phase is based on the observation of key performance indicators (KPIs).
- If some business processes dont exist within the enterprise, we applied another decision method to assess whether the cloud is suitable. This is not the focus of this paper and for more details we refer readers to our previous work [5].

In this paper, we focused on the depiction of business processes elected to be outsourced. To do so, we elaborated several essential steps: we identified KPIs for each business process running within the enterprise using business-GQM, then we monitored them to find out whether they attain the target value or not. BPO to the cloud is limited to business processes characterized by a degradation of their performance. Indeed, outsourcing business process may be a solution to enhance its relevant performance. A top-down analysis is applied then to extract related IT and business metrics that affect the business process performance. As already mentioned, we propose an adaptation of the GQM named the business-GQM. The GQM [6] is an analytic goal-oriented approach. The choice of this paradigm is thanks to its measurement-based property and the bottom-up characteristic [7,8]. The main strength of this approach is its ability to identify where an improvement is needed in software systems. Indeed, based on the identified goals, questions are posed to extricate the relevant metrics concerning the software system and then an evaluation of performance based on these metrics is done. We adapted the GQM so it can identify KPIs related to business processes and apply further analysis to identify the influential factors of the identified KPI such as IT and business metrics. The Business-GQM is presented in Fig. 2 and is applied for each running business process having a link with a strategic goal. The elaboration of the first step of the business-GQM for the business process Real estate credit request depicts the importance of monitoring the KPI Number of clients to find out whether it attain its strategic goal Have a good relation with clients. The monitoring phase in our project is based on events launched from BPEL (business process execution language) engines. These events are stored in an execution log database for subsequent analysis. The second level of the business GQM consists on defining influential factors affecting KPI. For our case, IT metrics influencing the KPI number of clients are datastorage size of data bases, the existence of security tools for infrastructure running the business process, and the availability of the service Evaluate client data. Two business metrics are found which are number of failed request and duration of the business process. The decision method purpose, is to evaluate whether cloud computing is suitable for the enactment of business processes and more precisely whether its adoption will enhance their performance. Obviously, benefits offered by cloud computing

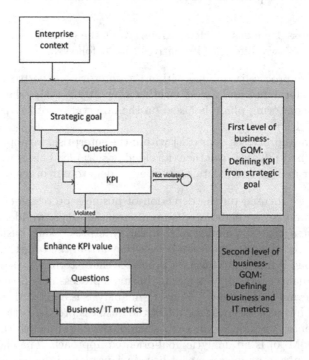

Fig. 2. Business-GQM

are limited to IT aspects such as the big capacity of data storage, the elasticity property, the time reduction, etc. For these reasons, when a KPI violation is detected, one needs to find out whether this fail is caused by IT or business factors. For this, the application of data mining tool is essential. We used the monitoring framework named QMODSev elaborated in our previous work [9,10] to monitor IT metrics.

Analysis of Business Process Performance. The main objective of this step is the evaluation of the influence of IT characteristics on the business processes performance and more precisely the previously depicted IT metrics. The idea is to apply data mining tool over the execution logs comprising different values of Influential factors and related KPI corresponding to each process instance. This step displays ranked influential factors started from one influencing the most process instances. The list of ranked influential factors is considered as input of the recommender system for searching most suitable cloud for executing the business process. It is to be noted that if the most influencing factor on the KPI is a business metric, the BPO to the cloud is not needed and the process of decision is stopped. The business analysts should focus on the assessment and improvement of business processes from a business perspective.

4 Conclusion

The decision of outsourcing business process to the cloud is not a trivial task. Cloud Computing environment is not a one-size-fits-all: the right approach depends on the enterprises needs, priorities and strategies. Several considerations should be taken so that appropriate decision is made such as the enterprise context elaboration, the business process performance identification and analysis and the assessment of cloud providers. In this paper, we presented our framework of the BPO to the cloud decision method. It encompasses steps and tools to assist experts on the business process outsourcing to the cloud. The elaborated decision method is characterized by its top down property as it goes from the study of the business aspects of the enterprise to the IT levels. Moreover, our decision method is flexible as it can be applied to different enterprise context and business processes. We are working on the elaboration of the recommender system for the selection of suitable cloud provider for the business process.

References

1. Vaquero, L., Merino, L., Caceres, J.: Towards a cloud definition. SIGCOMM Comput. Commun. Rev. **39**, 50–55 (2009)
2. Khajeh-Hosseini, A., Greenwood, D., Smith, J.W., Sommerville, I.: The cloud adoption toolkit: supporting cloud adoption decisions in the enterprise. Softw. Pract. Exp. **42**, 447–465 (2012)
3. Trigueros-Preciado, S., Perez Gonzlez, D., Solana Gonzlez, P.: Cloud computing in industrial SMEs: identification of the barriers to its adoption and effects of its application. Electron. Markets **23**, 105–114 (2013)

4. Braithwaite, F., Woodman, M.: Success Dimensions in Selecting Cloud Software Services the Software Engineering and Advanced Applications (SEAA) (2011)
5. Rekik, M., Boukadi, K. Ben Abdallah, H.: A decision method for business process outsourcing based on enterprise context. In: IEEE 22nd International Workshop on Enabling Technologies: Infrastructure for Collaborative Enterprises (WET-ICE), pp. 324–329 (2013)
6. Caputo, E., Corallo, A., Damiani, E., Passiante, G.: KPI modeling in MDA perspective. In: Meersman, R., Dillon, T., Herrero, P. (eds.) OTM 2010 Workshops. LNCS, vol. 6428, pp. 384–393. Springer, Heidelberg (2010)
7. Basili, V.R., Caldiera, G., Rombach, H.D.: The goal question metric approach. In: Marciniak, J.J. (ed.) Encyclopedia of Software Engineering, vol. 1, pp. 528–532. Wiley, New York (1994)
8. Basili, V.R., Weiss, D.M.: A Methodology for collecting valid software engineering data. IEEE Trans. Softw. Eng. **10**, 728–738 (1984). IEEE CS Press
9. Grati, R., Boukadi, K., Ben-Abdallah, H.: A QoS monitoring framework for composite web services in the cloud. In: Advcomp 2012, Barcelone, Spain, pp. 65–70 (2012)
10. Grati, R., Boukadi, K., Ben-Abdallah, H.: An event based approach to extract the run time execution path of BPEL process for monitoring QoS in the Cloud. In: CSSME 2012, pp. 1233–1239 (2012)
11. Del-Ro-Ortega, A., Resinas, M., Cabanillas, C., Corts, A.R.: On the definition and design-time analysis of process performance indicators. Inf. Syst. **38**(4), 470–490 (2013)
12. Del-Ro-Ortega, A., Resinas, M., Durn, A., Corts, A.R.: Using templates and linguistic patterns to define process performance indicators. Enterp. Inf. Syst. 1–34 (2014)
13. Popova, P., Sharpanskykh, A.: Modeling organizational performance indicators. Inf. Syst. **35**(4), 505–527 (2010)
14. Horkoff, J., Barone, D., Jiang, L., Yu, E., Amyot, D., Borgida, A., Mylopoulos, J.: Strategic business modeling: representation and reasoning. Softw. Syst. Model. **13**(3), 1015–1041 (2014)
15. Delgado, A., Weber, B., Ruiz, F., de Guzmn, I.G.-R., Piattini, M.: An integrated approach based on execution measures for the continuous improvement of business processes realized by services. Inf. Softw. Technol. **56**(2), 134–162 (2014)

CLIoT 2014

Preface of CLIoT

Maria Fazio[1]($\boxtimes$), Nik Bessis[2], and Massimo Villari[1]

[1] University of Messina, Messina, Italy
mfazio@unime.it
[2] University of Derby, Derby, UK

The Internet of Things (IoT) is an emerging paradigm that aims to represent the physical world, change the way we interact with the things around us. IoT describes every system through uniquely identifiable and interconnected objects (things). Things have the capacity for sensing, processing or actuating information about entities available from within the real world. Thus, information travels along heterogeneous systems, such as routers, databases, information systems and the Internet, leading in the generation and movement of enormous amounts of data which have to be stored, processed and presented in a seamless, efficient and easily interpretable form. At the same time, Cloud Computing is quickly becoming a pervasive technology, able to offer several types of services according to different business models.

Both IoT and Cloud Computing address two important goals for distributed system: high scalability and high availability. These features make the Cloud Computing a promising choice for supporting IoT services. IoT can appear as a natural extension of Cloud Computing implementations, where the Cloud allows to access IoT based resources and capabilities, to process and manage IoT environments and to deliver on-demand utility IoT services such as sensing/actuation as a service.

CLIoT 2014 is the second edition of the International Workshop on CLoud for IoT. It aimed at bringing together scientists, practitioners and PhD students in order to discuss the limits and/or advantages of existing Cloud solutions for IoT, and to propose original and innovative contributions for enhancing real world resources over Cloud environments. The topics of interest for CLIoT 2014 included but were not limited to: innovative models and system architectures, IoT Data abstraction and processing, Mobile Cloud, Cloud storage for IoT, interaction between sensor networks and Cloud, Discovery Service for IoT, Cloud Computing based IoT technologies, Wireless Sensor Networks into the Cloud, Big data management, Smart Environments, ubiquitous computing/pervasive computing, real-time communication with smart objects, applications based on IoT and Cloud, Inter-cloud management and Cloud Federation, security and privacy in Clouds and IoT.

All submitted manuscripts have been peer-reviewed by the international program committee members, having three or four reviews for each paper. The final acceptance rate of the manuscripts is 60 %.

The contributions accepted for presentation at the workshop include the work of Belli et al., which proposed a novel Cloud architecture for Big Stream applications that can efficiently handle data coming from deployed smart objects

© Springer International Publishing Switzerland 2015
G. Ortiz and C. Tran (Eds.): ESOCC 2014, CCIS 508, pp. 73–75, 2015.
DOI: 10.1007/978-3-319-14886-1_8

through a graph-based processing platform and deliver processed data to consumer applications with low latency. Ismail et al. presented an architectural model for decentralized self-adaptation to support the crosslayer and multi-cloud environment. They also proposed a planning model and method to enable the decentralized decision making. Mulfari et al. propose a new methodology to evaluate performances of applications running on virtual machines over the Cloud and accessed through Remote Desktop environments. They use such a methodology to analyze the behavior of a Cloud IaaS considering two different applications that can be widely adopted for IoT purposes.

The workshop program included one invited speaker, Orazio Tomarchio, Assistant Professor at the Department of Electrical, Electronic and Computer Engineering, University of Catania, Italy. His talk on "A semantic framework for matching business requirements in cloud markets" presented semantic languages used to build a new data models of the Cloud domain from the business perspectives of the provider and customer respectively.

Maria Fazio, Nik Bessis and Massimo Villari
Workshop Organizers
CLIoT 2014

Organization

Workshop Organizers

Maria Fazio, University of Messina, Italy
Nik Bessis, University of Derby, UK
Massimo Villari, University of Messina, Italy

Technical Program Committee

Liz Bacon	University of Greenwich, UK
Francisco J. Blaya Gonzlvez	University of Murcia, Spain
Antonio Celesti	University of Messina, Italy
Ciprian Dobre	University Politehnica of Bucharest, Romania
Teodor-Florin Fortis	West University of Timisoara, Romania
Antonio J. Jara	University of Applied Sciences Western Switzerland (HES-SO), Switzerland
Natalia Kryvinska	University of Vienna, Austria
Giovanni Merlino	University of Catania, Italy
Navonil Mustafee	Swansea University, UK
Zsolt Nemeth	MTA SZTAKI, Hungary
Chrysa Papagianni	National Technical University of Athens, Greece
Marco Picone	University of Parma, Italy
Florin Pop	University Politehnica of Bucharest, Romania

Evangelos Pournaras   Delft University of Technology, Netherlands
Orazio Tomarchio   University of Catania, Italy
Sergio Toral   University of Seville, Spain

Sponsoring Institutions

The event has been sponsored by the IEEE ComSoc IoT Emerging Technical Committee

Decentralized Planning for Self-Adaptation in Multi-cloud Environment

Azlan Ismail[1]([✉]) and Valeria Cardellini[2]

[1] Faculty of Computer and Mathematical Sciences,
Universiti Teknologi MARA (UiTM), Shah Alam, Malaysia
azlanismail@tmsk.uitm.edu.my
[2] Department of Civil Engineering and Computer Science Engineering,
University of Roma Tor Vergata, Roma, Italy
cardellini@ing.uniroma2.it

Abstract. The runtime management of Internet of Things (IoT) oriented applications deployed in multi-clouds is a complex issue due to the highly heterogeneous and dynamic execution environment. To effectively cope with such an environment, the cross-layer and multi-cloud effects should be taken into account and a decentralized self-adaptation is a promising solution to maintain and evolve the applications for quality assurance. An important issue to be tackled towards realizing this solution is the uncertainty effect of the adaptation, which may cause negative impact to the other layers or even clouds. In this paper, we tackle such an issue from the planning perspective, since an inappropriate planning strategy can fail the adaptation outcome. Therefore, we present an architectural model for decentralized self-adaptation to support the cross-layer and multi-cloud environment. We also propose a planning model and method to enable the decentralized decision making. The planning is formulated as a Reinforcement Learning problem and solved using the Q-learning algorithm. Through simulation experiments, we conduct a study to assess the effectiveness and sensitivity of the proposed planning approach. The results show that our approach can potentially reduce the negative impact on the cross-layer and multi-cloud environment.

Keywords: Cross-layer self-adaptation · Decentralized planning · Markov Decision Process · Multi-cloud · Reinforcement learning · Q-learning

1 Introduction

The smart environment concept concerns with the implementation of smart city technologies into the urban environment with the goal to benefit and improve people's daily lives. In the context of Internet computing, a smart city can effectively process networked information to improve outcomes on any aspect of city operations [3]. The key infrastructures to enable smart city technologies lie on Internet of Things (IoT) and Cloud computing. In principle, IoT comprises of

© Springer International Publishing Switzerland 2015
G. Ortiz and C. Tran (Eds.): ESOCC 2014, CCIS 508, pp. 76–90, 2015.
DOI: 10.1007/978-3-319-14886-1_9

three main components; sensors and actuators, data analytic tools, and visualization tools [9]. In a large-scale context, especially with sensor data streams [2], these components should be deployed and managed in a multi-cloud setting.

The layered and multi-cloud environment introduces a compelling challenge in the self-adaptation of IoT-oriented applications [11]. A possible approach to support such mechanism is the adoption of a decentralized control method [21], which is fundamentally based on the MAPE (Monitor, Analyze, Plan, and Execute) reference framework of autonomic computing [12]. MAPE provides a closed control loop capability which can enable an autonomic component to realize self-CHOP (Configuration, Healing, Optimization, Protection) properties as well as emergent self-* properties [18]. The decentralized approach promotes multiple MAPEs and thus a set of adaptation managers to control the adaptation while interacting between each other. Depending on the chosen decentralized pattern, some managers act as sensors and executors, while others analyze and make decisions, or all managers have a complete capability as defined in MAPE. By implementing this way, each manager is able to make and execute its own decision with its own environment. At the same time, it is aware of the other systems operating in the same global environment through coordinated interaction.

The benefits of the decentralized approach include flexibility, performance, and fault tolerance. Indeed, each adaptation component has flexibility in making its own plan and executing it; as a result, the performance of the adaptation mechanism can be speeded up, since the adaptation managers are able to plan and take the necessary actions within their scope (within a layer or a cloud environment). In addition, decentralization provides fault tolerance in the presence of some component failure. However, decentralized self-adaptation implies a communication overhead since the managers should coordinate their actions.

In this paper we present a conceptual decentralized self-adaptation architectural model that operates in a multi-cloud environment. The architecture supports the capability of information sharing pattern among the autonomic adaptation managers, that are responsible to manage the cross-layer as well as the multi-cloud environment.

We also address the decentralized planning problem in realizing the self-adaptation process. In decentralized settings, the adaptation manager will plan the adaptation by considering the information within its environment. However, it can occur that the executed plan impacts negatively on the other layers and cloud providers. Herein, the negative impact refers to the a situation where the predefined Service Level Agreements (SLAs) of a layer or a cloud provider are violated. For instance, rebinding a service at the application layer may increase the resource utilization at the infrastructure layer, thus causing a violation of the resource utilization at a certain period of time. Another example is rescaling the size of the virtual machines which may slow down the application; the slowing down of the application may in its turn affect the application layer, namely the application reliability. Furthermore, the effect of multiple cloud providers that may be involved need to be considered as well; for example, the migration of a processing service from one cloud to another with the goal to locate the service closer to the data sources can affect negatively the traffic load on the receiving cloud and thus its performance. Therefore, a planning solution that is aware of cross-layer and multi-cloud effects is required. To this end, we define a decentralized planning approach that is formulated as a Reinforcement Learning problem and solved using the Q-learning algorithm.

The rest of this paper is organized as follows. We discuss the challenges that require for a decentralized planning for self-adaptation in Sect. 2. Then, we present a conceptual decentralized self-adaptation architectural model in Sect. 3. In Sect. 4, we propose a decentralized planning approach for the self-adaptation. We then report the experimental study to show the effectiveness of the proposed approach in Sect. 5. In Sect. 6, we highlight related work. Finally, we conclude and provide hints for future work in Sect. 7.

2   Challenges for Self-Adaptation

2.1   Example Scenario

To motivate our work, we consider as example a traffic management system for an urban environment [14]. This kind of system consists typically of a set of sensing, data analysis and visualization capabilities. The sensing application collects the traffic condition data through sensors dispersed in the urban environment; the data analysis application analyzes and explores the data; finally, the visualization application is used to interpret data in a meaningful form.

In a multi-cloud setting, these applications can be located in different clouds due to non-functional requirements. For instance, the sensing application can be located in a proximate cloud facility that is typically at the network edges (the so called Fog computing [1]), the data analysis application in a distant and resource-rich cloud data center, and the visualization application in a different remote cloud providing high computing power.

In the multi-layer perspective, each type of cloud has more than one layer. In general, a cloud may have an application layer, the middleware layer (platform) to manage the runtime lifecycle of the application, and the infrastructure layer which comprises the virtualized computing, storage and network resources.

During runtime, fault conditions may occur [4] which can cause a specific layer or a cloud to become unresponsive, slow, failed, etc. Such problematic condition requires a self-adaptation mechanism to bring the entire traffic management system back into a healthy condition.

2.2   Motivation

Weyns et al. [21] have proposed several decentralized control patterns which are useful to support the self-adaptation process, i.e., information sharing patterns. Some benefits of the decentralized approach are related to its flexibility and performance. In a decentralized approach, each adaptation component has flexibility in making its own plan and executing the plan. As a result, the performance of the adaptation mechanism can be speeded up, since the adaptation managers are able to plan and take the necessary actions within their scope (within a layer or within a cloud environment).

However, there are issues to be addressed to successfully perform the planning mechanism. In this paper, we focus on the uncertainty impact caused by the future adaptation actions. This means, an adaptation action specifically targeted to a layer may cause a negative impact on other layers or clouds. Herein, the negative impact refers to the a situation where some non-functional requirement is violated. For instance, redeploying an application at the application layer may affect the infrastructure layer in such a way that the resources utilization at a certain period of time is violated. Another example is rescaling the size of the virtual machines which may cause the application to slow down. The slowing down of the application may in its turn affect the application layer, namely the reliability of the application. The uncertainty of the negative impact is caused by the limited knowledge and control obtained by the adaptation managers in producing their adaptation plan. It can be reduced by providing more predicted information to the respective adaptation manager in the planning phase. Therefore, in this paper, we focus on proposing a decentralized planning approach with the cross-layer and multi-cloud impact information.

3   Decentralized Self-Adaptation Architecture

In this section, we present the decentralized self-adaptation architecture for the multi-cloud environment in which IoT applications are deployed. The overall architecture is illustrated in Fig. 1 and consists of the layered and multi-cloud models.

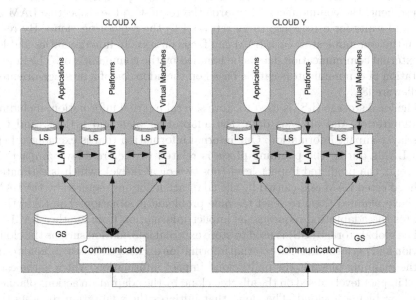

Fig. 1. Decentralized self-adaptation architecture

The layered model within each cloud represents the relationship between the adaptation managers, called Local Adaptation Manager (LAM), and the cloud layers, i.e., application, platform, and virtual machine (infrastructure) layers. This relationship is also viewed as an internal one within a given cloud environment. Each LAM has the capability to monitor, analyze, plan, and execute the proper adaptation actions on the layer it manages. It also has a local storage (LS) to keep the knowledge within its own environment. Whenever needed, LAMs can exchange information between each other. That is, each LAM may request information (or a portion of information) directly to another LAM. As a result, the respective LAM will respond with the required information. This internal communication between LAMs is essential to effectively plan for the adaptation. This kind of setting is called an information sharing pattern [21].

The multi-cloud model represents the relationship between LAMs and the external environment. This is essential since an IoT application can be deployed over multiple clouds. Hence, an adaptation performed by any LAM within its cloud environment can affect another cloud. Whenever needed, each LAM can make a request to the communicator component to get the relevant information from another cloud environment. By using some external information, which is stored in the global storage (GS), the adaptation plan can be improved. This external information sharing also represents the information sharing pattern.

The communicator in each cloud becomes the agent to support the external communication for requesting and receiving the relevant information about the adaptation impact on the other clouds. The request is triggered by LAM whenever an adaptation is needed. Upon receiving a request from LAM, the communicator submits the request to the respective clouds to obtain the impact information. After receipt of the required response, the communicator returns the information to the respective LAM. In case of receiving a request from another cloud environment, the communicator forwards the request to the respective LAM as well, and waits for a response to be returned to the requesting cloud. By relying on the communicator, each LAM can focus on its core functionalities and let the external communication details be handled by the communicator. The implementation of communicators can be based on the adoption of a message-oriented middleware [8].

The local storage (LS) is used to store several internal information, including the monitoring and analysis data, the adaptation plan and actions, and the cross-layer impact information. One internal information that is exchanged between LAMs during the planning phase is related to the cross-layer impact. It represents the predicted impact level (positive or negative), which is estimated by the affected LAM and caused by the adaptation actions required by the LAM that have planned them to react to some problematic situation. The LAM that initiates the adaptation requests the impact information from another LAM.

The global storage (GS) is used to store external information such as the cloud location and performance. An external information exchanged between clouds during the planning phase is the multi-cloud impact information, which is the estimated impact level caused on the affected cloud by the adaptation actions planned by the problematic cloud. The cloud that initiates the adaptation requests the impact information from the related clouds.

4   Local Adaptation Manager Planning

In this section, we present the design of the planning approach for LAM. We begin by introducing the planning process. Then, we present the model of the planning problem based on Markov Decision Process and the planning algorithm based on Q-learning [20].

4.1   Planning Process in MAPE Cycle

Herein, we define the normal scenario for the planning process. In the MAPE control loop, the adaptation is needed whenever a SLA violation is detected by the monitoring component. The LAM that triggered the detection will perform the analysis to estimate the impact level based on the pre-defined strategies.

In the initial cycle of adaptation, the analysis only provides the internal impact level information, since the planning has not yet been executed. This internal impact becomes the core input to the planning component. In the planning stage, a pre-processing of Q-value will be executed followed by the learning process. The aim is to identify the appropriate adaptation strategy which can minimize the impact. Once the strategy is determined, it is exchanged with other LAMs and the respective clouds. This is essential to enable other LAMs within the same cloud as well as other clouds to assess the impact in their environment. The exchange mechanism within the same cloud environment may utilize the sharing concept, which means all the estimated impact information will be made public by storing them in the global repository. A synchronization mechanism is needed to ensure the data consistency [5]. Meanwhile, the exchange mechanism between clouds may utilize a message-oriented middleware [8]. Upon receiving the external impact information, the LAM that initiated the adaptation process will replan the strategy aiming at the minimization of the impact level. If the expected strategy is found, then the LAM will notify the others to execute either concurrently or in a coordinated form. Otherwise, re-exchanging the information may be required within a certain period.

In the following section, we focus on modeling the planning for the k-MAPE cycle where k refers to any stage in the cycle.

4.2   Planning Problem Modeling

The planning problem is modeled within the context of a LAM. It consists of a set of elements, namely, the services, the states, the actions, the impact values, the Q-value and the policy. The details are provided as below.

Services. The services refer to the set of functionalities associated to the given layer. For instance, a service at platform layer is meant to control the execution of application.

The services are represented by a matrix $LE : L \times E$, where L is a set of layers and E is a set the services for each layer. Therefore, the services managed by a LAM can be represented as $E_l \in LE$, where l is a specific layer and E represents all services associated to layer l. It is assumed that $e_0 \in E_l$ and $e_0 \in E_k$ is associated to the same application.

States. The states refer to the condition of a specific service e in a specific layer l. The condition is referred to the non-functional requirement satisfactions. For instance, a state of the application layer's LAM could be "service A's availability is satisfied and its cost is violated".

In this model, the states of service e is a finite number which determines the limit of the adaptation cycle. The states are variables to be assigned with the satisfaction status, such as *satisfied* and *violated*. In the context of multiple LAMs, the states are represented as a matrix $SS : L \times E \times S$ where L is a set of layers, E is a set of services for each layer and S is a set of finite states for each service. Therefore, the states for a LAM can be represented as $S_{lE} \in SS$, where l is a specific layer and E represents all services associated to the layer.

We assume that the states are in a sequence order $(s_0, \ldots, s_n)$ with $s_i \in S_{lE}$, where the first state variable s_0 determines the initial state and the last state variable s_n the final state. The initial state should contain the violated status.

Actions. The actions refer to the possible adaptation actions that can be executed for the respective layer. For instance, adding or migrating a new virtual machine instance (infrastructure), updating or redeploying a Web server (platform), and reselecting different component services on the basis of the QoS properties (application).

In the context of multiple LAMs, the actions are represented as a matrix $AA : L \times E \times S$ where L, E, and S have been already defined. Therefore, the set of actions for a LAM can be represented as $A_{lES} \in AA$, where l is a specific layer, E represents all services associated to the layer, and S represents all states for each service E.

Impact Values. In this paper, the impact represents the consequence of performing an adaptation. The source of the impact can be either internal or external. The internal source refers to the cross-layer impact within a cloud, while the external source refers to the multi-cloud impact.

The impact level can be of two types: positive or negative. A positive impact means the entire service-based application in the multi-cloud setting can recover from a problematic condition, e.g., a SLA violation, while the negative impact is the opposite condition.

In this work, the impact values represent the impact level (positive or negative) which may be obtained from different sources (internal and external) and is associated to the SLA violation. The values are in the range $[0, 1]$, where 0 means absolutely positive impact and 1 means absolutely negative impact.

The impact values are kept in two matrixes, defined as $IL : L \times L \times E \times A$ for the cross-layer impact and $IC : C \times C \times A$, where $C : L \times E$. We define an impact function $imp(c, l, e, a)$ to compute the total impact of action a in relation to service e at layer l and cloud c. The impact function is formulated as follows:

$$imp(c, l, e, a) = \sum_{l=0, (l,k) \in L}^{l=m} y_{lkea} + \sum_{c=0, (c,z) \in C, c \neq z}^{z=n} x_{cza} \qquad (1)$$

In Eq. 1, the first term of the sum represents the cross-layer impact and the second term the multi-cloud impact. y_{lkea} is an element of matrix IL and x_{cza} an element of matrix IC. The parameters k and z represent the layer and the cloud that initiates the adaptation, respectively, while l represents the cross-layer relation and c the multi-cloud relation. Meanwhile, e denotes the service and a indicates the action under consideration.

Q-Value. The Q-value refers to the expected utility value of taking an action in a given state. It is essential to support the Q-learning algorithm [20], in particular to select the optimal action for the next state.

The Q-value is represented as a matrix $Q : L \times E \times S \times A$ where L, E, S and A have been already defined. A single Q-value can be represented as q_{lesa}, which represents the value for the adaptation action a at layer l of service e with state s.

The Q-value is obtained by a Q-function $Q(s_{le}, a_{les})$ which aims at estimating the value of taking action a_{les} at state s_{le}. The formulation is as follows:

$$Q(s_{le}, a_{les}) = q_{lesa} + \partial[imp(c, l, e, a) + \gamma \min_{a'} Q(s'_{le}, a'_{les}) - q_{lesa}] \qquad (2)$$

In Eq. 2, ∂ and γ are the learning rate and the discount factor respectively, where $0 \leq \partial, \gamma \leq 1$. Setting a higher value for the learning rate results in a quicker learning, while a higher value for the discount rate determines a less worth of future reward than immediate reward.

Policy. The policy refers to the generated plan, which comprises a set of appropriate actions from the initial state to the final state. It is generated from the learning process by selecting the best action based on the estimation of Q-value. It is formulated as follows:

$$\pi(s_{lE}) = \arg \min_a Q(s_{lE}, a_{lEs}) \qquad (3)$$

In Eq. 3, the best action is selected by considering the minimum Q-value for each iteration in the Q-learning process. Observe that we take the minimum value rather than the maximum one due to the impact level definition which is part of the Q-value estimation. Technically, a lower Q-value represents a lower impact level, which means a positive impact.

4.3   Planning Algorithm

Algorithm. We present the planning algorithm based on Q-learning by assuming that some inputs are made available. The algorithm requires a set of input parameters, namely, the states, the actions, and the impact values related to the respective layer. The algorithm outcome is an optimal policy which contains a set of optimal actions.

Require: $(E_l, S_{lE}, A_{lES}, Y_{lLEA}X_{lCEA})$
Ensure: $\pi(s_{lE})$
 1: set arbitrary for Q, ∂ and γ
 2: **for** each $e \in E_l$ **do**
 3:    **for** each $s \in S_{lE}$ **do**
 4:       select $a \in A_{lES}$ based on Eq. 3
 5:       get $l \leftarrow Y_{lLEA}$ and $c \leftarrow X_{lCEA}$
 6:       get total impact based on Eq. 1
 7:       estimate Q based on Eq. 2
 8:       assign $\pi(s_{lE}) \leftarrow a$
 9:    **end for**
10: **end for**

Algorithm 1: LAM's planning algorithm

The first step is to initialize the Q-value matrix, the learning rate ∂, and the discount factor γ. Then, a set of policies will be generated for each $e \in E$ in the respective layer l. Each service is associated with a finite set of states. Therefore, the policies to be generated are meant for each state of each service. The process of generating a policy begins with selecting an action on the basis of Eq. 3. Then, the total impact level is computed according to Eq. 1. After that, the Q-value is estimated based on Eq. 2. The selected action is then taken as part of the policy. This process is repeated until the policies for all services have been obtained.

5   Evaluation

In this section, we present an initial simulation-based evaluation of the proposed decentralized planning for IoT applications executed in a multi-cloud environment. The goal is to show the effectiveness of the proposed approach in producing a plan which minimizes the overall (cross-layer and multi-cloud) negative impacts. In addition, we present a sensitivity analysis to support our confidence of the simulated data.

5.1   Simulation Setup

We implemented a simplified Java-based multithreaded simulator of the decentralized planning scenario. The main thread acts as communicator, while the other threads represent LAMs and focus only on the planning stage; they receive a set of data inputs to produce the appropriate plans. The core data inputs are the impact and the initial Q-value matrixes, which are randomly generated. Table 1 shows the main simulation parameters and their basic setting. The simulation experiments were conducted on a HP Compaq 6005 PC equipped with 2.80 GHz AMD Phenom®II X4 B93 processor, 4 GB of RAM, and Windows 7 Professional.

Table 1. Main simulation parameters and their basic setting

Parameter	Value
Number of clouds	2
Number of layers per cloud	3
Number of services per layer	100 to 500
Number of states per service	5
Number of actions per service	5
Learning rate for Greedy strategy	0.5
Discount factor for Greedy strategy	0.9

5.2 Effectiveness Analysis

Overview. We evaluate the effectiveness of the proposed decentralized planning approach by analyzing the average impact level obtained through the optimal plan driven by two strategies, namely *Greedy* and *Random* strategy. The Greedy strategy represents the adaptation plan that is determined by utilizing the cross-layer and multi-cloud impact information as discussed in the previous section. On the other hand, the Random strategy represents a randomly generated adaptation plan and is therefore used for comparison. The average impact level data has been obtained by simulating the multiple LAM planning stages for both strategies.

Procedure. There were 5 simulation cycles for each strategy, where the cycles differed in the number of services, namely, 100, 200, 300, 400, and 500 services. The other simulation parameters shown in Table 1 were set identically. The simulation begun with the generation of the impact values and initial Q-value matrixes. This information was loaded into the main thread and distributed to the respective threads (LAM's layer). Each thread performed the planning process based on the LAM's planning algorithm to produce the appropriate adaptation plan.

We stored the generated plans for both strategies and for each simulation cycle and used them to calculate the average impact level achieved by each strategy in every simulation cycle. Finally, we normalized the collected average impact level data to obtain a value within the range $[0, 1]$, where 0 represents the most positive impact and 1 the most negative one. The normalization was computed based on the following formula:

$$av_\phi = \frac{av - im_{\min}}{im_{\max} - im_{\min}} \qquad (4)$$

In Eq. 4, av is the average total impact based for n services of a specific layer, $im_{\min}$ is the minimum impact value, $im_{\max}$ is the maximum impact value, and av_ϕ is the resulting normalized value.

Results and Findings. Figure 2 shows the average impact level values. The x-axis represents the LAM layer as well as the simulation cycle; the y-axis represents the impact level. From the table within Fig. 2, we can see that the Greedy strategy, which considers multiple impact information, contributes to a significant lower impact when the plan is executed at layer 0 except for 100 services. At layer 1, the generated plan based on the Greedy strategy contributes to a significant lower impact for each simulation cycle. At layer 2, the Greedy strategy contributes to a significant lower impact for 100, 200 and 400 services. Overall, the chart shows that the Greedy strategy contributes to a lower impact level as compared to the Random strategy. Furthermore, most of the impact levels are below 0.5 except for layer 2. These results indicate that the generated plan based on the Greedy strategy can potentially reduce the negative impact on the cross-layer and multi-cloud environment.

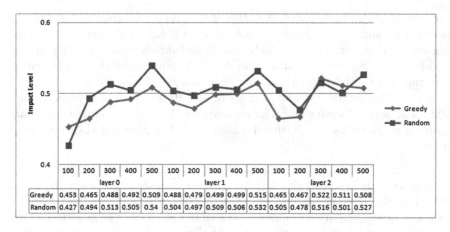

	100	200	300	400	500	100	200	300	400	500	100	200	300	400	500
			layer 0					layer 1					layer 2		
Greedy	0.453	0.465	0.488	0.492	0.509	0.488	0.479	0.499	0.499	0.515	0.465	0.467	0.522	0.511	0.508
Random	0.427	0.494	0.513	0.505	0.54	0.504	0.497	0.509	0.506	0.532	0.505	0.478	0.516	0.501	0.527

Fig. 2. Impact level for Greedy and Random strategies with respect to the LAM's layer and number of services

5.3   Sensitivity Analysis

Procedure. We now present a sensitivity of the planning approach to show that the simulated data were not dependent on the simulation settings used in the previous section and to confirm our confidence on the results. To perform the sensitivity analysis, we have chosen three parameters by focusing only on the effect at layer 0 (due to space constraints) and the Greedy strategy, as reported in Table 2. As shown in the table, a set of base values were identified, together with their low and high values. The base values were used to compute the impact level for the benchmark. The low and high values were used to compute the variation of the impact level. The simulations were carried out for each type of values; base, low and high. The generated plans were recorded and used to calculate the normalized average impact level as in Eq. 4.

Table 2. Configuration setting for sensitivity analysis

Factors	Base value	Low value	High value
Number of services	300	100	500
Number of states	5	3	8
Learning rate	0.5	0.1	0.9

Results and Findings. Figure 3 shows the average impact level generated for each parameter. The left bars represent the average impact level due to the low values, while the right bars represent the average impact level due to the high values. The line in the middle represents the impact level of the base values.

The top bar shows the variation of impact level associated to the number of states. Setting the low value of state number caused the impact level to reduce to 0.27 from the base impact level. Meanwhile, setting the high value of state number caused the impact level to increase to 0.67 from the base impact level. The variation of impact level indicates the values within −0.5 and +0.5 from the base impact level.

Very small variations are shown for the impact level related to the number of services (middle bar) and learning rate (bottom bar). Setting to low value for both parameters caused the impact level to reduce to a value within −0.5 from the base impact level. Meanwhile, setting to high value caused the impact level to increase to a value within +0.5 from the base impact level.

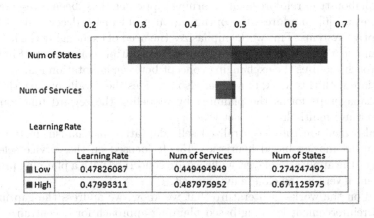

Fig. 3. Sensitivity analysis of configuration change for layer 0

In comparison, a slightly higher variation related to the change of state numbers is expected since the states represent the lifecycle of the adaptation process. The variations shown in Fig. 3 also supports our confidence level of 95 % that the simulated impact level is expected to variate within the range of −0.5 to +0.5.

6   Related Work

Learning-based approach has been applied in a few works to support the decision making of self-adaptive systems. The work by Elkhodary et al. [7] proposed a learning cycle for understanding the impact caused by an adaptation action against the system's goals. Sykes et al. [19] applied a learning-based approach to learn the appropriate rules for planning at the goal management layer of multi-tier adaptive systems. In comparison, our work is concerned with the application of the reinforcement learning-based approach since it is suitable to deal with incomplete or partial information of the environment.

Kim et al. [13] proposed a reinforcement learning-based approach for planning the reconfiguration architecture of a managed system. Panerati et al. [16] adopted the reinforcement learning-based approach to enable self-adaptive resource allocation. Although the core technique is similar, we consider an additional factor which is the complexity of the learning approach whenever multiple adaptation managers are involved.

The more recent work by Panerati et al. [17] applied a reinforcement learning-based approach to determine the appropriate configuration for coordinating multiple autonomic managers. In this context, we share the same problem motivation as addressed in our previous work [10]. The key idea is to have a centralized or global manager to control the adaptation of individual or local managers. Differently, in this work we apply the reinforcement learning-based approach for the decentralized autonomic managers where there is no centralized controller.

A collaborative reinforcement learning approach has been presented by Dowling et al. [6] to address the optimization problem for decentralized-based self-adaptive systems. This work emphasizes the need of exchanging the information to enable a collaborative learning process of multiple components. Similarly, our approach requires the exchanging concept between adaptation managers. To differentiate with this work, our paper also provides the details on how the individual manager performs the planning by modeling the reward function as a cross-layer and multi-cloud impact level.

We also mention the decentralized self-adaptation mechanism in the cloud context using market-based heuristics [15]. It focused on the service selection problem at the application layer, while we are concerned with a planning problem at different layers in the cloud environment.

Based on the works in literature that we know, we address the gap in providing a reinforcement learning-based planning approach for decentralized self-adaptive systems in a multi-cloud environment.

7   Conclusions and Future Work

In this paper, we presented an architectural model for decentralized self-adaptation of IoT applications operating in a multi-cloud environment. We also proposed a decentralized planning approach that aims at reducing the negative impact of adaptation actions. The evaluation study we conducted supports the fact that the proposed approach is reasonably effective in reducing the negative impact.

Our future work aims mainly at addressing two issues. First, a support for the decentralized planning approach to cater a conflicting problem among LAMs. This issue is essential since each LAM has the capability to make its own decision which can potentially affect the other LAMs. Therefore, an approach is needed to synchronize the generated plans which can thus benefit between each other, especially in the multi-cloud environment. Second, we plan an experimental study to understand the performance differences among decentralized control patterns, in particular the master-slave and information sharing patterns [21]. This understanding can assist in establishing an efficient and effective self-management capability that can be deployed in a real multi-cloud environment.

Acknowledgements. This work is supported by the Fundamental Research Grant Scheme (600-RMI/FRGS 5/3 (164/2013)) funded by the Ministry of Higher Education Malaysia (MOHE) and Universiti Teknologi MARA (UiTM), Malaysia.

V. Cardellini also acknowledges the support of the European ICT COST Action IC1304 Autonomous Control for a Reliable Internet of Services (ACROSS).

References

1. Bonomi, F., Milito, R., Zhu, J., Addepalli, S.: Fog computing and its role in the internet of things. In: Proceedings of 1st Workshop on Mobile Cloud Computing, MCC 2012, pp. 13–16 (2012)
2. Boyle, D., Yates, D., Yeatman, E.: Urban sensor data streams: London 2013. IEEE Internet Comput. **17**(6), 12–20 (2013)
3. Celino, I., Kotoulas, S.: Smart cities [guest editors' introduction]. IEEE Internet Comput. **17**(6), 8–11 (2013)
4. Chan, K., Bishop, J., Steyn, J., Baresi, L., Guinea, S.: A fault taxonomy for web service composition. In: Di Nitto, Elisabetta, Ripeanu, Matei (eds.) ICSOC 2007. LNCS, vol. 4907, pp. 363–375. Springer, Heidelberg (2009)
5. De Oliveira, F., Ledoux, T., Sharrock, R.: A framework for the coordination of multiple autonomic managers in cloud environments. In: Proceedings of 7th International Conference on Self-Adaptive and Self-Organizing Systems, SASO 2013, pp. 179–188, Sep 2013
6. Dowling, J., Cahill, V.: Self-managed decentralised systems using k-components and collaborative reinforcement learning. In: Proceedings of 1st ACM SIGSOFT Workshop on Self-managed Systems, WOSS 2004, pp. 39–43 (2004)
7. Elkhodary, A., Esfahani, N., Malek, S.: FUSION: a framework for engineering self-tuning self-adaptive software systems. In: Proceedings of 18th ACM SIGSOFT International Symposium on Foundations of Software Engineering, FSE 2010, pp. 7–16 (2010)
8. Fazio, M., Celesti, A., Villari, M.: Design of a message-oriented middleware for cooperating clouds. In: Canal, C., Villari, M. (eds.) ESOCC 2013. CCIS, vol. 393, pp. 25–36. Springer, Heidelberg (2013)
9. Gubbi, J., Buyya, R., Marusic, S., Palaniswami, M.: Internet of Things (IoT): a vision, architectural elements, and future directions. Future Gener. Comput. Syst. **29**(7), 1645–1660 (2013)
10. Ismail, A., Cardellini, V.: Towards self-adaptation planning for complex service-based systems. In: Lomuscio, A.R., Nepal, S., Patrizi, F., Benatallah, B., Brandić, I. (eds.) ICSOC 2013. LNCS, vol. 8377, pp. 432–444. Springer, Heidelberg (2014)

11. Issarny, V., Georgantas, N., Hachem, S., Zarras, A., Vassiliadist, P., Autili, M., Gerosa, M., Hamida, A.: Service-oriented middleware for the future internet: state of the art and research directions. J. Internet Serv. Appl. **2**(1), 23–45 (2011)

12. Kephart, J.O., Chess, D.M.: The vision of autonomic computing. IEEE Comput. **36**(1), 41–50 (2003)

13. Kim, D., Park, S.: Reinforcement learning-based dynamic adaptation planning method for architecture-based self-managed software. In: Proceedings of ICSE Workshop on Software Engineering for Adaptive and Self-Managing Systems, SEAMS 2009, pp. 76–85, May 2009

14. Kostakos, V., Ojala, T., Juntunen, T.: Traffic in the smart city: exploring city-wide sensing for traffic control center augmentation. IEEE Internet Comput. **17**(6), 22–29 (2013)

15. Nallur, V., Bahsoon, R.: A decentralized self-adaptation mechanism for service-based applications in the cloud. IEEE Trans. Softw. Eng. **39**(5), 591–612 (2013)

16. Panerati, J., Sironi, F., Carminati, M., Maggio, M., Beltrame, G., Gmytrasiewicz, P., Sciuto, D., Santambrogio, M.: On self-adaptive resource allocation through reinforcement learning. In: Proceedings of 2013 NASA/ESA Conference on Adaptive Hardware and Systems, AHS 2013, pp. 23–30, Jun 2013

17. Panerati, J., Maggio, M., Carminati, M., Sironi, F., Triverio, M., Santambrogio, M.D.: Coordination of independent loops in self-adaptive systems. ACM Trans. Reconfigurable Technol. Syst. **7**(2), 12:1–12:16 (2014)

18. Sterritt, R., Parashar, M., Tianfield, H., Unland, R.: A concise introduction to autonomic computing. Adv. Eng. Inform. **19**(3), 181–187 (2005)

19. Sykes, D., Corapi, D., Magee, J., Kramer, J., Russo, A., Inoue, K.: Learning revised models for planning in adaptive systems. In: Proceedings of 2013 International Conference on Software Engineering, ICSE 2013, pp. 63–71 (2013)

20. Watkins, C.J., Dayan, P.: Q-learning. Mach. Learn. **8**(3–4), 279–292 (1992)

21. Weyns, D., et al.: On patterns for decentralized control in self-adaptive systems. In: de Lemos, R., Giese, H., Müller, H.A., Shaw, M. (eds.) Software Engineering for Self-Adaptive Systems. LNCS, vol. 7475, pp. 76–107. Springer, Heidelberg (2013)

A Graph-Based Cloud Architecture for Big Stream Real-Time Applications in the Internet of Things

Laura Belli[✉], Simone Cirani, Gianluigi Ferrari, Lorenzo Melegari, and Marco Picone

Wireless Ad-Hoc and Sensor Network Laboratory, Department of Information Engineering, University of Parma, Viale G.P. Usberti, 181/A, 43124 Parma, Italy
laura.belli1@studenti.unipr.it,
{simone.cirani,gianluigi.ferrari,marco.picone}@unipr.it,
lorenzo.melegari@tlc.unipr.it

Abstract. The Internet of Things (IoT) will consist of billions of inter-connected heterogeneous devices denoted as *"smart objects."* Smart objects are generally sensor/actuator-equipped and have constrained resources in terms of: (i) processing capabilities; (ii) available ROM/RAM; and (iii) communication reliability. To meet low-latency requirements, real-time IoT applications must rely on specific architectures designed in order to handle and process gigantic (in terms of number of sources of information and rate of received data) streams of data coming from smart objects. We refer to this smart object-generated data stream as *"Big Stream,"* in contrast to traditional "Big Data" scenarios, where real-time constraints are not considered. In this paper, we propose a novel Cloud architecture for Big Stream applications that can efficiently handle data coming from deployed smart objects through a graph-based processing platform and deliver processed data to consumer applications with lowest latency.

Keywords: Internet of Things · Cloud · Real-time applications · Processing graph

1 Introduction

The actors involved in IoT scenarios will have extremely heterogeneous characteristics, (in terms of processing and communication capabilities, energy supply and consumption, availability, and mobility), spanning from constrained devices, also denoted as "smart objects," to smartphones and other personal devices, Internet hosts, and the Cloud. Smart objects are typically equipped with sensors and/or actuators and are thus capable to perceive and act on the environment where they are deployed. Billions of smart objects are expected to be deployed in urban, home, industrial, and rural scenarios, in order to collect relevant information, which may be used to build new applications. Shared

© Springer International Publishing Switzerland 2015
G. Ortiz and C. Tran (Eds.): ESOCC 2014, CCIS 508, pp. 91–105, 2015.
DOI: 10.1007/978-3-319-14886-1_10

and interoperable communication mechanisms and protocols are currently being defined and standardized, allowing heterogeneous nodes to efficiently communicate with each other and with existing Internet actors. The most prominent driver for interoperability in the IoT is the adoption of the Internet Protocol (IP), namely IPv6 [1,2]. An IP-based IoT will be able to extend and interoperate seamlessly with the existing Internet. Standardization institutions, such as the Internet Engineering Task Force (IETF) [3], and several research projects [4] are in the process of defining mechanisms to bring IP to smart objects, due to the need to adapt higher-layer protocols to constrained environments. However, not all objects will be supporting IP, as there will always be tiny devices that will be organized in closed/proprietary networks and rely on very simple and application-specific communication protocols. These networks will eventually connect to the Internet through a gateway/border router.

Sensed data are typically collected and sent uplink, namely from IoT networks, where smart objects are deployed, to collection environments (server or cloud), possibly through an intermediate local network element, which may perform some processing tasks, such as data aggregation and protocol translation. Processing and storing data at the edge of networks (e.g., on set-top-boxes or access points) is the basis for the evolution of Fog Computing [5] in IoT scenarios. Fog Computing is a novel paradigm that aims at extending Cloud computing and services to the edge of the network and, therefore, leverages on its proximity to end-users, its dense geographical distribution, and its support for mobility. The wide geographical distribution makes the Fog Computing paradigm particularly suited to real-time big data analytics. Densely distributed data collection points allow to add a fourth axis, low-latency, to the typical Big Data dimensions (volume, variety, and velocity). Figure 1 shows the hierarchy of layers involved in data collection, processing, and distribution in IoT scenarios.

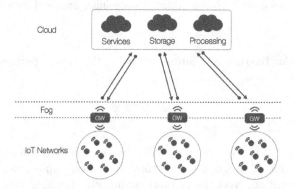

Fig. 1. The hierarchy of layers involved in IoT scenarios: the Fog works as an extension of the Cloud to the network edge to support data collection, processing, and distribution.

With billions of nodes capable of gathering data and generating information, the availability of efficient and scalable mechanisms for collecting, processing, and storing data is crucial. Big Data techniques, which were developed in the last few years (and became popular due to the evolution of online and social/crowd services), address the need to process extremely large amounts of heterogeneous data for multiple purposes. These techniques have been designed mainly to deal with huge volumes (focusing on the amount of data itself), rather than to provide real-time processing and dispatching. Cloud computing has found a direct application with Big Data analysis due to its scalability, robustness, and cost-effectiveness. The number of data sources, on one side, and the subsequent frequency of incoming data, on the other side, create a new need for Cloud architectures to handle such massive flows of information, thus shifting the Big Data paradigm to the Big Stream paradigm. Moreover, the processing and storage functions implemented by remote Cloud-based collectors are the enablers for their core business, which involves providing services based on the collected/processed data to external consumers. Several relevant IoT scenarios, (such as industrial automation, transportation, networks of sensors and actuators), require real-time/predictable latency and could even change their requirements (e.g., in terms of data sources) dynamically and abruptly. Big Stream-oriented systems could react effectively to changes and provide smart behavior for allocating resources, thus implementing scalable and cost-effective Cloud services. Dynamism and real-time requirements are another reason why Big Data approaches, due to their intrinsic inertia (i.e., Big Data typically works with batch-based processing), are not suitable for many IoT scenarios.

The main differences between Big Data and Big Stream paradigms are (i) the nature of data sources and (ii) the real-time/latency requirements of consumers. The Big Stream paradigm allows to perform real-time and ad-hoc processing in order to link incoming streams of data to consumers, with a high degree of scalability, fine-grained and dynamic configuration, and management of heterogeneous data formats. In brief, while both Big Data and Big Stream deal with massive amounts of data, the former focuses on the analysis of data, while the latter focuses on the management of flows of data, as shown in Fig. 2.

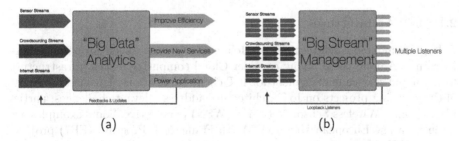

Fig. 2. (a) Data sources in Big Data systems. (b) The multiple data sources and listeners management in Big Stream system.

The difference is in the meaning of the term "Big," which refers to volume of data for Big Data and to global information generation rate of the data sources for Big Stream. This has an impact also on the data that are considered relevant to consumer applications. For instance, while for Big Data applications it is important to keep all sensed data in order to be able to perform any required computation, Big Stream applications might decide to perform data aggregation or pruning in order to minimize the latency in conveying the results of computation to consumers, with no need for persistence. Note that, as a generalization, Big Data applications might be consumers of Big Stream data flows.

For these reasons, in this paper we propose an architecture targeting Cloud-based applications with real-time constraints, i.e., Big Stream applications, for IoT scenarios. The proposed architecture relies on the concepts of *data listener* and *data-oriented processing graph* in order to implement a scalable, highly configurable, and dynamic chain of computations on incoming Big Streams and to dispatch data with a push-based approach, thus providing the lowest delay between the generation of information and its consumption.

The rest of this work is organized as follows. In Sect. 2, an overview of related works is presented. In Sect. 3, the proposed architecture is presented and detailed. Finally, in Sect. 4 we draw our conclusions and discuss future research directions.

2   Related Work

The IoT paradigm consists of a huge number of different and heterogeneous smart objects connected in a "Network of Networks." These nodes are envisioned as collectors of information from the environment in order to provide useful services to users. This ubiquitous sensing, enabled by the IoT in most areas of modern living, has led to information and communication systems invisibly embedded in the environment, thus making the technology disappear from the consciousness of the users. The outcome of this trend is the generation of a huge amount of data that, depending on the application scenario, should be aggregated, processed, stored, transformed, and delivered to the final users of the system, in an efficient and effective way, with traditional commodity services.

2.1   IoT Architectures

A large number of architectures for IoT scenarios have been proposed in the literature. Among these, many consider Cloud computing as the infrastructure for data and service management for IoT client applications. For instance, most of the outgoing projects on IoT architecture address relevant challenges, particularly from a Wireless Sensor Networks (WSN) perspective. Some examples are given by a few European Union (EU) 7th Framework Program (FP7) projects such as SENSEI [6] and Internet of Things-Architecture (IoT-A) [7].

The purpose of the SENSEI project is to create an open and business-driven architecture that addresses the scalability problems for a large number of globally distributed Wireless Sensor and Actuator (WS&A) networks devices. It provides necessary network and information management services to enable reliable and accurate context information retrieval and interaction with the physical environment. By adding mechanisms for accounting, security, privacy, and trust, SENSEI aims at enabling an open and secure market space for context-awareness and real world interaction.

The IoT-A project team has focused on the design of a IoT architecture, creating an Architectural Reference Model (ARM) with the definition of an initial set of key building blocks. The IoT-A ARM's aim is to connect vertically closed systems, architectures, and application areas in order to create open interoperable systems and integrated environments or platforms. It constitutes a foundation from which software companies can capitalize on the benefits of developing consumer-oriented platforms including hardware, software, and services.

"Connect All IP-based Smart Objects!" (CALIPSO) [4] is another EU FP7 project with relevant implications on the design of an IoT architecture. The main purpose of CALIPSO is to build IoT systems with IPv6-connected smart objects and to look for novel methods to achieve very low power consumption, thus providing both high interoperability and long lifetime. CALIPSO leans on the significant body of work on sensor networks to integrate radio duty cycling and data-centric mechanisms with the IPv6 [2]. The project entails three layers (network, routing, and application) using Contiki [8] open source Operating System (OS), Europe's leading OS for smart objects, as the target development environment for prototyping and experimental evaluation. CALIPSO focuses on three main use cases to drive its research activities: (i) Smart Infrastructures; (ii) Smart Cities; and (iii) Smart Toys applications.

In the work of Gubbi et al. [9], the success of IoT is attributed to three factors:

- shared understanding of the situation of its users and their appliances;
- software architectures and pervasive communication networks to process and convey the contextual information where it is relevant;
- IoT analytics tools aiming at autonomous and smart behaviors.

For the above reasons, the IoT architecture proposed therein is not based on WSNs and the focus is instead on the user and the Cloud. The consumer is the "center" and drives the use of data and infrastructure to develop new applications. The rest of the work discusses the key enabling technologies and the different future applications domains, describes a Cloud-centric architecture for IoT, and presents an implementation based on Aneka [10], a .NET-based application development Platform-as-a-Service (PaaS), which can utilize storage and computing resources of both public and private clouds.

Another framework for (IoT-based) Cloud systems is OpenStack [11], a global collaboration of developers producing an ubiquitous open source cloud computing platform for public and private clouds. The project aims to deliver solutions for all types of clouds by being simple to implement, massively scalable, and feature-rich. The technology consists of a series of interrelated projects delivering various components for a cloud infrastructure solution. The result is an open cloud OS that controls large pools of computing, storage, and networking resources. OpenStack can be used as a background to build other platforms. An example of this approach is given by the FI-WARE project [12], an open cloud-based infrastructure for the cost-effective creation and delivery of Internet applications and services. FI-WARE API specifications are public, royalty-free, and OCCI-compliant, driven by the development of an open source reference implementation which allows developers, service providers, enterprises, and other organizations to develop innovative products based on FI-WARE technologies.

While OpenStack can be seen as a framework with a vendor-driven model, OpenNebula [13] is an open-source Cloud platform that focuses efforts on the user. This project aims at delivering a simple feature-rich and flexible solution to build and manage enterprise clouds and virtualized data centers.

2.2   Big Data Processing Pattern

Big Data architectures generally use traditional processing patterns with a pipeline approach [14]. These architectures are typically based on a processing approach where the data flow goes downstream from input to output, to perform specific tasks or reach the target goal. Typically, the information follows a pipeline where data are sequentially handled, with tightly coupled pre-defined processing sub-units (static data routing). The described paradigm can be defined as "process-oriented:" a central coordination point manages the execution of sub-units in a certain order and each sub-unit provides a specific processing output, which is created to be used only within the scope of its own process without the possibility to be shared among different processes. This approach represents a major deviation from traditional Service Oriented Architectures (SOAs), where the sub-units are external web services invoked by a coordinator process rather than internal services [15].

2.3   Fog Computing

In the area of user-driven and Cloud IoT architectures, in [5] Fog computing is proposed as the novel and appropriate paradigm for a variety of IoT services and applications that require mobility support, low latency, and location awareness. The Fog can be described as a highly virtualized platform that provides computing, storage, and networking services between end-devices and traditional Cloud Computing. In other words, the Fog is meant to act as an extension of the Cloud, operating at the edge of the network to support endpoints by providing rich services that can fulfill real-time and low-latency consumers requirements. The Fog paradigm has specific characteristics, which can be summarized as follows:

- geographical distribution, in contrast with the centralization envisioned by the Cloud;
- subscriber model employed by the players in the Fog;
- support for mobility.

The architecture described by Bonomi et al. [5] is based on the Fog and Cloud interplay: the former provides localization, low latency, and context awareness to endpoints; the latter provides global centralization functionalities. In the presented IoT Fog scenario, collectors at the edge of the network ingest the data generated by sensors and devices: the portion of these data that require real-time processing (from milliseconds to tenths of seconds) are consumed locally by the first tier of the Fog. The rest is sent to the higher tiers for operations with less stringent time constraints (from seconds to minutes). The higher the tier, the wider is the geographical coverage and the longer the time scale. As a result, the Fog must support several types of storage: from ephemeral, at the lowest tier, to semi-permanent, at the highest tier. The ultimate and global coverage is provided by the Cloud, which is used as repository for data for a duration of months or years.

2.4 IoT Protocols and Models

As previously stated in Sect. 1, the most prominent driver to provide interoperability in the IoT is IPv6. Referring to the IP stack, at the application layer, the IoT scenario brings a variety of possible protocols that can be employed according to the specific applications requirements. The following are relevant options:

- HyperText Transfer Protocol (HTTP) [16]: mainly used for the communication with the consumer's devices;
- Constrained Application Protocol (CoAP) [17]: explicitly designed to work with a large number of constrained devices operating in LLNs. CoAP is built on the top of User Datagram Protocol (UDP) and follows a request-response paradigm;
- Extensible Messaging and Presence Protocol (XMPP) [18];
- MQ Telemetry Transport (MQTT) protocol [19]: a lightweight publish/subscribe protocol flowing over TCP/IP for remote sensors and control devices through low bandwidth, unreliable, or intermittent communications;
- Constrained Session Initiation Protocol (CoSIP) [20,21]: a version of the Session Initiation Protocol (SIP) [22] aiming at allowing constrained devices to instantiate communication sessions in a lightweight and standard fashion. Session instantiation can include a negotiation phase of some parameters which will be used for all subsequent communication.

Regardless of the selected application-layer protocol, most IoT/M2M applications will follow the REpresentational State Transfer Protocol (REST) architectural model [23], because (i) it provides simple and uniform interfaces and (ii) it is designed to build long-lasting and robust applications, resilient to changes that might occur over time.

3   Architecture

As stated in Sect. 1, a major difference between Big Data and Big Stream approaches resides in the real-time/low-latency requirements of consumers. The gigantic amount of data sources in IoT applications has mistakenly made Cloud-service implementors believe that re-using Big Data-driven architectures would be the right solution for all applications, rather than designing new paradigms specific for IoT scenarios. IoT application scenarios are characterized by a huge number of data sources sending small amounts of information to a collector service at a typically limited rate. Many services can be built upon these data, such as: environmental monitoring, building automation, and smart cities applications. These applications typically have real-time or low-latency requirements in order to provide efficient reactive/proactive behaviors, which could effectively be implemented especially in an IP-based IoT, where smart objects can be directly addressed.

3.1   Big Stream-Oriented Architecture

Applying a traditional Big Data approach for IoT application scenarios might bring to higher or even unpredictable latencies between data generation and its availability to a consumer, since this was not among the main objectives behind the design of Big Data systems. Figure 3 illustrates the time contributions introduced when data pushed by smart objects need to be processed, stored, and then polled by consumers. The total time required by any data to be delivered to a consumer can be expressed as $T = t_0 + t_1 + t_2$, where:

1. t_0 is the time elapsed from the moment a data source sends information, through an available API, to the Cloud service (1) and the service dispatches the data to an appropriate queue, where it can wait for an unpredictable time (2), in order to decouple data acquisition from processing;
2. t_1 is the time needed for data, extracted by the queue, to be pre-processed and stored into a Data Warehouse (DW) (3); this time depends on the number of concurrent processes that need to be executed and get access the common DW and the current size of the DW;
3. t_2 is the data consumption time, which depends on the remaining time that a polling consumer needs to wait before performing the next fetch (4), the time for a request to be sent to the Cloud service (5), the time required for lookup in the DW and post-process the fetched data (6), and the time for the response to be delivered back to the consumer (7).

It can be observed that the architecture described is not optimized to minimize the latency and, therefore, to feed (possibly a large number of) real-time applications, but, rather, to perform data collection and batch processing. Moreover, it is important to understand that data significant for Big Stream applications might be short-lived, since they are to be consumed immediately, while Big Data applications tend to collect and store massive amounts of data for an unpredictable time.

In this work, we propose a novel architecture explicitly designed for the management of Big Stream applications targeting IoT scenarios. The main design criteria of the proposed architecture are: (i) the minimization of the latency in data dispatching to consumers and (ii) the optimization of resource allocation. The main novelty in the proposed architecture is that the data flow is

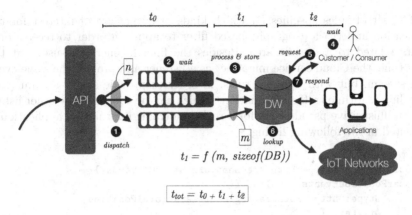

Fig. 3. Traditional Big Data architecture for IoT and delay contributions from data generation to applications information delivery.

"consumer-oriented", rather than being based on the knowledge of collection points (repositories) where data can be retrieved. The data being generated by a deployed smart object might be of interest for some consumer application, denoted as *listener*. A listener registers its interest in receiving updates (either in the form of raw or processed data) coming from a streaming endpoint (i.e., Cloud service). On the basis of application-specific needs, each listener defines a set of rules, which specify what type of data should be selected and the associated filtering operations. For example, in a smart parking application, a mobile app might be interested in receiving contents related only to specific events (e.g., parking sensors status updates, the positions of other cars, weather conditions, etc.) that occur in a given geographical area, in order to accomplish relevant tasks (e.g., find a covered free parking spot). The pseudo-code that can be used to express the set of rules for the smart parking application is shown in the following listing:

```
when
    $temperatureEvent = {@type:http://schema.org/Weather#temperature}
    $humidityEvent = {@type:http://schema.org/Weather#humidity}
    $carPositionEvent = {@type:http://schema.org/SmartCar#travelPosition}
    $parkingStatusEvent = {@type:http://schema.org/SmartParking#status}

    @filter: {
      location: { @type:"http://schema.org/GeoShape#polygon",
      coordinates: [ [
        [41.3983, 2.1729], [41.3986, 2.1729], [41.3986, 2.1734],
        [41.3983, 2.1734], [41.3983, 2.1729]
      ] ]
    }
then
    <application logic>
```

[Pseudo-code to express the set of rules for a smart parking application.]

The set of rules specifies (i) which kinds of events are of interest for the application and (ii) a geography-based filter to apply in order to receive only events related to a specific area. Besides the final listener (end-user), at the same time, the Cloud service might act as a listener and process the same event data stream, but with different rules, in order to provide a new stream (e.g., providing real-time traffic information), which can be consumed by other listeners. An illustrative pseudo-code for a real-time traffic information application is presented in the following listing:

```
when
    $cityZone = {@type:http://schema.org/SmartCity#zone}
    $carPositionEvents = collect({
        @type: http://schema.org/SmartCar#travelPosition,
        @filter: {
                location: cityZone.coordinates
        }
    }) over window:time(30s)
then
    emit {
        @type: http://schema.org/SmartCity#trafficDensity,
        city_zone: $cityZone,
        density: $carPositionEvents.size,
    }
```

[Pseudo-code to express the set of rules for a real-time traffic information application.]

The proposed Big Stream architecture guarantees that, as soon as data are available, they will be dispatched to the listener, which is thus no longer responsible to poll data, thus minimizing latencies and possibly avoiding network traffic.

The information flow in a listener-based Cloud architecture is shown in Fig. 4. With the new paradigm, the total time required by any data to be delivered to a consumer can be expressed as:

$$T = t_0 + t_1 \qquad (1)$$

where:

1. t_0 is the time elapsed from the moment a data source sends information, through an available API, to the Cloud service (1) and the service dispatches the data to an appropriate queue, where it can wait for an unpredictable time (2), in order to decouple the data acquisition from processing;
2. t_1 is the time needed to process data extracted from the queue and be processed (according to the needs of the listener, e.g., to perform format translation) and then deliver it to registered listeners.

It is clear that the inverse of perspective introduced by a listener-oriented communication is optimal in terms of minimization of the time that a listener must wait before it receives data of interest. In order to highlight the benefits brought by the Big Stream approach, with respect to a Big Data approach, consider an alerting application, where an event should be notified to one or more consumers in the shortest possible time. The traditional Big Data approach would require an unnecessary pre-processing/storage/post-processing cycle to be executed before the event could be made available to consumers, which would be responsible to retrieve data by polling. The listener-oriented approach, instead, guarantees that only the needed processing will be performed before data are being delivered directly to the listener, thus providing an effective real-time solution.

This general discussion proves that a consumer-oriented paradigm may be better suited to real-time Big Stream applications, rather than simply reusing existing Big Data architectures, which fit best applications that do not have critical real-time requirements.

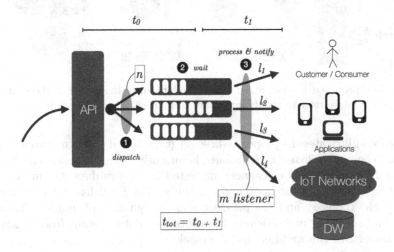

Fig. 4. The proposed listener-based architecture for IoT delay contributions from data generation to consumers information delivery are explicitly indicated.

3.2 Graph-Based Processing

In order to overcome the limitations of the "process-oriented" approach described in Sect. 2, and fit the proposed Big Stream Architecture, we have envisioned and designed a new Cloud Graph-based architecture built on top of basic building blocks that are self-consistent and perform "atomic" processing on data, but that are not directly linked to a specific task. In such systems, the data flows are based on dynamic graph-routing rules determined only by the nature of the data itself and not by a centralized coordination unit. This new approach allows the platform to be "consumer-oriented" and to implement an optimal resource allocation. Without the need of a coordination process, the data streams can be dynamically routed in the network by following the edges of the graph and allowing the possibility to automatically switch-off nodes when some processing units are not required at a certain point and transparently replicate nodes if some processing entities is consumed by a significant amount of concurrent consumers.

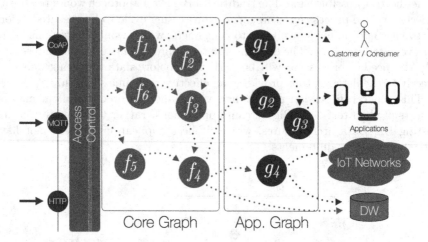

Fig. 5. The proposed listener-based Graph architecture: the nodes of the graph are listeners; the edges refer to the dynamic flow of information data streams.

Figure 5 illustrates the proposed directed graph-based processing architecture and the concept of listener. A listener is an entity (e.g., a processing unit in the graph or an external consumer) interested in the raw data stream or in the output provided by a different node in the graph. Each listener represents a node in the topology and the presence and combination of multiple listeners, across all processing units, defines the routing of data streams from producers to consumers. In this architectural approach:

- nodes are processing units (processes), performing some kind of computation on incoming data;
- edges represent flows of informations linking together various processing unit, which are thus able to implement some complex behavior as a whole;
- nodes of the graph are listeners for incoming data or outputs of other nodes of the graph.

The designed graph-based approach allows to optimize resource allocation in terms of *efficiency*, by switching off processing units that have no listeners registered to them (enabling cost-effectiveness), and *scalability*, by replicating those processing units which have a large number of registered listeners. The combination of these two functionalities and the concept of listener allow the platform and the overall system to adapt itself to dynamic and heterogeneous scenarios, by properly routing data streams to the consumers, and to add new processing units and functionalities on demand.

In order to provide a set of commonly available functionalities, while allowing to dynamically extend the capabilities of the system, the graph is composed by concentric levels:

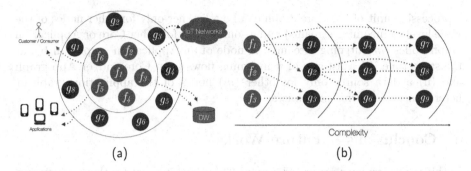

Fig. 6. (a) The concentric linked Core and Application Graphs. (b) Basic processing nodes build the Core Graph: the outer nodes have increasing complexity.

- *Core Graph*: basic processing provided by the architecture (e.g., format translation, normalization, aggregation, data correlation, and other transformations);
- one or more *Application Graphs*: listeners that require data coming from an inner graph level in order to perform custom processing on already processed data.

The complexity of processing is directly proportional to the number of levels crossed by the data. This means that data at an outer graph level must not be processed again at an inner level. From an architectural viewpoint, as shown in a representative scheme in Fig. 6, nodes at inner graph levels cannot be listeners of nodes of outer graph levels. In other words, there can be no link from an outer graph node to an inner graph node, but only vice versa. Same-level graph nodes can be linked together if there is a need to do so. Figure 7 illustrates incoming and outgoing listener flows between Core and Application graphs units. In particular,

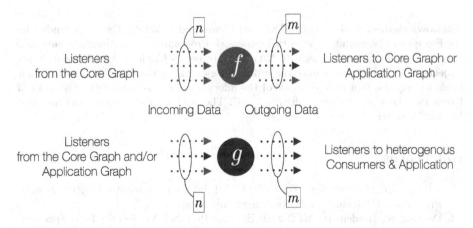

Fig. 7. Allowed input and output flows for Core Graph nodes and Application Graph nodes.

a processing unit of the Core graph can be a listener only for other nodes of the same level (n incoming streams) and a source both for other Core or Application graph nodes (m outgoing streams). A node of an Application graph can be, at the same time, (i) a listener of n incoming flows from Core and/or App graph and (ii) a data source only for other (m) nodes of the application graph or heterogeneous external consumers.

4   Conclusions & Future Works

In this paper, we have presented a novel Cloud architecture for the management of Big Stream applications in IoT scenarios. After defining the Big Stream paradigm and highlighting the main differences with the traditional Big Data paradigm, in terms of data sources and real-time requirements, we have described how a consumer-oriented architecture might lead to the minimization of the latency between the time instant of data generation and the time instant at which the processed data can be delivered to a consumer application. The proposed architecture is based on a data-driven processing graph, where data flows between processing units (graph nodes), denoted as *"listeners,"* which, collectively, perform consumer-oriented processing, thus implementing an architecture-wide push-based communication. The listener-oriented approach has to several benefits, such as: (i) lowest latency, as the push-based approach guarantees that no delay, due to polling and batch processing, is introduced; (ii) fine-grained self-configuration, as listeners can dynamically "plug" to those that output data of interest; (iii) optimal resource allocation, as processing units that have no listeners can be switched off, while those with many listeners can be replicated, thus leading to cost-effectiveness from a Cloud service perspective. As a next step of our work, we plan to start the implementation of the presented architecture modules with open-source technologies, and test them with data from real IoT scenarios.

Acknowledgments. The work of Simone Cirani and Gianluigi Ferrari is funded by the European Community's Seventh Framework Programme, area "Internetconnected Objects", under Grant no. 288879, CALIPSO project - Connect All IP-based Smart Objects. The work reflects only the authors views; the European Community is not liable for any use that may be made of the information contained herein. The work of Laura Belli is supported by Multitraccia SC. The work of Marco Picone is supported by Guglielmo srl.

References

1. Internet Engineering Task Force: RFC 791 Internet Protocol - DARPA Inernet Programm, Protocol Specification, September 1981
2. Deering, S., Hinden, R.: RFC 2460 Internet Protocol, Version 6 (IPv6) Specification. Internet Engineering Task Force, December 1998
3. IETF: The Internet Engineering Task Force. http://www.ietf.org/

4. EC FP7 Project: CALIPSO - Connect All IP-based Smart Objects. http://www. ict-calipso.eu/
5. Bonomi, F., Milito, R., Zhu, J., Addepalli, S.: Fog computing and its role in the internet of things. In: Proceedings of the First Edition of the ACM Workshop on Mobile Cloud Computing, New York, pp. 13–16 (2012)
6. EU FP7 project: SENSEI. http://www.ict-sensei.org/index.php
7. EU FP7 project: Internet of Things - Architecture (IoT - A) (2012–2015). http:// www.iot-a.eu/
8. Contiki Operating System. http://www.contiki-os.org/
9. Gubbi, J., Buyya, R., Marusic, S., Palaniswami, M.: Internet of Things (IoT): a vision, architectural elements, and future directions. Future Gener. Comput. Syst. **29**(7), 1645–1660 (2013)
10. Manjrasoft: Aneka. http://www.manjrasoft.com/aneka_architecture.html
11. Rackspace, NASA: OpenStack Cloud Software - Open source software for building private and public clouds. https://www.openstack.org/
12. EU FP7 project: FI-Ware (2011). http://www.fi-ware.org/
13. Open Source Project: OpenNebula. http://opennebula.org/
14. Hohpe, G., Woolf, B.: Enterprise Integration Patterns: Designing, Building, and Deploying Messaging Solutions. Addison-Wesley Longman Publishing Co., Inc., Boston (2003)
15. Isaacson, C.: Software Pipelines and SOA: Releasing the Power of Multi-Core Processing, 1st edn. Addison-Wesley Professional, Upper Saddle River (2009)
16. Fielding, R., Gettys, J., Mogul, J., Frystyk, H., Masinter, L., Leach, P., Berners-Lee, T.: Hypertext transfer protocol - http/1.1 (1999)
17. Shelby, Z., Hartke, K., Bormann, C., Frank, B.: Constrained Application Protocol (CoAP). Technical report, IETF Secretariat, Fremont, CA, USA (2011)
18. Saint-Andre, P.: Extensible messaging and presence protocol (xmpp): Instant messaging and presence. Internet RFC 3921, October 2004
19. MQTT: MQ Telemetry Transport. http://mqtt.org/
20. Cirani, S., Picone, M., Veltri, L.: CoSIP: a constrained session initiation protocol for the internet of things. In: Canal, C., Villari, M. (eds.) ESOCC 2013. CCIS, vol. 393, pp. 13–24. Springer, Heidelberg (2013)
21. Cirani, S., Picone, M., Veltri, L.: A session initiation protocol for the internet of things. Scalable Comput. Pract. Exp. **14**(4), 249–263 (2014)
22. Roach, A.B., Memo, S.O.T.: Session Initiation Protocol (SIP)-Specific Event Notification, RFC 3265 (2002)
23. Fielding, R.T.: Architectural styles and the design of network-based software architectures. Ph.D. thesis (2000)

An Approach to Evaluate Applications Running on Web-Based Remote Virtual Machines in Cloud Computing

Davide Mulfari$^{(\boxtimes)}$, Antonio Celesti, Maria Fazio, and Massimo Villari

DICIEAMA, University of Messina, Contrada Di Dio,
98166 Sant'Agata - Messina, Italy
{dmulfari,acelesti,mfazio,mvillari}@unime.it
http://mdslab.unime.it

Abstract. The exploitation of remote Virtual Machines (VM) over the Cloud gives new opportunities to both business and private clients for extending their processing and storage infrastructures. Typically, a remote VM can be accessed through consolidated technologies based on SSH or Remote Desktop Viewer. Regarding Remote Desktop Viewer, several solutions are emerging on the market to access remote VMs via web. However, evaluating performance of desktop applications running on remote VMs is quite hard, because CPU clocks of VMs are typically misaligned from physical devices. In addition, the overhead due to network latency can considerably degrade performance in terms of application responsivity. In this paper, we propose a new methodology that can help scientists and software developers to evaluate performance of applications running on Remote Web-Based VMs (RWVMs) over the Cloud by means of estimating the LAtency Gap (LAG). We use such a methodology to analyze the behavior of a Cloud IaaS considering two different applications running on RWVMs, which can be widely adopted for IoT purposes.

Keywords: Cloud computing · IaaS · Virtual machine · Remote desktop · Web · Performance

1 Introduction

Cloud computing allows users and developers to build on top of an Infrastructure as a Service (IaaS) layer different types of Platform as a Service (PaaS) and Software as a Service (SaaS) systems. IaaS Cloud providers allow a user to deploy in a VM a traditional desktop Operating System (OS), i.e., a guess OS, and other software applications.

To access VMs, clients can mainly use to approaches: the first is based on a CLI (Command Line Interface). Specifically, the client exploits a SSH connection to enter the VM and execute remote commands. The second approach is based on a *Remote Desktop* viewer, that is a GUI (Graphical User Interface) able to make

© Springer International Publishing Switzerland 2015
G. Ortiz and C. Tran (Eds.): ESOCC 2014, CCIS 508, pp. 106–117, 2015.
DOI: 10.1007/978-3-319-14886-1_11

the VM access more user-friendly. Some solutions are emerging on the market to integrate a Remote Desktop viewer into a web interface, such as Guacamole, noVNC, Remote Spark, and so on. These solutions typically deploy a Remote Desktop server into the VM and a Remote Desktop client on a web server. Users remotely access VMs using only a web browser, thus to avoid software installation on the client device and to make the accessing system more flexible. For simplicity, from now on, we will refer to the VMs in the Cloud accessed by using a Remote Desktop viewer with the term *Remote Web-based Virtual Machines* (RWVMs).

In RWVM, it is possible to easily deploy several types of applications. To meet IoT aims, RWVMs can host real-time applications able to interact with smart objects, collecting, processing, and displaying information coming from the environment through smart devices, sensors, and so on. These IoT oriented applications typically require to satisfy a minimum Quality of Service level. Thus, performance evaluation represents a key factor that have hindered the adoption of Cloud services in many contexts till now, especially in business, where companies are reluctant to move their applications over the Cloud since low performances can cause critical issues.

Evaluating performance of desktop applications running on VMs is not trivial at all because virtual CPUs and virtual I/O devices are often decoupled by the real hardware devices. In addition, using Remote Desktop technologies, applications responsivity is also affected by the network latency due to communication links: the link between the VM and the Remote Desktop client and the link between the web server and the browser at the client site. Thus, due to all these factors, the evaluation of usability of such VMs is quite hard.

In this paper, we deal with the evaluation of the usability of applications running on RWVM, focusing the attention on the resulting quality of experience of the final client. Specifically, we propose a methodology that can help scientists and software engineers to test the I/O performances of multimedia applications running on RWVM. To this aim, we evaluate the LAtency Gap (LAG) as performance metric. Indeed, as discussed in [1], LAG measures the time delay between an input action and an output response and, hence, it assesses the major bottleneck for usability of an interactive computer system available over the Internet. The main contributions of the paper are: (1) describing the phases required to make performance evaluation of applications running on RWVM; (2) providing a guideline to prepare and perform experiments, to process collected experimental data, and to present results through graphs; (3) showing effective benefits of the proposed methodology.

The rest of the paper is organized as follows. Section 2 describes background and related works. The reference scenario and our motivation are presented in Sect. 3. The proposed methodology for testing the usability of applications running on RWVMs is described in Sect. 4. Concrete cases of study to which we applied the methodology and our experimental results are described in Sect. 5, where we analyze two types of applications, that are audio and video playbacks. Our conclusions are summarized in Sect. 6.

2   Related Works

Some works on performance analysis of applications running on remote virtual machines are available in literature [2]. Studies on Amazon EC2 have highlighted how several services running on VMs, such as MapReduce tasks [3], Apple's Darwin Streaming Server and Doom 3 Game, are afflicted by significant performance overhead due to network latency delay [4]. In [5], the authors present a study to characterize the impact of virtualization techniques on the networking performance of EC2 data centers. Specifically, they evaluate processor sharing, packet delay, TCP/UDP throughput and packet loss among EC2 VMs [6]. In [7], the authors discuss a systematic approach for performance measurement and to characterize performance of servers that use virtualization technologies to perform software consolidation of multiple physical servers.

To evaluate Remote Virtual Desktops, an interesting solution is Xbench [8]. It consists in a benchmark tool for measuring performance of a graphic display system in a virtualized environment. The Xbench results on a Xeno-Linux system highlighted a subtle relationship between the performance of memory and of the graphic display system, as well as the relationship between the performance of virtual-CPUs and of graphic display systems.

Differently from the aforementioned approaches, here we deal with RWVMs. The benefits for the customers to exploit such type of remote interaction have been already discussed in our previous works [9–11]. In this paper we focus the attention on the performance of IoT oriented applications running on remote VMs in the Cloud, where VMs are accessed by end users through an HTML5 web interface, in order to assess issues related to both virtual environments and virtual/physical networks.

3   Reference Scenario and Motivations

As depicted in Fig. 1, a typical Cloud architecture to access RWVMs consists of three components: (1) Physical Client Machine (PCM), (2) Remote Desktop System and (3) IaaS Cloud system.

PCM is the physical device used by the user to access RWVMs. It runs a HTML5 web browsers, that is the only software interface for the user towards the Cloud. The Remote Desktop System comes between the PCM, and hence the user, and the virtual infrastructure offered by a IaaS provider. It runs a web server that hosts the web application acting as a HTML5 Remote Desktop client. Typically, the web application exchanges data with a Remote Desktop proxy (gateway) server: such a component acts as an interface between the Remote Desktop server process running on the VM and the HTML5 Remote Desktop client. The IaaS Cloud provides the virtual infrastructure by means of VMs managed by a middleware called Virtual Infrastructure Manager (VIM). VIM allows to arrange IaaS instances controlling several Virtual Machine Monitors (VMMs), i.e., hypervisors. Looking at the software equipment available on VMs, each one runs its own guest OS and several desktop applications, including

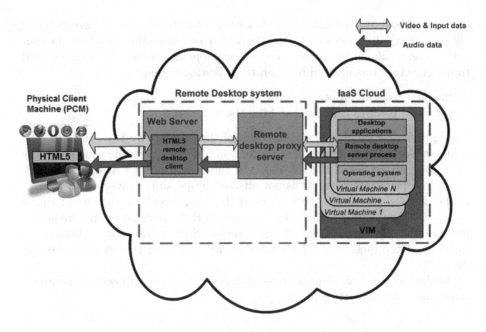

Fig. 1. Cloud architecture for RWVM provisioning.

customized programs. In order to support both audio and video transmissions, a valuable solution consists in configuring VMs Remote Desktop server to support the RDP (Remote Desktop Protocol). To this end, the web application acting as HTML5 remote viewer desktop client as to support RDP. In order to provide a RDP connection, each RWVM has to execute a RDP compliant Remote Desktop server process.

To evaluate the quality of service experienced by the end user at the PCM, several issues must be considered, such as performance at the Remote Desktop system and in Cloud data centers. However, carrying out independent performance measurements at the different involved sites can be very complex. Thus, we propose to analyze performance experienced by the end user measuring the LAG at the PCM. In the next section we provide details on how to perform such a LAG evaluation.

4   Methodology

In this Section, we introduce a new methodology to estimate the LAG when a RWVM technology is exploited. In our scenario, users access VMs using a HTML5 web browser to download an HTML5 Canvas tag able to show the VM's screen and to handle all the low-level input events occurring at the web page. According to such a system, whenever the user performs any mouse action on the Canvas or presses any key on the keyboard in its PCM, the Remote Desktop client web application turns the detected input events into specific commands to control the VM. Therefore, if a click occurs on the Canvas, a corresponding click action will be processed by the the VM. To evaluate the LAG that the user experiences while he/she manages a desktop application on a RWVM, we need to measure the time interval between the following actions:

1. the user gives an input on the PCM;
2. the PCM receives the response from the VM.

Such a time interval gives a measurement of the LAG. To evaluate the LAG, we configure some timestamps in the system, in order to catch the time necessary to perform an action on the RWVM. The timestamps are set at the PCM and, hence, the LAG measurement is not affected by possible unsynchronized clock in the involved physical/virtual nodes of the whole architecture. Considering a large set of LAG measurements for a specific action, we can draw the frequency histogram to aggregate different LAG values. Such a histogram allows us to understand the quality in Cloud responsivity according to end users requirements.

In the following, we discuss in details the steps of the proposed methodology to evaluate the RWVM responsivity.

Simulating the Input Action. At the first step of our methodology, we have to simulate an input event at periodic time intervals (e.g. mouse click or keyboard button pushing), thus to characterize the behavior of the system by changing the input frequency. To this aim, we used the Python script below to emulate the mouse click event at the PCM. The script retrieves the timestamp value in which each simulated click input action occurs.

```
1   \label{ls:phyton}
2   from pymouse import PyMouse
3   import time
4   import datetime
5   t=51
6   sl=10
7   m=PyMouse()
8   x, y = m.position()
9   for n in range(1,t):
10      m.click(x,y,1)
11      ts = time.time()
12      st = datetime.datetime.fromtimestamp(ts).
13      .strftime('%H:%M:%S:%f')
14      print st
15      time.sleep(sl)
```

Listing 1.1. This Python script allows to emulate single mouse click events that occur on the PCM running the web browser.

The code exploits PyMouse, that is a Python cross-platform module aimed at interfacing a mouse device. Specifically, code at lines 7–8 gives the absolute mouse positions (in terms of absolute coordinates) on the PCM's screen and code at line 9 performs a click action on that position. Code at lines 11–12 gets timestamp related to each mouse event.

Evaluating the LAG. The second step of the proposed methodology estimates the overall LAG. We assume that the RWVM executes a custom application. Specifically, in our use experiments, we analyzed the LAG measured running two different applications, that are: (1) screen update and (2) audio playback applications. We present details of such experiments in Sect. 5. However, the proposed methodology can be applied to whichever type of application running at the VM.

In order to retrieve at the PCM the timestamp values related to the input and output events, we execute a packet analyzer (such as Wireshark) in order to monitor the data processed by the HTML5 Remote Desktop web client. Both the simulated mouse click at the PCM and the output from the RWVM's are periodic events, thus we can numerically compute the difference, expressed in milliseconds, between the respective timestamp values. Such a time difference represents the overall time that a customer experiences while he/she works with the HTML5 Remote Desktop viewer (e.g., the web browser).

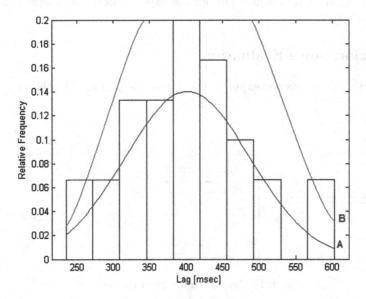

Fig. 2. Example of a frequency histogram. Curves A and B are normal probability functions for respectively successful and unsuccessful stochastic evaluation model.

Evaluating the Distribution of LAG Measurements. As step 3, the LAG test is performed several times in order to perform a statistical evaluation of the system behavior. The obtained sets of LAG values are analyzed by means

of *frequency histogram*, which allows us to show features about the distribution
of the LAG measurements. Indeed, frequency histograms summarize the data
set in order to understand general characteristics of value distribution (e.g., the
shape), thus to detect different types of and unusual system responses. The frequency histograms has discrete interval of LAG values on the x-axis, while the
number of occurrences of each LAG interval is represented on the y-axis (see the
example in Fig. 2). Over the histogram, the normal probability density function
estimated from the LAG data sets is drawn. Then, according to the results discussed in [12], a comparison between the frequency histogram and the normal
probability density function provides interesting information about the quality
of the RWVM evaluation. Specifically, the probability density function is a function that describes the relative likelihood for a random variable to take on a
given value. The probability of the random variable falling within a particular
range of values is given by the the area under the density function (but above
the horizontal axis) and between the lowest and greatest values of the range.
Also the frequency histogram provides information about the distribution of
LAG values in the range. Thus, the shapes of both the the normal probability
density function and the frequency histogram should be similar, such as the histogram and the density function A in Fig. 2. If the resulting graph shows different
shapes, such as the histogram and the function B in Fig. 2, we can not assume
the resulting histogram meaningful for the experimental characterization of the
system behavior.

5   Performance Evaluation

This Section describes our experiments to test the proposed methodology.

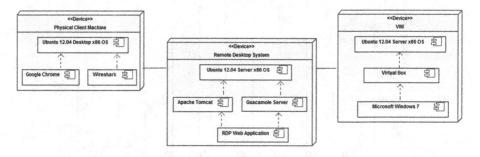

Fig. 3. Deployment diagram of the testbed.

5.1   Testbed Setup

We arranged our testbed over three physical nodes, as shown in the deployment
diagram in Fig. 3. We used Guacamole as Remote Desktop System. Guacamole
acts as both HTML5 remote desktop client web application and remote desktop proxy server. Further details about Guacamole and the used technology are

available in [13]. Software modules of the web application (Apache Web Server, Tomcat 6 extension, Guacamole remote desktop gateway) has been deployed on an IBM LS20 server blade with Ubuntu Server 12.04 64 bit as operating system. For simplicity, regarding the Iaas Cloud system, we did not considered a specific VIM middleware because the performance of applications running on RWVMs are not afflicted from the way they the are turned on. Thus, regarding the IaaS Cloud System block, we simply considered a different IBM LS20 server blade running Ubuntu Server 12.04 64 bit operating system and Oracle VM VirtualBox 4 as hypervisor. In particular, we have created a single VM supporting Microsoft Windows 7 Ultimate and we have configured the environment to execute the built-in RDP remote desktop viewer server. The two physical servers were connected by means of a Gigabit Ethernet connection. Such a high speed connection between physical nodes allows us to assume that the network latency is negligible. The PCM had the following software configurations: Ubuntu 12.04 x86 Operating system, equipped with the Google Chrome Web Browser and Wireshark as network packet analyzer. The PCM ran the Python script to simulate periodic mouse click events, as discussed previously. In addition, by using Guacamole as remote proxy gateway, we relied on a convenient way to detect all the single mouse click events on the HTML5 Canvas tag and the time in which they occur. This has been done by applying the following filter expression on the captured network data.

```
1  http && frame contains "POST" &&
2  frame contains "mouse," && frame contains "1.1;"
```

Listing 1.2. This Wireshark filter expression allows you to extract all the network packets regarding mouse click events.

5.2   Experimental Results

We performed our experiments considering two different applications running into the VMs: (1) a screen update and (2) an audio playback applications. In the following, we briefly describe the arrangement of the system to evaluate LAG and report the obtained experimental results for both the two use cases.

Screen Update Application on a RWVM. The application displays an empty full screen form listening for a single mouse click events. Whenever a click event is detected, a thread starts its execution and modifies the background color of the form. During our experiments, we noticed that each update of the background color on the VM produces notable throughput spikes in the Wireshark report, as shown in Fig. 4, where the time, expressed in seconds, is on the x-axis, while the amount of data processed by the web application and sent to the PCM, expressed in bytes, is on the y-axis. Thus, thanks to this graphical tool, we get the time of each spike to catch the output event timestamp. Then, we numerically compute the difference, expressed in milliseconds, between the input and the respective output timestamp values.

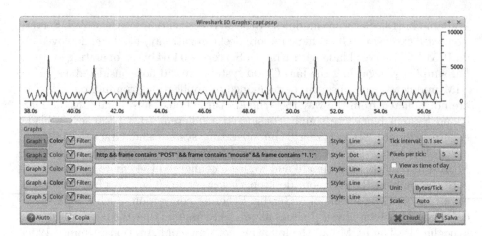

Fig. 4. Throughput graph in Wireshark to update the background color in a VM.

We show the LAG measurements for the screen update application in Fig. 5, where we can appreciate that the normal distribution has almost the same shape of the histogram and, hence, it describes a reasonable probabilistic model.

As shown in the plot, the LAG is negligible, so the RWVM responds immediately to the mouse action input and the end user does not feel too much delay in using the VM by means of the web interface.

Audio Playback Application on a RWVM. This kind of analysis is intended for RWVMs able to play on the PCM's speakers the sound effects generated by applications running on VMs. To this end the HTML5 Remote Desktop client has to support an audio redirection feature. In this way, the user can use just a common web browser to interact with multimedia pieces of software running on RWVMs, without having to install additional plugins at the PCM [10].

In the experiments, the PCM has an Ubuntu-based OS equipped with Pulse-Audio sound server and the Python script periodically simulates single mouse click events on the Canvas tag. Each mouse action produces a given live audio streaming coming from the VM. To catch the timestamp values at which the PCM receives the audio packets coming from the VM, we used the Freshfoo-Pulseaudio_monitoring tool able to monitor the audio levels and to get the time when the playback starts its execution at the PCM. By matching the obtained timestamp values with the time in which the simulated single mouse click events occur on the PCM, we can numerically estimated the LAG for the remote audio playback application. Experimental results are shown in Fig. 6, where the plot includes a smooth curve which highlights an estimated density for a normal distribution.

By looking at the distribution graph, the estimated density function and the density histogram do not match up. However, from the end user's perspective,

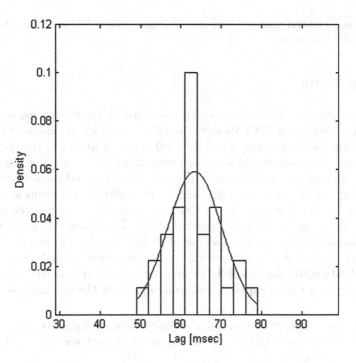

Fig. 5. LAG evaluation for the screen update application.

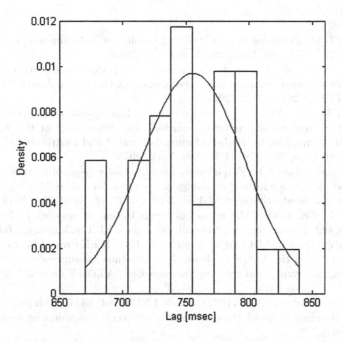

Fig. 6. LAG evaluation for the remote audio playback application.

the proposed testbed makes a multimedia running on a VM quite usable via the HTML5 web interface.

6 Conclusion

This paper presents a new methodology to perform qualitative evaluations of application running in RWVMs over the Cloud. This effort allowed us to support multimedia application oriented to IoT, since it abstracts the distributed architecture of hardware and software components, analyzing the responsivity of the whole system from the end user perspective. The performance evaluation methodology make use of the LAg metric, which allow to overcome some issues related to the distributed nature of Cloud systems. We described the proposed methodology in detail, including portion of code and script developed to make the methodology effective. We also tested the methodology in two different use cases, that are respectively characterized by a screen update and an audio playback application. We described the arrangement of the system to evaluate LAG and report the obtained experimental results for both the two use cases.

Acknowledgements. This work has been funded by the Project "Design and Implementation of a Community Cloud Platform aimed at SaaS services for on-demand Assistive Technology".

References

1. Hilbert, D.M., Redmiles, D.F.: Extracting usability information from user interface events. ACM Comput. Surv. **32**(4), 384–421 (2000)
2. Xu, F., Liu, F., Jin, H., Vasilakos, A.: Managing performance overhead of virtual machines in cloud computing: a survey, state of the art, and future directions. Proc. IEEE **102**(1), 11–31 (2014)
3. Bu, X., Rao, J., Xu, C.-Z.: Interference and locality-aware task scheduling for mapreduce applications in virtual clusters. In: Proceedings of the 22nd International Symposium on High-Performance Parallel and Distributed Computing, HPDC 2013, pp. 227–238. ACM, New York (2013)
4. Barker, S.K., Shenoy, P.: Empirical evaluation of latency-sensitive application performance in the cloud. In: Proceedings of the First Annual ACM SIGMM Conference on Multimedia Systems, MMSys 2010, pp. 35–46. ACM, New York (2010)
5. Wang, G., Ng, T.S.E.: The impact of virtualization on network performance of amazon ec2 data center. In: Proceedings of the 29th Conference on Information Communications, INFOCOM 2010, pp. 1163–1171. IEEE Press, Piscataway (2010)
6. Schad, J., Dittrich, J., Quiané-Ruiz, J.A.: Runtime measurements in the cloud: observing, analyzing, and reducing variance. Proc. VLDB Endow. **3**(1–2), 460–471 (2010)
7. Nambiar, R., Poess, M.: TPCTC 2010. LNCS, vol. 6417. Springer, Heidelberg (2011). Revised Selected Papers. LNCS Sublibrary: Programming and Software Engineering

8. Zhou, B., Zhang, Y.: Xbench: a benchmark evaluating the performance of graphic display system in virtual machines. In: 2010 5th International Conference on Computer Science and Education (ICCSE), August 2010, pp. 1730–1734 (2010)
9. Mulfari, D., Celesti, A., Villari, M., Puliafito, A.: Using virtualization and noVNC to support assistive technology in cloud computing. In: Third Symposium on Network Cloud Computing and Applications (NCCA) (2014)
10. Mulfari, D., Celesti, A., Villari, M., Puliafito, A.: Using virtualization and Guacamole/VNC to provide adaptive user interfaces to disabled people in cloud computing. In: 10th IEEE International Conference on Ubiquitous Intelligence and Computing (UIC), pp. 72–79 (2013)
11. Mulfari, D., Celesti, A., Puliafito, A., Villari, M.: How cloud computing can support on-demand assistive services. In: Proceedings of the 10th International Cross-Disciplinary Conference on Web Accessibility, W4A 2013, pp. 27:1–27:4. ACM, New York (2013)
12. MacKenzie, I.S., Ware, C.: Lag as a determinant of human performance in interactive systems. In: Proceedings of the INTERACT 1993 and CHI 1993 Conference on Human Factors in Computing Systems, CHI 1993, pp. 488–493. ACM, New York (1993)
13. von Suchodoletz, D., Rechert, K.: Efficient access to emulation-as-a-service – challenges and requirements. In: Aalberg, T., Papatheodorou, C., Dobreva, M., Tsakonas, G., Farrugia, C.J. (eds.) TPDL 2013. LNCS, vol. 8092, pp. 409–412. Springer, Heidelberg (2013)

CSB 2014

Cloud Service Brokerage - 2014: Towards the Multi-cloud Ecosystem

Anthony J.H. Simons[1(✉)], Alessandro Rossini[2],
Iraklis Paraskakis[3], and Jens Jensen[4]

[1] Department of Computer Science, University of Sheffield, Regent Court,
211 Portobello, Sheffield S1 4DP, UK
a.j.simons@sheffield.ac.uk
[2] Department of Networked Systems and Services, SINTEF,
P.O. Box 124 Blindern, 0314 Oslo, Norway
alessandro.rossini@sintef.no
[3] South-East European Research Centre, Proxenou Koromila 24,
54622 Thessaloniki, Greece
iparaskakis@seerc.org
[4] STFC, Chilton, Didcot, Oxfordshire OX11 0QX, UK
jens.jensen@stfc.ac.uk

Abstract. In the future multi-cloud ecosystem, many cloud providers and consumers will interact to create, discover, negotiate and use software services. Cloud service brokers will play a central role in bringing providers and consumers together, assisting with software service creation (from abstract models to platform-specific deployments), multi-cloud translation (model-driven adaptation and deployment of services) quality assurance (governance; functional testing and monitoring), service continuity (failure prevention and recovery) and market competition (arbitrage; service optimization; service customization). The emerging ecosystem will be supported by common standards, service models, methods and mechanisms that will operate across a wide variety of platforms and infrastructure, and across disparate service protocols.

Preface

This volume contains the proceedings of the 2nd International Workshop on Cloud Service Brokerage (CSB-2014), which was held on 2 September 2014 in the historic city of Manchester, the home of Computer Science, co-located with the 3rd European Conference on Service Oriented and Cloud Computing (ESOCC). The theme of this second workshop, which was organised and co-sponsored by the EU FP7 Broker@Cloud and PaaSage projects, is the role of Cloud service brokerage in catalysing the emergence of the multi-Cloud ecosystem.

Cloud service brokers will play a major role in matching providers with consumers. Industry analysts such as Gartner and Forrester have foreseen brokers playing the role of intermediaries, either integrating different partners, or aggregating their services, offering added value on brokered platforms. This was the motivation behind the EU FP7 Broker@Cloud project, whose goal is to investigate methods and mechanisms for continuous quality assurance and optimization for Cloud service brokerage.

© Springer International Publishing Switzerland 2015
G. Ortiz and C. Tran (Eds.): ESOCC 2014, CCIS 508, pp 121–123, 2015.
DOI: 10.1007/978-3-319-14886-1_12

122 A.J.H. Simons et al.

Furthermore, many potential Cloud consumers are challenged by the process of porting their business to the Cloud, particularly when the major vendors in the marketplace offer strictly incompatible interfaces to their platforms and services. Model-driven engineering has been suggested as one technology for keeping control of your software investment, while retaining the capability to deploy on many Clouds. This was the inspiration behind the EU FP7 PaaSage project, whose goal is to provide model-based Cloud platform "upperware", in a development and deployment environment for vendor-neutral Cloud software services.

This workshop reports recent research findings from these two projects; but also presents a number of papers from elsewhere. Altogether, nine papers were accepted from eighteen submissions, each of which was reviewed by at least three different referees from our international Programme Committee.

The first workshop session, entitled "Towards the Multi-Cloud Ecosystem", highlighted progress made towards overcoming vendor lock-in and increasing the predictability of service offerings. Baur et al. describe model-based Cloud platform "executionware", a model-based engine that enacts the provisioning, deployment, monitoring, and adaptation of Cloud-based applications in a multi-Cloud environment. In contrast, Gonidis et al. describe a framework-based approach, offering a homogeneous Java interface to heterogeneous Cloud services. Becker et al. argue that the Cloud computing paradigm reduces the impact of Quality-of-Service mismatch induced by interoperability errors, so reducing risk.

The second session, entitled "Service Composition - Verification and Testing", looked at economic incentives for composing services; and how to verify and test single and composed services. Brangewitz et al. explore the game-theoretic incentives affecting the design of composed service contracts. Lefticaru and Simons describe a method for complete functional test-generation from verified service specifications. Kiran and Simons show how intelligent test pruning and testing assumptions can reduce the size of test suites drastically, when testing composed services.

The third session, entitled "Service Description - Rules and Reasoning", looked at descriptive technologies for expressing business policies and rules. Domaschka et al. describe a Scalability Rule Language for specifying complex scalability rules for Cloud-based applications. Arampatzis et al. map business-level Linked USDL descriptions into checkable WS-Agreement templates. Friesen et al. derive Cloud service broker policies from the hosting platform's service descriptions in Linked USDL.

Altogether, the papers collected here represent a diverse range of analyses, ranging from the envisioning of the future, to the technical challenges and solutions and the measurement of economic benefits for Cloud Service Brokerage. We hope that you find these insights stimulating!

Anthony J.H. Simons
Alessandro Rossini
Iraklis Paraskakis
Jens Jensen

Acknowledgements. The research leading to these results has received funding from the European Union Seventh Framework Programme (FP7/2007-2013) under grant agreement no. 328392, the Broker@Cloud project (www.broker-cloud.eu) and under grant agreement no. 317715, the PaaSage project (www.paasage.eu).

CSB-2014 Workshop Organisation

Organising Committee

- Anthony J. H. Simons, University of Sheffield, UK
- Alessandro Rossini, SINTEF, Oslo, Norway
- Iraklis Paraskakis, SEERC, Thessaloniki, Greece
- Jens Jensen, STFC, Didcot, Oxfordshire, UK

Programme Committee

- Andreas Friesen, SAP, Karlsruhe, Germany
- Anthony Sulistio, HLRS, Stuttgart, Germany
- Antonia Schwichtenberg, CAS Software, Karlsruhe, Germany
- Brice Morin, SINTEF, Oslo, Norway
- Christian Perez, INRIA, Lyon, France
- Craig Sheridan, Flexiant, Edinburgh, UK
- Dimitris Dranidis, International Faculty of the University of Sheffield, CITY College, Thessaloniki, Greece
- Franck Fleurey, SINTEF, Oslo, Norway
- Gregoris Mentzas, ICCS NTUA, Athens, Greece
- Jörg Domaschka, University of Ulm, Germany
- Lutz Schubert, University of Ulm, Germany
- Nikos Parlavantzas, INRIA/IRISA, Rennes, France
- Panagiotis Gouvas, SingularLogic, Athens, Greece
- Petros Kefalas, International Faculty of the University of Sheffield, CITY College, Thessaloniki, Greece
- Raluca Lefticaru, University of Sheffield, UK
- Symeon Veloudis, SEERC, Thessaloniki, Greece
- Volker Kuttruff, CAS Software, Karlsruhe, Germany
- Yiannis Verginadis, ICCS NTUA, Athens, Greece

CSB-2014 Workshop Sponsors

http://www.paasage.eu/

http://www.broker-cloud.eu/

Towards a Model-Based Execution-Ware for Deploying Multi-cloud Applications

Daniel Baur[✉], Stefan Wesner, and Jörg Domaschka

Institute of Information Resource Management, University of Ulm,
Albert-Einstein-Allee 43, 89081 Ulm, Germany
{daniel.baur,stefan.wesner,joerg.domaschka}@uni-ulm.de
http://www.uni-ulm.de/in/omi

Abstract. The current cloud landscape is highly heterogeneous caused by a vast number of cloud offerings by different providers. This hinders the selection of a cloud provider and its divergent offerings based on the requirements of an application and ultimately its deployment. This paper introduces a model based execution-ware that helps coping with these challenges by allowing the deployment of applications in a multi-cloud environment, based on a high-level model created by the user. Based on our experiences with building an initial prototype, we discuss the fundamental challenges and solution approaches that the multi-cloud environment holds.

Keywords: Cloud computing · Multi-cloud · Cloud broker

1 Introduction

The cloud landscape as of today is characterized by a tremendous number of cloud offerings on various levels and involving several types of services including computing, storage, and networking [20]. The offerings do not only differ on the interface level, and the description model but also on their service type and tiers such as IaaS, PaaS, and SaaS.

As for IaaS, the variance leads to different abstract specifications of hardware that are hard to compare. Moreover, the abstraction level makes it difficult to select one of the offerings for one's own application. This leads to four main challenges from an application user's perspective [5]: *(i)* When using a particular cloud platform for the first time, the actual performance that will be received by a particular hardware configuration is hard to predict making a selection based solely on the provider's description insufficient. *(ii)* Consequently, the number of required resources and with it the actual costs cannot be reliably predicted. *(iii)* When eventually the actual costs are finally known, the user may already suffer from vendor lock-in so that it is barely possible to change the cloud provider. The same is true whenever new operators appear on the market or existing operators change system properties such as pricing or service levels. *(iv)* Finally, the availability offered by a single operator may not suffice for mission critical applications.

© Springer International Publishing Switzerland 2015
G. Ortiz and C. Tran (Eds.): ESOCC 2014, CCIS 508, pp. 124–138, 2015.
DOI: 10.1007/978-3-319-14886-1_13

Deploying an application over multiple clouds as proposed by the multi-cloud/federated cloud model promises to solve many of the performance and availability issues mentioned above according to [7,19]. In order to avoid that users have to handle, monitor, and interact with multiple cloud operators at the same time, the usage of cloud brokerage [23] appears worthwhile.

In this paper, we discuss fundamental challenges that a potential cloud brokerage operator has to face. We first propose a broker architecture allowing deployment of applications in a multi-cloud environment based on a model created by the user. We automatically transfer the model given by the user, into a deployment plan describing the placement of the application. Afterwards the plan is automatically executed resulting in a deployment of the application within the multi-cloud environment. Based on performance indicators given by the model, the proposed execution-ware evaluates the performance of the current deployment and allows it to revise the initial deployment plan. Based on this initial architecture we depict the challenges that the current implementation faces and hold a discussion proposing changes to overcome these challenges.

In Sect. 2 we give a short overview over the architecture required for building the model-based execution-ware, and explain the need for the single components by depicting an example deployment workflow. In Sect. 3 we describe the single components and their task within the execution-ware's architecture in more detail. Afterwards, Sect. 4 presents the current implementation status and discusses the experiences we gained from this first implementation of the execution-ware. In particular, we provide fundamental challenges our system faces in the multi-cloud environment. Finally, Sect. 5 summarizes related work on this topic and Sect. 6 concludes the paper by depicting our future work on this topic.

2 Overview

This section first gives a short architectural overview of the different components required for a model based multi-cloud execution-ware. Afterwards, the interaction of the single components is shown, using an example deployment workflow.

2.1 Architecture

The following components are required for building a execution-ware able to deploy an application described by a user's model in a multi-cloud environment:

Cloud Repository. The cloud repository stores the cloud offerings of different providers and additional meta information. It provides the information required for (i) the reasoning of the broker and (ii) the deployment done by the cloud managers using the abstraction layer.

User Models. In the user model the user describes his application and the requirements his application has. It consists of a description of the application and the required topology for the application. Based on the model the broker can select the best fitting cloud offering that should be used for the defined application. It also provides the necessary steps needed to deploy the application on the allocated VMs.

Model Repository. The model repository stores already created user models. Its task is to provide model templates, facilitating the initial entry for modeling applications by reusing already made models. In addition it allows to share models with other users.

Abstraction Layer. The abstraction layer wraps and translates the calls to the cloud provider interfaces. As nearly all cloud providers use their own definition of an interface, the abstraction layer is crucial for allowing the broker and the cloud managers to call these interfaces in a unified way.

Cloud Manager. The cloud managers are responsible for controlling the different clouds, where cloud represents one cloud provider offer selected for the multi-cloud deployment. They orchestrate this cloud, by executing the tasks given by the broker component and collect information provided by the agents.

Application VM and Agents. The agents will be installed on each VM allocated by the system. Their task is to deploy the application based on the description by the model and to collect monitoring information enriching the cloud repository with information about the applications' execution.

Broker. The broker is the controller of the single components. It takes the user model and the cloud repository as input and calculates the placement of the application within the cloud environment. It then coordinates the execution of the cloud managers, and collects the monitoring information used to calculate a new revision of the placement.

2.2 Example Deployment Workflow

The workflow will be depicted using a simple example. Assume the user wants to deploy a multi-tier application consisting of three well understood *application components (AC)* such as a database, a web server, and an application server. For the sake of simplicity, assume these are called *A1*, *A2* and *A3*. For the deployment, the three cloud providers *P1*, *P2* and *P3* are available. This example workflow is depicted in Fig. 1.

Preparation. The first step is the initial, one-time population of the repositories. For this purpose the user needs to enter his accounting information for the known cloud providers. Consequently, the repository retrieves the configurations the cloud providers offers, and stores them. In addition already created models are stored in the model repository.

Modelling. The next step for deploying a application is the description of the application and the desired topology using a model. As most multi-tier applications consist of standard ACs, the user can first access the model repository and retrieve a standard model template for each of his ACs. If the repository does not provide a model template, he needs to create one for himself. The next step is the

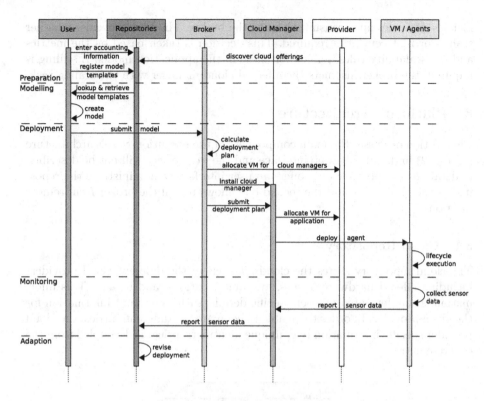

Fig. 1. Deployment workflow

customization of the model template to meet the specific requirements of each of the different application components. In addition, the user needs to define a topology description, including the required hardware (CPU, RAM, persistent storage, ephemeral storage), operating system image and location for each of the three application components. Finally the model is submitted to the broker.

Deployment. Based on the application and topology model and available data about the provided services in the cloud repository the broker calculates a deployment plan, depicting the placement of the different application components. In the example the deployment plan could place *A1* and *A2* on *P1* and *A3* on *P2*. The next step is the execution of the deployment plan. For this step the broker installs the cloud manager in the required cloud provider infrastructure (*P1* and *P2*). Afterwards, it initiates the installation of *A1* and *A2* to the cloud manager installed on *P1* and the installation of *A2* to the manager in *P2*. The cloud managers now acquire the required resources from the given providers using the abstraction layer and install the application as described in its model.

Adaption. After an initial deployment, the agents installed on each created application components' virtual machine (VM) monitor the defined application metrics and rules and transmit them to the broker. The broker decides whether scaling or replacement is required. This decision is taken based on the metrics and the scalability rules defined for these in the application model. If scaling is required, the broker instructs the affected cloud manager with the scaling task.

3   Platform Architecture

This section discusses the main components of the execution-ware's architecture (cf. Fig. 2) in detail. The web interface and the web service will not be described in detail, as the first one only offers an user interface to administrate the repositories and the broker and the second one allows to call the broker from remote locations.

3.1   Cloud Repository

The cloud repository stores the cloud offerings of the different cloud providers including offered hardware flavors, available locations, and images. This information is supplemented by user specific details, such as account information for the given provider. In order to be able to compare the different entries, the cloud provider specific information (e.g. unique identifiers, price) is decoupled from the concrete entries.

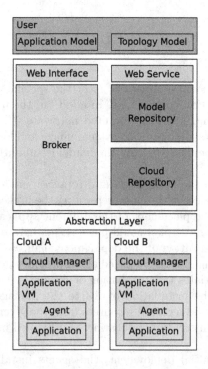

Fig. 2. Architecture of the execution-ware

Furthermore, the repository contains meta-data about the actual stored data. This includes for instance data protection information for the single locations or performance benchmarks. This allows the execution-ware to select cloud offerings based on requirements rather than a specific description. For the location this means e.g. that the user does not need to select a specific location but models his demands more like constraints in respect to data protection requirements.

3.2   User Models

The user's model consists of two main parts: a specification of the application behavior and a description of the desired topology.

Application model. The application model mainly consists of the application's lifecycle specification. For every event in the lifecycle of an application a corresponding action is defined, which is executed if the application enters this state. This allows the execution-ware to deploy, start and observe any described application. The executed action is a shell script or binary which can be customized based on the different environments of the virtual machine (e.g. FreeBSD or Linux). The application's lifecycle actions and their meaning are described in Table 1. Providing the application's lifecycle actions on this level, allows the user to either completely describe the application by himself, or rely on automation tools like chef [8] or puppet [27]. The template mechanism provided by the model repository facilitates this, by offering the possibility to provide ready to use templates for these solutions.

In addition, the model defines sensors by which the application's performance (metrics) will be measured during runtime. Based on this metrics, the deployer can describe scaling rules, if one of these metrics is out of the allowed range. An example for this would be the metric *Response Time* with a threshold constraint *not greater as 0.2 s.*

Topology model. The topological model depicts the required environment for the application on a per AC-basis. It describes the hardware required for the individual AC based on e.g. CPU, RAM, storage and location.

3.3   Model Repository

Most multi-tier applications are build on top of a selection of standard resources: For instance, any web-application is likely to include load balancers, application servers and one or multiple databases and will further add a container with the specific application. This allows the usage of model templates (generic models where single variables may be easily overwritten), which, in turn, enables the user to reuse other models. These may be either his own models, but more importantly this allows community building, the exchange of model templates with other users and business propositions for companies offering reference models reducing the obstacle of high initial modeling effort.

Table 1. The application lifecycle actions [11]

init	Invoked after the application VM is initialized; used for validating the system environment
preInstall	Used to retrieve the installation binaries
install	Extract or install the binaries
postInstall	Used for adaption of configuration files according to the environment
preStart	Used for checking that required operating system files are available, like files, disk space and port
start	Mandatory; launches the application process
startDetection	Used for notifying the agent that the application has started
locator	Used for checking the liveness of the application
stopDetection	Used for notifying the agent that the application stopped
postStart	Used for registration of the service instance with e.g. a load balancer
preStop	Unregister the service instance
stop	Used for manual stop logic
postStop	Used for releasing any allocated external resources
shutdown	Used for cleanup before the application VM shuts down

The same applies to the topology for the application. While the requirements targeting the hardware may vary between applications, the model of other comparable applications may provide a good starting point.

3.4 Abstraction Layer

Despite all differences across vendors the fundamental capabilities of the offerings are very similar. As a result different vendors seek differentiation of their offerings in the cloud application interfaces (API) as this makes it difficult to migrate an application to the infrastructure of a competitor. The abstraction layer provided by the broker has the task to map calls from the broker and cloud managers to the interfaces of the respective cloud provider.

To achieve this, the abstraction layer fulfills two different tasks: (i) It offers a standard language which it maps to the language used by the target provider's interface. (ii) It also unifies the different semantics used by the providers, offering a common semantic, which is used within the model (cf. Sect. 4.1).

3.5 Cloud Manager

A cloud manager is responsible for the orchestration within a respective cloud, meaning a specific cloud offered by one provider. While the broker (cf. Sect. 3.7) decides the placement of the application, the cloud managers are responsible for executing the deployment instructions by allocating the resources (i.e. the VMs) from the cloud provider. They also install and start the agents (cf. Sect. 3.6) on the target VM.

After the application has started, a cloud manager collects the monitoring information submitted by the agents, and transmits the information to the broker. If the broker decides to change the execution of the application (e.g. scale), the cloud managers are also responsible for the allocation of the new resources and the deployment.

Using a cloud manager per cloud infrastructure enhances isolation and autonomy. Application VMs hosting background services that must not be accessible from public networks can communicate using the provider's private network infrastructure achieving higher bandwidth, lower latency and reduced cost. In addition, the autonomy increases the reliability of the system, as otherwise the broker would be a single point of failure for the complete multi-cloud environment. As the cloud managers still represent a single point of failure for the specific cloud, this can be overcome by allowing their replication.

3.6 Application VM and Agents

On each created application components' VM the application will be started within an container for isolation and monitoring purposes. Additionally an agent will be started for communication with the cloud manager responsible for the given cloud. The agent is also responsible for the execution of the lifecycle events (cf. Table 1). In addition it transmits the monitoring information required for the metrics defined in the application's model.

3.7 Broker

The broker is the main actor of the proposed architecture. It processes the user input of application and topology model and the data provided by the cloud repository to calculate the placement of the individual ACs (reasoning).

Based on the model analysis the broker will start the installation of the required cloud managers. Afterwards, the installation instructions for the different application tiers are given to the cloud managers.

During execution of the application the broker will aggregate the runtime monitoring information from the different cloud managers and calculate metrics as required by the application model. If one of the defined metrics is out of the allowed range, the broker will recalculate the placement of the individual ACs and change the execution status of the ACs by adopting them to the new deployment plan.

However, this adaptability based on metrics makes the reasoning difficult. The space of possible configurations is immense (it grows exponentially with each variable like offered cloud solutions or performance of the offered solution). This makes it impossible to calculate and compare each configuration allowed by the given constraints. Therefore, an iterative approach is required, meaning that a "best-effort" first deployment is calculated which is later improved with experience gained by the monitoring information.

4   Discussion

During the implementation of a first prototype of the execution-ware several question and challenges regarding the components arose, when dealing with a multi-cloud setup. This section will therefore first of all describe the current implementation status in the first subsection, and afterwards depict these challenges in the remaining subsections, which are separated by the different components that are affected. Afterwards, the different challenges will be discussed on p a per-component basis, and possible solutions for a further implementation of the execution-ware will be drawn.

4.1   Implementation Status

The execution-ware is implemented in context of the FP7 PaaSage[1] project, which aims at facilitating the execution of applications within the multi-cloud environment. This means that some parts of the depicted architecture are implemented outside of the execution-ware, in particular the model and reasoning part. The model repository is currently missing, as it is designed but not yet implemented.

Cloud Repository. With our current implementation the user needs to enter the provider's cloud offerings and the related accounting information (username and password) by himself. This means that he needs to register for all available cloud providers, respectively deployment is limited to the providers for which an account is available.

User Models. Within PaaSage models are defined using a family of domain-specific languages (DSLs) called Cloud Application Modeling and Execution Language (CAMEL). Part of CAMEL are the Cloud Modeling Language (CLOUDML) [15], Saloon [28], WS-Agreement [1] and the Scalability Rule Language (SRL) [14]. CLOUDML is used for depicting the deployment of the application, Saloon for specifying its requirements and target goals, WS-Agreement for defining the SLAs and the SLR is used for defining the scalability rules.

Abstraction Layer. The current implementation of the abstraction layer is based on jclouds [3]. However, as not all features of jcloud are required, a second layer of abstraction is implemented, invoking the specific jclouds function. This reduces the complexity of the implementation as only the required jclouds functionality is present in the abstraction layer. Furthermore this allows an easier implementation of connectors for cloud providers not shipped with jclouds. Additionally, it enables the support of different multi-cloud toolsets, of which some are described in Sect. 5.

---

[1] www.paasage.eu.

Broker. Reasoning within PaaSage makes use of a model@runtime architecture as proposed by [6,24]. This means that based on the initial topology model, each iteration/adoption step based on the current context leads to a revision/ improvement, which is validated using monitored data. The current implementation of the execution-ware publishes the measured monitoring data using a time series database (KairosDB [21]), where the reasoning components can subscribe to the information. Afterwards the calculated revised model (deployment plan) is transmitted to the execution-ware via the RESTful web service, which is then executed by instantiating the cloud managers and transmitting the deployment information. The usage of a web service, makes it possible to use different reasoner implementations. A more detailed description for the reasoning within the PaaSage project can be found in [17].

Cloud Manager. The current implementation of the cloud managers provides a REST interface which is used by the broker to submit the installation requests of the single ACs. Afterwards, the cloud managers use the implemented abstraction layer to allocate required VMs from the provider. Subsequently, the agents are installed and started. Reporting data from the agents is collected, and written to the time series database residing within the cloud manager component.

Application VM and Agents. After the agents are started on the application VM, they receive the installation request from the cloud managers via web requests. Afterwards, they execute the lifecycles defined in the application model. Based on the defined actions they are able to detect the failure of a service and are able to restart it. Sensors like memory or CPU consumption are already implemented. A generic interface allows the implementation of application dependent sensors.

4.2   User Model

One of the main problems when modeling application and topology properties of an application, is the high initial workload for creating an application model. This initial effort can be reduced by offering a model repository (cf. Sect. 3.3), containing templates for the most important standard software. But the main obstacle regarding re-usability of existing models is the high diversity of existing solutions for describing application's properties. This does not only hinder the exchange of existing models, but makes it hard to migrate from one model driven engine to another, as all created models need to be transformed to the new modeling language. This results in moving the vendor lock-in from cloud provider level to the level of the used engine. Using a wide-spread standard for modeling the application could not only reduce the initial barrier, but also allow the user to switch between multiple model driven engines.

Furthermore, the modeling possibilities are currently limited by the interfaces offered by the providers. As available (meta) data and the services provided by the abstraction layer define the possibilities of the model, further modeling options need an improvement in these fields. The next section will depict this in more detail.

4.3 Abstraction Layer

While an abstraction layer for the unification of cloud provider interfaces is mandatory as a wide-spread standard is still missing, it introduces a vulnerability into the architecture. The APIs offered by providers are prone to changes, causing the failure of control for one cloud in worse cases.

In addition the computed deployment plan will never render the optimal plan, it will only represent the optimal solution considering the clouds supported by the abstraction layer. While a standard is needed due to these shortcomings, the individual features of different providers (e.g. spot-instances[2], consulting) will always diminish in the unification process, making the price-performance ratio the key indicator regarding resource selection. This will make it harder, especially for smaller providers, to compete in the cost dominated environment.

Regarding the model, the abstraction layer and the interfaces offered by cloud providers currently oppose the expressiveness of the model. As interfaces currently limit the selection to a simple selection of the CPU, RAM and disk (type and space) the model is also limited to these properties. As this may be enough for simple web application, complex applications, e.g. from the area of high-performance computing, crave for more specific placement options like direct selection and reservation of a host for compute intensive operations or a high bandwidth connection to storage for disk intensive tasks [16]. While this is surely a cost that is caused by the virtualization, it reduces the usefulness of cloud computing for these kind of applications. That is why a standard for allowing more specific placement of resources is needed.

With the current status of SLA and account interfaces the user needs to supply all his accounting information in advance as described in Sect. 4.1. This could be overcome with two possible solutions: *(i)* the broker negotiates for the user using a standard API or *(ii)* the broker uses a single broker account per cloud provider. As using a broker account introduces multiple other issues regarding e.g. billing and isolation, using an interface would be preferable.

4.4 Cloud Repository

Regarding the cloud repository, the user has to fill in all data regarding the different services offered by cloud providers, e.g. images, hardware. As this represents a high initial effort for the user and is also problematic regarding timely notice of changes, a service providing this data would be preferable. While CloudHarmony [9] or CloudMetric [29] offer such a service, those public databases can not include private clouds. The better solution would be a collection interface querying all known services offered by providers in real-time.

Another challenge is the comparison of the different cloud provider services. A selection solely based on the publicly available information by cloud provider interfaces, e.g. the number of CPU or RAM, can be implemented by solving the placement problem [26]. However performance unpredictability [5] and different

---

[2] http://aws.amazon.com/de/ec2/purchasing-options/spot-instances/.

requirements regarding applications hinder taking a correct decision based only on this information. Usage of a cloud comparison tool like CloudCMP [22] could offer a more sophisticated foundation for the comparison, as available performance data would allow the user to model application requirements based on needed performance.

In addition, there are additional constraints coming from the multi-cloud environment, e.g. bandwidth and latency for communication between the used cloud providers. While communication-intensive applications still are a challenge for cloud environments [18], in general not considering these constraints can lead to suboptimal placement of applications.

4.5 Broker

The first deployment of an application is mainly limited by the information given by the cloud repository as already described in Sect. 4.4. Allowing elasticity for applications by scaling the application based on monitoring information is only limited by the description and implementation of the lifecycle actions the user defined in his model.

The main challenge regarding deployments is the dynamic environment, meaning that the data used for the first deployment may be quickly outdated. There may be multiple reasons: pricing changes; changing requirements for the application result in a new model; new and more cost-efficient hardware flavors offered by a provider; and many more. While the detection of these changes is easy, a reaction upon them is challenging, as a calculation of a new deployment plan can include a different provider selection. This makes the transformation between the old and the new deployment plan challenging, as a migration between two different providers is needed. As migrations are not only hard to execute due to vendor specific virtualization formats, they are also expensive: As data transfer does not only cause costs at provider level (transfer costs), but also at application level due to downtime or higher load during migration. These additional costs add to the computing model, making a reaction on changes a complex model.

5   Related Work

Regarding the unification of the different infrastructure interfaces of the cloud providers several different approaches exist. The first approach is the standardization of the providers' interfaces. Two examples for such standards are the Cloud Infrastructure Management Interface (CIMI [12]) and the Open Cloud Computing Interface (OCCI [25]). While CIMI is already supported by popular open source cloud software such as OpenStack[3], it still lacks the support of the public cloud providers such as Amazon and many others.

---

[3] https://blueprints.launchpad.net/nova/+spec/cimi.

Another approach is unification due to programming interfaces supporting multiple cloud providers as offered by jclouds [3] or libcloud [4]. Apache's δ-cloud [2] offers a slightly different approach by offering a web service translating e.g. CIMI into other provider's interfaces. While these libraries are an enabler for the usage of multi-clouds, they do not offer automatization with respect to deployment of applications or the acquisition of resources.

More complex solutions like cloudify [10] not only include a translation layer, but also a domain specific language for modeling applications as well as an orchestration engine responsible for deployment and scaling of applications.

All above mentioned solutions only consider the management of cloud infrastructure and do not support the creation of accounts or negotiation of service level agreements. While WS-Agreement [1] and WS-Agreement Negotiation [30] define standards for this, they are not yet supported by public clouds.

When migrating instances, the Open Virtualization Format (OVF) provides portability of applications on the layer of virtualization allowing deployment in multiple cloud environments [13].

For the description of the topology and the application, CloudMF [15] introduces a domain-specific modeling language for modeling applications. In addition it provides a models@runtime environment, allowing to adapt the running system to changes in the model and vice versa.

The CACTOS[4] project addresses the problem that VMs perform significantly different on various hardware configurations and that performance prediction is often difficult as the application behavior is not well enough understood. By performing offline trace analysis, derived performance models and corresponding realtime trace analysis the scalability rules can be more complex than simple threshold misses [31].

6   Conclusions and Future Work

In this paper we have introduced a model based execution-ware allowing the deployment of applications across multiple clouds based on a model created by the user. The proposed architecture and a prototypical implementation are an initial step to ease the usage of the multi-cloud environment. However, there are still many challenges needed to overcome to fully take advantage of the versatile cloud offers. While the public cloud providers are still reluctant to implement already proposed standards which would facilitate the usage of multiple providers at once, many community driven solutions help by mitigating these shortcomings.

Our future work will try to overcome the challenges described in the discussion section. While some challenges like the missing interfaces for accounting and more specific deployment are only solvable by cloud providers themselves, implementations based on open-source cloud software like OpenStack[5] or Apache

---

[4] http://www.cactosfp7.eu/.
[5] https://www.openstack.org/.

CloudStack[6] could offer possibilities to overcome these limitations. Furthermore, additional requirements like security have to be considered. In addition experiments are required to evaluate the selected solutions in regard to their contribution in facilitating the deployment of applications in the multi-cloud environment.

Acknowledgments. The research leading to these results has received funding from the European Community's Seventh Framework Programme (FP7/2007-2013) under grant agreement no. 317715 (PaaSage) and grant agreement no. 610711 (CACTOS).

References

1. Andrieux, A., Czajkowski, K., Dan, A., Keahey, K., Ludwig, H., Nakata, T., Pruyne, J., Rofrano, J., Tuecke, S., Xu, M.: Web Services Agreement Specification (WS-Agreement). Open Grid Forum (2007)
2. Apache Deltacloud. https://deltacloud.apache.org/
3. Apache jClouds. http://jclouds.apache.org/
4. Apache libcloud. https://libcloud.apache.org/
5. Armbrust, M., Fox, A., Griffith, R., Joseph, A.D., Katz, R.H., Konwinski, A., Lee, G., Patterson, D.A., Rabkin, A., Stoica, I., Zaharia, M.: Above the clouds: a Berkeley view of cloud computing, Technical report UCB/EECS-2009-28. University of California, Berkeley, EECS Department (2009)
6. Blair, G., Bencomo, N., France, R.B.: Models@Run.Time. Computer **42**(10), 22–27 (2009)
7. Buyya, R., Ranjan, R., Calheiros, R.N.: InterCloud: utility-oriented federation of cloud computing environments for scaling of application services. In: Hsu, C.-H., Yang, L.T., Park, J.H., Yeo, S.-S. (eds.) ICA3PP 2010, Part I. LNCS, vol. 6081, pp. 13–31. Springer, Heidelberg (2010)
8. Chef. http://www.getchef.com/chef/
9. Cloud Harmony. https://cloudharmony.com
10. Cloudify. http://getcloudify.org/
11. Cloudify Lifecycles. http://getcloudify.org/guide/2.7/developing/lifecycle_events.html
12. DMTF: Cloud Infrastructure Management Interface (CIMI) Model and RESTful HTTP-based Protocol. http://dmtf.org/standards/cloud
13. DMTF: Open Virtualization Format 2.1.0 (2013). http://www.dmtf.org/sites/default/files/standards/documents/DSP0243_2.1.0.pdf
14. Domaschka, J., Kritikos, K., Rossini, A.: Towards a generic language for scalability rules. In: CSB 2014: 2nd International Workshop on Cloud Service Brokerage (2014, accepted for publication)
15. Ferry, N., Chauvel, F., Rossini, A., Morin, B., Solberg, A.: Managing multi-cloud systems with CloudMF. In: Proceedings of the Second Nordic Symposium on Cloud Computing & Internet Technologies, pp. 38–45 (2013)
16. Gupta, A., Milojicic, D., Kalé, L.V.: Optimizing VM placement for HPC in the cloud. In: Proceedings of the 2012 Workshop on Cloud Services, Federation, and the 8th Open Cirrus Summit, pp. 1–6 (2012)

---

[6] http://cloudstack.apache.org/.

17. Horn, G.: A Vision for a stochastic reasoner for autonomic cloud deployment. In: NordiCloud 2013 Proceedings of the Second Nordic Symposium on Cloud Computing & Internet Technologies, pp. 46–53 (2013)
18. Jackson, K.R., Ramakrishnan, L., Muriki, K., Canon, S., Cholia, S., Shalf, J., Wasserman, H.J., Wright, N.J.: Performance analysis of high performance computing applications on the amazon web services cloud. In: 2010 IEEE Second International Conference on Cloud Computing Technology and Science (CloudCom), pp. 159–168 (2010)
19. Jrad, F., Tao, J., Streit, A.: A broker-based framework for multi-cloud workflows. In: MultiCloud 2013 Proceedings of the 2013 International Workshop on Multicloud Applications and Federated Clouds, pp. 61–68, New York (2013)
20. Kächele, S., Spann, C., Hauck, F.J., Domaschka, J.: Beyond IaaS and PaaS: an extended cloud taxonomy for computation, storage and networking. In: UCC 2013: IEEE/ACM 6th International Conference on Utility and Cloud Computing, pp. 75–82 (2013)
21. KairosDB. https://code.google.com/p/kairosdb/
22. Li, A., Yang, X., Kandula, S., Zhang, M.: CloudCmp: comparing public cloud providers. In: IMC 2010 Proceedings of the 10th ACM SIGCOMM Conference on Internet Measurement, pp. 1–14, New York (2010)
23. Liu, F., Tong, J., Mao, J., Bohn, R.B., Messina, J.V., Badger, M.L., Leaf, D.M.: NIST Cloud Computing Reference Architecture, Special Publication 500–292, National Institute of Standards and Technology Gaithersburg (2011)
24. Morin, B., Barais, O., Jézéquel, J.-M., Fleurey, F., Solberg, A.: Models@Run.Time to support dynamic adaption. Computer **42**(10), 44–52 (2009)
25. Open Cloud Computing Interface (OCCI). http://occi-wg.org/
26. Pawluk, P., Simmons, B., Smit, M., Litoiu, M.: Introducing STRATOS: a cloud broker service. In: 2012 IEEE Fifth International Conference on Cloud Computing, pp. 891–898 (2012)
27. Puppet. http://puppetlabs.com/
28. Quinton, C., Haderer, N., Rouvoy, R., Duchien, L.: Towards multi-cloud configurations using feature models and ontologies. In: Proceedings of the 2013 International Workshop on Multi-cloud Applications and Federated Clouds, pp. 21–26 (2013)
29. Smit, M., Pawluk, P., Simmons, B., Litoiu, M.: A web service for cloud metadata. In: 2012 IEEE Eighth World Congress on Services, pp. 361–368 (2012)
30. Waeldrich, O., Battrè, D., Brazier, F., Clark, K., Oey, M., Papaspyrou, A., Wieder, P., Ziegler, W.: WS-Agreement Negotiation Version 1.0, Open Grid Forum (2011)
31. Wesner, S., Groenda, H., Byrne, J., Svorobej, S., Hauser, C., Domaschka, J., Optimised Cloud data centre operation supported by simulation, eChallenges (2014, in print)

A Development Framework Enabling the Design of Service-Based Cloud Applications

Fotis Gonidis[1(✉)], Iraklis Paraskakis[1], and Anthony J.H. Simons[2]

[1] South-East European Research Centre (SEERC),
International Faculty of the University of Sheffield, City College,
24 Proxenou Koromila Street, 54622 Thessaloniki, Greece
{fgonidis,iparaskakis}@seerc.org
[2] Department of Computer Science, The University of Sheffield,
Regent Court, 211 Portobello Street, Sheffield S1 4DP, UK
A.Simons@dcs.shef.ac.uk

Abstract. Cloud application platforms gain popularity and have the potential to change the way applications are developed, involving composition of platform basic services. In order to enhance the developer's experience and reduce the barriers in the software development, a new paradigm of cloud application creation should be adopted. According to that developers are enabled to design their applications, leveraging multiple platform basic services, independently from the target application platforms. To this end, this paper proposes a development framework for the design of service-based cloud applications comprising two main components: the meta-model and the Platform Service Manager. The meta-model describes the building blocks which enable the construction of Platform Service Connectors in a uniform way while the Platform Service Manager coordinates the interaction of the application with the concrete service providers and further facilitates the administration of the deployed platform basic services.

Keywords: Platform basic services · Abstract service models · Multi-cloud

1 Introduction

The emergence of the cloud application platforms has been accompanied by a growing number of platform basic services being provisioned via them. In addition to the traditional platform resources such as programming environment and data stores [1], a cloud application platform provisions a range of platform basic services that developers can leverage to accelerate the software development process [2]. A platform basic service, in the Platform as a Service level [1], can be considered as a piece of software which offers certain functionality and can be reused by multiple users. It is typically provisioned via a web Application Programming Interface (API) either REST [3] or SOAP [4]. Examples of such services are the message queue, the e-mail, the authentication and the payment service.

The rise of the platform basic services has the potential to lead to a paradigm of software development where the services act as the building blocks for the creation of

© Springer International Publishing Switzerland 2015
G. Ortiz and C. Tran (Eds.): ESOCC 2014, CCIS 508, pp. 139–152, 2015.
DOI: 10.1007/978-3-319-14886-1_14

service-based cloud applications. Applications do not need to be developed from ground-up but can rather be synthesised from various platform basic services increasing rapidly this way the productivity. This paradigm of software development can be considered as an evolution of the Service Oriented Architecture (SOA) [5] approach, where the applications are composed of various web services. In that case, established frameworks, such as the Business Process Execution Language (BPEL) [6] and the Web Service Resource Framework (WSRF) [7] assist developers during the integration process of the web services. However, the advent of the cloud application platforms and the platform basic services has resulted in multiple software vendors offering the same type of service such as authentication service, mailing service and payment service. Therefore, developers should not only be enabled to effortlessly integrate the platform basic services but also to choose seamlessly the concrete service providers, overcoming the heterogeneity among them.

Towards this direction, a new approach for the design of service-based cloud applications must be adopted. The key concept is for users not to develop applications directly against proprietary cloud provider's environment. Rather, they should use either standard and widely adopted technologies or abstraction layers which decouple application development from specific target technologies and Application Programming Interfaces (APIs).

To this end the paper proposes a development framework which promotes uniform access to platform basic services via the use of abstract Platform Service Connectors (Fig. 1). It is composed of three main parts: (i) the Platform Service Manager (PSM), which handles the execution of the services, (ii) the Platform Service Connectors (PSC), which contain an abstract description of the functionality of the services and (iii) the Provider Connectors (PC), which include the detailed implementation required by each provider.

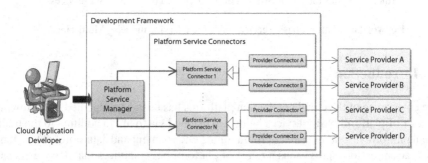

Fig. 1. Cloud application development framework

The key objective of the proposed solution is two-fold. First, it introduces a reference meta-model which enables the integration of platform basic services in a consistent way through the construction of the PSCs. Second, it decouples application development from vendor specific implementations by encapsulating the latter in the PCs components. In addition to the reference meta-model, the proposed framework automates the workflow execution of the platform service operations.

The remainder of the paper is structured as follows. The next Section reviews established work in the field. Section 3 describes the way platform basic services may be consumed and motivates the need for a meta-model for constructing the PSCs in a uniform manner. Subsequently, Sect. 4 states the high-level components of the meta-model and the framework which manages the execution of the PSC. In order to illustrate how the proposed solution can be utilised to enable uniform access to platform basic services, Sect. 5 illustrates the case of the cloud payment service.

2 Related Work

The constant increase in the offering of platform basic services has resulted in a growing interest in the field of cross platform development and deployment of service-based cloud applications. Significant work has been carried out in the field which can be grouped into three high-level categories: library based solutions [8, 9], middleware platforms [10] and Model-Driven Engineering (MDE) [11] based initiatives [12–15]. Representative work on each of the three categories is presented.

Library-based solutions such as jclouds [8] and LibCloud [9] provide an abstraction layer for accessing specific cloud resources such as compute, storage and message queue. While, library-based approaches efficiently abstracting those resources, they have a limited application scope which makes it difficult to reuse them for accommodating additional services.

Middleware platforms constitute middle layers which decouple application development from directly being developed against specific platform technologies and deployed on specific platforms. Rather, cloud applications are deployed and managed by the middleware platform which has the capacity to exploit multiple cloud platform environments. mOSAIC [10] is such a PaaS solution whose main target is to facilitate the design and execution of scalable component-based applications. The main application building block in the mOSAIC platform is the cloudlet. A platform container manages the cloudlets and has the ability to spawn or destroy instances with respect to the load. Additionally mOSAIC offers an open source API in order to enable the applications to use common cloud resources offered by the target environment such as virtual machines, key/value stores and message queues. mOSAIC adopts a particular programming style based on the cloudlets which impose that applications abide by this style. Thus, although the mOSAIC platform is able to exploit multiple cloud environments, the applications which leverage mOSAIC's benefits, are tightly connected with the specific technology. Furthermore, middleware solutions often are complex environments which may impose an unnecessary overhead, should the applications not exploit all of their features.

Initiatives that utilise MDE techniques present meta-models which can be used for the creation of cloud platform independent applications. The notion in this case is that cloud applications are designed in a platform independent manner and specific technologies are only infused in the models at the last stage of the development. MODAClouds [12] and PaaSage [13] are both FP7 initiatives aiming at cross-deployment of cloud applications. Additionally, they offer monitoring and quality assurance capabilities.

They are based on CloudML [16], a modelling language which provides the building blocks for creating applications deployable in multiple IaaS and PaaS environments. Hamdaqa et al. [14] have proposed a reference model for developing applications which make use of the elasticity capability of the cloud infrastructure. Cloud applications are composed of CloudTasks which provide compute, storage, communication and management capabilities. MULTICLAPP [15] is a framework employing MDE techniques during the software development process. Cloud artefacts are the main components that the application consists of. A transformation mechanism is used to generate the platform specific project structure and map the cloud artefacts onto the target platform. Additional adapters are generated each time to map the application's API to the respective platform's resources.

The solutions listed in this Section focus mainly on eliminating the technical restrictions that each platform imposes, enabling this way cross-deployment of cloud applications. Additionally, they offer monitoring and quality assurance capabilities as well as the creation of elastic applications. On the contrary, the vision of the authors is to facilitate the use of platform basic services and concrete providers from the various cloud application platforms in a seamless and transparent manner. To this end, rather than focusing on the obstacles imposed during the deployment of cloud applications we focus on the commonalities and differences exposed by the various platform service providers during the consumption of those by the cloud applications. The proposed solution may be positioned in the intersection of the work presented in this Section. A reference meta-model is introduced to enable the consistent modelling and integration of the various platform basic services such as the authentication, payment, e-mail service. Additionally, a middleware framework handles the execution of the workflow and accommodates the abstraction of the various concrete providers so that application developers are not bound to specific vendor implementations.

3   The Need for a Platform Service Meta-model

Before describing the proposed framework and the meta-model for constructing the Platform Service Connectors (PSCs), we motivate the need for such a solution. We do so by examining various implementations of platform service clients. Preliminary work of the authors on several platform service providers [17] offered by Heroku [18], Google App engine [19], AWS marketplace [20] have shown that platform services may be distinguished into two categories: stateless and stateful [21].

Stateless services offer operations which are completed in one step. This means that the user of the service initiates a request and the latter responds with the result of the operation. The requests are performed using the web API exposed by the service providers and usually are in the form of a REST or SOAP call. Examples of such services include the message queue and the e-mail services. For example, in case that the user wants to send an e-mail using an e-mail service provider, he merely needs to submit a web request with a minimum set of required fields: recipient, sender, subject and body. Upon the successful post of the e-mail, the provider responds with a confirmation message.

On the other hand, stateful services require two or more steps in order to complete an operation. Therefore, contrary to the first category, a coordination mechanism is required to handle the operation flow. Additionally, the process involves incoming requests originated either by the client of the application or the service provider and which needs to be handled by the application.

Such an example is the payment service that enables developers to accept payments through their application. In this case the client initiates the purchase flow by sending a request to the application via the user interface. The latter receives the request and subsequently notifies the payment provider about the purchase operation. The provider responds to the application with information regarding the purchase transaction. Afterwards the client fills in the payment card details and transmits the data to the payment provider. Once the validation of the card is completed the provider responds to the application with the result of the payment transaction.

In this process two types of requests are implied. The first one includes the requests performed by the application towards the payment providers and which are executed using the web API offered by the providers. They are the similar to those described in the stateless services. The second type involves incoming requests submitted to the cloud application either by the client or the payment provider and which need to be received and handled by the cloud application.

In addition to the variety of the requests described above, platform basic services in both categories share some common characteristics. Certain configuration settings and credentials are required when a cloud application interacts with a platform service. For example in the case of the payment service, among others, a "redirect URL" needs to be specified to inform the service provider how to perform a request to the application. Regarding the requests performed using the web API of the service provider, authorization information and knowledge of the endpoints are required to execute the web call.

As it became clear a cloud application may interact with several platform basic services in various ways. If we count in the large number of services that an application may be composed of, one can realize that the integration and management of the services may become a time consuming and strenuous process. In order to enable the consistent modelling and integration of services as well as the decoupling from vendor specific implementations, a reference meta-model is required.

The meta-model should be platform and service independent so that it facilitates the design and implementation of a wide range of PSCs. Towards this direction the abstract description of the platform basic service functionality is modelled. Then, the technical details and the specific implementation of each service providers are infused in a transparent to the cloud application manner. Additionally, the Platform Service Manager (Fig. 1) keeps track of the platform basic services consumed by the application and coordinates the interaction between the application and the services.

4   The Development Framework

In this Section the high-level components of the development framework are described (Fig. 1). This can be further decomposed into (i) the meta-model used to create the

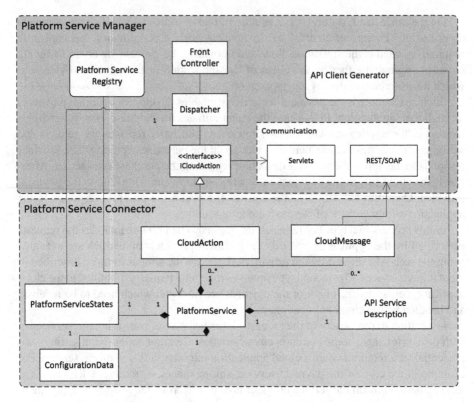

Fig. 2. High level overview of the development framework

Platform Service Connectors (PSCs) and (ii) the Platform Service Manager (PSM) which handles the interaction between the cloud application and the platform service (Fig. 2).

4.1 Meta-model Components

This Section states the components of the meta-model. In essence the meta-model describes the building blocks of which a PSC is composed. As depicted in the lower component of the Fig. 2 there are 5 main concepts:

1. **CloudAction.** Cloud Actions are used to model stateful platform basic services as described in Sect. 3, which define more than one step in order to complete an operation. The whole process required to complete the operation can be modelled as a state machine. Each step can be modelled as a concrete state that the platform service can exist in. When the appropriate event arrives an action is triggered to handle the event and subsequently causes the transition to the next state. The events in this case are the incoming requests arriving either by the application user or the service provider. A separate Cloud Action is defined to handle each incoming request and subsequently signals the transition to the next state.

2. **CloudMessage.** CloudMessages can be used to model requests performed by the cloud application towards the service provider. In this case the web API exposed by the provider is used, usually implemented with the REST or the SOAP protocol. CloudMessages can be used in platform services where the operation can be completed in one step, namely one REST/SOAP request to the service provider. Example of such a request, as mentioned in the previous section, is the e-mail service. A CloudMessage can be defined to send the web request along with the required fields: recipient, sender, title and body. In addition, CloudMessages can be used within Cloud Actions when the latter are required to submit a request to the service provider.

3. **PlatformServiceStates.** The PlatformServiceStates description file holds information about the states involved in an operation and the corresponding Cloud Actions which are initialised to execute the behavior required in each state. A part of a state description file describing the states involved in the payment transaction of a particular service provider is shown here:

```
<StateMachine>
  <State name="PaymentForm"
    action="org.paymentservice.FillOutFormCloudAction"
    nextState="SendTransaction" />
  <State name="SendTransaction"
    action="org.paymentservice.SendTransactionCloudAction"
    nextState="Finish" />
</StateMachine>
```

Two states are described here. For each state the following information is provided: (a) The name of the state, (b) The CloudAction which needs to be initialised in order to handle the incoming requests and (c) the next state which follows when the action finishes the execution. The state named "Finish" signals the completion of the operation.

4. **ConfigurationData.** Certain configuration settings are required by each platform service provider. That information is captured in the ConfigurationData. Example of settings which needs to be defined are the clients' credentials required to perform web requests and the redirect URL parameter which is often requested by the service provider in order to perform requests to the cloud application.

5. **API Service Description File.** The API service description file describes the functionality offered by the service provider via the web interface. The concrete operations, parameters and endpoints are stated in the file. It is consumed by the framework in order generate the client adapter which is used by the Cloud-Messages to communicate with the service provider.

The concepts listed in this Section enable the modelling of the PSCs and contribute to the first objective of the proposed solution which is to facilitate the integration of platform basic services in a consistent way. Additionally, the consistent modelling of the PSC enables the automation of the workflow execution of the platform service operations.

4.2 Framework Components

In this Section the high level components comprising the PSM, handling the PSCs, are described. As seen in the upper part of the Fig. 2, it essentially consists of the following components:

(1) **Front Controller.** The Front Controller [22] serves as the entry point to the framework. It receives the incoming requests by the application user and the service provider.

(2) **Dispatcher.** The dispatcher [23] follows the well-known request-dispatcher design pattern. It is responsible for receiving the incoming requests from the Front Controller and forwarding them to the appropriate handler, through the ICloudAction which is explained below. As mentioned in Sect. 4.1, the requests are handled by the CloudActions. Therefore the dispatcher forwards the request to the proper CloudAction. In order to do so, he gains access to the platform service states description file and based on the current state it triggers the corresponding action.

(3) **ICloudAction.** ICloudAction is the interface which is present at the framework at design time and which the Dispatcher has knowledge about. Every CloudAction implements the ICloudAction. That facilitates the initialisation of the new CloudActions during run-time.

(4) **Communication patterns.** Two types of communication pattern are supported by the framework: The first one is the Servlets and particularly the Http Servlet Request and Response objects [23] which are used by the CloudActions in order to handle incoming requests and respond back to the caller. The second type of communication is via the use of the REST/SOAP protocol which enable the CloudMessages to perform external requests to the service providers.

(5) **Cloud Service Registry.** The Cloud Service Registry, as the name implies, keeps track of the services that the cloud application consumes.

(6) **API Client Generator.** Based on the API Service Description file, the API client generator maps the provider's specific API to the abstract one defined in the PSC. In case the provider offers additional functionality, the respective client is updated. The updated client is used by the CloudMessages to communicate with the service provider.

The components of the framework listed in this Section facilitate the workflow execution of the platform service operations and further automate the generation of the Web API clients required to interact with the platform services. Along with the PSCs, they contribute to the second objective of the proposed solution which is to decouple the cloud application from directly interacting with the vendor specific implementations and thus enabling developers to choose seamlessly the concrete service providers.

5 The Case of the Cloud Payment Service

In order to illustrate how the meta-model and the Platform Service Manager (PSM) can be utilised to facilitate the consumption of platform basic services by the applications, the case of the cloud payment service is presented. The payment service enables a website or an application to accept online payments via electronic cards such as credit or debit cards. The added value that such a service offers is that it relieves the developers from handling electronic payments and keeping track of the transactions. The payment provider undertakes the task to verify the payment and subsequently informs the application about the outcome of the transaction. The payment service has been chosen because of its inherent relative complexity compared to other services such as e-mail or message queue service. The complexity lies in the fact that the purchase transaction requires more than one state to be completed and there is a significant heterogeneity among the available payment providers with respect to the involved states.

In order to enable the cloud application developer to choose seamlessly the optimal payment provider, the various provider implementations need to be modelled and added to the framework so that the latter can handle the flow of the operations. This way the application developers are relieved from implementing explicitly the interactions with each payment provider.

The process can be divided into three steps:

(1) Modelling of the states of the cloud payment service. Several payment service providers need to be studied in order to extract a common state chart capturing the operation flow.
(2) Based on the state chart constructed in the previous step, a model is created utilising the meta-model described in Sect. 4.
(3) Capturing of the provider specific data and mapping on the abstract model built in step 2.

5.1 State Modelling of the Platform Service

The first step towards modelling the states of the cloud payment service is to explore the concrete payment providers and extrapolate the common states in which they may co-exist. For that reason 9 major payment service providers have been studied [24–32], provisioned either via a major cloud platform such as Google App Engine and Amazon AWS or via platform service marketplaces such as Heroku add-ons and Engineyard add-ons. These providers can be grouped into three main categories. An exhaustive listing of the characteristics of each payment provider is out of the scope of this paper. Rather, we focus on demonstrating how concrete providers can be mapped on the abstract model. Therefore, in this paper we present the case of one category, the "transparent redirect" and use as the concrete payment provider, the Spreedly [30], a payment provider offered via Heroku platform.

Transparent redirect is a technique deployed by certain payment providers in which, during a purchase transaction, the client's card details are redirected to the provider who consequently notifies the cloud application about the outcome of the transaction.

Figure 3 describes the steps involved in completing a payment transaction, while Fig. 4 shows the state chart of the cloud application throughout the transaction. Two states are observed. While the cloud application remains in the first state, it waits for a payment request. Once the client requests a new payment, the cloud application should display the fill out form where the user enters the payment details.

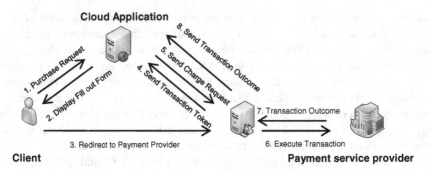

Fig. 3. Cloud payment service

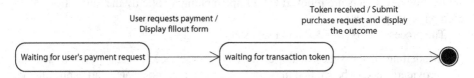

Fig. 4. State chart of the cloud payment service

Subsequently, the cloud application moves to the next state where it waits for the transaction token issued by the payment provider. The transaction token uniquely identifies the current transaction and can be used by the cloud application to complete the purchase. Once the user submits the form, she is redirected to the payment provider who validates the card details. Then a request to the cloud application is submitted including the transaction token. Once the token is received the application submits a request to the provider with the specific amount to be charged. The provider completes the transaction and responds with the outcome. Depending on the outcome, the cloud application displays a success or failure page to the client.

5.2   Mapping of the State Model on the Meta-model

Based on the state chart mentioned in the previous Section a provider independent model is constructed using as building blocks the meta-model described in Sect. 4.

The model is constructed as follows:

(1) For each state where the application waits for an external request, a CloudAction is defined to handle the request.
(2) For each request initiated by the cloud application targeting the service provider a CloudMessage is defined.

As seen in Fig. 5, the following blocks are defined:

a. **FilloutForm.** The FilloutForm receives the request for a new purchase transaction and responds to the client with the fill out form in order for the latter to enter the card details. The communication is realised using the servlet technology.

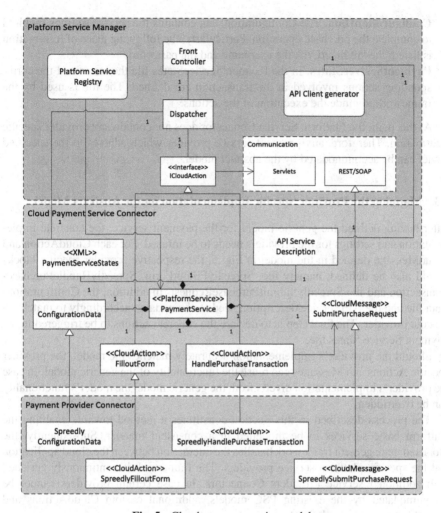

Fig. 5. Cloud payment service model

b. **HandlePurchaseTransaction.** The HandlePurchaseTransaction receives the request from the service provider containing the transaction token. Then, a request is submitted to the provider including the transaction token and the amount to be charged. The provider replies with the outcome of the purchase and subsequently the action responds to the client with a success or fail message accordingly.

c. **SubmitPurchaseRequest.** The SubmitPurchaseRequest is a CloudMessage used internally by the HandlePurchaseTransaction action. Its purpose is to model the request to the service provider, using the exposed web API, to complete the purchase transaction. It receives the provider's respond stating the outcome and forwards it to the action.

d. **ConfigurationData.** The ConfigurationData contains the service settings required to complete the purchase operation. Particularly, the following piece of information is listed: the "redirectUrl", the username and the password.

e. **PaymentSerivceStates.** In the PaymentServiceStates file the states and the corresponding actions involved in the transaction are defined. The file is used by the framework to guide the execution of the actions.

At this point the Platform Service Connector does not contain any provider specific information. Therefore, any payment service provider which adheres to the specified model can be accommodated by the abstract model.

5.3 Mapping the Provider Specific Implementation on the Abstract Model

After having defined the generic model for the payment service, the concrete implementation and settings for the providers needs to be infused. For each CloudAction and CloudMessage defined in the model in Fig. 5, the respective provider specific blocks should also be defined, namely the: SpreedlyFilloutForm, SpreedlyHandlePurchase-Transaction and the SpreedlySubmitPurchaseRequest. In addition, the Conifguration-Data file and the API service description needs to be updated accordingly to match the specific provider. The final step is to declare the concrete actions to be triggered in the Payment Service States file.

Should the provider's implementation accurately matches the model, the provider specific Actions and Messages can reuse the functionality of the generic model. In case the provider's implementation diverts from the generic model the model's functionality can be overridden.

The process described in this Section constitutes a method towards enabling the platform basic services to be modelled in a consistent manner. Subsequently, the proposed management framework handles the interaction between the cloud application and the specific platform service providers. The framework is continuously enriched with additional service Providers Connectors. In case certain providers cannot be accommodated by the existing PSC models, additional custom CloudActions and CloudMessages can be defined.

6 Conclusions

This paper proposed a development framework and a meta-model for designing service-based cloud applications. Platform basic services are becoming increasingly popular and have the potential to act as building blocks for the development of applications. As a result, developers should be enabled to integrate platform basic services in a consistent way and choose seamlessly the concrete service providers.

Towards this direction, the meta-model presented in Sect. 4 expedites the modelling of abstract Platform Service Connectors. The latter constitutes the intermediate layer between the cloud application and the concrete service Provider Connectors. The main components of the meta-model are the CloudActions and the CloudMessages. The former facilitates the modelling of the incoming requests which needs to be handled by the application, while the latter are used for the requests initiated by the application targeting the service providers. The case of the cloud payment service illustrated how the proposed solution can facilitate the modelling of the platform basic services and accommodate concrete service providers.

In addition, the Platform Service Manager described in this work coordinates the interaction between the application and the service providers. At the same time it paves the way for an integrated solution which enables the application developers efficiently managing the platform basic services they consume. Future work involves refining the components of the framework such as the API Client Generator and the PlatformService Registry and applying the proposed solution to a variety of platform basic services.

Acknowledgment. The research leading to these results has received funding from the European Union Seventh Framework Programme (FP7/2007-2013) under grant agreement n°264840, the RELATE project (http://www.relate-itn.eu).

References

1. Mell, P., Grance, T.: The NIST definition of cloud computing. Nat. Inst. Stand. Technol. **53**(6), 50 (2009)
2. Kourtesis, D., Bratanis, K., Bibikas, D., Paraskakis, I.: Software co-development in the era of cloud application platforms and ecosystems: the case of CAST. In: Camarinha-Matos, L.M., Xu, L., Afsarmanesh, H. (eds.) Collaborative Networks in the Internet of Services. IFIP AICT, vol. 380, pp. 196–204. Springer, Heidelberg (2012)
3. Fielding, R.T.: The REpresentational State Transfer (REST). Ph.D. dissertation, Department of Information and Computer Science, University of California, Irvine (2000). http://www.ics.uci.edu/fielding/pubs/dissertation/top.htm
4. Box, D., Ehnebuske, D., Kakivaya, G., Layman, A., Mendelsohn, N., Nielsen, H.F., Thatte, S., Winer, D.: Simple Object Access Protocol (SOAP) 1.1. (2000). http://www.w3.org/TR/SOAP/
5. Erl, T.: Service-Oriented Architecture: Concepts, Technology, and Design. Prentice Hall PTR, Upper Saddle River (2005)
6. Andrews, T., Curbera, F., Dholakia, H., Klein, J., Leymann, F., Liu, K., Roller, D., Smith, D., Thatte, S., Trickovic, I., Weerawarana, S.: Business Process Execution Language for Web Services Version 1.1. Technical Report (2003). http://xml.coverpages.org/BPELv11-20030505-20030331-Diffs.pdf
7. Web Services Resources Framework (WSRF 1.2). Technical Report, OASIS (2006). https://www.oasis-open.org/committees/tc_home.php?wg_abbrev=wsrf
8. jclouds (2014). http://www.jclouds.org
9. Apache LibCloud (2014). https://libcloud.apache.org/index.html
10. Petcu, D.: Consuming resources and services from multiple clouds. J. Grid Comput. **10723**, 1–25 (2014)
11. Kent, S.: Model driven engineering. In: Butler, M., Petre, L., Sere, K. (eds.) IFM 2002. LNCS, vol. 2335, pp. 286–298. Springer, Heidelberg (2002)
12. Ardagna, D., Di Nitto, E., Casale, G., Petcu, D., Mohagheghi P., Mosser, S., Matthews, P., Gericke, A., Ballagny, C., D'Andria, F., Nechifor, C. S., Sheridan, C.: MODAClouds: a model-driven approach for the design and execution of applications on multiple clouds. In: Workshop on Modeling in Software Engineering, Zurich, Switzerland (2012)

13. Jeffery, K., Horn, G., Schubert, L.: A vision for better cloud applications. In: Proceedings of the 2013 International Workshop on Multi-cloud Applications and Federated Clouds, Prague, Czech Republic, pp. 7–12 (2013)

14. Hamdaqa, M., Livogiannis, T., Tahvildari, L.: A reference model for developing cloud applications. In: 1st International Conference on Cloud Computing and Services Science, Noordwijkerhout, The Netherlands, pp. 98–103 (2011)

15. Guillen, J., Miranda, J., Murillo, J.M., Cana, C.: Developing migratable multicloud applications based on MDE and adaptation techniques. In: The 2nd Nordic Symposium on Cloud Computing & Internet Technologies, Oslo, Norway, pp. 30–37 (2013)

16. Ferry, N., Chauvel, F., Rossini, A., Morin, B., Solberg, A.: Managing multi-cloud systems with CloudMF. In: The 2nd Nordic Symposium on Cloud Computing & Internet Technologies, Oslo, Norway, pp. 38–45 (2013)

17. Gonidis, F.: Experimentation and categorisation of cloud application platform services. SEERC Technical Report, South East European Research Centre (SEERC), Thessaloniki, Greece (2013)

18. Heroku (2014). http://heroku.com

19. Google App Engine (2014). https://developers.google.com/appengine

20. AWS Marketplace (2014). https://aws.amazon.com/marketplace

21. Pautasso, S., Zimmermann O., Leymann F.: Restful web services vs. "big" web services: making the right architectural decision. In: 17th International Conference on World Wide Web, pp. 805–814. ACM, New York (2008)

22. Alur, D., Crupi, J., Malks, D.: Core J2EE Patterns. Sun Microsystems Press, Upper Saddle River (2001)

23. Hunter, J., Crawford, W.: Java Servlet Programming. O'Reilly & Associates Inc., Sebastopol (2001)

24. Amazon Flexible Payments (2014). https://payments.amazon.com/developer

25. AuthorizeNET (2014). http://developer.authorize.net/api/sim/

26. Braintree (2014). http://chargify.com/

27. Chargify (2014). https://www.braintreepayments.com/

28. Google Wallet For Digital Goods (2014). https://developers.google.com/wallet/digital/

29. Paypal Express Checkout (2014). https://www.paypal.com/gr/webapps/mpp/express-checkout

30. Spreedly (2014). https://spreedly.com/

31. Stripe (2014). https://stripe.com/

32. Viva Payment Services (2014). https://www.vivapayments.com/en/

Cloud Computing Reduces Uncertainties in Quality-of-Service Matching!

Matthias Becker[✉], Marie Christin Platenius, and Steffen Becker

Software Engineering Group, Heinz Nixdorf Institute,
University of Paderborn, Paderborn, Germany
{matthias.becker,m.platenius,steffen.becker}@upb.de

Abstract. Cloud computing resulted in a continuously growing number of provided software services to be used by consumers. Brokers discover services that fit best to consumers' requirements by matching Quality-of-Service (QoS) properties. In order to negotiate Service-Level Agreements (SLAs), a provider has to determine the provided QoS based on QoS analyses. However, the risk for the provider to violate the SLA is high as the service's actual quality can deviate from the specified QoS due to uncertainties that occur during the provider's quality analysis. In this paper, we discuss current software engineering paradigms like cloud computing and service-oriented computing with respect to the amount of uncertainty they induce into service matching and SLA negotiations. As a result, we explain, why cloud computing reduces such uncertainties.

Keywords: Cloud computing · Quality-of-service matching · Uncertainty

1 Introduction

Cloud computing resulted in a growing number of service providers providing software components in the form of deployed, ready-to-use services. A provider gains profit by selling services to consumers. Such a transaction takes place based on Service-Level-Agreements (SLAs) [7]. In such an SLA, a provider promises certain quality properties to a consumer. Since an SLA violation is subject to penalty, a provider is motivated to pass an SLA that complies to the actual quality of the provided service (Quality-of-Service, QoS).

For example, imagine a consumer that searches for an online bookstore service that offers functionality for browsing books and putting books into a shopping cart. Furthermore, she wants the service to have a maximum response time of 3 s. At the provider side, a company provides such a bookstore service and guarantees each consumer (e.g., local book shops) with an average request rate with up to 50 requests per minute (e.g., 50 customers with each one putting one book into the shopping cart) a response time of 2 s (e.g., putting one book into a shopping cart takes 2 s). A broker acting as an intermediary between consumer and providers applies matching techniques that compare the consumer's requirements to the

G. Ortiz and C. Tran (Eds.): ESOCC 2014, CCIS 508, pp. 153–159, 2015.
DOI: 10.1007/978-3-319-14886-1_15

provider's offer. This also includes QoS matching, in order to determine whether the provided quality is as least as high as the requested quality. In the current example, the broker determines that the provided service is a potential match (2 s < 3 s). Thus, the consumer and the provider both agree to the SLA and enter into a contract.

However, by agreeing to such an SLA, the provider takes the risk of SLA violations. The reason for this is that the prediction of quality properties like performance properties is relying on the context of a service. However, this context is not always available to the provider at negotiation time. For example, the actual response time of a service depends on the workload as well as the platform it is deployed on. If this context is not available to the provider, QoS analyses have to be performed based on incomplete or estimated service descriptions, e.g., unknown request rates. This leads to false positives: a service that has been predicted to be a good match actually does not match, i.e., the risk for SLA violations is very high.

QoS analysis techniques, like performance prediction for software components [3], support the provider in determining the response time based on probability functions. In our work, we combined QoS matching with such QoS analyses in order to support providers in SLA negotiations. However, current analysis approaches are inflicted with uncertainties, e.g., uncertainty about the service's actual workload at runtime or the runtime platform. Therefore, the provider still cannot completely assess the risk for SLA violations. Since cloud computing provides features like elasticity and scalability, some of these uncertainties do not apply for cloud services. However, a detailed analysis has not been conducted until now.

In this position paper, we classify and discuss current software engineering paradigms (component-based software engineering, service-oriented software engineering, cloud computing) according to the potential amount of uncertainty. In particular, we explain why cloud computing reduces uncertainties in SLA negotiations and also why there are still uncertainties left. As a benefit, we provide a better understanding of the benefits of cloud computing with respect to service matching and SLA negotiations.

The remainder of this paper is organized as follows. Section 2 discusses how QoS matching and QoS analysis are combined, while Sect. 3 explains the problems with this approach and why these problems are minimized in cloud computing. Section 4 lists open challenges. Related work is discussed in Sect. 5, and in Sect. 6, we conclude the paper.

2   Perfect World QoS Matching

Current service matching approaches decide whether the specification of a provided service matches the requirements given by a service consumer. Typically, these requirements include functional requirements, e.g., signatures or protocols, as well as non-functional requirements, e.g., QoS properties. In this paper, we focus on matching performance properties as one example for QoS matching.

In particular, the provided specification of the bookstore service has to be compared to the consumer's requirement that the response time of the service should be less than 3 s.

A provider can determine her service's quality based on QoS analyses. Thus, we combine QoS matching with performance analysis [3]. This results in the process depicted in Fig. 1: First of all, the provider needs to create a specification of the bookstore using a service description language (e.g., USDL [13]) or a component model (e.g., PCM [3]). For QoS matching, it is important that this specification includes a model that can be used to analyze the properties to be matched. For example, for performance properties, the control flow within a service in addition to its resource demands as well as resource and deployment information is needed to be specified. These specifications are then translated into specific analysis models, e.g., queueing networks, which are optimal to perform QoS analyses (see [2] or [6] for an overview of appropriate model transformation approaches). The QoS analysis delivers the predicted performance properties of a service as analysis results (e.g., response time = 2 s). These analysis results can then be compared to the given requirements.

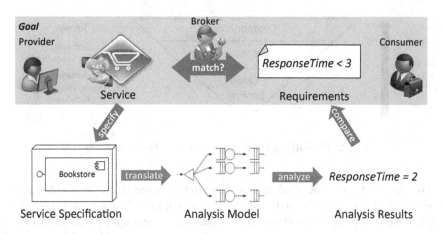

Fig. 1. QoS Matching Process

3   How Cloud Computing Closes Gaps Between the Real World and the Perfect World

The process described in Sect. 2 leads to several gaps. First of all, there is always a gap between the specification of a service and the specified, real world service itself. This is due to the abstraction needed to formally represent the service omitting properties irrelevant for matching and further analyses. Similarly, there is a second gap between the service specification and the analysis model. Again, the translation abstracts from details in order to enable a decidable and efficient analysis. As a result, there is also a gap between the properties of the

real world service (e.g., the bookstore service's actual response time is 4 s) and
the analysis results (e.g., 2 s). This gap can lead to wrong matching results (our
example service actually does not match but the matching result says it does).
This again leads to a high risk of SLA violations because the SLA has been made
based on wrong information.

The reason for this problem is uncertainty during the analysis. In order to
deliver an analysis result like "response time = 2 s", much knowledge about the
service is needed. However, this knowledge is not completely available at negotiation time. For example, the actual CPU time a service call takes to complete
cannot be exactly predicted without knowing the CPU schedule which is only
decided by the operating system dynamically at runtime. The actual request
rates of the consumer, as well, have to be estimated because they are not known
at negotiation time. These two properties are often estimated to be exponentially
distributed random variables around mean values (taken from measurements or
estimations). On the one hand, this estimation leads to efficiently computable
analysis models, on the other hand, it is often only a coarse abstraction and
unrealistic estimation. Thus, the certainty of the prediction is again reduced.

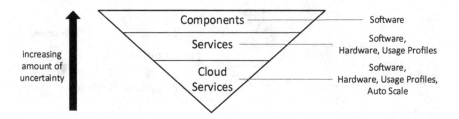

Fig. 2. Classifying Paradigms into Specification Levels

We analyzed the mentioned gaps in more detail based on the available knowledge about the service. As a result, we created a classification as depicted in
Fig. 2. We classify the different software engineering paradigms according to their
level of uncertainty playing a role in QoS analysis and matching. The width of
the levels in the reversed pyramid illustrate the level of uncertainty, i.e., the
higher the level in the pyramid the higher the level of potential uncertainty.

QoS analyses are based on components. Components are independent software fragments that are designed to work in various software, hardware, and
usage contexts [12]. That is, a component is designed and implemented to be
decoupled from a concrete software. QoS properties, however, cannot be predicted in isolation for components because context information of the component
is missing, e.g., the hardware it is deployed on, and its usage. Hence, a matching
of components, relying on the QoS predictions, is not possible.

Software services can be interpreted as self-contained and deployed components, i.e., a software component without unbound required interfaces deployed
on a runtime environment and a hardware platform. Hence, for a service, more
QoS-analysis-relevant information is known at design-time than for a component.

The actual usage of a service, however, is still uncertain at design-time. This is due to the fact, that the usage of a service may vary over time. For example, our bookshop may have higher usage during the time before the holidays, because many customers are looking for gifts. During the summer, the bookshop then has fewer clients and less usage. Thus, the usage context of a service can only be estimated. The QoS properties can also only be predicted for these estimated usage contexts. Consequently, the uncertainty in matching services depends on the accuracy of the usage context estimation.

In cloud computing, software services are deployed in dynamic resource environments, i.e., Infrastructure-as-a-Service (IaaS) environments with resources like virtual machines, virtual CPUs, etc. that scale autonomously with the resource demand. We will refer to this kind of service also as cloud service. In these cloud services, QoS properties can be achieved for arbitrary usage contexts by taking advantage of the auto-scaling of IaaS environments. QoS properties can be predicted for cloud services using the fully available set of context information. Hence, the matching of cloud computing services can be fully supported by QoS predictions.

In conclusion, with cloud computing, services providers are able to base their SLA negotiations on reliable, certain context information. Thus, also the risk of SLA violations can be reduced in comparison to earlier paradigms, like Service-Oriented Computing.

4   Open Research Challenges

This paper's classification of uncertainties in different software engineering paradigms can be extended in several directions.

First, there are still uncertainties left, also in newer software engineering paradigms like cloud computing. For example, service providers will still not be willing to publish many details of their services in order to protect business interests. Furthermore, consumers can have fuzzy requirements. Newly introduced matching concepts like Fuzzy Matching [8,11] do a first attempt to cope with such uncertainties. The benefit of advanced Fuzzy Matching approaches is the idea of measuring the extent of induced uncertainty and classifying it based on different sources (e.g., "requester-induced" and "provider-induced") [10]. Thereby, such approaches are able to return the measured uncertainty as part of the matching result, increasing transparency for both consumer and provider. This allows for a more informed decision-making and provides both consumer and provider with the possibility of reacting based on the identified uncertainties.

Second, cloud computing may close the gap that introduces uncertainties in performance analyses, but new challenges arise in handling dynamic contexts within QoS analysis for this class of systems. Initial analyses [1] take auto-scaling of IaaS environments into account. Thus, these analyses provide more realistic and less uncertain performance predictions for cloud services. However, these analyses require more inputs, e.g., the auto-scaling rules of an IaaS provider. We expect that matching benefits from the more realistic predictions and thus reduces the risks in SLA negotiations.

Third, when QoS analyses for cloud computing systems exist, research has to study further potential uncertainties introduced with the cloud computing paradigm. For example, in multi-tenant cloud computing environments the performance isolation of single tenants may not be guaranteed and hence has to be considered as an uncertainty factor in analysis and SLA negotiations. We expect that these uncertainties are low compared to the prior discussed uncertainties. However, these uncertainties could be considered in analysis as well by taking them into account as random disturbances.

Finally, we created and discussed our classification for the performance property response time. In future work, it has to be evaluated whether this classification also applies for other service properties, e.g., availability, reliability, costs, etc. We expect that our classification also applies for these properties. The shift from the component-based software engineering to cloud computing has not only effected performance, but also other properties, like costs due to the pay-as-you-go paradigm or availability due to the heavy use of visualization in cloud computing.

5   Related Work

Becker et al. [4] discussed different classifications of software component interoperability errors. Amongst others, they elaborated the hierarchical interface model introduced by Beugnard et al. [5]. In that approach, interfaces models are classified into four levels: Syntactic, Behavioral, Synchronization, and QoS. Such classifications are related to ours in a sense that they reflect the differences between specification levels and what they mean for QoS matching in contrast to traditional component matching. However, these works have been published years ago and, thus, could not take into account the changes cloud computing introduced, as our approach does.

In a more recent published work, Perez-Palacin and Mirandola [9] discuss sources of uncertainty in modeling self-adaptive systems. The authors provide a taxonomy of uncertainty which is also applicable for cloud computing. However, in contrast to our work the impact of uncertainty on matching and analysis is not discussed in this paper.

6   Conclusions

In this paper, we presented a classification and discussion of software engineering paradigms in relation to uncertainties in Quality-of-Service analysis and matching that have an impact on SLA violations. Furthermore, based on the discussion, some open research challenges are presented.

All in all, we came to the conclusion that in cloud computing, in comparison to ealier paradigms, Quality-of-Service analysis and matching are inflicted with less uncertainties. This is due to the increased amount of information. This raises hopes for a complete and efficient automation of desired long-term challenges like fully automated service composition and automated or analysis-supported SLA negotiations.

Acknowledgments. This work was supported by the German Research Foundation (DFG) within the Collaborative Research Center "On-The-Fly Computing" (CRC 901).

References

1. Becker, M., Luckey, M., Becker, S.: Performance analysis of self-adaptive systems for requirements validation at design-time. In: 9th International Conference on Quality of Software Architectures. ACM (2013)
2. Becker, S.: Model transformations in non-functional analysis. In: Bernardo, M., Cortellessa, V., Pierantonio, A. (eds.) SFM 2012. LNCS, vol. 7320, pp. 263–289. Springer, Heidelberg (2012)
3. Becker, S., Koziolek, H., Reussner, R.: The palladio component model for model-driven performance prediction. J. Syst. Softw **82**(1), 3–22 (2009)
4. Becker, S., Overhage, S., Reussner, R.: Classifying software component interoperability errors to support component adaption. In: Crnković, I., Stafford, J.A., Schmidt, H.W., Wallnau, K. (eds.) CBSE 2004. LNCS, vol. 3054, pp. 68–83. Springer, Heidelberg (2004)
5. Beugnard, A., Jézéquel, J.-M., Plouzeau, N., Watkins, D.: Making components contract aware. Computer **32**, 38–45 (1999)
6. Cortellessa, V., Di Marco, A., Inverardi, P.: From software models to performance models. In: Cortellessa, V., Di Marco, A., Inverardi, P. (eds.) Model-Based Software Performance Analysis, pp. 79–140. Springer, Heidelberg (2011)
7. Hasselmeyer, P., Koller, B., Schubert, L., Wieder, P.: Towards SLA-supported resource management. In: Gerndt, M., Kranzlmüller, D. (eds.) HPCC 2006. LNCS, vol. 4208, pp. 743–752. Springer, Heidelberg (2006)
8. Patiniotakis, I., Rizou, S., Verginadis, Y., Mentzas, G.: Managing imprecise criteria in cloud service ranking with a fuzzy multi-criteria decision making method. In: Lau, K.-K., Lamersdorf, W., Pimentel, E. (eds.) Service-Oriented and Cloud Computing, vol. 8135, pp. 34–48. Springer, Heidelberg (2013)
9. Perez-Palacin, D., Mirandola, R.: Uncertainties in the modeling of self-adaptive systems: a taxonomy and an example of availability evaluation. In: Proceedings of the 5th ACM/SPEC International Conference on Performance Engineering, ICPE '14, pp. 3–14. ACM, New York (2014)
10. Platenius, M.C.: Fuzzy service matching in on-the-fly computing. In: Proceedings of the Doctoral Symposium of the 9th Joint Meeting of the European Software Engineering Conference (ESEC) and the ACM SIGSOFT Symposium on the Foundations of Software Engineering (FSE). ACM (2013)
11. Platenius, M.C., von Detten, M., Becker, S., Schäfer, W., Engels, G.: A survey of fuzzy service matching approaches in the context of on-the-fly computing. In: 16th International Symposium on Component-based Software Engineering. ACM (2013)
12. Szyperski, C.: Component Software: Beyond Object-oriented Programming. Pearson Education, Harlow (2002)
13. Terzidis, O., Oberle, D., Friesen, A., Janiesch, C., Barros, A.: The internet of services and usdl. In: Barros, A., Oberle, D. (eds.) Handbook of Service Description, pp. 1–16. Springer, New York (2012)

Contract Design for Composed Services in a Cloud Computing Environment

Sonja Brangewitz[✉], Claus-Jochen Haake, and Jochen Manegold

Department of Economics, University of Paderborn, Paderborn, Germany
{sonja.brangewitz,claus-jochen.haake,jochen.manegold}@wiwi.upb.de

Abstract. In this paper, we study markets in which sellers and buyers interact with each other via an intermediary. Our motivating example is a market with a cloud infrastructure where single services are flexibly combined to composed services. We address the contract design problem of an intermediary to purchase complementary single services. By using a non-cooperative game-theoretic model, we analyze the incentives for high- and low-quality composed services to be an equilibrium outcome of the market. It turns out that equilibria with low quality can be obtained in the short run and in the long run, whereas those with high quality can only be achieved in the long run. In our analysis we explicitly determine the according discount factors needed in an infinitely repeated game. Furthermore, we derive optimal contracts for the supply of high- and low-quality composed services.

Keywords: Composed services · Contract design · Cloud computing · Service quality · Asymmetric information · Repeated games

1 Introduction

On the worldwide market for IT services with a huge number of single services clients are often searching from a solution-oriented point of view. Moreover, the evolution of the "cloud" as an infrastructure with flexible and on demand access to applications has the effect that "[...] the computing world is rapidly transforming towards developing software for millions to consume as a service, rather than to run on their individual computers." [4, p.599]. Our article analyzes the interaction between providers of such single services and an intermediary. The intermediary combines these services and sells them as a composed service on the market. We contribute to a broader research agenda called "On-The-Fly (OTF) Computing" which investigates the economic and technical challenges for dynamic automated service composition in a cloud computing environment. The main goal of OTF computing is to configure and provide individual IT services in a flexible way to overcome inefficiencies related to traditional software solutions. On such a market an intermediary is indispensable, since clients

---

This work was partially supported by the German Research Foundation (DFG) within the Collaborative Research Centre "On-The-Fly Computing" (SFB 901).

G. Ortiz and C. Tran (Eds.): ESOCC 2014, CCIS 508, pp. 160–174, 2015.
DOI: 10.1007/978-3-319-14886-1_16

usually do not have the necessary knowledge and expertise to find the desired services themselves and, moreover, to combine them flexibly. The task of the intermediary is to create a link between clients and service providers producing single services. The intermediary proposes composed services as solutions that combine different single services to a new product. The vision of OTF computing is briefly presented in [9]. As [17] points out "Aggregating service providers is very challenging in the Cloud due to complex relationship among Cloud service providers that are built via subcontracting."

More specifically, in this article we focus on the contract design problem of one intermediary and two service providers who strategically interact on the market. We use a non-cooperative game-theoretic approach for our analysis. The service providers deliver complementary services which they can choose to produce in either high or low quality. For services in a cloud computing environment this quality decision may be an important factor. It crucially influences the performance of the service composition and results in additional costs or effort for the service providers. Examples are the bandwidth provided, resources made available for the execution of a service as well as the priority given to the inquiry of the intermediary. Besides choosing the quality, the service providers may deliver their single services in various quantities, such as number of licenses to use the provided service, number of instances, utilization time available for execution, or the amount of storage space. The intermediary receives the single services and combines them to a composed service. The quality of the composed service depends on the inputs' qualities and can also be either high or low. The intermediary strategically reports the quality of the composed service to his input suppliers and pays them accordingly. We assume that he is only able to observe the quality of the composed service, but is not aware of the two single services' qualities. A typical feature of a composed service is that its quality properties are dependent on those of the single services and their interaction when the composed service is executed. Quality properties of the single services can only be tested to a limited extent prior to composition. For example, in a cloud computing environment it may technically be difficult or too costly to individually test the quality of a software service or of a hardware service that is used for execution. On the demand side we suppose that clients have a demand for both composed services of high and low quality (usually at different prices).

Besides considering a one-shot game we analyze a repeated interaction between the intermediary and his suppliers. Here, the intermediary initially offers contracts to the sellers in which he specifies the payment he is willing to make, depending on the reported quality of the composed service. While in the short run producing low-quality composed services is always a Nash equilibrium (*Proposition* 1) and producing high-quality composed services is never a Nash equilibrium (*Proposition* 2), the long run situation is more promising. We identify conditions on the time preferences (discount factors) under which high quality is a subgame-perfect equilibrium on the market in the long run. The main finding is that even if selling high quality is profitable for the intermediary, the emergence of high-quality composed services on the market still crucially depends on the intermediary's discount factor (*Proposition* 3). We identify optimal payments of the intermediary to implement high- or low-quality composed services (*Propositions* 4 *and* 5).

2 Related Literature

Our model is related to the literature on principal-agent relationships as well as on reputation and repeated interaction. We use this section to describe similarities and differences in comparison to our approach.

The price model in the procurement situation that we study is related to the modeling of contracts in principal-agent relationships. For example, if the agent's contribution to the firm's value is not directly observable, [2] addresses how to design compensation contracts consisting of a base salary and a bonus payment in a repeated setting. A similar procurement problem with respect to price and quality considerations is also discussed by [1]. They derive the optimal procurement mechanism and compare it with alternatives such as scoring auctions and (sequential) bargaining. The procurement situation in [11] is related to the one we assume here, but the focus of the analysis is different. Having several intermediate-input suppliers they study the incentives of vertical integration in a dynamic model. In comparison to the approaches just mentioned, even if the relationship between the intermediary and its service providers resembles a principal-agent model, we additionally incorporate the influence of the clients' demand on the intermediary's profit function. Therefore, the profit is influenced simultaneously by two aspects: on the one hand the effort or quality choice of the service provider and on the other hand the resulting client's demand in dependence on the quality of the composed service. Moreover, by considering composed services we are interested in the right coordination of the service providers' quality choices.

In a setting with repeated interaction, experiences that were made with a certain product in the past have an influence on its future evaluations as well as future sales opportunities. [7] refers to this as "reputation". Similarly, already [16] argues:

> "When product attributes are difficult to observe prior to purchase, consumers may plausibly use the quality of products produced by the firm in the past as an indicator of present or future quality. In such cases a firm's decision to produce high quality items is a dynamic one: the benefits of doing so accrue in the future via the effect of building up a reputation. In this sense, reputation formation is a type of signaling activity: the quality of items produced in previous periods serves as a signal of the quality of those produced during the current period."

We follow this definition of reputation for our analysis. Similar to our approach, [5] analyzes the influence of the market structure on the incentives to produce high quality in a repeated game setting. While they focus on the comparison of different market structures, our analysis highlights the interaction and contract design of an intermediary and its suppliers. In addition, we relax the assumption that customers have a unit-demand. [18] consider a market in which an intermediary offers a composed service. In their setting, a user has to decide to buy two complementary web services either from a web service intermediary or directly from its providers. Optimal location and price choices of the web service intermediary are analyzed in a spatial model, more precisely in a linear and circular city model. Contrary to their approach we focus on the optimal contract design between the intermediary and its service providers.

Reputation systems for online markets are explicitly addressed by [7]. He studies the mechanism design problem of a reputation system where buyers and sellers directly interact with each other. A monopolistic seller exerts an effort that influences the quality of the product. After having experienced the quality of the good the buyer reports his satisfaction of the product. These reports are summarized in the reputation profile of the seller. A repeated game setting is used to analyze efficiency and seller payoffs by varying the number of observations in the reputation profile and by extending his model to multi-values including incomplete reports and multiple competing sellers. Our analysis, however, does not include a reputation system. We assume that the seller is always able to sell his products at the market by adapting prices to demand. From an architectural perspective, including reputation information in the OTF computing process has been discussed in [3]. Intermediaries selling composed services are also analyzed in the literature on Cloud Services Brokerage as for example in [8,10,17]. We complement previous works by considering contract design issues from an economic perspective.

The analysis proceeds as follows: First, we present the model. Then we analyze the different decisions considering the trade of services and the contract design. Finally, we conclude and comment on further extensions.

3   The Model

In our setting we consider three types of market participants: clients, intermediaries, and service providers. Our focus is on modeling the strategic interaction of one intermediary and two service providers. The intermediary chooses a long run contract that he offers to the service providers. Then the service providers strategically choose the quality and quantity of the service they would like to provide. The intermediary afterwards reports (not necessarily truthful) the quality of the composed service he produced from the service providers' inputs. The clients are assumed to be non-strategic.

3.1   Long Run Contracts

Before services are actually traded the intermediary makes a decision on the quality he is willing to deliver to the market and the long run contracts he offers to the service providers. He privately observes his clients' demands for the composed service which is demanded in low (L) and high quality (H). Furthermore, he is aware of the service providers' cost functions for producing (single) services in high or low quality. Therefore, he is able to determine his expected profit possibilities for the "two" markets. He compares them and afterwards chooses the quality he prefers to deliver to his clients.

Based on this strategic quality choice, the intermediary designs contracts specifying the way the service providers are paid. These contracts are of the following form: for delivering a service a service provider receives a base payment independently of the quality of his service. This payment is equivalent to the payment for a low quality service. Furthermore, the intermediary *promises* him an additional payment, if the observed quality of the composed service, which is dependent on the quality of both inputs, is high. For the interaction with his client the intermediary takes the client's demand functions as given and determines the sales prices as well as the sales quantities that maximize his profits. Then, using the contract design and the optimal sales quantities, he explicitly determines the transfer payments and offers them in the form of contracts to the service providers. More precisely, the transfer payments towards a service provider depend on the observable quantity of the single service he delivered and the quality of the composed service reported by the intermediary.

3.2   Market Interaction

In the next step, the services are traded on the market. We start to describe the *procurement side*. For simplicity, we suppose that the intermediary needs one unit of each service to produce one unit of composed service. In every period, each service provider decides on which of the demanded quantities, the optimal sales quantity for either high or low quality, he delivers and if the service is of quality L or H. Service provider i's cost function is denoted by $C_{\theta^i}^i : \mathbb{R}_+ \to \mathbb{R}_+$ for quality $\theta^i \in \{H, L\}$ and $i \in \{1, 2\}$. We assume convex cost functions and higher cost to deliver high quality services, $C_H^i(\cdot) > C_L^i(\cdot)$. Convexity means that marginal costs are non-decreasing, i.e., providing an additional instance (or unit) is at least as expensive as the previous one. The quality of the composed service depends on the quality choices of the service providers and is defined as follows[1]

$$\theta^0 : \{L, H\}^2 \to \{L, H\} \quad \text{with } \theta^0\left(\theta^1, \theta^2\right) = \begin{cases} H & \text{if } \left(\theta^1, \theta^2\right) = (H, H) \\ L & \text{otherwise.} \end{cases} \quad (1)$$

The intermediary is able to directly observe the delivered quantities. The suppliers' quality choices are not directly observable and can only be uniquely determined in certain cases by considering the quality of the composed service. The intermediary decides whether to report this quality truthfully or not. The reported quality is defined by $\hat{\theta}^0 : \{L, H\} \to \{L, H\}$ such that $\theta^0 \mapsto \hat{\theta}^0\left(\theta^0\right)$.

---

[1] The superscript 0 indicates that the quality of the composed service is observed by the intermediary, denoted in the following as player 0.

According to the report he rewards the service providers with a transfer payment of $T_H^i, T_L^i : \mathbb{R}_+ \to \mathbb{R}_+$ for $i \in \{1,2\}$ specified in the long run contract.[2] We assume convex transfer payments that are differentiable at 0 and suppose $T_H^i(\cdot) \geq T_L^i(\cdot) \geq C_L^i(\cdot)$. This reflects the idea, that in any case the intermediary pays $T_L^i(\cdot)$ and if he reports high quality the service providers receive $T_H^i(\cdot) - T_L^i(\cdot)$ additionally as a bonus. The actions of the service providers, i.e., choosing the quantity and quality of the delivered services, as well as of the intermediary whether to report truthfully or not are assumed to be chosen simultaneously.

On the *demand side* the intermediary is facing a client who has a certain demand for both composed services of quality H and of quality L. The client's demand functions (for low and high quality) assign to any positive price P the demanded quantities and are given by $D_{\theta^0} : \mathbb{R}_+ \to \mathbb{R}_+$ with $P \mapsto D_{\theta^0}(P)$ for quality $\theta^0 \in \{L, H\}$ of the composed service. Thus, when charging a price of P for the composed service, the intermediary faces a demand of his client of $D_{\theta^0}(P)$ units of the composed service with quality θ^0. For our subsequent analysis we make some technical assumptions related to the client's demand functions. Suppose $D_{\theta^0}(P)$ is twice continuously differentiable, non-increasing, strictly decreasing whenever $D_{\theta^0}(P) > 0$ and satisfies $D_{\theta^0}''(P)D_{\theta^0}(P) - 2\left(D_{\theta^0}'(P)\right)^2 < 0$. The inverse demand function assigning a price to a given demand is denoted by $P_{\theta^0}(D)$.[3] Suppose for a given price P we always have $D_H(P) > D_L(P)$. Moreover, demand and transfer payments are assumed to satisfy $P_{\theta^0}(0) > T_{\theta^0}'(0)$.

Our focus for the succeeding analysis is on the information asymmetries between the intermediary and the service providers. We assume complete information on the demand side, the intermediary delivers the demanded quality of the final product truthfully to his clients.

The remainder of this section is used to explain the assumptions we made by means of an example illustrated in Fig. 1. Suppose a client has an own program routine and wants to analyze a huge data set by running simulations. As the computations are complex and resource-intense, the client is not able to execute his program within his own infrastructure. Therefore, he decides to make use of cloud services. He approaches an OTF intermediary who is offering a composed service that is able to process the client's demand. The OTF intermediary flexibly combines a service for storage with a service for computing that he purchases from other service providers. For a given price per instance, the quantity demanded by the client is the number of instances he is willing to book for the execution of his simulations. Clearly, a higher price triggers a lower demanded quantity. Quality properties of the single services are the access time for the

---

[2] Note that the subscript relates to the reported quality $\hat{\theta}^0\ (\theta^0) \in \{H, L\}$.

[3] The third assumption on the demand function is related to its curvature and can be equivalently expressed in terms of elasticities as $D_{\theta^0}''(P)P/D_{\theta^0}'(P) > 2D_{\theta^0}'(P)P/D_{\theta^0}(P)$. This assumption ensures that $DP_{\theta^0}(D)$ is strictly concave and is derived from $DP_{\theta^0}''(D) + 2P_{\theta^0}'(D) < 0$, using the derivative of the inverse demand function. The three assumptions on the demand function are also made in [6], for example.

storage and the time needed by the computing service. The quality of the composed service is the overall time per instance to run the client's simulations. If the composed service is of high quality, e.g. the total process time is short, the client has a high willingness to pay. Accordingly, in case of a low quality composed service he accepts a longer processing time while having a lower willingness to pay. A comprehensive analytical example for specific demand and cost functions to illustrate our results of the next sections can be found in Appendix A.

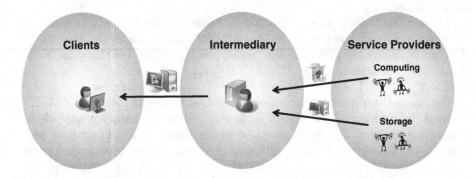

Fig. 1. Composed services consisting of hardware and software services

4   Trading Services

4.1   Optimal Sales Prices and Quantities

Given the contract $T = (T_L^i(\cdot), T_H^i(\cdot))_{i=1,2}$ the intermediary determines the optimal quantity $D_{\theta^0}^{T*}$ he is willing to sell to his client for a fixed quality θ^0 of the composed service. This is the client's demanded quantity that maximizes the intermediary's profit. With this optimal demand the optimal sales price denoted by $P_{\theta^0}^{T*} := P_{\theta^0}(D_{\theta^0}^{T*})$ can be computed. Hereby, the intermediary assumes that both service providers deliver him services of the same quality $\theta^1 = \theta^2$ and therefore the resulting quality of the composed service is $\theta^0 = \theta^1 = \theta^2$. Formally, the intermediary $D_{\theta^0}^{T*} = \text{argmax}_{D \in \mathbb{R}_+} DP_{\theta^0}(D) - \sum_{i=1}^{2} T_{\theta^0}^i(D)$. Note that due to our assumptions a maximizer $D_{\theta^0}^{T*}$ exists and is unique. The function $DP_{\theta^0}(D)$ is strictly concave and the transfer payments $T_\theta^i(\cdot)$ are convex. Therefore, the objective function is strictly concave. Moreover, we have $P_{\theta^0}(0) > T_{\theta^0}'(0)$ ensuring positive profits. Using the contract design and the optimal sales quantities the intermediary offers the following contracts to the service providers $\left(T_L^i\left(D_L^{T*}\right), T_L^i\left(D_H^{T*}\right), T_H^i\left(D_L^{T*}\right), T_H^i\left(D_H^{T*}\right)\right)_{i=1,2}$. The service providers decide whether to choose a quantity D_L^{T*} or D_H^{T*} as well as the quality, either L or H, they deliver to the intermediary.

4.2 Trading once

We use a non-cooperative game in strategic form with three players, which we first consider as a one-shot game and in the next subsection as a repeated game. We denote the intermediary as player 0 and the two service providers as players 1 and 2. The strategy sets are $\{(L, D_L^{T*}), (L, D_H^{T*}) (H, D_L^{T*}), (H, D_H^{T*})\}$ for the service providers and $\{truthful, not\ truthful\}$ for the intermediary. The intermediary's strategy "truthful" indicates that he reports the composed service's quality honestly and "not truthful" means that he always pretends to have seen low quality. He chooses the strategy to be $truthful$ if $\hat{\theta}^0(L) = L$ and $\hat{\theta}^0(H) = H$. If he reports $\hat{\theta}^0(L) = L$ and $\hat{\theta}^0(H) = L$, we say that he is $not\ truthful$. From now on we refer to the composed service's quality θ^0 and reported quality $\hat{\theta}^0$ for short. For a delivered quantity $D^i \in \{D_L^{T*}, D_H^{T*}\}$ of service provider $i \in \{1, 2\}$ we define $D_{\min} := \min_{i \in \{1,2\}} D^i$. Given a strategy profile the payoff of service provider $i \in \{1, 2\}$ is his profit $\Pi^{T,i}\left(\hat{\theta}^0, (\theta^1, D^1), (\theta^2, D^2)\right) = T_{\hat{\theta}^0}^i(D^i) - C_{\theta^i}^i(D^i)$. With the quantities the intermediary receives from the service providers he is able to produce maximally $D_{\min}$ units of the composed service. Therefore, the intermediary needs to reconsider his revenue maximization problem. He chooses the sales price of the composed service such that his profits are maximized given the capacity constraint $D_{\min}$, that is $P_{\theta^0}^{T**} = P_{\theta^0}\left(D_{\theta^0}^{T**}\right)$ with $D_{\theta^0}^{T**} = \text{argmax}_{D_{\theta^0}^T \leq D_{\min}} P_{\theta^0}\left(D_{\theta^0}^T\right) D_{\theta^0}^T - \sum_{i=1}^2 T_{\hat{\theta}^0}^i(D^i)$ yielding a profit of $\Pi^{T,0}\left(\hat{\theta}^0, (\theta^1, D^1), (\theta^2, D^2)\right) = P_{\theta^0}^{T**} D_{\theta^0}^{T**} - \sum_{i=1}^2 T_{\hat{\theta}^0}^i(D^i)$ with $P_{\theta^0}^{T**} := P_{\theta^0}\left(D_{\theta^0}^{T**}\right)$.[4]

The most well-known solution concept for non-cooperative games is the Nash equilibrium [13]. A Nash equilibrium is a collection of strategy choices of the OTF provider and the service providers such that no one has an incentive to unilaterally change his strategy given the others' strategies. For the OTF market this means that in an equilibrium the OTF provider cannot increase his profit from changing his report for given quality choices of the service providers and each service provider cannot increase his profit from unilaterally changing the produced quality or quantity. We observe the following equilibrium result, when services are traded just once.

Proposition 1. *Given the other service provider delivers low quality services, then producing the correct quantity of* **low quality** *services is a Nash equilibrium strategy if and only if* $T_L^i\left(D_L^{T*}\right) - C_L^i\left(D_L^{T*}\right) \geq T_L^i\left(D_H^{T*}\right) - C_L^i\left(D_H^{T*}\right)$ *for* $i = 1, 2$.

Proof of Proposition 1. First, note that the intermediary is indifferent in being truthful or not. The condition in Proposition 1 is immediately derived from comparing the profits of the service providers in case of a deviation from $\left(L, D_L^{T*}\right)$. □

---

[4] Note that if $\theta^0 = \theta^1 = \theta^2$ and the service providers deliver $D_{\theta^0}^{T*}$, then $D_{\theta^0}^{T**} = D_{\theta^0}^{T*}$ and $P_{\theta^0}^{T**} = P_{\theta^0}^{T*}$.

Proposition 1 demonstrates that there exists the possibility to choose the properties of the transfer payments and cost functions in such a way that producing low-quality composed services is a Nash equilibrium of the static game. If we choose $T_L^i(\cdot) = C_L^i(\cdot)$ in Proposition 1 we obtain immediately that independently of the transfer payments for high quality $T_H^i(\cdot)$, producing low quality services is a Nash equilibrium strategy.

Proposition 2. *Producing **high-quality** composed services is not a Nash equilibrium.*

Proof of Proposition 2. If $T_H^i(\cdot) > T_L^i(\cdot)$, the intermediary has an incentive to deviate to not being truthful. For $T_H^i(\cdot) = T_L^i(\cdot)$ service provider i has an incentive to deviate in producing low quality as $C_H^i(\cdot) > C_L^i(\cdot)$. Moreover, if the service providers are not rewarded with a bonus for high quality, then each of them has an incentive to deviate to produce low quality as $C_H^i(\cdot) > C_L^i(\cdot)$.   □

In contrast to Proposition 1, Proposition 2 shows that in the static game the intermediary has no possibility to end up with a high-quality composed service as there are always possibilities for improvement for either the intermediary or the service providers. In the next section we analyze if high-quality composed services can be obtained by considering the described one-shot trading game repeatedly.

4.3   Trading Repeatedly

The previous section showed that producing high-quality composed services is not an equilibrium if the services are traded only once. Therefore, in this section we consider repeated interaction between the intermediary and the service providers assuming an infinite time horizon. Once agreed to produce either high- or low-quality composed services in the optimal quantities, the intermediary and the service providers repeatedly trade services accordingly. We analyze if the right incentives can be provided such that this agreement is sustainable in the long run even if it is supposed to be non-binding. In our setting neither demand nor cost structures vary over time.

A refinement of the Nash equilibrium concept that fits a repeated interaction structure is the subgame-perfect Nash equilibrium [14,15]. Applied to our context, in a subgame-perfect Nash equilibrium neither the OTF provider nor the service providers are willing to unilaterally change their long run strategies at any point in time, while taking the others' (equilibrium) strategies as given. We consider the long run profits of the OTF provider and the service providers and technically apply the "one-shot deviation principle" [12, Proposition 2.2.1 p.25] to determine subgame-perfect Nash equilibria.

A composed service with *low quality* may constitute a Nash equilibrium of the trading game as shown in Proposition 1. If this is the case, it is also a subgame-perfect Nash equilibrium of the repeated trading game. Concerning **high-quality** composed services, suppose that the objective of the intermediary and the service providers is to maximize their discounted profits by using a personal discount factor $\delta_i \in (0, 1)$ $(i = 0, 1, 2)$ from trading *high-quality* services. Suppose for the rest of this section that the condition of Proposition 1 is satisfied and, therefore, producing low-quality composed services in the correct quantities is a Nash equilibrium of the one-shot trading game.

Within the repeated trading game we assume that the intermediary commits himself to report his observation of the quality of the composed service *truthfully* whereas the two service providers agree to deliver him the *optimal quantity* of *high quality* services: $\left(\text{truthful}, \left(H, D_H^{T*}\right), \left(H, D_H^{T*}\right)\right)$. From this agreement the intermediary can deviate in reporting his observation *not truthfully* or the service providers can deviate in delivering *low quality* services or a *different quantity* of services. Cheating in one period is followed by an according punishment in the periods thereafter. In case, one of the service providers does not deliver high quality, the other service provider will also not be rewarded for the high quality he produced. Therefore, he is no longer willing to deliver high quality services in future. Similarly, if the intermediary does not report his observation truthfully, the punishment of the service providers is to deliver low quality services from now on. The punishment strategy profile is therefore denoted by: $\left(\text{not truthful}, \left(L, D_L^{T*}\right), \left(L, D_L^{T*}\right)\right)$. Taking this behavior into account, we obtain the following:

Proposition 3. *If* $T_L^i\left(D_L^{T*}\right) - C_L^i\left(D_L^{T*}\right) \geq T_L^i\left(D_H^{T*}\right) - C_L^i\left(D_H^{T*}\right)$, *then producing high quality services (in the demanded quantities) and the intermediary reporting truthfully is a subgame-perfect Nash equilibrium of the repeated game if and only if the following conditions hold for the intermediary*

$$\left(P_H^{T*} D_H^{T*} - \sum_{i=1}^{2} T_H^i\left(D_H^{T*}\right)\right) \geq (1 - \delta_0)\left(P_H^{T*} D_H^{T*} - \sum_{i=1}^{2} T_L^i\left(D_H^{T*}\right)\right)$$

$$+ \delta_0 \left(P_L^{T*} D_L^{T*} - \sum_{i=1}^{2} T_L^i\left(D_L^{T*}\right)\right), \qquad (2)$$

and for the service providers

$$T_H^i\left(D_H^{T*}\right) - C_H^i\left(D_H^{T*}\right)$$
$$\geq (1 - \delta_i) \max\left\{T_L^i\left(D_L^{T*}\right) - C_L^i\left(D_L^{T*}\right), T_H^i\left(D_L^{T*}\right) - C_H^i\left(D_L^{T*}\right),\right.$$
$$\left. T_L^i\left(D_H^{T*} - C_L^i\left(D_H^{T*}\right)\right)\right\} + \delta_i \left(T_L^i\left(D_L^{T*}\right) - C_L^i\left(D_L^{T*}\right)\right). \qquad (3)$$

Proof of Proposition 3. The first condition implies that the punishment strategy after a deviation is a Nash equilibrium strategy if the services are traded once as shown in Proposition 1. The conditions on the discount factors are derived by comparing the discounted long run payoffs (for an infinite time horizon). □

Proposition 3 gives us conditions on the critical discount factors needed to ensure that high-quality composed services are produced in the long run. These depend on the transfer payments, cost functions and implicitly on the client's demand function.

5   Contract Design

The intermediary offers long run contracts which specify the way the service providers are paid in dependence on the (reported) quality of the composed service. The optimal contracts for the intermediary crucially depend on his strategic decision on whether to sell high- or low-quality products to his clients. Therefore, we first analyze the optimal contract design for both cases separately.

5.1   Contracts for Low-Quality Composed Services

Proposition 4. *To produce low-quality composed services the intermediary optimally chooses the transfer payments to be* $T^{L*} = \left(T_L^{L*,i}(\cdot), T_H^{L*,i}(\cdot) \right)_{i=1,2} = \left(C_L^i(\cdot), C_L^i(\cdot) \right)_{i=1,2}$.

Given T^{L*} the service providers are always paid exactly their costs for producing low quality services and therefore have zero profits. They have no interest in producing high quality services since they are not rewarded accordingly and would thus suffer a negative profit. In contrast to the zero profits of the service providers, the intermediary is able to extract all the generated surplus and his profit is equal to $P_L^{T^{L*}} * D_L^{T^{L*}} * - \sum_{i=1}^{2} C_L^i \left(D_L^{T^{L*}} \right)$.

5.2   Contracts for High-Quality Composed Services

Using the conditions for the service providers from Proposition 3 we obtain:

Proposition 5. *To give the appropriate incentives to the service providers in order to produce high-quality composed services in the long run, the intermediary optimally chooses the transfer payments to be* $T^{H*} = \left(T_L^{H*,i}(\cdot), T_H^{H*,i}(\cdot) \right)_{i=1,2} = \left(C_L^i(\cdot), C_H^i(\cdot) + \varepsilon^i \right)_{i=1,2}$ *with small* $\varepsilon^i > 0$.

Given these transfer payments the service providers are paid exactly their costs for producing low quality services and strictly more than their costs for producing high quality services. Therefore, they have a strict interest in producing high quality services in the long run. The intermediary is able to extract almost all the generated surplus and his profit is equal to $P_H^{T^{H*}} * D_H^{T^{H*}} * - \sum_{i=1}^{2} C_H^i \left(D_H^{T^{H*}} \right) - \sum_{i=1}^{2} \varepsilon^i$. Hence, the parameter ε^i is chosen to be strictly positive, but as small as possible. Using Proposition 3 with $T_L^{H*,i}(\cdot) = C_L^i(\cdot)$ and $T_H^{H*,i}(\cdot) = C_H^i(\cdot) + \varepsilon^i$ we have:

Corollary 1. *If the intermediary's discount factor satisfies*

$$\delta_0 > \frac{\sum_{i=1}^{2} C_H^i \left(D_H^{T^{H*}} * \right) + \sum_{i=1}^{2} \varepsilon^i - \sum_{i=1}^{2} C_L^i \left(D_H^{T^{H*}} * \right)}{\left(P_H^{T^{H*}} * D_H^{T^{H*}} * - \sum_{i=1}^{2} C_L^i \left(D_H^{T^{H*}} * \right) \right) - \left(P_L^{T^{H*}} * D_L^{T^{H*}} * - \sum_{i=1}^{2} C_L^i \left(D_L^{T^{H*}} * \right) \right)},$$

(D0)

then there exist transfer payments such that the intermediary is interested in producing high-quality composed services.

Adding and subtracting the term $\sum_{i=1}^{2} C_H^i \left(D_H^{T^{H*}*} \right)$ in the denominator on the lower bound for δ_0 in Corollary 1 gives the following interpretation: The evaluation of future payoffs of the intermediary represented by his personal discount factor δ_0 needs to be strictly greater than the difference in the transfer payments the intermediary has to make (for $D_H^{T^{H*}*}$) relative to this difference plus the advantage in his profits for high-quality composed services.

5.3 Long Run Quality Choice

Using the optimal contract design, the intermediary compares the profits on the market of low-quality composed services with the profits on the market for high-quality composed services. We can distinguish three different situations on the market. If the following condition holds

$$P_H^{T^{H*}*} * D_H^{T^{H*}*} - \sum_{i=1}^{2} C_H^i \left(D_H^{T^{H*}*} \right) - \sum_{i=1}^{2} \varepsilon^i > P_L^{T^{L*}*} * D_L^{T^{L*}*} - \sum_{i=1}^{2} C_L^i \left(D_L^{T^{L*}*} \right)$$

(HIGH)

and the intermediary's discount factor δ_0 is sufficiently large, he prefers to deliver high-quality composed services to his clients and the service providers have the right incentives to produce high quality. In contrast, if condition (HIGH) holds but the intermediary's personal discount factor is not high enough, he intends to be willing to reward the delivery of high quality services, but as soon as the service providers deliver high quality services the intermediary does not pay the bonus as promised. This is anticipated by the service providers. Consequently, only low-quality composed services are produced. If the following condition holds

$$P_H^{T^{H*}*} * D_H^{T^{H*}*} - \sum_{i=1}^{2} C_H^i \left(D_H^{T^{H*}*} \right) - \sum_{i=1}^{2} \varepsilon^i < P_L^{T^{L*}*} * D_L^{T^{L*}*} - \sum_{i=1}^{2} C_L^i \left(D_L^{T^{L*}*} \right)$$

(LOW)

the intermediary prefers to deliver low-quality composed services.

6 Concluding Comments

With our model we analyzed the incentives for high and low quality to be an equilibrium outcome of the market for composed services in a cloud computing environment. Hereby, the intermediary's discount factor is crucial even if the market for high-quality composed services is advantageous in terms of expected profits. Therefore, as a first implication for the OTF market, not only the profitability of composed services is important but also the evaluation of future profits. Hence, we have shown that if the intermediary's discount factor is lower than the payments for the single services relative to the advantage of high-quality composed services, only composed services of low quality may appear on the market.

However, we made several simplifying assumptions and therefore our model can be extended in various directions. For our theoretical analysis we suppose that the quality of the composed service and the single services is either high or low. An obvious extension is to introduce a finite or infinite number of different quality levels. Such a modification enlarges the set of possible strategic choices of the services providers, has the effect that the composed services may be available in these numerous quality levels and requires that the client's demand is defined to take this into account. A different direction for future research is the extension of asymmetric information issues to the client-intermediary relation. So far each client had a demand for high- and low-quality composed services. Differently, we may assume that there are several types of clients and the intermediary faces a client type who either demands high- or low-quality composed services. Moreover, a different reasonable assumption, especially for cloud services, is that demand and cost structures vary over time. In this case the intermediary might have to renew his contracts from time to time or the contracts might have a specific durability during which services can be flexibly demanded and delivered at a certain price. Up to now the services we considered were complementary and the intermediary needed exactly one service of each type. Adding substitute services and along with this competition is another direction to extend the current model.

A   Analytical Example

The client's demand typically decreases if the price of the composed service increases. As composed services of high quality are more valuable we suppose that for a given price they are demanded in greater quantities than composed services of low quality. The demand functions $D_{\theta^0}(P) = \frac{1}{\beta_{\theta^0}^2} \frac{1}{P^2}$ for $\theta^0 \in \{L, H\}$ with $\beta_L > \beta_H > 0$ have these properties. The service providers' costs are typically increasing in the quality they provide. Linear cost functions $C_{\theta^i}^i \left(D^i\right) = \gamma_{\theta^i} D^i$ for $\theta^i \in \{L, H\}$ with $\gamma_H > \gamma_L > 0$ for $i = 1, 2$ describe the service providers' costs. The profit from producing composed services of quality θ^0 from the optimal contracts of Proposition 4 and 5 is given by

$$PD_{\theta^0}(P) - (1 + \tilde{\varepsilon}_{\theta^0}) \sum_{i=1}^{2} C_{\theta^0}^i \left(D_{\theta^0}(P)\right) = \frac{P - 2\gamma_{\theta^0} \left(1 + \tilde{\varepsilon}_{\theta^0}\right)}{\beta_{\theta^0}^2 P^2} \qquad (A.1)$$

with $\tilde{\varepsilon}_L = 0$ and $\tilde{\varepsilon}_H > 0$. To simplify the calculations we use $\tilde{\varepsilon}_H$ as a multiplicative and not as an additive term (Proposition 5). Profit maximization yields

$$P_{L*}^{T^{L*}*} = P_{H*}^{T^{L*}*} = P_{L*}^{T^{H*}*} = 4\gamma_L \quad \text{and} \quad D_L^{T^{L*}*} = D_H^{T^{L*}*} = D_L^{T^{H*}*} = \frac{1}{16\gamma_L^2 \beta_L^2}$$

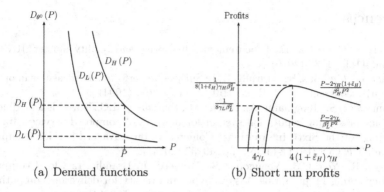

(a) Demand functions   (b) Short run profits

Fig. 2. Example for $\beta_H = \frac{1}{2}$, $\beta_L = 1$, $\gamma_H = \frac{1}{3}$, $\gamma_L = \frac{1}{8}$, $\tilde{\varepsilon}_H = \frac{1}{100}$

and for high-quality composed services

$$P_H^{T^{H*}*} = 4\left(1+\tilde{\varepsilon}_H\right)\gamma_H \quad \text{and} \quad D_H^{T^{H*}*} = \frac{1}{16\left(1+\tilde{\varepsilon}_H\right)^2\gamma_H^2\beta_H^2}.$$

By the choice of the parameter $\gamma_L < \gamma_H$ we observe immediately that the price the intermediary charges for high quality is strictly greater than the price he charges for low quality, whereas the effect on the quantity remains ambiguous. Figure 2(a) illustrates the client's demand functions and Fig. 2(b) the short run profits of the OTF provider for low- and high-quality composed services.

Consider the long run quality choice of the intermediary. The conditions derived in Sect. 5.3 and Corollary 1 are for our example

$$\frac{1}{\left(1+\tilde{\varepsilon}_H\right)\gamma_H\beta_H^2} > \frac{1}{\gamma_L\beta_L^2}, \tag{Ex-HIGH}$$

$$\frac{1}{\left(1+\tilde{\varepsilon}_H\right)\gamma_H\beta_H^2} < \frac{1}{\gamma_L\beta_L^2}, \tag{Ex-LOW}$$

$$\delta_0 \geq \frac{\left(1+\tilde{\varepsilon}_H\right)\gamma_H - \gamma_L}{\left(1+\tilde{\varepsilon}_H\right)\gamma_H - \gamma_L + \left(1+\tilde{\varepsilon}_H\right)^2\gamma_H^2\beta_H^2\left(\frac{1}{\left(1+\tilde{\varepsilon}_H\right)\gamma_H\beta_H^2} - \frac{1}{\gamma_L\beta_L^2}\right)}. \tag{Ex-D0}$$

The three possible market situations are as follows: If (Ex-HIGH) and (Ex-D0) hold, high-quality composed services are produced. If (Ex-HIGH) holds and (Ex-D0) does not hold, low-quality composed services are produced even if high-quality composed services yield a higher profit for the intermediary if the services are traded once. If (Ex-LOW) holds, low-quality composed services are produced. Inserting the values from Fig. 2 yields that high-quality composed services are produced if $\delta_0 \geq 0.66$. This means as soon as future profits are considered to be sufficient attractive high-quality composed service will be the equilibrium outcome of the market.

References

1. Asker, J., Cantillon, E.: Procurement when price and quality matter. RAND J. Econ. **41**(1), 1–34 (2010)
2. Baker, G., Gibbons, R., Murphy, K.J.: Subjective performance measures in optimal incentive contracts. Q. J. Econ. **109**(4), 1125–1156 (1994)
3. Brangewitz, S., Jungmann, A., Petrlic, R., Platenius, M.C.: Towards a flexible and privacy-preserving reputation system for markets of composed services. In: Proceedings of the Sixth International Conferences on Advanced Service Computing (SERVICE COMPUTATION), pp. 49–57 (2014)
4. Buyya, R., Yeo, C.S., Venugopal, S., Broberg, J., Brandic, I.: Cloud computing and emerging IT platforms: Vision, hype, and reality for delivering computing as the 5th utility. Future Gener. Comput. Syst. **25**(6), 599–616 (2009)
5. Dana, J.D.J., Fong, Y.F.: Product quality, reputation, and market structure. Int. Econ. Rev. **52**(4), 1059–1076 (2011)
6. Dana Jr., J.D.: Monopoly price dispersion under demand uncertainty. Int. Econ. Rev. **42**(3), 649–670 (2001)
7. Dellarocas, C.: Reputation mechanism design in online trading environments with pure moral hazard. Inf. Syst. Res. **16**(2), 209–230 (2005)
8. Giovanoli, C., Pulikal, P., Gatziu Grivas, S.: E-marketplace for cloud services. In: CLOUD COMPUTING 2014, The Fifth International Conference on Cloud Computing, GRIDs, and Virtualization, pp. 76–83 (2014)
9. Happe, M., Kling, P., Plessl, C., Platzner, M., Meyer auf der Heide, F.: On-the-fly computing: A novel paradigm for individualized it services. In: Proceedings of the 9th Workshop on Software Technology for Future embedded and Ubiquitous Systems (SEUS) (2013)
10. Jula, A., Sundararajan, E., Othman, Z.: Cloud computing service composition: a systematic literature review. Expert Syst. Appl. **41**(8), 3809–3824 (2014)
11. Laussel, D., Long, N.V.: Strategic separation from suppliers of complementary inputs: a dynamic markovian approach. In: Working Paper No. 2011s–41, Centre interuniversitaire de recherche en analyse des organisations (CIRANO), April 2011
12. Mailath, G.J., Samuelson, L.: Repeated Games and Reputations: Long-Run Relationships. Oxford University Press, Oxford (2006)
13. Nash, J.: Non-cooperative games. Ann. Math. **54**(2), 286–295 (1951)
14. Selten, R.: Spieltheoretische Behandlung eines Oligopolmodells mit Nachfrageträgheit: Teil I: Bestimmung des dynamischen Preisgleichgewichts. Zeitschrift für die gesamte Staatswissenschaft **121**(2), 301–324 (1965)
15. Selten, R.: Spieltheoretische Behandlung eines Oligopolmodells mit Nachfrageträgheit: Teil II: Eigenschaften des dynamischen Preisgleichgewichts. Zeitschrift für die gesamte Staatswissenschaft **121**(4), 667–689 (1965)
16. Shapiro, C.: Premiums for high quality products as returns to reputations. Q. J. Econ. **98**(4), 659–680 (1983)
17. Sundareswaran, S., Squicciarini, A., Lin, D.: A brokerage-based approach for cloud service selection. In: 2012 IEEE 5th International Conference on Cloud Computing (CLOUD), pp. 558–565, June 2012
18. Tang, Q.C., Cheng, H.K.: Optimal location and pricing of web services intermediary. Decis. Support Syst. **40**(1), 129–141 (2005)

X-Machine Based Testing for Cloud Services

Raluca Lefticaru[1,2](✉) and Anthony J.H. Simons[1]

[1] Department of Computer Science, The University of Sheffield,
Regent Court, Portobello Street, Sheffield S1 4DP, UK
{r.lefticaru,a.j.simons}@sheffield.ac.uk
[2] Department of Computer Science, University of Bucharest,
Str. Academiei Nr. 14, 010014 Bucharest, Romania

Abstract. In this article we present a tool designed for cloud service testing, able to generate test cases from a formal specification of the service, in form of a deterministic stream X-machine (DSXM) model. The paper summarizes the theoretical foundations of X-machine based testing and illustrates the usage of the developed tool on some examples. It shows in detail how the specification should be written, which are the design for test conditions it should satisfy, in order to assure the generation of high quality test suites for the cloud service.

Keywords: Cloud service testing · State-based testing · X-machine

1 Introduction

As cloud computing has emerged as a new paradigm for hosting and delivering services over the Internet [16], the enterprise IT environment has been transformed into a matrix of interwoven infrastructure, platform and application services which are delivered from different service providers. In this context, Cloud Service Brokers will play an important role by serving as intermediaries between providers and consumers, ensuring the quality of software-based enterprise cloud services.

This paper provides a powerful model-based testing approach for cloud services, which aims to increase the confidence in the quality of service behaviour, previously tested using a specification in the form of a *stream X-machine* (SXM). The testing methodology based on SXMs is more general and can be applied to other types of software, not only cloud services, but cloud ecosystems would substantially benefit from this approach, which would allow testing and trusting all the services that agreed on implementing the same SXM specification and passed the generated test sets.

A stream X-machine [11,12] is a particular type of X-machine [9], a state model which has been investigated for many years, because of perceived advantages in: (1) its modelling capability, e.g. has been used in high performance agent based simulators like FLAME [7]; and (2) its associated testing methods [8,11,12]. In essence, an SXM is a class of extended finite state machine

© Springer International Publishing Switzerland 2015
G. Ortiz and C. Tran (Eds.): ESOCC 2014, CCIS 508, pp. 175–189, 2015.
DOI: 10.1007/978-3-319-14886-1_17

(EFSM), having an internal memory and transitions labelled by processing functions, which might have input parameters and can update the machine internal memory. An SXM can model not only the control part of a system, but also the data processing. And, if certain design for test conditions are satisfied, from the SXM specifications one can derive test suites able to establish the correctness of the implementation under test (IUT). Much recent research has been focused on obtaining theoretical results, such as relaxing the conditions the SXM should satisfy (determinism, nondeterminism, controllability), in order to produce high quality test suites.

In this paper we use a deterministic SXM to model the cloud service that will be tested and we present a tool, which assists the user in writing the SXM specification, validating it and generating test data.

The paper is structured as follows: Sect. 2 introduces the theoretical foundations of stream X-machine testing, Sect. 3 presents the tool developed, some examples are summarized in Sect. 4, related work is presented in Sect. 5 and finally conclusions are drawn in Sect. 6.

2   Theoretical Background

In this section we present the foundations of stream X machine testing. We will use ε to denote the empty sequence. For a finite alphabet Σ, Σ^* represents the set of all finite sequences with members in Σ. For $a, b \in \Sigma^*$, ab denotes the concatenation of the two sequences a and b. For $U, V \in \Sigma^*$, $UV = \{ab | a \in U, b \in V\}$; U^n is defined by $U^0 = \{\varepsilon\}$ and $U^n = U^{n-1}U, n \geq 1$. Furthermore, $U[n] = \bigcup_{0 \leq i \leq n} U_i$.

2.1   Stream X-Machines

A Stream X-Machine (SXM) is an extended form of state machine, capable of modelling both the data and the control of the system [11,12]. Compared to Finite State Machines (FSMs), SXMs enrich them with: (1) internal storage or *memory* (the internal variables of the machine), (2) *processing functions* instead of input/output symbols which traditionally labelled the transitions of FSMs.

Definition 1. *An SXM [12] is a tuple* $Z = (\Sigma, \Gamma, Q, M, \Phi, F, q_0, m_0)$ *where:*

- Σ *is the finite* input alphabet
- Γ *is the finite* output alphabet
- Q *is the finite* set of states
- M *is a (possibly infinite) set called* memory
- Φ *is a finite set of distinct* processing functions; *a processing function is a non-empty (partial) function of type* $M \times \Sigma \longrightarrow \Gamma \times M$
- F *is the (partial) next-state function,* $F : Q \times \Phi \longrightarrow Q$
- $q_0 \in Q$ *is the* initial state
- $m_0 \in M$ *is the* initial memory value

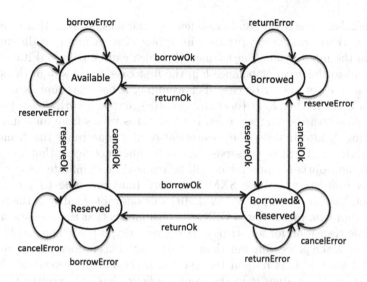

Fig. 1. A state transition diagram for an SXM modelling a book service

When representing a certain system, it is frequently helpful to abstract and think of an SXM as a finite automaton with the arcs labelled by functions from the set Φ. The automaton $A_Z = (\Phi, Q, F, q_0)$ over the alphabet Φ is called the *associated finite automaton of Z*.

Usually, the processing functions of Φ specify the components or the possible operations of the system specified by Z. The memory typically represents the variables used by the modelled system. It is formed from tuples, where each element of the tuple corresponds to either a global variable or a parameter that may be passed between the elements of Φ.

When modelling a real system, the input alphabet Σ consists of the names of the operations which should be triggered and their parameters, if applicable. For example, a simplified book lending service, shown in Fig. 1, could have operations like *borrow(id)*, *return(id)*, *reserve(id)*, *cancel(id)*, where *id* is a number representing the customer which attempts to do the operation, with values taken from a finite set. However, providing an actual value for the parameters, and depending on the current state and value of the SXM memory, there might exist different processing alternatives. For example, the SXM can have two processing functions, labelled *borrowOk* and *borrowError* (in order to differentiate them as distinct branches of the operation *borrow(id)* from the implementation). These two processing functions can be triggered if the value of the *id* is adequate for the first case or if the value of *id* is incorrect in the second case (e.g., the book is reserved by another customer, represented by the internal memory variable *res_id*, and *res_id* $\neq$ *id*).

There are cases in which the number of processing alternatives is more than two (success/error). For example, a bank account is modelled in [8] as a SXM having $\Sigma = \{open(), deposit(a), withdraw(a), close()\}$, where a represents a positive number. The SXM can have different functions, such as *WithdrawAll*, *Withdraw*, *WithdrawError* (written in upper case, in order to differentiate them from the input symbol *withdraw(a)*), which can be triggered if the value of a is equal to the account balance b in the first case, $0 < a < b$ in the second case and $b < a$ for the error case. For example, a bank account is modelled in [8] as a SXM having $\Sigma = \{open(), deposit(a), withdraw(a), close()\}$, where a represents a positive number. Even if $a > 0$ takes values from an infinite set, thus making Σ also infinite, the theoretical results concerning the X-machine test generation will still be preserved, the only difference being that the search process for appropriate input values will be realized in an infinite set.

In this context, when the SXM has more functions able to process the same input, like *borrow(id)* or *withdraw(a)*, one desirable quality of the SXM is to be *deterministic* (abbreviated DSXM) which means that there exists at most one possible transition for any triplet (state, memory, input). This implies that the domains of the processing functions are disjoint. This property is not unusual for a cloud service, it is normal to expect a deterministic, repeatable behaviour, whenever the system is in the same configuration and receives the same input values. However, there exist also testing methodologies developed for non-deterministic X-machines [2] where the non-determinism can be caused either by overlapping functions domains or by non-determinism of the associated automation A_Z, i.e. $F : Q \times \Phi \longrightarrow 2^Q$.

Definition 2. *An SXM Z is said to be* deterministic *if for every $\phi_1, \phi_2 \in \Phi$, if there exists $q \in Q$ such that $(q, \phi_1), (q, \phi_2) \in domF$ then either $\phi_1 = \phi_2$ or $dom\phi_1 \cap dom\phi_2 = \emptyset$;*

A sequence $p \in \Phi^*$ of processing functions induces a function $||p||$ that shows the correspondence between a (memory, input sequence) pair and the (output sequence, memory) pair produced by the application, in turn, of the processing functions in the sequence p.

Definition 3. *Given $p \in \Phi^*$, $||p|| : M \times \Sigma^* \longrightarrow \Gamma^* \times M$ is defined by:*

- *$||\epsilon||(m, \epsilon) = (\epsilon, m), m \in M$*
- *Given $p \in \Phi^*$ and $\phi \in \Phi$, $||p\phi||(m, s\sigma) = (g\gamma, m')$, for $m, m' \in M$, $s \in \Sigma^*$, $g \in \Gamma^*$, $\sigma \in \Sigma$, $\gamma \in \Gamma$ such that there exists $m'' \in M$ with $||p||(m, s) = (g, m'')$ and $\phi(m'', \sigma) = (\gamma, m')$.*

A computation of the SXM represents the traversal of all sequences of transitions in the associated automaton A_Z and the successive application of the corresponding processing functions (using the actual parameters provided to each of them) to the initial memory value for the first function and to the resulting memory value for the following processing functions. The correspondence between the input sequence applied to the machine and the output produced gives rise to the relation (function) computed by the Z.

Definition 4. *The relation computed by Z, $f_Z : \Sigma^* \longleftrightarrow \Gamma^*$ is defined by: $(s, g) \in f_Z$ if there exist $p \in \Phi^*$ and $m \in M$ such that $(q_0, p) \in domF^*$ and $||p||(m_0, s) = (g, m)$.*

Definition 5. *An SXM Z is said to be* completely-defined *if dom$f_Z = \Sigma^*$.*

In other words, an SXM is completely-defined if every sequence of inputs can be processed by at least one sequence of functions accepted by the associated automaton. In the case when the SXM has some "refused" (or ignored) inputs, it can be transformed into a completely-defined one by adding a designated error output, which is not in the output alphabet of Z and completing the automaton with self-looping transitions or transitions to an extra (error) state.

2.2   Reaching and Distinguishing States in a DSXM

When testing from finite state machines (FSMs) or from finite automata, some important notions are:

- *state cover*, a set S consisting of sequences that reach every state of the machine;
- *transition cover*, a set T consisting of sequences that reach every state of the machine and exercise every transition from that state; if S is a state cover and X the input alphabet, then the transition cover can be computed by $T = S \cup SX$
- *characterization set*, usually labelled W, that distinguishes between every pair of states in the FSM.

Considering the automaton from Fig. 1, where the input alphabet is $X = \{borrowOk, borrowError, returnOk, returnError, reserveOk, reserveError, cancelOk, cancelError\}$, a state cover can be $S = \{\varepsilon, borrowOk, reserveOk, borrowOk\,reserveOk\}$, and a characterization set $W = \{returnOk, cancelOk\}$.

Using these sets, test suites of the form $Y = TX[k]W$ can be produced, according to the W-method [6], where S is a state cover, $T = S \cup SX$ a transition cover, X is the input alphabet of the machine, W the characterization set and $k \geq 0$ is the difference between the estimated number of states in the implementation and the number of states of the specification. The W-method is the most general testing method (that does not rely on the existence of direct state inspection). For this method to be applicable, there must be a reliable *reset* in the implementation, that correctly puts the system specified by the FSM into its initial state before each test sequence is executed.

The idea behind the test suite $Y = TX[k]W$ is that $T = S \cup SX$ ensures that all the states and transitions in the specification are also present in implementation, the set $X[k]W$ verifies that the implementation is in the same state as the specification after triggering each transition. In case the implementation contains up to k extra states, the set $X[k]W = X^kW \cup \ldots \cup \{\varepsilon\}W$ ensures that each of them would be reached by some input sequence of length up to k and that they behave the same way as the corresponding specification states (by applying the sequences from W, which can distinguish between states).

Many adaptations of the W-method exist in the literature, such as the *round trip* approach [1], based on a transition tree constructed in a depth-first fashion, which includes all the transition sequences that begin and end with the same state. Other authors [4] preferred to use a reliable state-reporting oracle instead of the characterization set W, in order to check the current state of the implementation under test.

The testing methods for simple FSMs have been adapted to SXM testing [2,10–12], and consequently corresponding notions have been proposed to build the theoretical framework, such as realisable sequences, r-state cover, separating sets (which are sets of sequences of processing functions that differentiate between every pair of separable states of the machine [12]).

Because the transitions in the state diagram of an SXM are labelled not by simple input/output symbols as in FSMs, but by functions, with restrictions on their input/memory which prevent them from firing unconditionally, there might exist states that are reachable in the associated automaton, but which cannot be reached by any input sequence applied to the machine. This is why the state cover from the FSM should be replaced, when applying testing methods from SXM, with an r-state cover, which is a minimal set of realisable sequences, that reaches every r-reachable state in Z [11,12].

Analogously, there may be pairs of distinguishable states in the associated automaton for which the sequences of processing functions that distinguish between them can never be applied.

2.3   Design for Test Conditions

The first approach on testing using X-machines, the so called "DSXM integration testing" [2,10,13,15], was inspired by the W-method, and it can guarantee the conformance of the implementation, with respect to the SXM specification. The method was originally developed for testing the control structure of a system, modelled by a DSXM and it can be applied under some design for test conditions and the assumption that the processing functions of the X-machine have been correctly implemented (and previously tested).

The two design for test conditions necessary in this approach are: *output-distinguishability* and *input-completeness*.

Definition 6. *An SXM Z is said to be* output-distinguishable *if for all $\phi_1, \phi_2 \in \Phi$, whenever there exist $m, m_1, m_2 \in M, \sigma \in \Sigma, \gamma \in \Gamma$ such that $\phi_1(m, \sigma) = (\gamma, m_1)$ and $\phi_2(m, \sigma) = (\gamma, m_2)$, then $\phi_1 = \phi_2$.*

This property, which states that the output produced in response to any given input determines which processing function has been applied, is important for testing purposes and in practice can be easily achieved by adding, if needed, some extra output symbols.

Definition 7. *An SXM Z is called* input-complete *if $\forall \phi \in \Phi, m \in M, \exists \sigma \in \Sigma$ such that $(m, \sigma) \in dom(\phi)$.*

The input-completeness (or controllability) of an SXM assures that any sequence of processing functions in the associated finite automaton (FA) can be triggered by suitable input sequences, so they can be tested against the implementation.

This property is rather strict; and most specifications corresponding to real systems are not by default input-complete.

Definition 8. *A test function of an SXM Z is a function* $t : \Phi^* \longrightarrow \Sigma^*$ *that satisfies the following conditions:*

- $t(\varepsilon) = \varepsilon$ (1)
- *Let* $p = \phi_1 \dots \phi_k \in \Phi^*$, $k \geq 1$
    - *Suppose* $\phi_1 \dots \phi_{k-1} \in L_{A_Z}$ *and there exists* $\sigma_1, \dots, \sigma_k \in \Sigma$, $\gamma_1, \dots, \gamma_k \in \Gamma$ *and* $m_1, \dots, m_k \in M$ *such that* $\phi_i(m_{i-1}, \sigma_i) = (\gamma_i, m_i)$, $1 \leq i \leq k$. *Then* $t(p) = \sigma_1 \dots \sigma_k$ *for some* $\sigma_1 \dots \sigma_k$ *that satisfy this condition* (2)
    - *Otherwise,* $t(p) = t(\phi_1 \dots \phi_{k-1})$. (3)

As the initial design conditions for DSXM integration testing were quite restrictive, in further works they have been relaxed, for example the *controllability* has been replaced by *input-uniformity* in [11]. This property of the X-machine suggests that, having a sequence of processing functions in the FA, one can determine an input sequence that drives this sequence of functions by simply selecting appropriate input symbols for each processing function in the sequence, one at a time, without needing to know the processing functions to be applied next.

2.4 The Test Suite

As mentioned previously, the test suites derived from X-machines are mainly inspired from FSM testing and many derivation approaches are extensions of the *W*-method.

After applying a certain methodology, some "abstract" test sequences in the associated FA are produced and in order to obtain a corresponding test suite in the X-machine, the input values that trigger the processing functions should be generated according to Definition 8.

It might be the case that the sequences produced are not all feasible and consequently they cannot be mapped into a set of transitions with actual input values. In this case, as Definition 8 case (3) specifies, only the longest subsequence will be mapped into actual input values.

However, in the SXM-testing literature there is no suggestion how to automatically obtain these input values. The problem of how to generate feasible paths and their corresponding input values is in general an NP-complete problem. This is why a tool that automatically generates these complete test suites is desirable, first, because one could rely on the theoretical results that assure the quality of test suite derived according to the SXM testing methodologies and, second, the human effort would be limited to writing good SXM specifications.

3 Tool Presentation

Based on the SXM testing framework, a tool[1] has been developed, in order to help users specify X-machine models, verify, validate them and automatically

---

[1] http://staffwww.dcs.shef.ac.uk/people/A.Simons/broker/.

generate high-level functional test suites from these specifications. The tool aims to be used for testing cloud services, after specifying them using the DSXM formalism.

The software developed consists of three main modules:

- *The validation component*, responsible for checking the X-machine specified and announce the user if there are non-reachable states or missing transitions.
- *The verification component*, responsible mainly for checking the operations of the service protocol, in order to assure determinism.
- *The test generation component*, which will deliver high quality test suites, providing also the actual value for each parameter of the processing functions.

3.1 Validation Component

The XML specification of a service consists firstly of a functional part, which defines the constants and variables used in the service model, the signatures of the service's operations and their inputs, outputs, branching conditions and state update effects on the memory variables [14]. For a complete description of the service specification language, the BNF of the language may be consulted [14].

The second part of the XML specification is represented by a state machine, which captures the high-level control states of the service and shows its allowed transitions, labelled with the names of distinct request/response (event/action) pairs taken from the operations [14], which correspond to the processing functions of the SXM.

For example, an excerpt from a web service specification representing the system for Book reservation and borrowing from Fig. 1 would look like this:

```
<State name="Available" initial="true">
 <Transition name="borrow/ok" source="Available" target="Borrowed"/>
 <Transition name="borrow/error" source="Available" target="Available"/>
 <Transition name="reserve/ok" source="Available" target="Reserved"/>
 <Transition name="reserve/error" source="Available" target="Available"/>
</State>
```

The validation module allows users to cross-check the design of their state machine against the service's operations, and to determine whether all events are appropriately handled.

The output of this module is an XML file containing the analysed state machine specification. The root Machine node will contain a *Notice* node, which may contain further Analysis or Warning nodes. For example

```
<Notice id="1" text="Validation report for machine: BookServiceMachine">
 <Analysis id="2" text="Events are ignored in state: Available"/>
 ...
</Notice>
```

A *Warning* is issued if there are states that cannot be reached in the machine, or if known events (service's operations) are not handled by the machine. These are *faults* in the specification that should be rectified. An *Analysis* is issued if any state ignores certain events. This is not necessarily a fault, and it is provided for further information.

A *Notice* is then also attached to each State node, giving an Analysis of which events are ignored by that state. A state may legitimately choose to ignore certain events; but the analysis allows the user to check that events are handled as it was intended. The Warning is repeated for each unreachable state, as a reminder.

```
<State id="6" name="Available" initial="true">
  <Notice id="7" text="Completeness check for state: Available">
    <Analysis id="8" text="State ignores the events:">
      <Event id="9" name="return/ok"/>
      <Event id="10" name="return/error"/>
      <Event id="11" name="cancel/ok"/>
      <Event id="12" name="cancel/error"/>
    </Analysis>
  </Notice>
</Notice>
```

3.2 Verification Component

This module is responsible for checking a specification for *completeness* and *consistency*. As explained before, some operations of the service can have different behaviours or branches, depending on the values of the operation's inputs, or internal memory variables. For example, the withdraw operation from a bank account can have different branches, for error (when the amount requested is higher than the current balance) or for success (when the value is less or equal to balance). These different behaviours are specified in the XML model of the X-machine as "scenarios" of the same operation, corresponding to different processing functions of the X-machine. The difference between these scenarios is given by the *condition* of each one, which is an expression restricting the domain of the processing function, for example an excerpt of the account service contains the following:

```
<Scenario name="withdraw/ok">
  <Condition>
    <Proposition name="and">
      <Comparison name="moreThan">
        <Input name="amount"/>
        <Constant name="zero"/>
      </Comparison>
      <Comparison name="notMoreThan">
        <Input name="amount"/>
        <Variable name="balance"/>
      </Comparison>
    </Proposition>
```

```
</Condition>
  ...
</Scenario>
```

The verification module checks each operation, to ensure that whatever the current state of variables in memory, and whatever values are supplied as inputs, there will always be exactly one path that is executable.

The verification process uses symbolic evaluation to determine possible partitions in the input space and symbolic subsumption to check which path is enabled. The verification process can detect whether the specification exhibits *nondeterminism* (more than one scenarios enabled, this is equivalent to several processing functions having overlapping input domains) or *blocking* (no path is enabled, or no function can process the input) for particular inputs and states.

The output of the verification is an XML file containing the analysed protocol specification. The root Protocol node will contain a *Notice* node, which may contain further Analysis or Warning nodes. An *Analysis* node is issued if the memory is correctly initialised and each operation is found to be deterministic. A *Warning* node is issued if the memory is not fully initialised, operation inputs are not all bound, or known events are not handled by the protocol specification. A *Warning* is also issued if an operation is found to be blocking, or non-deterministic under certain inputs. These warnings indicate faults in the specification that should be corrected. For example:

```
<Notice id="1" text="Verification report for protocol: BookService">
  <Analysis id="2" text="Memory is correctly initialised"/>
  <Warning id="3" text="Operation is blocking: borrow(id)"/>
  <Warning id="4" text="Operation is blocking: reserve(id)"/>
  <Analysis id="5" text="Operation is deterministic: return(id)"/>
  <Analysis id="6" text="Operation is deterministic: cancel(id)"/>
</Notice>
```

A *Notice* node is then attached to each Operation node, describing the analysed behaviour of that operation. If the operation is sensitive to different inputs, another Notice node is attached, containing an Analysis node for each input partition. Otherwise an Analysis node reports that the operation accepts universal input. Then, for each input partition, an Analysis node is created if one scenario accepts this input; and a Warning node is issued if no scenarios accept the input (blocking); or if multiple scenarios accept the input (non-determinism) - the multiple scenarios are identified in appended Analysis nodes under the warning. In blocking and non-deterministic cases, the specification is faulty and should be corrected.

3.3 Test Generation Module

This module aims to systematically explore the paths through a specification, according to the methodology presented in Sect. 2 and to generate complete test suites from a cloud software service specification.

High-Level Test Suite Generator. The internal mechanism of the module is described in the following. It will generate first a reachable state cover set S_r for the X-machine (which can be different from the one of the associated automaton, which in case of X-machines could be infeasible). Then, a transition cover $T = S_r \cup S_r \Phi$ is generated and, according to the W-method, a test set $Y = T\Phi[k]W$ should be constructed. In practice, if the current state can be checked using an abstract or a precise oracle, the W characterisation set can disappear from the previous formula, resulting in a reduction in test set size. This is at the cost of inserting a call to the oracle function to inspect the reached state. The tool considers then for generation only sets of the form $Y' = S_r\Phi[k]$. Test sequences are generated to a finite bounded depth k, given by the user, to avoid an explosion of cases.

The maximum path depth k can be arbitrarily chosen. When $k = 0$ the generated test suite is the state cover; and when $k = 1$, it is the transition cover of the associated automaton. Since all complete paths through the FA are not necessarily realizable in the SXM, the tool warns the user if states are not reached, or transitions not covered, for any given value of k.

```
<Warning id="6" text="Specification is not fully covered by the test
  suite">
  <Analysis id="7" text="Suggest increasing the path length"/>
</Warning>
<Warning id="8" text="These transitions were not tested:">
  <Transition id="9" name="borrow/error" source="Available" target=
    "Available"/>
  <Transition id="10" name="reserve/error" source="Available" target=
    "Available"/>
  <Transition id="11" name="return/ok" source="Borrowed" target=
    "Available"/>
  ...
```

The output will be an XML file containing the high-level tests, its root node *TestSuite* will contain a *Notice* node, whose children nodes consist of Advice nodes describing the stages in generating and filtering the resulting tests, and *Warning* nodes describing any transitions and states that were not covered in the specification, for the chosen depth k of exploration. The remaining *TestSequence* nodes are the paths to test, presented as an ordered set, for example:

```
<TestSequence id="39" state="BorrowedReserved" path="0">
  <TestStep id="40" name="create/ok" state="Available">
    <Operation id="41" name="create"/>
  </TestStep>
  <TestStep id="42" name="borrow/ok" state="Borrowed">
    <Operation id="43" name="borrow">
      <Input id="44" name="id" type="Integer">1</Input>
      <Output id="45" name="result" type="Boolean">true</Output>
    </Operation>
  </TestStep>
```

```
<TestStep id="46" name="reserve/ok" state="BorrowedReserved"
  verify="true">
  <Operation id="47" name="reserve">
    <Input id="48" name="id" type="Integer">2</Input>
    <Output id="49" name="result" type="Boolean">true</Output>
  </Operation>
</TestStep>
</TestSequence>
```

Each TestSequence describes a unique scenario to test, consisting of a sequence of TestSteps. Typically, the early *TestSteps* in a sequence denote set-up actions and the final TestStep is the particular step under observation, to be verified. However, if multi-objective tests were selected, some TestSequences may also have intermediate verified TestSteps. This is where shorter tests have been merged into longer tests, where the shorter sequence is a prefix of the longer sequence.

Low-Level Test Suite Grounding. The returned high-level test suite is intended for service providers to develop their own bespoke grounding to concrete tests. A grounding is a transformation from high-level abstract tests to low-level concrete, executable tests. This may be performed by programs that understand the XML format of the generated high-level tests, and the expected implementation technology of the cloud service to be tested.

It is fairly simple to build a grounding and the process is described in [14]. Each TestSequence starts with a freshly-created (or reset) instance of the service. The TestSequence then describes a particular scenario to test, shown as a sequence of TestStep interactions. Each TestStep represents a single interaction with the service, in which a given operation is called with particular concrete inputs that should trigger the given scenario. Typically, the early TestSteps in a sequence constitute the set-up actions for the desired scenario and the final Test-Step is the step to be verified. Whenever a TestStep is flagged for verification, then the grounding should generate code to verify, through assertions, that:

- a request triggers the expected named scenario in the operation
- the service subsequently enters the state named by the step
- any outputs returned in the response are the expected outputs

Positive tests are indicated by the scenario's response-name, for example, *ok* for a normal response, or *error* for a planned error handler. Negative test sequences are always indicated by the response *ignore*, which is generated automatically. No outputs are simulated for negative tests, but the implementation should flag that the request was refused. Negative tests always arise from refusals by the state machine, since failing a guard for one scenario always triggers a different scenario (positively), so long as the guards are mutually exclusive and exhaustive.

In the above, we presume that software services are designed respecting the mentioned design-for-test criteria. Each response from a service must indicate, in addition to the usual returned value, metadata about which branch of an operation (scenario) executed, and what abstract state the service entered afterwards. This information could be supplied as extra header information, or as additional query-operations upon the service, which could be interleaved with the tested operations above.

4   Example XML Service Specifications.

The testing tool is offered as a web service, able to receive XML specifications of the cloud software services under test. The web standard for specifying the functional behaviour of the system under test is also provided and it has been presented in [14]. To assist users understanding how a valid service specification may be defined according to this schema, several XML service specifications are also given as examples, as valid implementations of the schema and provided on the tool web page[2]. Due to space constraints we will briefly summarize them, more details and complete specification can be found online.

- A simple *login service*, with two states and no memory updates, illustrating a state machine, guarded scenarios and default ignore transitions, inserted during test generation.
- A bank *account service*, with two states and integer balance updates in memory. This example illustrates how to initialise and update memory variables and design guards with compound conditions.
- A *contact list service* with data stored as two lists in memory. This is a more complex example, illustrating the need to complete functions with enough scenarios to trigger all memory-dependent branches; more variants are provided in order to illustrate how a specification can be improved for testability reasons.
- A simple *shopping cart* that represents the state of the cart and the level of stock as two maps in memory. This example illustrates the pure functional style of updates to data structures in memory.
- A simple *book lending service*, modelling the constraints on borrowing and reserving books. This example illustrates the discovery of incomplete operations, where the given scenarios do not cover all input and memory cases.
- A simple *Cloud data storage service*, with document versioning and a limit set on the volume of data to be stored. This example illustrates the use of an extra local variable in memory to assist with version numbering.

5   Related Work

Different approaches to cloud service testing can be consulted in two excellent surveys about testing and verification of service oriented architectures [3,5]. Among these, only a few only a few approaches have used the state-based nature of services for testing purposes; and this research has not led to a mature testing tool.

---

[2] http://staffwww.dcs.shef.ac.uk/people/A.Simons/broker/specify.html.

The current paper is extending the work from [14] in the following aspects. It introduces the theoretical X-machine background, needed to understand the test suite generation mechanism and the properties (or design for test conditions) the specifications should satisfy. Secondly, compared to previous variant of the tool, the *validation* and the *verification* modules have been added, in order to help the user design proper specifications. Also, some improvements in the test generation algorithm, regarding the search for input values that trigger every transition on the path, have been realized.

Another tool, called JSXM [8], was developed and used for SXM based testing, using the theoretical foundations from [12]. JSXM supports the animation of SXM models, described in an XML-based language with Java in-line code, and the automatic generation of test suites from the SXM specifications. However, the user modelling the system should provide the r-state cover S_r and a separating set W_s (its construction for more complex machines can be tedious).

6   Conclusions and Further Work

This paper presents a tool for model based testing cloud services, using as formal specification the stream X-machine model. It summarizes the theoretical background of SXM testing and explains what properties the specification must satisfy in order to obtain high quality test suites.

Future work will focus on automatic groundings for certain standard service implementation technologies. Another interesting research direction is to apply metaheuristic search algorithms to generate the concrete input parameter values which can trigger the given functions from a generated sequence.

Acknowledgements. The research leading to these results has received funding from the European Union Seventh Framework Programme (FP7/2007-2013) under grant agreement no 328392, the Broker@Cloud project (www.broker-cloud.eu).

References

1. Binder, R.V.: Testing Object-oriented Systems: Models, Patterns, and Tools. Addison-Wesley Longman Publishing Co., Inc., Boston (1999)
2. Bogdanov, K., Holcombe, M., Ipate, F., Seed, L., Vanak, S.K.: Testing methods for X-machines: a review. Formal Asp. Comput. **18**(1), 3–30 (2006)
3. Bozkurt, M., Harman, M., Hassoun, Y.: Testing and verification in service-oriented architecture: a survey. Softw. Test. Verif. Reliab. **23**(4), 261–313 (2013)
4. Briand, L.C., Di Penta, M., Labiche, Y.: Assessing and improving state-based class testing: a series of experiments. IEEE Trans. Softw. Eng. **30**(11), 770–793 (2004)
5. Canfora, G., Di Penta, M.: Service-oriented architectures testing: a survey. In: De Lucia, A., Ferrucci, F. (eds.) ISSSE 2006–2008. LNCS, vol. 5413, pp. 78–105. Springer, Heidelberg (2009)
6. Chow, T.S.: Testing software design modeled by finite-state machines. IEEE Trans. Softw. Eng. **4**(3), 178–187 (1978)

7. Coakley, S., Gheorghe, M., Holcombe, M., Chin, S., Worth, D., Greenough, C.: Exploitation of high performance computing in the FLAME agent-based simulation framework. In: Min, G., Hu, J., Liu, L.C., Yang, L.T., Seelam, S., Lefevre, L. (eds.) HPCC-ICESS, pp. 538–545. IEEE Computer Society (2012)
8. Dranidis, D., Bratanis, K., Ipate, F.: JSXM: a tool for automated test generation. In: Eleftherakis, G., Hinchey, M., Holcombe, M. (eds.) SEFM 2012. LNCS, vol. 7504, pp. 352–366. Springer, Heidelberg (2012)
9. Eilenberg, S.: Automata, Languages, and Machines. Academic Press Inc, Orlando (1974)
10. Holcombe, M., Ipate, F.: Correct Systems - Building a Business Process Solution. Applied Computing. Springer, London (1998)
11. Ipate, F.: Testing against a non-controllable stream X-machine using state counting. Theor. Comput. Sci. **353**(1–3), 291–316 (2006)
12. Ipate, F., Holcombe, M.: Testing data processing-oriented systems from stream X-machine models. Theor. Comput. Sci. **403**(2–3), 176–191 (2008)
13. Ipate, F., Holcombe, M.: An integration testing method that is proved to find all faults. Int. J. Comput. Math. **63**, 159–178 (1997)
14. Kiran, M., Friesen, A., Simons, A.J.H., Schwach, W.K.R.: Model-based testing in cloud brokerage scenarios. In: Lomuscio, A.R., Nepal, S., Patrizi, F., Benatallah, B., Brandić, I. (eds.) ICSOC 2013. LNCS, vol. 8377, pp. 192–208. Springer, Heidelberg (2014)
15. Laycock, G.T.: The Theory and Practice of Specification Based Software Testing. Ph.D. thesis, University of Sheffield (1993)
16. Zhang, Q., Cheng, L., Boutaba, R.: Cloud computing: state-of-the-art and research challenges. J. Internet Serv. Appl. **1**(1), 7–18 (2010)

Model-Based Testing for Composite Web Services in Cloud Brokerage Scenarios

Mariam Kiran[1] and Anthony J.H. Simons[2(✉)]

[1] School of Electrical Engineering and Computer Science,
University of Bradford, Bradford BD7 4DP, UK
m.kiran@bradford.ac.uk
[2] Department of Computer Science, University of Sheffield,
Regent Court, 211 Portobello, Sheffield S1 4DP, UK
a.j.simons@sheffield.ac.uk

Abstract. Cloud brokerage is an enabling technology allowing various services to be merged together for providing optimum quality of service for the end-users. Within this collection of composed services, testing is a challenging task which brokers have to take on to ensure quality of service. Most Software-as-a-Service (SaaS) testing has focused on high-level test generation from the functional specification of individual services, with little research into how to achieve sufficient test coverage of composite services. This paper explores the use of model-based testing to achieve testing of composite services, when two individual web services are tested and combined. Two example web services – a login service and a simple shopping service – are combined to give a more realistic shopping cart service. This paper focuses on the test coverage required for testing the component services individually and their composition. The paper highlights the problems of service composition testing, requiring a reworking of the combined specification and regeneration of the tests, rather than a simple composition of the test suites; and concludes by arguing that more work needs to be done in this area.

1 Introduction

Cloud computing is becoming a prevalent business paradigm for software delivery and services, allowing businesses to save on the costs of infrastructure, maintenance and personnel [1]. To enable this, complex cloud computing environments are emerging that support new business models for cloud service and infrastructure providers, to help manage this increase in demand. Among the various cloud scenarios such as private, public and multi-cloud scenarios, cloud brokerage is one which is quickly becoming popular and difficult to manage.

Cloud brokerage is still an active research area, bringing challenges of risk, security and trust [2, 3] and further issues in terms of how brokers handle services, recommend optimal infrastructures and perform cloud service quality checking when they link customers to cloud environments [4]. By acting as an intermediary between the service consumers and providers, the brokers are expected to ensure that all requirements of the services are met and delivered on time.

© Springer International Publishing Switzerland 2015
G. Ortiz and C. Tran (Eds.): ESOCC 2014, CCIS 508, pp. 190–205, 2015.
DOI: 10.1007/978-3-319-14886-1_18

Given the need for mechanisms to assure the quality of service for risk and security, testing of the services is another challenging and expensive task, with brokers scrutinizing infrastructures and applications over issues of reliability, functionality and performance. Cloud services consist of using service-oriented architecture applications which focus on Software-as-a-Service (SaaS) functionality. A large body of literature exists focusing on how various functional attributes of services can be tested using approaches like fault-based testing, model-based testing and interoperability testing [11]. However, these approaches have focused on specific individual services being used independently.

This paper contributes to the area of service testing by focusing on the principles of functional testing for composed cloud services. The paper describes how the specification of the composite service needs to be reworked and the service tested again, even after the individual services have passed all test cases. This is due to issues of interoperability and integration of the components in the new composite service, which interact in ways not anticipated in the original component specifications. A model-based testing tool [30] is used to demonstrate systematically the kind of test coverage required to achieve the same levels of quality assurance for simple and composed software services. The tool attempts to automate the testing procedure as much as possible.

The paper has been organized in the following manner: Sect. 1 presents an introduction to cloud brokerage and the testing challenges for individual web services. Section 2 discusses the related work in this domain, discussing cloud environments and the test research used to produce test suites for services. Section 3 describes the model based testing approach, with examples of two web services: the login and the shopping services. Section 4 discusses the issues when the two services are composed to produce a composite shopping cart service. Finally Sects. 5 and 6 present the problems encountered, leading to the conclusions of this paper and the future work in this domain.

2   Related Work

2.1   Testing in Cloud Brokerage Ecosystems

Cloud computing adopts three broad styles of software architecture, when communicating between nodes. These are as follows:

- HTTP requests and responses, known as Representational State Transfer (REST). This is a "lightweight" approach, where the client is a simple web-browser and data is transferred in compact HTTP formats; but it requires bespoke server-side processing to dispatch requests.
- Service-Oriented Architecture (SOA) adopts XML standards, using SOAP for message communication, WSDL and UDDI for service description and discovery. SOA technology supports open, extensible, federated and composable architecture and fosters the separate development of autonomous, modular software components, which can be reconfigured in various ways before usage [5]. In this respect, SOA is vendor-diverse, offering the prospect of reusable, interoperable web-services [6], also offering a means of describing and measuring the Quality-of-Service (QoS) arising out of the distributed nature of services [7, 8].

- An increasingly popular style uses bespoke rich-client desktops, providing app-like services that use continuous information trickle via AJAX to communicate with back-end servers. Rich-client applications are developed in client-side scripting languages, such as JavaScript, resulting in *thick client* MVC applications. This architecture presents a different set of testing challenges [9, 10] and like RESTful services, does not lead to homogeneity.

Much research has been conducted into developing tools to test SOA, which arguably may also apply to the cloud [11]. However, clouds are more challenging due to their heterogeneous nature, involving many different kinds of stakeholders, integrating many packages that operate asynchronously. Cloud brokers are faced with merging services of more than one of the above kinds, to assess the trustworthiness of composite applications desired by consumers. This involves assessing and certifying complex service oriented applications which are composed of distributed software services that can be selected dynamically, assembled together and executed to produce evolving software ecosystems.

2.2 Functional Testing Approaches for Composite Web Services

Web services use open standards and are quite flexible to accommodate fault tolerance, security or performance requirements [12]. A few approaches [9–11] have developed finite state-based testing methods, recognizing the state-based nature of services, but find it necessary to augment web standards and provider-based testing of services, using translations from agreed web standards [7]. Further work [29] has used labelled transition systems to define the testing of web services, based on their protocols. While web services may be used individually, accessed through simple HTTP or SMTP protocols, a more interesting prospect is when they are combined in more complex applications.

Figure 1 describes a typical service-oriented architecture, in which communication takes place between three actors: the service provider, the service requester (also known as the consumer) and the service broker. The service provider publishes (1) a service interface (WSDL) to the broker's UDDI registry. The service requester then contacts the UDDI registry to discover (2) a suitable service and find out who the provider is; and then the broker acts as intermediary (3) in closing the deal. The service requester thereafter communicates with the service provider directly (4) using the SOAP message protocol. Since all SOAP data is transmitted as XML, the service provider may validate service requests; likewise the requester may validate the response from the provider, using a suitable XSD file (XML Schema).

In cloud computing environments, the providers are responsible for providing the necessary SOA infrastructure middleware and infrastructural mechanisms for service discovery, discovery to service providers, consumers and integrators. Brokers can act as service integrators, using existing services to create composite services to create an end user application. In such cases, brokers are responsible for developing guidelines for testing composites of various types. This involves employing a range of composition mechanisms (e.g. WSBPEL, application-embedded, WS-CDL).

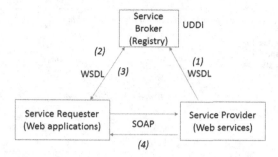

Fig. 1. Interaction between provider, requester and broker in SOA c.f. [31].

Testing composed services involves a workflow management to make interoperability possible by focusing on the interfaces for data transfer. Researchers have used Mealy models for defining complex state based operations in services [14] or data driven approaches to OWL-S [15, 16], however these fail to describe how different test suites for services can be merged if individual services are tested.

3   Towards a Methodology for Composite Service Testing for Cloud Brokerage

3.1   Testing During the Cloud Service Lifecycle

Kiran et al. [17] have described the use of model-based testing for cloud brokerage scenarios. Model-based testing depends on some kind of model specification, either a state-based specification, or a functional specification, or a combination, such as UML with OCL[1] pre- and post-conditions; essentially using any modelling formalism with a formal language grammar [18, 19]. The model serves as an oracle when generating tests for the system, linking specific test inputs with expected outputs [11, 20], deriving the correct results for the tests. The test generation algorithm also uses the model to determine the necessary and sufficient test coverage, given some reasonable assumptions about the system-under-test [20].

Figure 2 illustrates how broker-managed testing might be organised during the onboarding phase of the service lifecycle. The diagram shows the development stages for service *specification*, which describes the service formally, *test generation*, which produces abstract test sequences directly from the specification, and *grounding*, which translates the high-level tests into concrete tests capable of execution on a given service architecture [17], after which the concrete test suite may be used to test a service implementation to produce pass/fail test reports. Testing during the service onboarding phase is likely to be an important part of service certification by brokers. Testing will still be carried out as usual by service providers during the service engineering phase; and potential service consumers may also wish to re-test the services that they include in service compositions, for added quality assurance.

---

[1] Object Constraint Language, part of the Unified Modelling Language.

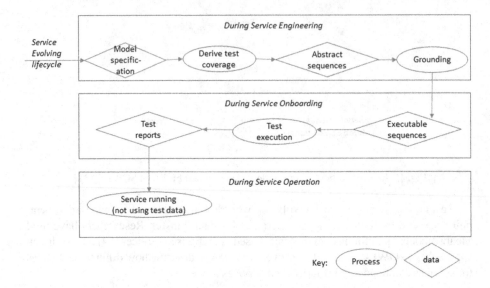

Fig. 2. Service evolution through the lifecycle when services are engineered, tested during onboarding, and when deployed to execute on the infrastructure.

3.2 Testing Considerations for Composed Web Services

The following general quality assurance considerations apply to platforms offering service discovery, conformance testing, and service composition [13, 24], where test case generation, execution and verdict assignment can be focused according to the service lifecycle stage:

1. Testing service discovery, as part of the Service Engineering phase.

   a. Define what properties should be described.
   b. Define how to query against them efficiently.

2. Testing service composition, as part of the Service Engineering phase.

   a. Specify the goals of a composition.
   b. Specify the constraints on a composition.
   c. Build a composition from component services.
   d. Analyse the composition.

3. Testing data flows, during the Service Onboarding phase.

   a. How to keep initial data separated
   b. How to track data movement between services
   c. How to provide the transactional guarantees.

During composite service testing, component services are treated as pieces to be glued together. This gives rise to the naïve idea that composed test-sets might be derived cheaply by considering how the services are combined. Services can be combined in three ways: (1) *sequentially,* by ordering services one after the other - this is equivalent to joining two services on their respective final and initial states; (2) *concurrently,* when the combined services are executing together in parallel - this is not tractable, since every action of one service could interleave at any point with the actions of the other; and (3) *decision-based,* a variant of sequential combination, where the path to follow depends on a condition [25] (Fig. 3).

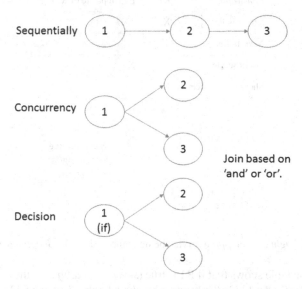

Fig. 3. Sequential, concurrent and decision arrangement when composing services.

Other researchers have used various approaches for composite testing using model checking for temporal logic using finite state machines [21] or using rule-based services [22]. Enkatraman et al. [23] showed a dynamic verification of protocol compliance in commitments modelled using auction behaviour. Tsai et al. [26] used rank and fault detection to find the capability of test scripts to establish an oracle for most test inputs to test the complete composite service. Endo et al. [27] employed an event-driven model approach to support the test model and generation, to test the environment and also support test concretization (grounding) and test execution.

4   Generating Model-Based Test Suites for Composite Services

The eventual goal of composite service testing is to make it easier for the average developer to produce high-quality tests for composed services, possibly on-the-fly at run-time. In the naïve approach, tests are created and archived for each component service, but are combined by rule at a later stage. The example in Fig. 4 presumes that a *Login* service and simple *Shopping* service are to be composed as an authenticated *ShoppingCart* service. Decision-based composition initially seems to be appropriate, under the condition specified in Table 1:

Table 1. Decision Table for *ShoppingCart* service.

		Rules	
Constraints		R1	R2 (opposite of R1)
Server is Ready		X	¬X
Next Action			
Login service			X
Shopping Service		X	

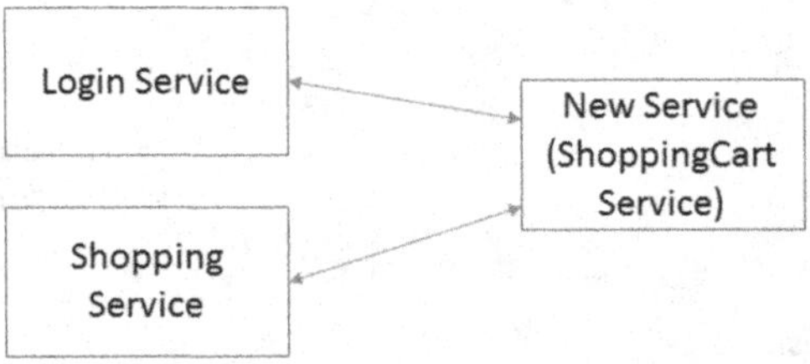

Fig. 4. The *Login* and *Shopping* service being combined for the *ShoppingCart* service.

The decision table shows that if R1 is true (*server is ready*) then the *Shopping* initial state is reached, else the *Login* final state is reached. Such a decision table can help build composed services, based on the constraint rules, by conditionally joining their state transition graphs. The testing procedure could be something like:

1. Generate test cases.

   a. Generate and store all paths for the *Login* service.
   b. Generate and store all paths for the *Shopping* service.

2. Combine test cases.

   a. Generate a decision table for the combined *ShoppingCart* service.
   b. Create joined test sequences by combining paths.
   c. Create concrete test inputs for the combined paths.

We will show that this approach is inadequate, because of a faulty intuition about sequential (and hence decision-based) composition. A different model of composition is required to express faithfully what happens when services are joined.

4.1 Login and Shopping Services Modelled Separately

First we introduce the FSM concepts briefly to show how the test suites for each web service are generated. FSMs consist of a finite number of states, one of which is an initial

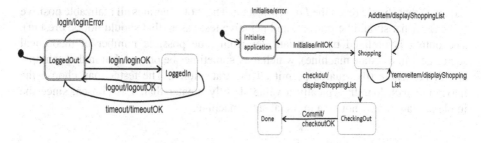

Fig. 5. FSM for *Login* Service and *Shopping* Service

```
<TestSuite id="0" testDepth="1">
  <Notice id="1" text="Generated test suite for service: LoginService">
    <Analysis id="2" text="Exploring all paths up to length: 1"/>
    <Analysis id="3" text="Number of theoretical sequences: 9"/>
    <Analysis id="4" text="Number of infeasible sequences: 0"/>
    <Analysis id="5" text="Number of executable sequences: 9"/>
  </Notice>
  <TestSequence id="6" state="LoggedOut" path="0">
    <TestStep id="7" name="create/ok" state="LoggedOut" verify="true">
      <Operation id="8" name="create"/>
    </TestStep>
  </TestSequence>
  <TestSequence id="9" state="LoggedOut" path="1">
    <TestStep id="10" name="create/ok" state="LoggedOut">
      <Operation id="11" name="create"/>
    </TestStep>
    <TestStep id="12" name="login/ok" state="LoggedIn" verify="true">
      <Operation id="13" name="login">
        <Input id="14" name="userName" type="String">Jane Good</Input>
        <Input id="15" name="password" type="String">serendipity</Input>
      </Operation>
    </TestStep>
  </TestSequence>

  <!-- other sequences omitted for brevity -->
</TestSuite>
```

Fig. 6. Fragment of a test suite generated for the *Login* Service. Some data from the above XML has been omitted for reasons of brevity.

state and the rest are intermediate and final states. To model the execution of a web service, every transition in a FSM corresponds to a web request/response cycle. Figure 5 shows the FSMs for two component services, the *Login* service and the simple *Shopping* service. These figures are the visual representation of the specifications, developed in a model-based specification language [30], which defines all states, transitions, service requests and responses received. Based on these specifications, the model-based testing tool creates test suites for both the *Login* and the *Shopping* service.

Figure 6 shows a fragment of the transition cover test set generated for the *Login* service. This reaches every state, and explores every single transition from each state. This fragment shows just the first two sequences from this test set, which represent the initial (empty) sequence that should reach the *LoggedOut* state; and a valid login sequence that should reach the *LoggedIn* state. The tool generates all realizable positive test cases (that should be present) and negative test cases (that should not be present). The output is prefixed by metadata describing the possible number of theoretical sequences (in the state machine), which may sometimes be pruned, but in this example are all realizable (the guards permit all the transitions). The tester may choose the maximum path length; typically a value slightly greater than 1 is chosen, since the implementation may not be a minimal state machine.

4.2   Composing the Two Services as a ShoppingCart Service

When these two services are merged together to produce a composed service, they are *not* actually joined in any linear fashion on their initial and final states, but rather, the entire behaviour of the *Shopping* state machine is embedded inside the *LoggedIn* state of the *Login* machine. The correct composition model for this is to use nested state machines, known as *Compound FSMs* or *Hierarchical FSMs* [28].

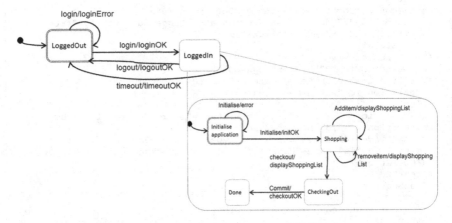

Fig. 7. *ShoppingCart* Service FSM (Composite service of *Login* and *Shopping* Services)

If we adopt the semantics from Harel and UML state machines, then any transition entering the *LoggedIn* superstate is deemed to enter the initial substate of the embedded *Shopping* machine; and any transition exiting this superstate is deemed to exit every contained substate. It is then possible to flatten this hierarchical FSM, to remove the superstate and create an equivalent flat state machine. According to Ipate [28], there are two possible strategies for generating tests for hierarchical FSMs:

- Flatten the hierarchical model and generate tests for the flattened machine – this is adequate, but produces much larger test sets, as a result of the transition explosion resulting from longer paths to reach all states;
- Treat the state hierarchy as a kind of refinement, and develop separate test suites for the external and internal FSMs, finding some way to integrate the expanded sequences for paths that traverse a superstate boundary.

The first approach was applied to the model in Fig. 7, yielding the flattened model in Fig. 8. The *login/loginOK* transition to the *LoggedIn* superstate was replaced by a transition from *LoggedOut* to the *InitialiseApplication* initial state of the embedded *Shopping* service. All of the *Shopping* service's substates were then given exit transitions for every exit transition leaving the *LoggedIn* superstate in the *Login* machine. They acquired additional transitions *timeout/timeoutok* and *logout/logoutok* as shown in Fig. 8.

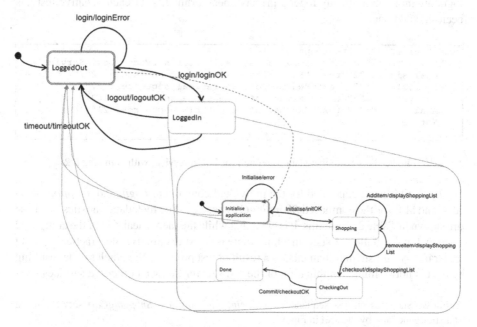

Fig. 8. Flattening the *ShoppingCart* Service FSM. For brevity, the substate exit transitions for timeout/timeoutOK and logout/logoutOK are each represented by single arrow.

5   Experimental Test Generation Results

The objective of this research was to investigate the two testing methods described by Ipate [28], using our testing tool for software services [30]. Initially, we expected the flattening approach to be computationally expensive, resulting from an exponential growth in test suite size. The hierarchical FSM modelling approach then might point the way towards a smarter refinement testing strategy.

In practice, the testing tool reduces the number of theoretical sequences generated for flattened examples, by pruning tests that either cannot be executed, or which replicate the results of other tests. Initially the tool generates all positive paths (which must exist) and all negative paths (which must not). However, once a negative transition has been proven absent, then all longer sequences containing this as a prefix may be pruned (assuming that memory is unchanged when an event is ignored). Similarly, the set of all positive paths includes some unrealizable sequences (blocked by guards on the current input and memory); so these are impossible, even in the specification, and are also pruned.

Figure 9 shows the metadata generated by a longer test of the *Login* service, where the maximum path length has been increased to 2 (anticipating one redundant state per desired state in the implementation). The count of infeasible sequences includes all pruned sequences; in this case, paths containing negative prefixes (such as a repeated login attempt when already logged in) have been pruned, after each negative test has been satisfied once.

```
<TestSuite id="0" testDepth="2">
  <Notice id="1" text="Generated test suite for service: LoginService">
    <Analysis id="2" text="Exploring all paths up to length: 2"/>
    <Analysis id="3" text="Number of theoretical sequences: 37"/>
    <Analysis id="4" text="Number of infeasible sequences: 16"/>
    <Analysis id="5" text="Number of executable sequences: 21"/>
  </Notice>
  ...
```

Fig. 9. Test Suite metadata generated for Login service, with path length 2.

Test suites were generated for the individual component *Login* and *Shopping* services, and also for the composed *ShoppingCart* service. The metadata statistics for these are shown in Table 2. From this, it is clear that while the theoretical size of the composed test set for the flattened state machine increases exponentially, the practical test set generated is a lot smaller than this, as a result of test pruning. Nonetheless, the resulting test set is not a simple combination of the test sets for the two composed services.

Table 2. Statistics on test sequences for *Login*, *Shopping* and *ShoppingCart* services using statistics generated by the tool in Fig. 9.

	LoginService (depth = 1)	LoginService (depth = 2)	Shopping Service (depth = 2)	Shopping Service (depth = 3)	Shopping Cart Service (depth = 2)	Shopping Cart Service (depth = 3)
Theoretical Sequences	9	37	151	907	511	5111
Infeasible sequences	0	16	120	846	372	4735
Executable sequences	9	21	31	61	139	376

The testing tool reported that a path length of 3 was eventually necessary to cover all the transitions of the *ShoppingCart* service. This is because operations depended on particular values of memory variables, such as an item necessarily being present in the cart, before proceeding to checkout. Because of the longer paths explored through the combined machine, we expected a steep rise in the number of test sequences generated.

The theoretical test suite size grows exponentially with longer paths; an upper bound[2] may be estimated from the recurrence relation: $C*\Sigma\alpha^k$, where C is the size of the state cover, α is the size of the event alphabet, and k increments from zero to the maximum path length. Nonetheless, Table 2 shows that in some cases (as with this example), it might be tractable to compose state-based specifications by embedding and then generate tests from the equivalent flattened specification; after all, a test suite consisting of 376 tests sequences is not actually terrible, particularly if test generation and test execution are automated.

Looking at the degree of pruning in the original component services, it is clear that the greatest reduction in test suite size was contributed by the simple *Shopping* service, for which the tool pruned 93 % of the theoretical test paths (at *depth* = 3), which were found to be either redundant or non-realizable. This is intuitively due to the "staged" nature of a shopping application, where many operations are disabled in particular states; and this only needs to be proved once for each operation. By contrast, fewer paths were pruned for the *Login* service. For the composite service, 92 % of paths were pruned (at *depth* = 3), which is highly useful.

Considering the theoretical test explosion in Table 2, it is attractive to speculate whether it might be possible to generate test suites for composite services by composing (in a more principled fashion) the test suites generated for the component services. It is clear that this will be no simple pooling of the component test suites; one would need to generate additional "glue sequences" to verify that the two machines were correctly joined together. Ipate previously speculated on the idea of refining the paths of the outer machine, by splicing in all paths through the nested machine, when the outer paths traverse the relevant superstate boundary [28]. In the conclusions below, we suggest an approach in which certain simplifying assumptions about the composed services allow you to identify sets of "glue sequences".

6   Conclusions and Future Work

This paper set out to determine whether it was tractable to develop test suites for composite software services either by reusing the test suites generated for the component services, or by reusing the component specifications in some way. From the theory of testing FSM-based specifications, we expected to find that there was no easy way of reusing the component test suites to achieve the same level of coverage of the composite service. However, we found that it is possible to compose and flatten state machine specifications, and from this, regenerate all-new tests for the composite service, to the same level of coverage. The test suites for the composite service turned out to be more tractable than anticipated, due to the test path pruning behaviour of the testing tool [30], which eliminates redundant paths with null-op transitions in the prefix, and unrealizable paths for which tests cannot be executed.

---

[2] Some sequences computed by the recurrence relation already exist in the state cover; the actual test suite is a set and contains no duplicate sequences.

To achieve any better reduction than this requires making quite strong assumptions about the services being composed. The most important assumption is that the *sets of events processed by each service do not intersect*; this allows consideration of the behaviour of each service in isolation. Without this assumption, when testing the composite service, the events of both FSMs must be pooled and many more negative tests are required, to demonstrate a lack of mutual interference between the FSMs. However, if the non-intersection assumption holds, then it is feasible to consider an approach where a composite test suite consisting of the component test suites, plus some additional "glue sequences", might be thought satisfactory. For the composed *Shopping Cart* service, the glue sequences would have to ensure that:

- Every transition of the *Login* service entering the *LoggedIn* state also enters (or enters instead) the initial state of the *Shopping* service.
- Every transition of the *Login* service exiting the *LoggedIn* state also exits every state in the *Shopping* service and targets the *LoggedOut* state.

Depending on whether the *LoggedIn* state is preserved, or expanded away in the composition, the first glue sequence may be considered additional, or a replacement for one of the *Login* service's sequences. The remaining glue sequences must reach the state cover of the inner nested FSM, and then exercise the "glue transitions" leading back to the outer machine. This "extended state cover" is easily constructed by prefixing the state cover of the nested *Shopping* machine by the sequence from the *Login* machine that reaches the *LoggedIn* superstate. Altogether, in this example, there would be nine "glue sequences": one path to verify that the *login/loginOK* entry transition reaches the *Shopping* initial state; and two paths for each *Shopping* state, to verify that the *logout/logoutOK* and *timeout/timeoutOK* exit transitions lead back to the *LoggedOut* state.

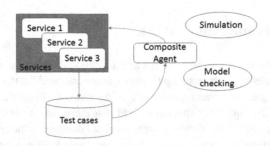

Fig. 10. Using composite agents to test composite web services.

Figure 10 sketches one possible architecture for testing composite services. The idea is based around a composition tool, here called a *Composite Agent*, that is able to reason in the manner described above, when composing FSM specifications. The agent would have access to the database of service specifications (the specifications include a high-level FSM describing control states, plus a more detailed description of the service's operations and their effects on memory [30]), and from this, would be able to calculate the additional "glue sequences" required, when services were composed by embedding one service's FSM inside a state of the other FSM. These "glue sequences" could be returned, on demand, along with the available test-suites for testing each of the individual component services.

The advantages of such an approach includes the fact that "glue sequences" could be generated on-the-fly, as services were composed dynamically. This would be very useful for creating "late integration" test suites, assuming that the components had already been tested. Secondly, the approach is very flexible: in principle, any service could be embedded inside any state of any other service; and multiple services could be composed, by embedding each component service in a different superstate of the composite service. This approach is also fully compositional, in that FSMs could be nested to arbitrary depths.

The drawbacks of this approach include the strong assumption that must be made about the non-interference of FSMs. This is partly mitigated by the fact that the *Composite Agent* may check that the alphabets of each composed machine do not intersect (assuring the separation of machines, in principle). As described above, the "glue transitions" do not anticipate any redundancy in the implementation. They only verify every single-step test obligation needed to show that the composed services appear to be properly connected. However, it would also be possible to generate slightly longer sequences that guarantee this with a higher level of confidence (c.f. testing redundant EFSM implementations with slightly longer paths [20]).

Compound services are a complex and interesting proposition for testing. Further work needs to explore how full automated test suites can be generated from individual test suites plus "glue sequences". The ideal solution should make use of component specifications, which may be composed on-the-fly. Such a capability would be of great advantage to cloud service brokers.

Acknowledgment. The research leading to these results has received funding from the European Union Seventh Framework Programme (FP7/2007-2013) under grant agreement no. 328392, the Broker@Cloud project (http://www.broker-cloud.eu).

References

1. Buyya, R., Yeo, C.S., Venugopal, S., Broberg, J., Brandic, I.: Cloud computing and emerging IT platforms: vision, hype, and reality for delivering computing as 5th utility. Future Gener. Comput. Syst. **25**, 599–616 (2008)
2. Khan, A.U., Kiran, M., Oriol, M., Jiang, M., Djemame, K.: Security risks and their management in cloud computing. In: CloudCom, pp. 121–128 (2012)
3. Kiran, M., Jiang, D., Armstrong, K., Djemame, K.: Towards a service life cycle-based methodology for risk assessment in cloud computing. In: Cloud and Green Computing (2011)
4. Plummer, D.C., Lheureux, B.J., Karamouzis, F.: Defining Cloud Services Brokerage: Taking Intermediation to the Next Level. Report ID G00206187, Gartner Inc. (2010)
5. Bell, M.: Introduction to service-oriented modeling. In: Bell, M. (ed.) Service-Oriented Modeling: Service Analysis, Design, and Architecture, p. 3. Wiley, Hoboken (2008). ISBN 978-0-470-14111-3
6. Arcitura Education Inc.: Service Orientation. http://serviceorientation.com/ (2012)

7. Norton, D., Feiman, J., McDonald, N., Pezzini, M., Natis, Y., Sholler, D., Heiden, G., Karamouzis, F., Young, A., James, G.A., Knipp, E., Duggan, J., Murphy, T., Valdes, R., Blechar, M., Driver, M., Young, G., Vining, J., Knox, R., Feinberg, D., Hart, T., Patrick, C., Forsman, J., Basso, M., Simpson, R., Adachi, Y., Clark, W., King, M., Hill, J., Gootzit, D., Bradley, A., Kenney, L., Stang, D.: Hype Cycle for Application Development, Gartner (2009)
8. Mei, H., Zhang, L.: A framework for testing web services and its supporting tool. In: Proceedings of IEEE International Workshop on Service-Oriented System Engineering, pp. 199–206. Computer Society (2005)
9. Marchetto, A., Tonella, P., Ricca, F.: State-based testing of Ajax web applications. In: Proceedings of the International Conference on Software Testing, Verification and Validation, pp. 121–130. IEEE Computer Society (2008). doi:10.1109/ICST.2008.22
10. Mesbah, A., Roest, D.: Invariant-based automatic testing of modern web applications. IEEE Trans. Softw. Eng. **38**(1), 35–53 (2012)
11. Bozkurt, M., Harman, M., Hassoun, Y.: Testing & verification in service-oriented architecture: a survey. Softw. Test. Verification Reliab. (2009). doi:10.1002/000
12. Web Services Architecture (W3C Working Group)
13. Hull, R., Su, J.: Tools for Design of Composite Web Services, Presented Version, 17 June 2004. http://www.cs.ucsb.edu/~su/tutorials/sigmod2004.html
14. Mealy, G.H.: A method to synthesizing sequential circuits. Bell Syst. Tech. J. **34**, 1045–1079 (1955)
15. Klusch, M., Gerber, A.: Evaluation of Service Composition Planning with OWLS-XPlan. http://www-ags.dfki.uni-sb.de/~klusch/i2s/klusch-evaluation-owlsXPlan.pdf
16. Norton, B., Foster, S., Hughes, A.: A Compositional Operational Semantics for OWL-S. www.dip.deri.org/documents/Norton-et-al-A-Compositional-Semantics-for-OWL-S.pdf
17. Kiran, M., Friesen, A., Simons, A.J., Schwach, W.K.: Model-based testing in cloud brokerage scenarios. In: Lomuscio, A.R., Nepal, S., Patrizi, F., Benatallah, B., Brandić, I. (eds.) ICSOC 2013. LNCS, vol. 8377, pp. 192–208. Springer, Heidelberg (2014)
18. Utting, M., Legeard, B.: Practical Model-Based Testing: A Tools Approach. Morgan-Kaufmann, Burlington (2007)
19. Pretschner, A., Philipps, J.: 10 methodological issues in model-based testing. In: Broy, M., Jonsson, B., Katoen, J.-P., Leucker, M., Pretschner, A. (eds.) Model-Based Testing of Reactive Systems. LNCS, vol. 3472, pp. 281–291. Springer, Heidelberg (2005)
20. Holcombe, W.M.L., Ipate, F.: Correct Systems - Building a Business Process Solution. Applied Computing Series. Springer, Berlin, Heidelberg, New York (1998)
21. Fu, X., Bultan, T., Su, J.: Analysis of interacting Bpel web services. In: Proceedings of the 13th International Conference on World Wide Web, pp. 621–630. ACM Press (2004)
22. Deutsch, S., Vianu, A.: Specification and Verification of Data Driven Web Services (2004)
23. Venkatraman, M., Singh, M.P.: Verifying compliance with commitment protocols. Auton. Agent. Multi-Agent Syst. **2**, 217–236 (1999)
24. Cao, T., Felix, P., Castanet, R., Berrada, I.: Online testing framework for web services. In: Proceedings 3rd International Conference on Software Testing, Verification and Validation, pp. 363–372. IEEE Computer Society (2010). doi:10.1109/ICST.2010.11
25. Belli, F., Linschulte, M.: An Event-Based Approach, April 2009
26. Tsai, W.T., Chen, Y., Paul, R., Liao, N., Huang, H.: Cooperative and Group Testing in Verification of Dynamic Composite Web Services (2011)
27. Endo, A.T., Silveira, M.B., Macedo, E., Simao, R., de Oliveiray, F.M., Zorzo, A.F.: Using models to test web service-oriented applications: an experience report (2012)
28. Ipate, F.: Test selection for hierarchical and communicating finite state machines. Comput. J. **52**(3), 334–347 (2009)

29. Bertolino, A., Frantzen, L., Polini, A., Tretmans, J.: Audition of web services for testing conformance to open specified protocols. In: Reussner, R., Stafford, J.A., Ren, X.-M. (eds.) Architecting Systems with Trustworthy Components. LNCS, vol. 3938, pp. 1–25. Springer, Heidelberg (2006)
30. Simons, A.J.H.: Cloud Service Quality Control: Broker@Cloud Verification and Testing Tool Suite (2014). http://staffwww.dcs.shef.ac.uk/people/A.Simons/broker/
31. Wu, B., Zhou, B., Xi, L.: Remote multi-robot monitoring and control system based on MMS and web services. Ind. Robot: Int. J. **34**(3), 225–239 (2007)

Towards a Generic Language
for Scalability Rules

Jörg Domaschka[1]([✉]), Kyriakos Kritikos[2], and Alessandro Rossini[3]

[1] Institute of Information Resource Management, University of Ulm, Ulm, Germany
joerg.domaschka@uni-ulm.de
[2] FORTH, Heraklion, Greece
kritikos@ics.forth.gr
[3] Department of Networked Systems and Services, SINTEF, Oslo, Norway
alessandro.rossini@sintef.no

Abstract. The PaaSage project aims at facilitating the specification and execution of cloud-based applications by leveraging upon model-driven engineering (MDE) techniques and methods, and by exploiting multiple cloud infrastructures and platforms. Models are frequently specified using domain-specific languages (DSLs), which are tailored to a specific domain of concern. In order to cover the necessary aspects of the specification and execution of multi-cloud applications, PaaSage encompasses a family of DSLs called Cloud Application Modelling and Execution Language (CAMEL). In this paper, we present one DSL within this family, namely the Scalability Rules Language (SRL), which can be regarded as a first step towards a generic language for specifying scalability rules for multi-cloud applications.

Keywords: Model-driven engineering · Domain-specific language · Metamodel · Cloud computing · Scalability rule

1 Introduction

Model-driven engineering (MDE) is a branch of software engineering that aims at improving the productivity, quality, and cost-effectiveness of software development by shifting the paradigm from code-centric to model-centric. MDE promotes the use of models and model transformations as the primary assets in software development, where they are used to specify, simulate, generate, and manage software systems. This approach is particularly relevant when it comes to the specification and execution of multi-cloud applications (*i.e.*, applications that can be deployed across multiple private, public, or hybrid cloud infrastructures and platforms), which allow for exploiting the peculiarities of each cloud service and hence optimising performance, availability, and cost of the applications.

According to MDE, a system may be modelled as a combination of models specified through general-purpose languages, which cover generic information such as requirements and use cases, along with models specified through domain-specific

© Springer International Publishing Switzerland 2015
G. Ortiz and C. Tran (Eds.): ESOCC 2014, CCIS 508, pp. 206–220, 2015.
DOI: 10.1007/978-3-319-14886-1_19

languages (DSLs), which cover specific information such as domain knowledge. Through this interplay of general-purpose and domain-specific languages, the different models cover all aspects of a system, including the aspects that are tailored to a specific domain of concern, at all the required levels of abstraction. As such, in order to cover the necessary aspects of the specification and execution of multi-cloud applications, the PaaSage project[1] encompasses a family of DSLs called Cloud Application Modelling and Execution Language (CAMEL) which have been specified in EMF Ecore [18] (the de-facto reference implementation of OMG's Essential Meta-Object Facility (EMOF) [10]). This family includes the Cloud Modelling Language (CLOUDML) [3,4], for modelling and enacting the provisioning and deployment of multi-cloud applications; Saloon [11–13], for specifying requirements and goals of multi-cloud applications; WS-Agreement [1], for modelling SLAs of web/cloud services; and Scalability Rules Language (SRL), for specifying scalability rules.

In this paper, we present SRL, which can be regarded as a first step towards a generic language for specifying scalability rules for multi-cloud applications. It comprises the appropriate modelling concepts for specifying noteworthy behavioural patterns of multi-cloud applications as well as the corresponding actions to change the provisioning and deployment model in response to these patterns. It is adopted in PaaSage in the life-cycle phase of execution for guaranteeing quality of service (QoS) levels (*cf.* D2.1.1 [15] and D2.1.2 [14]).

In general, scalability rules are associated with event patterns that lead to their triggering. In order to identify patterns in the application behaviour, component instances need to be monitored. Therefore, SRL provides mechanisms that can be used to: (a) express which components of an application will be monitored by which metrics or metric aggregators (aggregating measurements through formulas involving one or more metrics), (b) define patterns on the monitoring data, and (c) express actions that have to be executed when events occur that match the patterns.

SRL is based on scalability capabilities of existing cloud platforms and middleware. In particular, Amazon CloudWatch[2] and Cloudify's Automatic Scaling Rules[3] have served as a primary source of inspiration. Nevertheless, SRL goes beyond these two mechanisms as it is multi-cloud capable and does not depend on the capabilities offered by each cloud provider. Moreover, it enables combining existing metrics and associating them to event patterns to be assessed. The metric description used in SRL as well as parts of the terminology are taken from OWL-Q [8].

Compared to other related languages, SRL is more expressive and allows specifying behavioural patterns that only sophisticated complex event processing (CEP) languages can cover. Moreover, it allows specifying other kinds of required information, such as the concrete metrics to measure or the adaptation actions to perform. Furthermore, while most related languages assume the

---

[1] http://www.paasage.eu.

[2] http://aws.amazon.com/cloudwatch/.

[3] http://getcloudify.org/guide/2.7/developing/scaling_rules.html.

existence of predefined metrics, SRL enables the specification of custom metrics, which can then be used by monitoring systems to assess service level objectives (SLOs) and respective event patterns and by provisioning systems to perform the corresponding adaptation actions. Finally, although highly expressive, SRL caters for the specification of scalability rules at different levels of abstraction, depending on the goals of the modellers and their level of expertise: (a) either little information is modelled and predefined elements are used (*i.e.*, instances of classes) or (b) much information is modelled to customise the monitoring and assessment process.

The remainder of the paper is organised as follows. The next four sections concentrate on analysing the main information aspects of SRL, while Sect. 6 provides particular examples of its usage. Section 7 reviews related work. Finally, the last section concludes the paper and draws directions for further research.

2   Events

An SRL model consists of scalability rules. A scalability rule is associated with an event that leads to its triggering, and with actions that are performed when the scalability rule is triggered. Figure 1 shows the portion of the SRL metamodel that is related to events. This metamodel is specified in Ecore, and the basic attribute types such as **EString** and **EInt** are Ecore types that correspond to the respective **String** and **Integer** classes of Java.

An **Event** can be a **SimpleEvent** or a **CompositeEvent**. A **SimpleEvent** can either be functional (*i.e.*, functional error or failure of a component/cloud service; *e.g.*, a VM is down), or non-functional (*i.e.*, a violation of an SLO related to a particular QoS metric; *e.g.*, average availability SLO threshold was violated for a particular

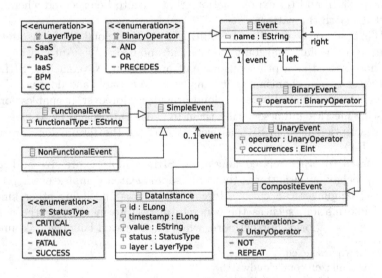

Fig. 1. Events portion of the SRL metamodel

component). We are currently investigating how to extend SRL to enable the specification of additional actions associated with functional events.

A CompositeEvent can either be a BinaryEvent or a UnaryEvent. A Binary-Event connects two other Events by a binary operator. These include common, logical operators such as AND and OR, but also time-based operators such as PRECEDES, which indicates that an event has to occur prior to another one. For instance, the condition A AND $(B$ OR $C)$ can be expressed as a BinaryEvent X_1 that comprises a SimpleEvent A and another BinaryEvent X_2 both connected by the AND operator. X_2, in turn, comprises two SimpleEvents B and C connected by the OR operator. A UnaryEvent is associated with just one event along with an operator such as NOT, which indicates that the negation of this event is required, or REPEAT, which indicates that its repetition is required. The attribute occurrences of UnaryEvent represents the number of repetitions for the latter case.

A DataInstance represents the actual (measurement) data associated with the events that occurred in the system (*e.g.*, the actual value measured, the component that produced the event, etc., see Sect. 4). Moreover, the attribute status represents the status of the event. This attribute may provide useful insight (*e.g.*, for performing off-line evaluation of the application performance) and also enables the evaluation/assessment of the events. The attribute layer represents the layer in the cloud stack where the event has occurred. IaaS or PaaS indicate that the event relates to IaaS or PaaS services used by an application, respectively, while SaaS indicates that the event relates to the application as a whole, or to a third-party SaaS (*e.g.*, Amazon Simple Email Service[4]). Additional (sub-)layers have been included in order to further distinguish different types of SaaS services: SCC (short for Service Composition) indicates that a service composition is concerned, while BPM (short for Business Process Management) indicates that business processes are concerned. The difference between these two layers lies on the fact that business processes are usually realised through service compositions and are therefore at a higher level of abstraction. For instance, a violation of a key performance indicator (KPI), which is critical for a business organisation, may be caused by a violation of an SLO threshold at the service composition layer that realises this business process.

3   Scheduling and Conditions

Figure 2 shows the portion of the SRL metamodel related to scheduling and conditions.

A Schedule represents any aspect of the operations (*e.g.*, measurements) that need to be executed on a regular, timely basis, such as when an operation will be run and when the scheduling shall end. The attribute type represents whether successive (operation) runs happen at a fixed rate or with a fixed delay. Moreover, the attribute intervalUnit represents the time unit used for a Schedule's interval. The difference between an interval-based and a rate-based scheduling is as follows: an interval-based scheduling ensures that the time between the end of

---

[4] http://aws.amazon.com/ses/.

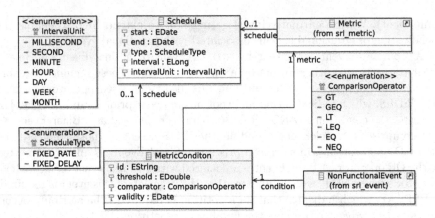

Fig. 2. Scheduling and Conditions portion of the SRL metamodel

one iteration and the start of the successive iteration is fixed, while a rate-based scheduling uses a constant time between the starts of two consecutive iterations.

Simple, non-functional events (see Sect. 2) are associated with MetricConditions, which are derived from the SLOs defined using WS-Agreement [1,14]. A MetricCondition is used to compare the measurement of a Metric (see Sect. 4) represented by the attribute value of DataInstance (see Sect. 2) to a threshold represented by the attribute threshold of MetricCondition. The comparison between the measured value and the threshold is performed according to a ComparisonOperator. The ComparisonOperator encompasses all possible comparison operators that can be used, *i.e.*, greater than or less than (including and excluding equality) as well as (in)equality. The point in time when a MetricCondition is evaluated is a choice of configuration. In case the MetricCondition is associated with a Schedule this evaluation is done based on time. Otherwise, it happens on every new measurement created for the metric of the associated event.

4   Sensors and Metrics

Figure 3 shows the portion of the SRL metamodel related to sensors and metrics.

A Metric represents a generic metric that can be associated with either raw measurements or aggregations on them. A MetricTemplate represents common metric information that might have been redundant if included directly in Metrics. Therefore, multiple Metric instances (mapping to different concrete metrics) can be associated with the very same MetricTemplate instance. A MetricTemplate does not include dynamic details such as how often the respective metric measurements are produced and which component instances on which cloud are concerned, which are attributed to the concept of a Metric. In contrast, the attribute type represents the kind of template and hence the kind of associated Metrics. RAW indicates that the associated metric refers to raw measurements, while COMPOSITE indicates that the associated metric is computed from other

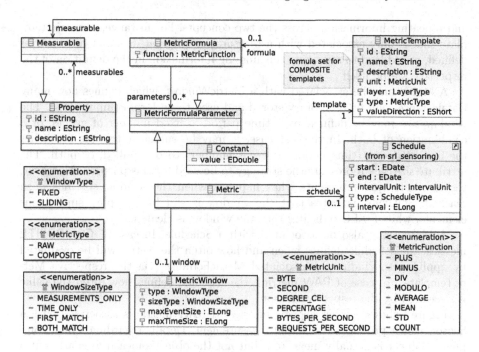

Fig. 3. Sensors and Metrics portion of the SRL metamodel

metrics. In the latter case, a MetricTemplate is associated with a MetricFormula, which represents the function that computes a metric template from other metric templates (*i.e.*, the formula from which one or more potential composite metrics that instantiate the metric template can be measured). A MetricTemplate is also associated with Measurable, which represents the attribute that the MetricTemplate (actually its associated metrics) measures.

For its computing task, a MetricFormula may be associated with one or more MetricFormulaParameters, which can be Constants or other MetricTemplates. The parameters are used as input to the function for computing the composite metric.

The need for a metric template is better illustrated by the following example. Assume that a COMPOSITE MetricTemplate *MT* is associated with a Measurable representing availability, as well as a MetricFormula representing the function to compute the availability. This MetricForumla is associated with MetricsFormulaParameters, which are another MetricTemplate representing uptime and a Constant representing the total measurement time space, and its result is the division of the metric template with the constant. Now, *MT* can be associated with different metrics that determine the availability for different components at different schedules. By associating *MT* with these metrics, it is not necessary to repeat any common information, such as the function to compute the availability, the measured attribute, and the value direction in these metrics. Please note that the common information specified by a metric template is the minimal one and cannot be further broken down without violating the respective semantics and repeating information across the two concepts. For instance, a metric template that is only associated with a Measurable, but that does not have a layer defined, would lead to repeating this missing information in the definition of the respective Metric itself.

A Metric may be associated with a MetricWindow, which defines how many DataInstances will be temporary stored and used to perform computations. The window size may be defined by a time period, a fixed number of events, or a combination of both. In the last case, it may be sufficient to wait for either the first attribute (time period or event number) to be fulfilled, or both. The attribute sizeType represents the strategy to be used for this purpose. Moreover, the attribute type represents what happens when the window size has been reached: SLIDING indicates that the window is slid by dropping superfluous elements, while FIXED indicates that the window is cleared.

A Metric may also be associated with a Schedule. In case of COMPOSITE metrics, the schedule defines when and how often the metric will be evaluated by applying the indirectly associated MetricFormula (via the respective MetricTemplate). In case of RAW metrics, the schedule defines how often the value is measured by the respective sensor.

Figure 4 shows further aspects metrics. A RAW metric is associated with a Sensor, which produces the actual measurement. Details regarding which component/object is actually measured (but not the object's measurable attribute) are exclusively covered by the MetricObjectBinding associated with the Metric. In particular, different components can be measured depending on the respective type of MetricObjectBinding, such as the application as a whole, one or more of its component instances, or one or more of the underlying virtual machine instances in a particular cloud.

Please note that the SRL metamodel enables to specify whether values are polled from the sensor by the metric (*i.e.*, by the service responsible for the collection of the metric measurements) or pushed by the sensor itself. Thus, it has been designed to cater for the two alternative realisations of a measurement architecture: either the measurement components (which produce aggregated

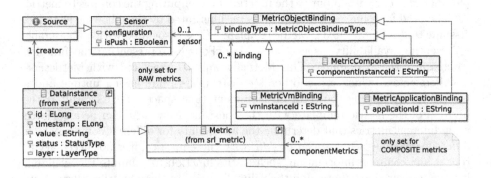

Fig. 4. Additionally modelled metric information in the SRL metamodel

measurement information) pull information from sensors, or the sensors push information to them.

5   Scalability Rules and Actions

Figure 5 illustrates the portion of the SRL metamodel related to scalability rules and actions.

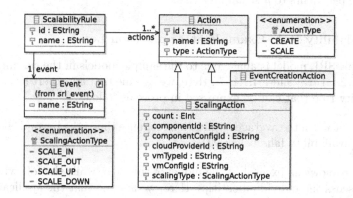

Fig. 5. Scalability Rules and Actions portion of the SRL metamodel

As mentioned, a ScalabilityRule is associated with an Event that leads to its triggering, and with Actions that are performed when the scalability rule is triggered. An Action can either be ScalingActions or EventCreationActions. A ScalingAction defines which entities of an application will be modified and how. The attribute scalingType represents how the affected entities will be changed, whereby SCALE_OUT, SCALE_IN, SCALE_UP, and SCALE_DOWN indicate the corresponding type of changes. The other attributes of ScalingAction reference the affected entities and also indicate their number (*e.g.*, the specific number of component instances to be added). The affected entities are actually associated (through an identifier) to their respective definition in the corresponding CLOUDML [3,4,14] provisioning and deployment model and can be associated with component and virtual machine instances, which carry respective configuration information. In this way, a ScalingAction encompasses all the necessary details to execute the four types of scaling action envisioned in PaaSage. An EventCreationAction, in contrast, represents that the application has reached a state where the current provisioning and deployment model may need to be checked by a component responsible for global rather than provider-specific adaptation. For instance, the scalability limit on a particular component has been reached and this component cannot be further adapted with a scale-out action.

6   Examples

In this section, we present how two common scalability requirements are represented in sample SRL models. The first example operates at the level of the application as a whole and considers the actions to take when availability drops below- or when response time exceeds a corresponding threshold. The second example operates at the level of a single component, namely a Couchbase distributed database, and maps empirical knowledge about the database gained through experiments to a scalability rule.

6.1   Scalability Rule Example at Application Level

This sample SRL model is analogous to the sample models in the running example from D2.1.1 [15] and D4.1.1 [7]. Here, we assume that an expert has provided a scalability rule that can be expressed in prose as follows:

> Scale out when the average application response time goes beyond 300 ms or its availability falls below 99 %.

Figure 6 shows an excerpt of the model of this rule, while the following paragraphs discuss the individual entities. Here, we assume that the application has an application identifier 12345.

The scalability rule requirements lead to a single BinaryEvent associated with two non-functional SimpleEvents connected by an OR operator. Each of the SimpleEvents is associated with an MetricCondition. The respective SLO conditions specify the thresholds of 300 ms and 99 %, respectively.

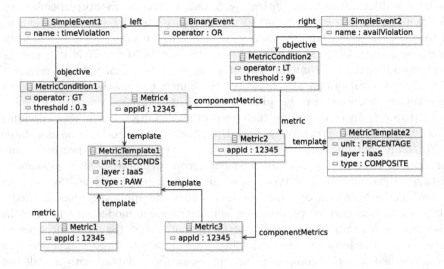

Fig. 6. A sample SRL model on application availability and response time (excerpt)

The two events above lead to two high-level metrics, respectively: Metric1 represents the response time and Metric2 represents the availability of the application. Both metrics are associated with their respective MetricTemplates. The response time is a RAW metric, as the response time is directly measured by a sensor. The availability, in contrast, is a COMPOSITE metric, as it is computed by dividing Metric3, which represents the uptime, with a constant Constant1, which represents the total measurement time. In order to compute this metric, Metric2 is associated with a MetricFormula. We do not show the formula in this example but show one in the next example.

The metrics above lead to a single rule that is associated with a single Action. Yet, it is unknown to the rule processor how the scale out described in prose should take place. Therefore, the action will be an EventCreationAction that leaves the right decisions to a reasoning engine (*cf.* D1.6.1 [6]). We do not show the action in this example.

6.2 Scalability Rule Example at Component Level

A pattern that has been found particularly useful for scaling the Couchbase[5] distributed database [17] is the following: scale out the Couchbase component when all instances of that component deployed to a particular cloud have a CPU load beyond 50 % and at the same time at least one instance has a load beyond 85 %. The average over 5 min and 1 min need to be computed for the metrics mapping to the 50 % and 85 % thresholds, respectively. The sensors need to be queried once per second.

Figure 7 shows an excerpt of the SRL model of the above pattern, while the following paragraphs discuss the individual entities. In order to avoid clutter, this figure omits some composite metrics, which, however, are symmetric to the ones shown; it also omits the events created for this example. Here, we assume that: Couchbase has a component identifier 99-99; the cloud on which Couchbase is deployed has a cloud identifier 88-88; the 3 instances of Couchbase have component instance identifiers 1, 2, 3, respectively; and a CPU sensor is associated with each of these instances.

The scalability rule requirements lead to six simple, non-functional Events (see Table 1). In particular, these Events correspond to the condition that either of the three instances exceed the 50 % and 85 % threshold, respectively. The overall event connects the SimpleEvent by either AND or OR operators.

The events above lead to a RAW metric per monitored sensor, *i.e.*, to three symmetric Metrics, with a single, common MetricTemplate. The layer of this MetricTemplate is IaaS. Each of the Metrics is associated with the same Schedule gathering new data once per second. Each RAW metric is referred to by two COMPOSITE metrics that share a common MetricTemplate (*e.g.*, the metric measuring the raw CPU load for Couchbase instance 3 is associated with two composite CPU load metrics, which in turn are associated with the two different conditions that have to be assessed for the same instance). Furthermore, each of the last two

---

[5] http://www.couchbase.com/.

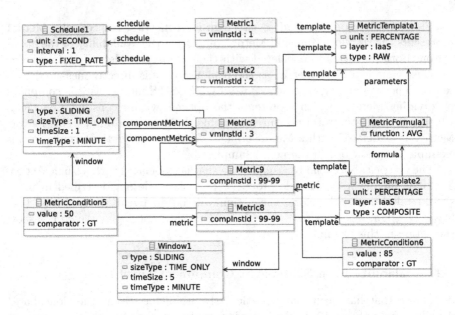

Fig. 7. A sample SRL model for Couchbase scalability rule (excerpt). Please note that for the sake of readability we put the information of the *MetricObjectBinding* in the Metrics.

Table 1. Events created for database scalability rule

NonFunctionalEvent	BinaryEvent
#e1: avg 50% load for 1 in 5 min	#e7: #e1 AND #e2
#e2: avg 50% load for 2 in 5 min	#e8: #e3 AND #e7
#e3: avg 50% load for 3 in 5 min	#e9: #e4 OR #e5
#e4: avg 85% load for 1 in 1 min	#e10: #e6 OR #e9
#e5: avg 85% load for 2 in 1 min	#e11: #e10 AND #e8
#e6: avg 85% load for 3 in 1 min	

component metrics is associated with a different Window (as the respective conditions enforce). Figure 7 only shows the three RAW metrics (Metric1–Metric3) together with two COMPOSITE metrics (Metric8 and Metric9 mapped to the same Couchbase instance and having as a component the third raw metric). The two other pairs of metrics ((Metric4, Metric5) and (Metric6, Metric7)) are symmetric to the pair (Metric8, Metric9), but refer to raw metrics Metric2 and Metric1, respectively.

The scalability rule requirements lead to six MetricConditions (each pertaining to a different composite metrics, see Table 2). In particular, three conditions check for a 50 % threshold and three conditions checking for an 85 % threshold over the respective metrics. Whenever the metrics associated with these Metric-Conditions have values that violate the MetricCondition, the non-functional event associated with the MetricCondition is triggered.

Table 2. MetricConditions created for database scalability rule

MetricCondition						
#sloc1	value	50		#sloc4	value	85
	comparator	GT			comparator	GT
	metric	Metric4			metric	Metric7
#sloc2	value	85		#sloc5	value	50
	comparator	GT			comparator	GT
	metric	Metric5			metric	Metric8
#sloc3	value	50		#sloc6	value	85
	comparator	GT			comparator	GT
	metric	Metric6			metric	Metric9

The occurrence/triggering of a sufficient subset of non-functional events according to the respective logical operator semantics and priorities activates the BinaryEvent #e11. The ScalabilityRule for this example requires that when event #e11 occurs, a single SCALE_OUT action for Couchbase 99–99 on cloud 88–88 is triggered, which adds an additional instance to the database cluster.

7 Related Work

The most relevant work related to SRL is the one of SYBL [2] which specifies a scalability rule language that considers three main levels: (a) application, (b) component, and (c) programming. The programming level uses annotations on code level. This language can express logical combinations of constraints on metric values, which can lead to triggering specific strategies encompassing particular scalability actions, such as scale-in and scale-out. Compared to SRL, SYBL is not able to express complex constraints and conditions as well as complete definitions of metrics. Moreover, there is no information about how units are handled, besides showing some conditions on metrics where the respective metric value is accompanied with a specific unit.

In the context of European research projects, particular service description languages [5, 16] have been proposed to specify simple scalability rules that map simple conditions on metrics values to just one scalability action. Similar to SYBL, the expressiveness and completeness of these languages is lower than the one of SRL.

In [9], a reactive and proactive approach to cloud elasticity is proposed, which includes a language to define scalability rules. This language allows specifying simple scalability rules that include the metric condition (metric, operator, value and aggregation function on metric), the scope (which components to affect), the metric sliding window, the scalability limit (which can be regarded as a scalability policy) and scaling action details (*e.g.*, scale type). Therefore, the language seems to complement a limited metric definition with additional metric details specified in the scalability rule, while it also mixes scalability policies and rules together. In contrast, SRL has been designed in a modular way, where all metric information is specified through a metric (and the respective metric template), while policies are defined at the CAMEL level (*cf.* D2.1.2 [14]) to express the case that different limits are posed on different components, more expressive metric conditions can be expressed and different types of scaling actions can be defined with the capability to associate more than one action to a specific rule.

The Drools rule engine[6] includes a highly expressive language that allows specifying complex conditions on events and domain objects. Apart from supporting logical combinations of conditions, the language also includes rich timing comparison operators that allow specifying different timing relations between events, such as that event A happens before or after event B. The operators can be accompanied with a particular time space to explicitly quantify the relationship and thus be able to, *e.g.*, express that A happened 3 to 4 seconds before B. The same considerations hold for the Esper Processing Language (EPL)[7]. Apart from windowing and timing relation assessment, EPL can also evaluate event patterns taking various kinds of databases into account. Compared to event processing languages, SRL lacks some expressiveness in terms of timing relationships (not all are covered) and generality. On the other hand, it provides a pre-defined terminology particular suited for expressing scalability rules. This includes sensors that gather the raw data as well as actions that have to be executed when the elasticity rule is triggered. With general-purpose languages, the modeller has to concretise these abstractions by him/herself, making it even more complex to express scalability concerns. In particular, SRL shields the modeller from having to deal with technical low-level details such as where monitoring streams are emitted from and how they are being processed. On the other hand, we consider general rules engines as a beneficial implementation option for SRL in terms of event assessment and corresponding scalability rule triggering.

8   Conclusions and Future Work

In this paper, we have presented the metamodel of the Scalability Rule Language (SRL). This DSL is centred around the two fundamental concepts of metrics and events. A metric defines how to process, aggregate, and compute samples of data. It may be associated with an SLO condition, which in turn is associated with an event. Once the values generated by the metric lead to a violation of the SLO condition, the corresponding event is triggered. Events can be connected via operators. The trigger for a composite event depends on the operator and the status of its composing events. Moreover, events are associated with actions via scalability rules. When the event associated with a scalability rule is triggered, the associated action is executed.

Future work with respect to SRL includes the following tasks. First, time-based event connectors such as PRECEDES require the specification of some time-bounds. This helps avoiding that a CompositeEvent is fired when an event e_2 occurs a long time after an initial event e_1. Second, more rich timing relations

---

[6] http://docs.jboss.org/drools/release/6.0.1.Final/drools-docs/html/index.html.
[7] http://esper.codehaus.org/.

will be included. Third, the evaluation of SRL in the context of the PaaSage platform integration as well as its evaluation through use cases will lead to new requirements that will be integrated in the DSL. Finally, a specification of formal semantics for SRL will be considered.

Acknowledgements. The research leading to these results has received funding from the European Community's Seventh Framework Programme (FP7/2007–2013) under grant agreement number 317715 (PaaSage). We would like to thank the PaaSage consortium and the reviewers for their constructive feedback that improved the quality of this work.

References

1. Andrieux, A., Czajkowski, K., Dan, A., Keahey, K., Ludwig, H., Nakata, T., Pruyne, J., Rofrano, J., Tuecke, S., Xu, M.: Web Services Agreement Specification (WS-Agreement). Technical report, Open Grid Forum (March 2007)
2. Copil, G., Moldovan, D., Truong, H.L., Dustdar, S.: SYBL: an extensible language for controlling elasticity in cloud applications. In: CCGrid 2013: 13th IEEE/ACM International Symposium on Cluster, Cloud, and Grid Computing, pp. 112–119. IEEE Computer Society (2013)
3. Ferry, N., Chauvel, F., Rossini, A., Morin, B., Solberg, A.: Managing multi-cloud systems with CloudMF. In: Solberg, A., Babar, M.A., Dumas, M., Cuesta, C.E. (eds.) Proceedings of NordiCloud 2013: 2nd Nordic Symposium on Cloud Computing and Internet Technologies, pp. 38–45. ACM (2013)
4. Ferry, N., Rossini, A., Chauvel, F., Morin, B., Solberg, A.: Towards model-driven provisioning, deployment, monitoring, and adaptation of multi-cloud systems. In: O'Conner, L. (ed.) Proceedings of CLOUD 2013: IEEE 6th International Conference on Cloud Computing, pp. 887–894. IEEE Computer Society (2013)
5. Galán, F., Vaquero, L.M.: D4.X.1 - Resources and Services Virtualization without Barriers. Reservoir project deliverable, January 2010
6. Jeffery, K., Kirkham, T.: D1.6.1 - Initial Architecture Design. Paasage project deliverable, October 2013
7. Kritikos, K., Korozi, M., Kryza, B., Kirkham, T., Leonidis, A., Magoutis, K., Massonet, P., Ntoa, S., Papaioannou, A., Papoulas, C., Sheridan, C., Zeginis, C.: D4.1.1 - Prototype Metadata Database and Social Network. Paasage project deliverable, March 2014
8. Kritikos, K., Plexousakis, D.: OWL-Q for Semantic QoS-based Web Service Description and Discovery. In: Noia, T.D., Lara, R., Polleres, A., Toma, I., Kawamura, T., Klusch, M., Bernstein, A., Paolucci, M., Leger, A., Martin, D.L. (eds.) SMR² 2007: Workshop on Service Matchmaking and Resource Retrieval in the Semantic Web, CEUR Workshop Proceedings, vol. 243. CEUR (2007)
9. Moore, L.R., Bean, K., Ellahi, T.: A coordinated reactive and predictive approach to cloud elasticity. In: CLOUD COMPUTING 2013: 4th International Conference on Cloud Computing, GRIDs, and Virtualization. IARIA (2013)
10. Object Management Group: Meta-Object Facility Specification, April 2014. http://www.omg.org/spec/MOF/2.4.2

11. Quinton, C., Haderer, N., Rouvoy, R., Duchien, L.: Towards multi-cloud config-
    urations using feature models and ontologies. In: MultiCloud 2013: International
    Workshop on Multi-cloud Applications and Federated Clouds, pp. 21–26. ACM
    (2013)
12. Quinton, C., Romero, D., Duchien, L.: Cardinality-based feature models with con-
    straints: a pragmatic approach. In: Kishi, T., Jarzabek, S., Gnesi, S. (eds.) SPLC
    2013: 17th International Software Product Line Conference, pp. 162–166. ACM
    (2013)
13. Quinton, C., Rouvoy, R., Duchien, L.: Leveraging feature models to configure vir-
    tual appliances. In: CloudCP 2012: 2nd International Workshop on Cloud Com-
    puting Platforms, pp. 2:1–2:6. ACM (2012)
14. Rossini, A., Nikolov, N., Romero, D., Domaschka, J., Kritikos, K., Kirkham, T.,
    Solberg, A.: D2.1.2 - CloudML Implementation Documentation (First version).
    Paasage project deliverable, April 2014
15. Rossini, A., Solberg, A., Romero, D., Domaschka, J., Magoutis, K., Schubert, L.,
    Ferry, N., Kirkham, T.: D2.1.1 - CloudML Guide and Assesment Report. Paasage
    project deliverable, October 2013
16. Rumpl, A., Rasheed, H., Waeldrich, O., Ziegler, W.: Service Manifest: Scientific
    Report. Optimis project deliverable, June 2010
17. Seybold, D.: Design und Implementierung eines skalierenden Database-as-a-Service
    Systems (in German). Mastersthesis vs-m05-2014, Institute for Distributed Sys-
    tems, University of Ulm, April 2014
18. Steinberg, D., Budinsky, F., Paternostro, M., Merks, E.: EMF: Eclipse Modeling
    Framework 2.0, 2nd edn. Addison-Wesley Professional, Reading (2008)

Linked USDL Business Policy Specifications as WS-Agreement Templates

Ioannis Arampatzis(✉), Simeon Veloudis, and Iraklis Paraskakis

South East European Research Centre (SEERC), International Faculty
of the University of Sheffield, CITY College, 24 Proxenou Koromila,
54622 Thessaloniki, Greece
{iarampatzis,sveloudis,iparaskakis}@seerc.org

Abstract. With the increasing adoption of cloud computing, the enterprise IT environment is progressively transformed into a complex ecosystem of diverse interrelated services typically delivered by a multitude of providers. Such complexity calls for service governance and quality control activities. Ideally, such activities must be performed in a generic and platform-agnostic manner, one which demands an ontology-based approach for the specification and enforcement of the relevant governance *policies* and the service-level objectives that they entail. At the same time, such governance policies must be expressed in a suitable serialisation format in order to be exposed to the relevant stakeholders and, ultimately, form the basis of Service Level Agreements (SLAs). This paper presents an approach for the automatic translation of governance policies expressed in Linked USDL, our chosen ontological framework, into WS-Agreement templates.

Keywords: SLA · WS-Agreement · Linked USDL · Cloud computing · Governance · Governance policies · Quality control

1 Introduction

The enterprise IT environment is rapidly being transformed through the adoption of cloud computing, with significant advantages in terms of cost, flexibility and business agility [1, 2]. Cloud computing crucially discards the currently prevalent monolithic business software systems and advocates an integrated enterprise software environment composed of highly distributed, task-oriented, self-contained, modular, and collaborative services which are remotely delivered over the Internet as a service, and which are entrusted by users with data, software, and computation. Evidently, the enterprise IT environment is progressively transformed into an ecosystem of interwoven infrastructure, platform, and application services, typically delivered by a multitude of diverse service providers. Such an inherently complex environment calls for service *governance* and *quality control* activities. These activities are primarily focused on checking the compliance of services with a set of enterprise policies concerning the technical, business, and legal aspects of service delivery. In addition, they are concerned with testing services for conformance with their expected behaviour, and with continuously monitoring their operation for conformance to service level agreements (SLAs).

© Springer International Publishing Switzerland 2015
G. Ortiz and C. Tran (Eds.): ESOCC 2014, CCIS 508, pp 221–232, 2015.
DOI: 10.1007/978-3-319-14886-1_20

Nevertheless, the proliferation of externally-sourced infrastructure, platform, and application services, adds to the inherent complexity of the enterprise IT environment, hindering the performance of governance and quality control activities. For example, it becomes increasingly difficult for enterprises to keep track of how and when consumed services evolve over time, either through intentional changes, initiated by service providers, or through unintentional changes, such as variations in service performance and availability. Moreover, it becomes increasingly difficult for enterprises to accurately predict the potential repercussions that such an evolution has on the compliance of a service with enterprise policies and regulations, and their conformance to SLAs.

In order to deal effectively with this complexity, future enterprises are anticipated to delegate policy-based governance and quality control activities to cloud service brokerage frameworks [3]. These frameworks must ideally offer generic mechanisms that automate the performance of such activities in a manner which is agnostic to the underlying cloud delivery platform. This calls for an *ontology-based* approach for the specification and enforcement of governance policies. In this work, we rely on Linked USDL [4] for the provision of such an approach. More specifically, we advocate the use of Linked USDL SLA specification templates for the conceptualisation and expression of governance policies.

Governance policies must naturally be exposed to service providers in order to guide the creation of SLAs, possibly through a negotiation process. As we would expect, these SLAs incorporate service-level objective (SLO) specifications such as, for example, the bounds of service response times or of service availability. Nevertheless, governance policies exposed in an ontologically-expressed format (e.g. as Linked USDL templates) may hinder the creation of SLAs for such a format: (i) may not be readily understandable by service providers; (ii) have not been designed to form an adequate basis for a subsequent negotiation process. Today, the dominant framework for the advertisement of SLOs, and for providing a suitable basis for SLA negotiation, is OGF's WS-Agreement standard [5]. It offers an extensible XML language for specifying agreement templates that facilitate the negotiation of SLAs between service providers and consumers.

This paper reports on the development of an approach which paves the way for the automatic translation of governance policies, expressed as Linked USDL templates, into corresponding WS-Agreement templates. The purpose of such a translation is twofold. On the one hand it allows the conceptualisation, and subsequent expression, of governance policies at an ontological level (i.e. in the form of Linked USDL SLA specification templates). This crucially enables the capturing of the *meaning* of the various SLOs, with the significant advantage of explicitly representing service-level objective interrelations. On the other hand, it allows SLOs to be exposed to stakeholders in a diffused and commonly understandable serialisation format such as the one offered by the WS-Agreement standard. Evidently, we anticipate that our approach will facilitate the overall process of policy-driven governance and quality control in enterprise IT environments.

This paper is structured as follows. Section 2 proposes a methodology for creating governance policies which serve as Linked USDL SLA templates. Section 3 provides an overview of the WS-Agreement standard. Section 4 presents a methodology for translating Linked USDL SLA policy templates into WS-Agreement templates. Section 5 presents related work. Finally, Sect. 6 presents conclusions and future work.

2 Linked USDL

Linked USDL [4] is a remodelled version of USDL [6] which builds upon the principles of Linked Data. In this respect, it re-expresses USDL specifications in terms of an RDF(S) vocabulary that provides better support for automatic trading of web services. Linked USDL relies on existing RDF(S) vocabularies, such as GoodRelations [7], whilst it can be easily extended through linking to further existing, or new, RDF(S) ontologies. For the purposes of this work, we concentrate on Linked USDL's SLA specification. An outline of this specification is provided in Sect. 2.2; a motivating fictional scenario is, however, first in order.

2.1 Motivating Scenario

CloudX is a state-of-the-art cloud platform that allows end-users to subscribe to, and consume, a variety of on-demand enterprise applications developed by its network of ecosystem partners and offered through its marketplace. CloudX also allows advanced users to develop and deploy their own custom applications on the platform, as well as to create rich compositions of applications offered by third-party cloud service providers (known as mash-ups). We assume that a brokerage framework is integrated into CloudX in order to augment its capabilities with respect to policy-based governance and quality control. Suppose that an ecosystem partner decides to offer a new service on CloudX which provides cloud storage. In order for the new service to become available through CloudX's marketplace, a number of entry-level criteria must be satisfied (see Table 1). These crucially capture a set of SLOs expressed in terms of restrictions on relevant service-level attributes. They essentially form CloudX's *business policy* with respect to onboarding the new service. As we would expect, this policy is exposed to service providers (SPs) in order to inform them of the available service deployment options and guide the creation of SLAs.

The brokerage platform formulates its business policy with respect to service onboarding by specifying a number of service-level objectives. This policy essentially represents a *template* by which SP-submitted service descriptions (SDs) must abide. It is beneficial to describe this template in Linked USDL SLA as it allows a causal relationship to be established between the expectations of CloudX with respect to the pertinent SLOs on the one hand, and the commitments made by SPs relative to these SLOs, on the other.

Table 1. Entry-level criteria

Service-level attribute	Acceptable values	SLO	Comments
Storage	[100, 1000)	High storage	Size measured
	[10, 100)	Medium storage	in TB
	[0, 10)	Low storage	
Availability	[0.99999, 1)	High availability	Total uptime ratio
	[0.9999, 1)	Medium availability	
	[0.999, 1)	Low availability	

2.2   Linked USDL SLA Specification

The Linked USDL SLA specification provides a simple vocabulary for describing SLAs. To this end, it introduces the classes Variable, Service Level Expression, Service Level, and Service Level Profile, along with a number of relevant object properties, as depicted in the upper rectangle of Fig. 1.

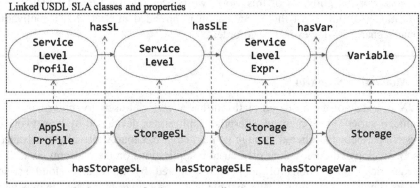

Fig. 1. Business policy in Linked USDL SLA

SLOs reside in the class Service Level. They are defined in terms of *service-level expressions* which represent the conditions that must be satisfied in order for the SLOs to be met; in fact, each SLO is associated with a service-level expression through the object property has service level expression (hasSLE) of Fig. 1. Now service-level expressions are formulated in terms of *service-level attributes* from the class Variable. A service-level expression is associated with its corresponding attributes via the property has variable (hasVar) of Fig. 1. Service-level attributes draw their values from appropriate intervals from the GoodRelations classes gr: QuantitativeValue and gr:QualitativeValue. Exactly which attributes characterise a service is determined by the *service-level profile* to which the service adheres. Such a profile characterises a particular type of service offering (e.g. 'transaction-based services', 'CPU-intensive services', etc.). SLOs can only be defined relative to a particular service-level profile to which they are associated via the has service level (hasSL) property; service-level profiles reside in the relevant Linked USDL SLA class of Fig. 1.

2.3   Modelling Business Policies in Linked USDL SLA

A business policy may be specified by defining suitable subclasses and sub-properties of the Linked USDL SLA classes and properties outlined in Sect. 2.2. The lower rectangle of Fig. 1 illustrates our approach with reference to the storage service-level attribute of the scenario of Sect. 2.1 (the perforated arrows indicate a subclass or sub-property relation); the `availability` attribute of Table 1 may be specified analogously. Note that for simplicity, albeit without loss of generality, the business policy presented here assumes that all service-level attributes adhere to a single service-level profile, namely `AppSLProfile`.

Subsequently, a number of value classes are specified (as instances) in order to define the allowable quantitative values for each service-level attribute. Figure 2 illustrates the specification of the value class `cpx:LowStorage` which defines, through the data properties `gr:hasMinValueInteger` and `gr:hasMaxValueInteger`, a range of allowable values for the `storage` attribute; it also defines an appropriate unit of measurement through the property `gr:hasUnitOfMeasurement`. Analogous instances (say `cpx:MediumStorage` and `cpx:HighStorage`) may be defined for the remaining allowable value ranges of the `storage` attribute (see Table 1). Value classes for the `availability` attribute may be specified analogously.

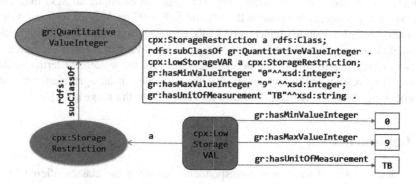

Fig. 2. Value class specification

3 WS-Agreement

The Web Services Agreement (WS-Agreement) Specification [5] defines an XML-based language for expressing SLAs, and a basic protocol for exposing service-level descriptions, validating service-level requests and, ultimately, reaching agreements between service providers and consumers.

An agreement *template* encompasses several sections. The `Name` section contains an optional name for the agreement. It is followed by the `Context` section which includes relevant meta-data such as the names of the involved participants and the agreement's expiration date. The `Terms` section (see Fig. 3) forms the main body of an agreement as it captures the defined consensus or obligations of a party [5]. Two kinds of term are discerned: `Service Description Terms` (SDTs) and `Guarantee Terms`. SDTs are a fundamental ingredient of an agreement as they identify the service that the agreement is about and may also include a description of the service. Each SDT may be associated with a set of `Service Properties` which are used to define measurable characteristics of a service that are of interest to the agreement.

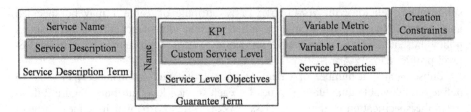

Fig. 3. WS-Agreement Terms section structure

Service Properties are expressed in terms of Variables which represent service-level attributes (e.g. service availability and response time).

Guarantee Terms describe SLOs. An SLO expresses an assurance relative to a particular Key Performance Indicator (KPI) which is, in turn, expressed in terms of the variables associated with Service Properties. For example, an SLO may assert that "service availability is between 0.9999 and 0.99999" or "service response time is less than 2 ms". Such an assurance is typically expressed through a condition which is formulated as a Custom Service Level. Finally, Agreement Creation Constraints optionally define acceptable values for the agreement terms outlined above. They restrict the value ranges that the variables in an agreement term may assume – e.g. "service availability draws its values from the range [0, 1]".

4   Implementation

As depicted in Fig. 4 there is a correspondence between the classes offered by the Linked USDL SLA specification on the one hand, and the sections of a WS-Agreement template, on the other. This work aims at exploiting this correspondence by providing a method for automatically mapping Linked USDL SLA class instances into WS-Agreement (WSAG) terms. Such a mapping brings about the significant advantage of exposing SLOs to the relevant stakeholders in a diffused and commonly understandable serialisation format, such as the one offered by WSAG templates. At the same time, it enables an adequate capturing of the meaning of the various SLOs within an ontological framework such as the one offered by Linked USDL SLA.

In this work we use the Java Architecture for XML Binding (JAXB) [8] in order to map the WSAG XML Schema components into Java content classes. These classes provide access to the content of the corresponding schema components via an appropriate set of JavaBean-style accessor methods. Instances of the Linked USDL SLA specification classes are accessed via the Apache Jena framework [9] in the form of RDF triples through the use of appropriate SPARQL queries.

As explained in Sect. 2.2, the SLOs of a business policy reside in the Linked USDL SLA class Service Level. They are defined in terms of service-level expressions which represent the conditions that must be satisfied in order for the SLOs to be met. Both SLOs and their corresponding service-level expressions are represented as Guarantee Terms in a WSAG template. The code listing of Table 2 creates such Guarantee Terms.

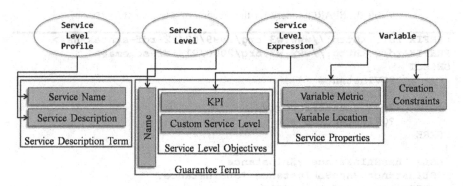

Fig. 4. Linked USDL SLA and WSAG template correspondence

Table 2. Code listing for the creation of a `Guarantee Term`

```
1.   List<SLO> SLOList =
             SLO.getSLOsFromModel(model,serviceLevelProfile);
2.   for( SLO slo : SLOList ){
3.      GuaranteeTermType GTT = new GuaranteeTermType();
4.      GTT.setName(slo.getName());
5.      ServiceLevelObjectiveType SLOType = new
        ServiceLevelObjectiveType();
6.      KPITargetType KPITargetValue = new KPITargetType();
7.      KPITargetValue.setKPIName(slo.getServiceName());
8.      SLOType.setKPITarget(KPITargetValue);
9.      CustomServiceLevelType slType = new
        CustomServiceLevelType();
10.     slType.setMinValue(slo.getMinValue());
11.     slType.setMaxValue(slo.getMaxValue());
12.     slType.setUnitOfMeasurement(slo.getUnit());
13.     SLOType.setCustomServiceLevel(slType);
14.     GTT.setServiceLevelObjective(SLOType);
15.     JAXBElement<GuaranteeTermType> jaxbGTT =
        objectFtory.createTermCompositorTypeGuaranteeTerm(GTT);
16.     termCompositor.getExactlyOneOrOneOrMoreOrAll()
        .add(jaxbGTT);
     }
```

More specifically, the 1st line executes the SPARQL query shown in Table 3 which generates a list of SLO elements, one for each `Service Level` instance appearing in a Linked USDL SLA business policy specification. Each element opaquely encompasses: (i) the name of the corresponding service-level instance, (ii) the name of the pertinent service-level expression instance, (iii) the minimum and maximum allowable values imposed by the service-level expression, along with a unit of measurement for these values.

Table 3. SPARQL query for the creation of a Guarantee Term

```
PREFIX rdf: <http://www.w3.org/1999/02/22-rdf-syntax-ns#>
PREFIX rdfs:<http://www.w3.org/2000/01/rdf-schema#>
SELECT
        ?QVInstance
        ?SLEInstance
        ?QVInstanceProperty
        ?QVInstanceObject
WHERE
{
  <SL> ?hasSLInstance ?SLInstance.
  ?SLInstance ?hasSLEInstance ?SLEInstance.
  ?SLEInstance rdf:type ?SLE.
  ?SLEInstance ?hasVarInstance ?varInstance.
  ?varInstance ?hasQVInstance  ?QVInstance.
  ?QVInstance rdf:type ?QVclass.
  ?QVclass rdfs:subClassOf ?GoodRelationsQV.
  ?QVInstance ?QVInstanceProperty ?QVInstanceObject
}
```

The for loop of line 2 traverses the list of SLO elements and extracts, from each one of them, the necessary information for creating a corresponding WSAG Guarantee Term. To this end, line 3 creates the GTT object that represents such a Guarantee Term, and line 4 sets the name attribute of this object to be equal to the corresponding service level name which appears as an attribute of the resulting XML wsag:GuaranteeTerm element. This is depicted in Table 4 for the LowStorageSL service level[1] of the example of Sect. 2.1.

Subsequently, line 5 creates the object SLOType which is incorporated within the GTT object in line 14. The SLOType object encompasses two main attributes: the KPITarget and the CustomServiceLevel. The KPITarget attribute contains the name of the corresponding service-level expression. This name is obtained in line 8 through the application of the method setKPITarget to the object KPITarget-Value. This latter object is created in line 6 and primed in line 7 with the appropriate service-level name. This is depicted in Table 4 for the service-level name LowStorageSLE from the example of Sect. 2.1. The CustomServiceLevel attribute contains the minimum and maximum allowable values imposed by the service-level expression, along with an appropriate unit of measurement. These values are set by the code in lines 9–13. Finally, lines 15–16 use the JAXB object factory to generate the XML serialisation that expresses the Guarantee Term as depicted in Table 4.

Service-level attributes are the building blocks of service-level expressions. They appear as instances of the class Variable in Linked USDL SLA, and are rendered as Service Properties in WSAG. For each variable, a corresponding WSAG metric is created and set to the pertinent data type extracted from the Linked USDL SLA

---

[1] Recall that the same SLO was also modelled in Linked USDL SLA in Sect. 2.3.

Table 4. WS-Agreement Guarantee Term for the Storage

```
<wsag:GuaranteeTerm wsag:Name="LowStorageSL">
  <ServiceLevelObjective>
   <KPITarget>
     <KPIName>LowStorageSLE</KPIName>
   </KPITarget>
   <CustomServiceLevel xsi:type="customServiceLevelType">
     <UnitOfMeasurement>TB</UnitOfMeasurement>
     <MinValue>0</MinValue>
     <MaxValue>9</MaxValue>
   </CustomServiceLevel>
  </ServiceLevelObjective>
</wsag:GuaranteeTerm>
<CreationConstraints>
   <Item wsag:Name="StorageRestriction">
       <delimiter>
           <MinValue>0</MinValue>
           <MaxValue>999</MaxValue>
       </delimiter>
   </Item>
</CreationConstraints>
```

specification. The code that creates Service Properties is analogous to the code described above and it is thus omitted.

The service-level attributes that characterise a service are determined on the basis of the service-level profile to which the service adheres. Such a profile is expressed in WSAG templates as an SDT. The code that sets SDTs is analogous to the one described for the creation of guarantee terms and it is thus omitted.

Moreover, service-level attributes draw their values from appropriate intervals which are expressed in Linked USDL SLA as instances of the class gr:Quantitativevalue. In WSAG, these intervals are associated with the corresponding variables through appropriate XPATH expressions that point to the relevant Creation Constraints. Table 4 depicts an example of such a constraint for the storage variable of the example of Sect. 2.1.

5   Related Work

This section revolves around two main themes: languages and frameworks for the specification and management of SLAs; different strands of service description languages and standardisation efforts. We begin with the first theme and by outlining works directly related to the WS-Agreement specification. WS-Agreement for Java (WSAG4 J) [10] is a generic implementation of the WS-Agreement protocol. It provides an easy-to-use Java framework for creating and monitoring SLAs expressed in the WS-Agreement language. The framework is deployable in any Web container (e.g. Apache Tomcat). Reference [11] proposed the WS-Agreement Negotiation protocol, an extension to WS-Agreement that offers multi-round negotiation capabilities in a manner compliant with the original WS-Agreement specification.

Turning now turn to other languages and frameworks for SLA specification and management, WSLA [12] provides a flexible and extensible XML-based language for defining and monitoring a wide variety of SLAs; it also encompasses a runtime architecture comprising several SLA monitoring services which may be outsourced to third parties to increase objectivity. Upon receipt of an SLA specification, the WSLA monitoring services are automatically configured to enforce the SLA. SLAng [13] provides a method for the negotiation of QoS properties, as well as a language to unambiguously capture these properties in SLAs. Both WSLA and SLAng offer tools for the automatic management of SLAs. The SLA@SOI project [14] aims at providing a framework for complete SLA management in Service Oriented Architectures. More specifically, it aims at: (i) predicting and enforcing at run-time seminal quality characteristics of a service; (ii) transparently managing SLAs across the business and IT stack; (iii) offering a method for automated SLA negotiation and service monitoring allowing for highly dynamic and scalable service consumption.

Turning to our second theme, namely service description languages, syntactic service descriptions were introduced along with the Service Oriented Architecture (SOA) model aiming at facilitating the interoperable data exchange between service registries (notably UDDI) and service providers and consumers. An outcome of this standardisation effort was WSDL [15], along with a number of additional platform-neutral WS-* standards. Nevertheless, syntactic service descriptions can only aid *manual* discovery and selection of services. In an attempt to automate these processes, and to promote automatic web service composition, a second strand of service description languages that enable *Semantic Web Services* emerged [16]. Prominent examples of standardization efforts in this area are WSMO [17] and OWL-S [18]. W3C proposed SAWSDL [19] which uses XML attributes to link tags in arbitrary XML Schema documents with concepts or relations expressed in an arbitrary ontology; a similar idea is adopted by W3C's SA-REST [20] and by OASIS's Reference Ontology for Semantic SOA [21].

Recently, a third strand of description languages has emerged, one which focuses on the business aspect of services. A prominent example in this area is the Unified Service Description Language (USDL) [6, 22]. It aims at unifying the business aspects of a service, as well as pertinent operational and technical details, in one coherent service description. In this respect, it provides a framework for describing services across the entire human-to-automation continuum. Finally, USDL-Agreement [23] is a novel Linked USDL extension module for capturing service agreements. It provides a number of suitable RDF(S) classes for expressing agreement conditions and representing the service-level agreement terms encompassed in such conditions. It also provides suitable classes for identifying the parties responsible for guaranteeing the terms of an agreement, as well as for identifying appropriate compensation actions in case these terms are not fulfilled. These classes are informed by SLAs expressed in the WS-Agreement language. To the best of our knowledge, no tools are available for the automatic translation of WS-Agreement specifications into the USDL-Agreement.

6 Conclusions and Future Work

This work has presented an approach for the automatic translation of governance policies, expressed in Linked USDL SLA, into corresponding WS-Agreement templates. This allows for the SLOs entailed by these policies to be exposed in a diffused and commonly understandable - by the relevant stakeholders – format. At the same time, the ontological expression of governance policies, allows for a proper separation of concerns between the definition of governance policies, and of their pertinent SLOs, on the one hand, and the enforcement of these policies, on the other. This enables a generic representation of the meaning of SLOs, one which is decoupled from any software components that check for potential policy violations, and which brings about the following significant advantages: increased portability and reusability of governance policies; ability to capture the interrelations between SLOs, as well as their associations with relevant underlying service-level attributes.

We anticipate that our approach will facilitate the negotiation of SLAs between service providers and consumers thus paving the way for the adoption of policy-driven governance and quality control mechanisms in the enterprise IT environment. This is particularly significant today, as cloud computing eventually transforms such environments into complex ecosystems of distributed, task-oriented, self-contained, and collaborative services.

In the future, we shall investigate the automatic expression of SLOs captured in the WS-Agreement language as Linked USDL SLA instances. This is expected to further promote multi-round negotiation and renegotiation capabilities, especially in connection with the recent USDL-Agreement extension module [23].

Acknowledgements. This research is funded by the EU 7th Framework Programme under the Broker@Cloud project (www.broker-cloud.eu), grant agreement n°328392, and under the RELATE project (FP7-PEOPLE-2010-ITN), grant agreement n°264840.

References

1. Cloud: What an Enterprise Must Know. Technical report, Cisco White Paper (2011)
2. Vaquero, L.M., Rodero-Merino, L., Caceres, J., Lindner, M.: A break in the clouds: towards a cloud definition. ACM SIGCOMM Comput. Commun. Rev. **39**(1), 50–55 (2008)
3. Liu, F., Tong, J., Mao, J., Bohn, R., Messina, J., Badger, L., Leaf, D.: Cloud Computing Reference Architecture. Technical report, NIST (2011)
4. Linked USDL. http://www.linked-usdl.org/
5. Andrieux, A., Czajkowski, K., Dan, A., Keahey, K., Ludwig, H., Nakata, T., Pruyne, J., Rofrano, J., Tuecke, S., Xu, M.: Web Services Agreement Specification (WS-Agreement). Technical report, Open Grid Forum Document GFD.107 (2007)
6. Barros, A.P., Oberle, D., Kylau, U., Heinzl, S.: Design overview of USDL. In: Barros, A.P., Oberle, D. (eds.) Handbook of Service Description: USDL and its Methods, pp. 187–225. Springer, New York (2012)
7. GoodRelations: The Professional Web Vocabulary for E-Commerce. http://www.heppnetz.de/projects/goodrelations/

8. Fialli, J., Sekhar, V.: The Java Architecture for XML Binding (JAXB). Technical report, Java Specification Request, JCP (2003)
9. Apache Jena. http://jena.apache.org/
10. WSAG4 J – WS-Agreement for Java. https://packcs-e0.scai.fraunhofer.de/wsag4j/
11. Battre, D., Brazier, F., Clark, K., Oey, M., Papaspyrou, A., Waldrich, O., Wieder, P., Ziegler, W.: A proposal for WS-Agreement negotiation. In: 2010 11th IEEE/ACM International Conference Grid Computing (GRID), pp. 233–241 (2010)
12. Keller, A., Ludwig, H.: The WSLA framework: specifying and monitoring service level agreements for web services. J. Netw. Syst. Manage. 11(1), 57–81 (2003)
13. The SLAng SLA Language – A Language for ASP SLAs. http://uclslang.sourceforge.net/
14. SLA@SOI. http://sourceforge.net/apps/trac/sla-at-soi/
15. Christensen, C., Curbera, F., Meredith, G., Weerawarana, S.: Web Services Description Language (WSDL) 1.1, W3C (2001). http://www.w3.org/TR/wsdl
16. McIlraith, S.A., Son, T.C., Zeng, H.: Semantic web services. IEEE Intel. Syst. 16(2), 46–53 (2001)
17. Lausen, H., Polleres, A., Roman, D. (eds.) Web Service Modeling Ontology (WSMO). W3C (2001). http://www.w3.org/Submission/WSMO/
18. Martin, M., Burstein, M., Hobbs, J., Lassila, O., McDermott, D., McIlraith, S., Narayanan, S., Paolucci, M., Parsia, B., Payne, T., Sirin, E., Srinivasan, N., Sycara, K.: OWL-S: Semantic Markup for Web Services. W3C (2004). http://www.w3.org/Submission/OWL-S/
19. Farrell, J., Lausen, H.: Semantic Annotations for WSDL and XML Schema (SAWSDL), W3C Recommendation (2007). http://www.w3.org/TR/sawsdl/
20. Gomadam, K., Ranabahu, A., Sheth, A.: SA-REST: Semantic Annotation of Web Resources, W3C Member Submission (2010). http://www.w3.org/Submission/SA-REST/
21. Norton, B., Kerrigan, M., Mocan, A., Carenini, A., Cimpian, E., Haines, M., Scicluna, J., Zaremba, M.: Reference Ontology for Semantic Service Oriented Architectures. OASIS Public Review Draft 0.1 (2008). http://docs.oasis-open.org/semantic-ex/ro-soa/v1.0/pr01/see-rosoa-v1.0-pr01.html
22. Oberle, D., Barros, A., Heinzl, S., Kylau, U.: A unified description language for human to automated services. Inf. Syst. 38, 155–181 (2013)
23. USDL-Agreement. https://github.com/linked-usdl/usdl-agreement

Derivation of Broker Policies from Cloud Hosting Platform Service Descriptions

Andreas Friesen[1](✉), Simeon Veloudis[2], and Iraklis Paraskakis[2]

[1] SAP AG, Vincenz-Priessnitz-Strasse 1, 76131 Karlsruhe, Germany
andreas.friesen@sap.com
[2] South-East European Research Centre (SEERC), The University of Sheffield,
24 Proxenou Koromila Street, 54622 Thessaloniki, Greece
{sveloudis,iparaskakis}@seerc.org

Abstract. Cloud service brokerage leads to creation of ecosystems of highly distributed, task-oriented, modular, and collaborative cloud services managed by a broker. A broker is striving to create optimized cloud service consumption lifecycle in terms of cost, flexibility and business agility. In order to effectively manage the complexity inherent in such ecosystems, enterprises are anticipated to crucially depend upon cloud service brokerage (CSB) mechanisms. This work focuses on the management of hosting platforms participating in the ecosystem of a cloud service brokerage platform. The hosting platforms are as any other actor of a cloud service brokerage ecosystem evolving over time. The hosting platforms may join or leave the ecosystem, add or remove hosting services to the ecosystem or change characteristics of the available hosting services. The broker is thereby confronted with the issue of keeping its business policy offered to the service providers and service consumers up to date concerning the hosting alternatives in the ecosystem. We present a strategy for derivation of business policies from service descriptions of hosting services. The strategy is showcased in Linked USDL – our chosen technical specification for enabling platform-agnostic data exchanges.

Keywords: Cloud computing · Cloud service brokerage · Service description languages · Linked USDL · Policy-based governance

1 Introduction

The increasing adoption of cloud computing is altering the way in which IT resources have traditionally been managed and consumed, bringing about significant advantages for enterprises in terms of cost, flexibility and business agility [1, 2]. The cloud computing paradigm crucially involves the use of computing resources that are remotely delivered over the Internet as a service, and which are entrusted by users with data, software and computation. Evidently, cloud computing progressively transforms the enterprise IT environment into an ecosystem of interwoven infrastructure, platform, and application services, typically delivered by a multitude of diverse service providers.

As the number of externally-sourced services proliferates, it becomes increasingly difficult to keep track of them. Additionally, services evolve over time, either through intentional changes initiated by service providers, or through unintentional changes,

G. Ortiz and C. Tran (Eds.): ESOCC 2014, CCIS 508, pp 233–244, 2015.
DOI: 10.1007/978-3-319-14886-1_21

such as variations in service performance and availability. Moreover, it becomes increasingly difficult to accurately predict the potential repercussions that such an evolution has with respect to a service's compliance to policies and regulations, and its conformance to Service Level Agreements (SLAs).

In addition, the proliferation of cloud services that offer similar functionality under comparable terms of provision, despite the obvious benefits, is adding to the overall complexity as the onus of discovering suitable alternatives to a currently-consumed service inevitably falls on the service consumer. Furthermore, service providers relying on PaaS for development of their services are often offering the services to customers as packaged applications that are deployable on a potentially large number of hosting platforms.

In order to deal effectively with the ensuing complexity with respect to the above described aspects, future enterprises are anticipated to increasingly rely on cloud service brokerage (CSB) [3]. This work focuses on the management of hosting platforms participating in the ecosystem of a cloud service brokerage platform.

The hosting platforms are as any other actor of a cloud service brokerage ecosystem evolving over time. The hosting platforms may join or leave the ecosystem, add or remove hosting services to the ecosystem or change characteristics of the available hosting services. The broker is thereby confronted with the issue of keeping its business policy offered to the service providers and service consumers up to date concerning hosting alternatives available in the ecosystem.

Hosting alternatives can be described on a brokerage platform as cloud services. They have, however, a specialized purpose within the cloud service brokerage ecosystem namely to host packaged applications (services) of the service providers. Hosting services are therefore in a general sense IaaS services with a more or less strong specialization of their characteristics and capabilities with respect to the packaged applications they are able to host.

Obviously, the service descriptions of hosting services and service descriptions of packaged applications have to be compatible to enable successful deployment and hosting. To successfully mediate between customers, service providers and hosting platforms, a broker needs to establish a shared vocabulary in a business policy for all actors of the ecosystem. We present a strategy for derivation of business policies from service descriptions of hosting services. The strategy is showcased in Linked USDL – our chosen technical specification for enabling platform-agnostic data exchanges.

The rest of this paper is structured as follows. Section 2 presents related work. Section 3 presents a motivating usage scenario. Section 4 outlines the overall process of building business policies for hosting platforms and derivation of business policies for service providers from service descriptions of hosting platforms. Section 5 shows how the methodology can be grounded to a service description language on example of Linked USDL. Section 6 presents conclusions and future work.

2 Related Work

This section provides an overview of the different strands of service description languages and standardisation efforts. More specifically, it outlines approaches that:

(i) focus on syntactic service descriptions; (ii) consider the underlying semantics of web services; (iii) capture the business aspects of services.

Syntactic service descriptions were introduced along with the Service Oriented Architecture (SOA) model as part of a standardisation effort aiming, primarily, at facilitating the interoperable data exchange in interactions between service registries (notably UDDI [22]) on the one hand, and service providers and consumers, on the other. The most prominent outcome of this standardisation effort was, perhaps, the development of WSDL [5], together with a number of additional platform-neutral WS-* standards (e.g. WS-Security, WS-Policy, WS-BPEL). Syntactic service descriptions do not offer vocabulary for discovery by semantic content. A second strand of service description languages is offering a richer vocabulary that enable *Semantic Web Services* [6]. These use ontologies to semantically annotate web services in order to capture their functionality in terms of an underlying, domain-specific, vocabulary. The basic tenet is that since both service descriptions and *consumer goals* rely on a common semantics expressed through a shared (or mediated), domain-specific, vocabulary), automatic service discovery and composition is, in principle, feasible. Prominent examples of standardization efforts in this area are the Web Service Modelling Ontology (WSMO) [7] and OWL-S (the Ontology Web Language) [8]. In a similar spirit, the W3C has proposed the recommendation Semantic Annotations for WSDL (SAWSDL) [9] and the Semantic Annotations for REST (SA-REST) [10]. OASIS has proposed the Reference Ontology for Semantic Service-Oriented Architectures, an abstract framework for capturing significant concepts and service interrelations within a semantically-enabled service-oriented environment [11]. Other research efforts in the area of Semantic Web Services are focused on Linked Open Data concepts, RESTful services, and Linked Services [12], e.g., WSMO-Lite [13] and MicroWSMO [14].

Whilst focusing on aspects which are important for the automatic composition and invocation of web services, the aforementioned approaches neglect any pertinent business details or, at best, address them as non-functional properties. This renders service descriptions cumbersome for service consumers, but also for third-party intermediaries who are interested in both business details and technical specifications in order to create added value by deploying, aggregating, customizing, and integrating services, or by optimising their delivery. A third strand of description languages has therefore emerged, one which focuses on the business aspect of services. A prominent example in this area is the Unified Service Description Language (USDL) [15, 16]. USDL aims at unifying the business aspects of a service (such as pricing, service-level, and legal/licensing information), as well as pertinent operational and technical details, in one coherent service description. In this respect, it provides a framework for describing services across the entire human-to-automation continuum; service behaviour is described in terms of interaction protocols whilst operational specifications offer grounding mechanisms to WDSL and REST specifications.

3   Motivating Usage Scenario

To exemplify the potential effect that the adoption of our framework could have on the operation of an enterprise cloud service delivery platform, let us consider the following fictional scenario. CPx (stands for "Cloud Service Brokerage Platform x") is a state-of-the-art cloud service brokerage platform that allows end-users to subscribe to, and consume, a variety of on-demand packaged enterprise applications offered through the platform's marketplace. The marketplace offers to hosting platforms an opportunity to host packaged enterprise applications offered on the marketplace. In order to create win-win situations for providers of packaged applications and their consumers, the CPx uses mediation services to find the hosting service for a packaged application with the best cost-performance ratio for the customer.

In order to be able to offer effective mediation services CPx needs:

- to know and understand the configuration parameters, and pricing of the hosting services;
- to communicate the available parameters and configuration options to service providers;
- to analyse the hosting requirements from the service descriptions of packaged applications and to match them with the offerings of hosting services to find the best value for money for customers;
- to maintain the service lifecycle for services of hosting platforms and packaged applications of service providers through consistent business policy.

Table 1. SLO structure specification

Service-level attribute	Available properties	Valid value	Comments
main-memory	*minValue*	Positive integer	Min/max valid values for main memory measured in GB
	maxValue	Positive integer	
	unitOfMeasurement	GB	
number-of-CPUs	*minValue*	Positive integer	Min/max number of CPUs
	maxValue	Positive integer	
	unitOfMeasurement	Qty	
Bandwidth	*minValue*	Positive integer	Min/max bandwidth in GB/s
	maxValue	Positive integer	
	unitofMeasurement	GB/s	

Suppose that some class of packaged applications to be offered on CPx relies basically on the following IaaS-related configuration parameters required for successful deployment and scaling: main memory, number of CPUs, and bandwidth of the network connection. These parameters crucially capture a set of IaaS *service-level objectives* (SLOs) that need to be described in the same shared vocabulary by the broker, the hosting platforms and the service providers with respect to the naming and structure of these parameters. Table 2 summarises an example specification for these SLOs. This specification essentially forms CPx's *business policy* towards hosting platforms with respect to description of hosting services interpretable by CPx.

We assume that a hosting partner platform describes the hosting services and their configuration options in terms of the structures specified in Table 1. Table 2 provides an example of a hosting service *host@cloud* with 3 different configuration options for all SLOs expressed as T-Shirt sizes (S, M, and L). The valid values for different T-Shirt sizes are specified as intervals [minvalue, maxvalue] that are bound to dynamic pricing and represent at the same time validity restrictions which may be used for SLA monitoring. These aspects are however not further discussed here.

Table 2. *host@cloud* configuration options

Service-level attribute	Acceptable values	SLO	Comments
main-memory	[256, 512]	L	Size measured in GB
	[128, 256]	M	
	[64, 128]	S	
number-of-CPUs	[8, 32]	L	Number of CPUs
	[5, 8]	M	
	[2, 4]	S	
Bandwidth	[512, 1024]	L	Bandwidth at server port in GB/s
	[128, 512]	M	
	[16, 128]	S	

To make the example as simple as possible we specified the three T-Shirt sizes of host@cloud service as complementing intervals.

Table 3. Business policy for service providers

Service-level attribute	Validity ranges	Comments
main-memory	[64, 512]	Size measured in GB
number-of-CPUs	[2, 32]	Number of CPUs
Bandwidth	[16, 1024]	Bandwidth at server port in GB/s

Hence, CPx business policy towards service providers derived from host@cloud service description can take a very simple form by aggregating the complementing intervals for each of the SLAs into one corresponding interval as shown in Table 3. Obviously, for the case that the intervals do not overlap the validity ranges have to be partitioned in order to take this into account. Imagine, the acceptable values for the T-Shirt size L of the SLA "number-of-CPUs" in Table 2 would be specified at the interval [16, 32]. This would lead to the specification of two validity ranges [2, 8] and [16, 32] for the SLA "number-of-CPUs" in Table 3. The two partitioned intervals would indicate to the providers of packaged apps that specification of application hosting requirements with respect to "number-of-CPUs" SLA in the range [9, 15] would not be optimally served according to the current business policy of the broker. This is because the next valid hosting option [16, 32] is oversized and hence potentially more expensive than necessary.

Based on the business policy as specified in Table 3 service providers of packaged applications have the maximum possible freedom to specify scaling options for their offerings with respect to available hosting options. In the given example CPx is able to match the scaling requirements of the customers to available scaling options of service providers and to figure out the hosting configuration with the best available price-performance ratio. In the next section we generalise the approach introduced in the motivating scenario to cover the service lifecycle process.

4 Policies and Service Descriptions in the Broker Policy Lifecycle

We distinguish between two types of broker's business policies within the scope of this paper: business policies for hosting platforms and business policies for service providers of packaged applications.

Business policy for hosting platforms specifies the names and structure of attributes to be used in the service descriptions of hosting services.

Business policy for service providers specifies the validity ranges of attributes related to hosting services offered to service providers.

The creation of broker's business policies and related artefacts follows the following process:

1. Broker: Specify the names and structure of attributes obligatory for description of hosting services (business policy for hosting platforms).
2. Hosting platforms: use the attribute specification from business policy for hosting platforms to specify the validity ranges and configuration options of a hosting service
3. Broker: Derive business policy for service providers from the analysis of all available hosting service descriptions by identifying complementing and overlapping validity ranges for single attributes and merging them to a unified validity range.
4. Service Providers: respect the restrictions of the business policy for service providers to specify the validity ranges and configuration options in the service description of a packaged application with respect to hosting-related attributes.

The lifecycle of hosting platforms definitely impacts the broker's business policy for service providers. Hosting platforms may join or leave the ecosystem, add or remove hosting services to the ecosystem or change the characteristics of the available hosting services. Hence, each time a change occurs in the available hosting services the third step above needs to be repeated. Furthermore, the broker has to verify if the already published service descriptions of the packaged apps are consistent with the new business policy for service providers and inform the eventually impacted service providers to repeat step four above to reestablish consistency of their service descriptions with respect to the new broker policy for service providers.

5   Specification of Policies and Service Descriptions in Linked USDL

We propose to use Linked USDL for specification of all above mentioned artefacts [6]. Linked USDL is a remodelled version of USDL [15] which builds upon the principles of Linked Open Data in order to promote its use in a 'web of data'. In this respect, it re-expresses USDL specifications in terms of an RDF(S) vocabulary that provides better support for automatic trading of web services. Linked USDL relies on existing RDF(S) vocabularies, such as GoodRelations [17], the Minimal Service Model [20], and FOAF [19], whilst it can be easily extended through linking to further existing, or new, RDF (S) ontologies.

Linked USDL comprises a Core specification (see Fig. 1) which provides a schema specifying basic interrelations between the various concepts pertaining to a service description, as well as between the various involved actors (i.e. the involved business entities along with their associated business roles). The Core schema also covers the operational aspects of a service by offering an interaction schema specification,[1] as well as the necessary grounding to lower-level technical service interface specifications (e.g. WSDL and REST). It can thus be readily used for the description of web services which offer these types of interface.

Linked USDL Core extends the GoodRelations ontology (gr) by introducing the concepts Service, ServiceModel, ServiceIndividual, and ServiceOffering, as subclasses of the corresponding concepts in gr (see Fig. 1). Linked USDL Core also introduces the EntityInvolvement class specifying the business entities, and their associated roles, involved in the definition and delivery of a service. The applicable role taxonomies are specified using the Concept Scheme of the Simple Knowledge Organization System (SKOS) ontology [18]; business entities are described as instances of the gr:BusinessEntities class. The property hasClassification relates a service to a particular classification taxonomy specified as a SKOS Concept Scheme. The use of the above mentioned concepts within our framework for the purposes of specification of business policies for service providers and service descriptions is documented in [21].

In the scenario of Sect. 2, the brokerage platform formulates its business policy with respect to hosting services by specifying a structure for a number of service-level objectives to be followed in the service description of a hosting service. This policy (referred to above as 'broker's business policy for hosting platforms') essentially represents a *template* by which service descriptions submitted by hosting platforms

---

[1] The operational interface is not directly related to the work reported in this paper and thus it shall not further concern us here; to avoid clutter, it is omitted from Fig. 1.

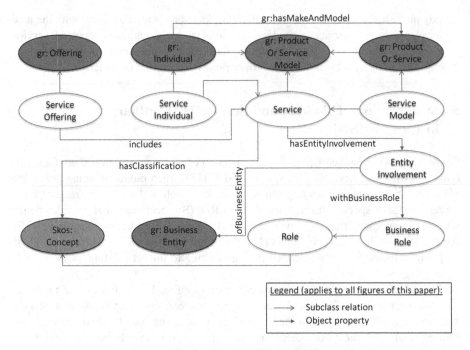

Fig. 1. Linked USDL Core

must abide. It is beneficial to describe such a template in Linked USDL as it renders the business policy referenceable from within SDs. This allows a clear causal relationship to be established between the expectations of the brokerage platform with respect to the structure of the pertinent SLOs on the one hand, and the commitments made by hosting platforms relative to these SLOs, on the other.

A broker's business policy for hosting platforms is specified in Linked USDL as an instance of the `ServiceModel` class, with the `BusinessRole` class instantiated to `Intermediary`. More specifically, referring to the scenario of Sect. 2, the broker policy `cpx:BusinessPolicyHostingCPx` is specified as an instance of the `cpx:ServiceModelHostingCPx` subclass of `ServiceModel` (see Fig. 2); the `cpx:ServiceModelHostingCPx` subclass is created to accommodate CPx's business policy for hosting platforms.

Similarly, a SD takes the form of an instance of the class `ServiceIndividual` with the `BusinessRole` class instantiated to `Hoster`; this instance refers, through the `gr:hasMakeAndModel` property, to the corresponding business policy. Referring to the scenario of Sect. 2, Fig. 2 depicts such an instantiation (`esp-y:host@cloud`) for the "host@cloud" service; the example code indicates an RDF(S) implementation of the discussion above.

The approach described above establishes, at the level of Linked USDL Core, a global reference between a SD and the relevant business policy. The specification of the structure of the SLOs relies on building a subclass in the `gr:QuantitativeValue` class hierarchy for each of the SLOs in the broker policy. `gr:QuantitativeValue`

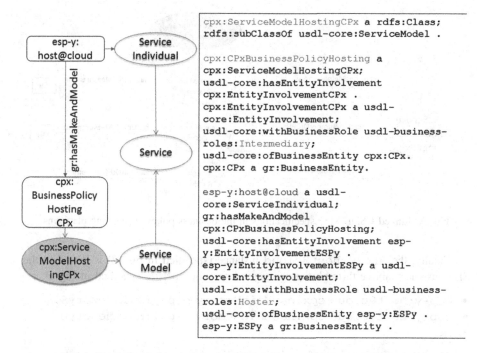

```
cpx:ServiceModelHostingCPx a rdfs:Class;
rdfs:subClassOf usdl-core:ServiceModel .

cpx:CPxBusinessPolicyHosting a
cpx:ServiceModelHostingCPx;
usdl-core:hasEntityInvolvement
cpx:EntityInvolvementCPx .
cpx:EntityInvolvementCPx a usdl-
core:EntityInvolvement;
usdl-core:withBusinessRole usdl-business-
roles:Intermediary;
usdl-core:ofBusinessEntity cpx:CPx.
cpx:CPx a gr:BusinessEntity.

esp-y:host@cloud a usdl-
core:ServiceIndividual;
gr:hasMakeAndModel
cpx:CPxBusinessPolicyHosting;
usdl-core:hasEntityInvolvement esp-
y:EntityInvolvementESPy .
esp-y:EntityInvolvementESPy a usdl-
core:EntityInvolvement;
usdl-core:withBusinessRole usdl-business-
roles:Hoster;
usdl-core:ofBusinessEnity esp-y:ESPy .
esp-y:ESPy a gr:BusinessEntity .
```

Fig. 2. Business policy and SD for hosting platforms in Linked USDL Core

class offers four properties gr:hasMinValue, gr:hasMaxValue, gr:has-Value, and gr:hasUnitOfMeasurement. gr:hasValue is a short link if discrete values have to be specified instead of intervals. Furthermore there are already two specified subclasses of gr:QuantitativeValue namely gr:QuantitativeValueInteger (for integer intervals) and gr:QuantitativeValueFloat (for float intervals) These properties are all what we need to specify the SLO structure of the Table 1. We specify three subclasses of gr:QuantitativeValueInteger class cpx:MainMemory, cpx:NumberOfCPUs, and cpx:Bandwidth and set the property gr:hasUnitOfMeasurement to the corresponding values.

The Linked USDL specification of the broker's business policy for hosting platforms is finalized by binding cpx:ServiceModelHostingCPx to the specified subclasses through corresponding properties cpx:hasMainMemory, cpx:hasNumberOfCPUs, and cpx:hasBandwidth specified as subproperties of gr:quantitativeProductOrServiceProperty. This is done by specifying cpx:ServiceModelHostingCPx as the domain of all the subproperties and the corresponding subclass as the range of the subproperty. Figure 3 illustrates the specified artefacts and relationships.

The SLAs of the host@cloud service from Table 2 can now be simply expressed in terms of the SLO structure specified in Fig. 3 by instantiating the corresponding concepts. Figure 4 illustrates this on example of the "main-memory" SLA from Table 2.

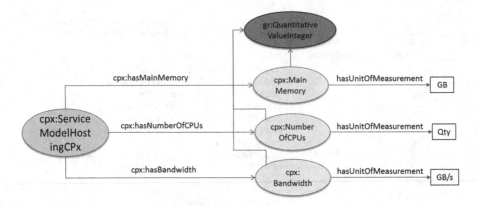

Fig. 3. Linked USDL SLO specifications in the business policy for hosting platforms

Finally, the `esp-y:host@cloud` instance (specified in Fig. 2) is bound to the SLA instances above through the corresponding subproperties specified in Fig. 3:

- `esp-y:host@cloud cpx:hasMainMemory esp-y:MainMemoryS.`
- `esp-y:host@cloud cpx:hasMainMemory esp-y:MainMemoryM.`
- etc.

The SLA specification of business policies for service providers and service descriptions for packaged apps is very similar to the SLA specification of business policies for hosting platforms and service descriptions for hosting services. However, the business policies for service providers specify not only SLA attribute types but also the validity ranges as has been shown in Table 3. The Linked USDL methodology for these specifications is in detail documented in [21] so that we do not further detail it in this contribution.

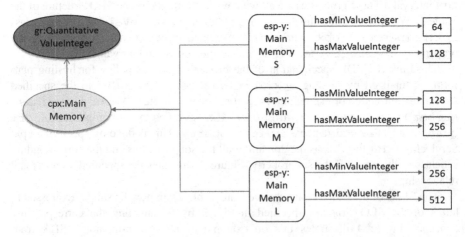

Fig. 4. Linked USDL specification of SLAs in the SD of a hosting service

6 Conclusions and Future Work

This work has presented a conceptual foundation, as well as a set of design guidelines and extensibility principles, for specification of broker policies for hosting platforms and basic strategy for derivation of broker policies for service providers of packaged apps from service descriptions of hosting services. In this respect, we have formulated a set of modifications and extensions to Linked USDL – our chosen technical specification for enabling platform-agnostic data exchange between the actors of a cloud service brokerage ecosystem.

With the proliferation of cloud computing, enterprises are anticipated to increasingly rely on CSB in order to manage the complex IT ecosystems of manifold services that ensue as a result. We anticipate that strategies for mediation of hosting services on CSB platforms require such platform-agnostic data description methods as introduced in this paper and will pave the way for the provision of efficient mediation mechanisms offered by CSBs.

In the future, more research is needed to elaborate on more sophisticated methods and strategies for specification and derivation of broker policies and service descriptions within the lifecycle of a cloud service brokerage ecosystem that would be able to cope with continuous change of actors, services, and their characteristics within an ecosystem.

Acknowledgment. The research leading to these results has received funding from the European Union Seventh Framework Programme (FP7/2007-2013) under grant agreement no. 328392, the Broker@Cloud project (www.broker-cloud.eu).

References

1. Cloud: What an Enterprise Must Know, Cisco White Paper (2011)
2. Vaquero, L.M., Rodero-Merino, L., Caceres, J., Lindner, M.: A break in the clouds: Towards a cloud definition. SIGCOMM Comput. Commun. Rev. **39**(1), 50–55 (2008)
3. Cloud computing reference architecture. Technical report, NIST (2011)
4. Linked USDL. http://www.linked-usdl.org/
5. Christensen, C., Curbera, F., Meredith, G., Weerawarana, S.: Web Services Description Language (WSDL) 1.1, W3C (2001). http://www.w3.org/TR/wsdl
6. McIlraith, S.A., Son, T.C., Zeng, H.: Semantic Web Services. IEEE Intel. Syst. **16**(2), 46–53 (2001)
7. Lausen, H., Polleres, A., Roman, D. (eds) Web Service Modeling Ontology (WSMO). W3C (2001). http://www.w3.org/Submission/WSMO/
8. Martin, M., Burstein, M., Hobbs, J., Lassila, O., McDermott, D., McIlraith, S., Narayanan, S., Paolucci, M., Parsia, B., Payne, T., Sirin, E., Srinivasan, N., Sycara, K.: OWL-S: Semantic Markup for Web Services. W3C (2004). http://www.w3.org/Submission/OWL-S/
9. Farrell, J., Lausen, H.: Semantic Annotations for WSDL and XML Schema (SAWSDL), W3C Recommendation (2007). http://www.w3.org/TR/sawsdl/
10. Gomadam, K., Ranabahu, A., Sheth, A.: SA-REST: Semantic Annotation of Web Resources, W3C Member Submission (2010). http://www.w3.org/Submission/SA-REST/

11. Norton, B., Kerrigan, M., Mocan, A., Carenini, A., Cimpian, E., Haines, M., Scicluna, J., Zaremba, M.: Reference ontology for semantic service oriented architectures. OASIS Public Review Draft 0.1 (2008). http://docs.oasis-open.org/semantic-ex/ro-soa/v1.0/pr01/see-rosoa-v1.0-pr01.html

12. Pedrinaci, C., Domingue, J.: Towards the next wave of services: linked services for the web of data. J. UCS **16**(13), 1694–1719 (2010)

13. Fensel, D., Fischer, F., Kopecký, J., Krummenacher, R., Lambert, D., Vitvar, T.: WSMO-Lite: Lightweight Semantic Descriptions for Services on the Web, W3C Member Submission (2010). http://www.w3.org/Submission/WSMO-Lite

14. Kopecky, J., Vitvar, T., Pedrinaci, C., Maleshkova, M.: RESTful services with lightweight machine-readable descriptions and semantic annotations. In: Wilde, E., Pautasso, C. (eds.) REST: From Research to Practice. Springer, New York (2011)

15. Barros, A., Oberle, D.: Handbook of Service Description: USDL and its Methods. Springer, New York (2012)

16. Oberle, D., Barros, A., Heinzl, S., Kylau, U.: A unified description language for human to automated services. Inf. Syst. **38**, 155–181 (2013)

17. GoodRelations: The Professional Web Vocabulary for E-Commerce. http://www.heppnetz.de/projects/goodrelations/

18. SKOS – Simple Knowledge Organization System. http://www.w3.org/2004/02/skos/

19. The Friend of a Friend (FOAF) Project. http://www.foaf-project.org/

20. http://iserve.kmi.open.ac.uk/ns/msm/msm-2013-05-03.html

21. https://sites.google.com/site/brokeratcloud/documents/deliverables/d30-2-methods-and-tools-for-brokerage-enabling-description-of-enterprise-cloud-services

22. https://www.oasis-open.org/committees/tc_home.php?wg_abbrev=uddi-spec

SeaCloudS 2014

Workshop on Seamless Adaptive Multi-cloud Management of Service-Based Applications (SeaCloudS): Preface

Antonio Brogi[1] and Ernesto Pimentel[2(✉)]

[1] University of Pisa, Pisa, Italy
brogi@di.unipi.it
[2] University of Málaga, Málaga, Spain
ernesto@lcc.uma.es

Deploying and managing in an efficient and adaptive way complex service-based applications across multiple heterogeneous clouds is one of the problems that have emerged with the cloud revolution. The current lack of universally accepted standards supporting cloud interoperability is severely affecting the portability of cloud-based applications across different platforms. The objective of the workshop was to provide a forum to discuss problems, solutions and perspectives of ongoing research activities aimed at enabling an efficient and adaptive management of service-based applications across multiple clouds.

The Program Committee of the workshop (please see below) included twelve internationally recognized experts from nine different countries (France, Germany, Ireland, Italy, Norway, Portugal, Romania, Spain, UK). Five contributions were submitted in response to the call for papers. The originality and relevance of those contributions was evaluated with a peer-review process carried over by the Program Committee, which unanimously decided to accept only one of those contributions as a regular paper, and three others contributions were accepted as presentations of work in progress (with a shorter time for presentation and fewer pages in the proceedings).

Besides the presentations of the contributed papers, the program included the shared opening keynote by Simon Moser (IBM) on "From TOSCA landscapes to the Foundry - A walkthrough", an invited talk by Alex Heneveld (Cloudsoft) on "Going to CAMP via Apache Brooklyn", and a round table on multi-cloud interoperability with the participation of K. Djemame (Univ. of Leeds), E. Gelenbe (Imperial College), A. Heneveld (Cloudsoft), S. Moser (IBM), and C. Pezuela (ATOS). The program also included a final session devoted to presentations of ongoing EU research projects, which included a presentation of the SeaClouds project (by F. D'Andria, ATOS), of the Panacea project (by E. Gelenbe and G. Gorbil, Imperial College), of the PaaSage project (by A. Rossini, SINTEF), of the MODAClouds project (by G. Casale, Imperial College), of the ARTIST project (by C. Pezuela, ATOS), of the Eco2Cloud project (by U. Wajid, Univ. of Manchester), and of the ASCETIC Project (by K. Djemame, Univ. of Leeds).

The workshop was promoted by the ongoing European research project EC-FP7-ICT-610531 SeaClouds.

G. Ortiz and C. Tran (Eds.): ESOCC 2014, CCIS 508, pp 247–248, 2015.
DOI: 10.1007/978-3-319-14886-1_22

We would like to thank all the people who contributed to the success of the workshop: the authors of the contributed papers, the program committee members, the invited speakers, the panelists of the round of table, and the presenters of the EU projects.

Antonio Brogi
Ernesto Pimentel
Program Chairs

Organization

Program Chairs

Antonio Brogi, University of Pisa, Italy
Ernesto Pimentel, University of Málaga, Spain

Program Committee

Marcos Almeida, Softeam, France
Jorge Cardoso, University of Coimbra, Portugal
Martin Chapman, Oracle, Ireland
Tommaso Cucinotta, Bell Labs, Alcatel-Lucent, Ireland
Javier Cubo, University of Málaga, Spain
Francesco D'Andria, ATOS, Spain
Elisabetta Di Nitto, Politecnico di Milano, Italy
Christoph Fehling, University of Stuttgart, Germany
Nicolas Ferry, SINTEF, Norway
Alex Heneveld, Cloudsoft, UK
Simon Moser, IBM, Germany
Dana Petcu, West University of Timisoara, Romania
Achim Streit, Karlsruhe Institute of Technology, Germany
PengWei Wang, University of Pisa, Italy

Publicity Chair

Michela Fazzolari, University of Pisa, Italy

Webmaster

Adrian Nieto, University of Málaga, Spain

Orthogonal Variability Modeling to Support Multi-cloud Application Configuration

Pooyan Jamshidi and Claus Pahl[✉]

IC4 – The Irish Centre for Cloud Computing and Commerce,
Dublin City University, Dublin, Ireland
{pooyan.jamshidi,claus.pahl}@computing.dcu.ie

Abstract. Cloud service providers benefit from a vast majority of customers due to variability and making profit from commonalities between the cloud services that they provide. Recently, application configuration dimensions has been increased dramatically due to multi-tenant, multi-device and multi-cloud paradigm. This challenges the configuration and customization of cloud-based software that are typically offered as a service due to the intrinsic variability. In this paper, we present a model-driven approach based on variability models originating from the software product line community to handle such multi-dimensional variability in the cloud. We exploit orthogonal variability models to systematically manage and create tenant-specific configuration and customizations. We also demonstrate how such variability models can be utilized to take into account the already deployed application parts to enable harmonized deployments for new tenants in a multi-cloud setting. The approach considers application functional and non-functional requirements to provide a set of valid multi-cloud configurations. We illustrate our approach through a case study.

Keywords: Multi-cloud · Variability · Multi-tenancy · Cloud architecture

1 Introduction

In the delivery model of software systems, a frequently studied shift [1] can be observed in which software products are no longer delivered to customers as packages or deployed in-house, however, they are deployed at a central location and offered to customers online (Software-as-a-Service; SaaS). In on-premise deployments, users access only one instance of an application that is developed in a software house and deployed on-premises. Obviously, such application can be tailored regarding specific customer needs in case the standard product functionalities do not perfectly fit with the very specific customer's requirements (in terms of business process support or particular non-functional requirements) [2]. However, this approach will not be profitable if customers request large number of variations. To make this more cost-beneficial and yet to satisfy particular customer needs, a novel approach has been proposed by which different products, based on a product core containing general requirements shared by all customers, can be generated in a software product line [3].

© Springer International Publishing Switzerland 2015
G. Ortiz and C. Tran (Eds.): ESOCC 2014, CCIS 508, pp. 249–261, 2015.
DOI: 10.1007/978-3-319-14886-1_23

The concept of software variability was first studied in the software product lines community [4]. Traditionally, variability only considers on-premise single-tenant software. This approach follows the idea that software products containing specific features have to be built before shipping the software (i.e., design-time binding). Software products that are delivered through online channels, however, only profits from runtime binding since it would be undesirable to restart or redeploy a version whenever changes are made (such case is a norm in design-time binding, for example). In software products, which are accessible online, the higher the configurability of a product is, the more variable a product would be. A variable product aims to provide customers with a set of options using a single code base in such a way that each tenant is able to have a unique configuration. Since the software instance is now deployed in one location, multiple customers can potentially use the same instance of the software. Sharing a software instance with multiple users, however, makes it impossible to have customized products for specific customers. In other words, multi-tenant software is able to fulfil all different customer requirements, while still taking advantage of shared resources [5]. In this setting, tenants are customers using the application and usually consisting of multiple users within the same organizational context or common interests [6].

The work reported in [7] use the concept of external runtime variability in software product line to represent the variability management in SaaS context. They refer to such type of variability as customer-driven variability. Such usage of external variability to represent tenant-based variability is also shown in several other research work, e.g., [5, 8–10]. One of the commonalities within such varieties of work is that they use a sort of variability model to represent very specific needs of tenants to make the online software product a configurable entity to allow for the varying requirements. However, with the new type of development in the accessibility options as well as deployment variability in the cloud, the application configuration and customization becomes a complex and unmanageable process due to the large variability in the solution space. These dimensions are orthogonal to the tenant-specific configuration and, in this paper, we propose to use a multi-dimensional variability management to address the newly raised concerns that we discuss in the following.

Multi-cloud configuration. Multi-cloud deployment [6, 11] is particularly effective in dealing with the situations where users are widely distributed around multiple data centers, country regulations limit options for storing data in specific data centers, and circumstances where public clouds are used jointly with on-premises resources. The main difficulty is to deal with the wide range of deployment options at different layers on different cloud platforms [12]. Such dimensions are orthogonal to the application architecture and make a large solution space for the deployment architecture. Consequently, there is a need to enable multi-cloud deployment specific configuration.

Multi-device configuration. With the raise of smartphones and devices in one hand and heterogeneity in the platforms, tenants are required to access to the cloud-based services on specific devices. Consequently, there is a need to enable multi-device and cross platform configuration, which is also orthogonal to both the application and deployment architectures.

To address these challenges, we propose $3OVM$, a model that integrates three variability models each addressing specific challenges regarding tenant-specific, multi-device and multi-cloud configuration. Cloud application variability can thus be described using $3OVM$. We use a video processing application as a running example to describe the approach. This application contains more than 10,000 different configurations. However, the approach proposed here is not specific to this application and can cover different cloud-enabled application domains that can benefit from multi-cloud deployment, such as process-aware applications [13].

2   Research Challenges

With the rise of multi-tenant cloud-based applications, the dimensions for configuring the software that is usually offered as a service has been also increased dramatically. The functionality and quality that individual tenants need from a software application are typically different from each other. As a consequence, in order to attract enough customers, cloud service providers are required [5, 7, 9, 10, 12]: **(i)** To cater for the varying requirements of potential tenants by providing tenant-specific configurations. **(ii)** To make sure that they can handle the varieties of the deployment options in terms of, for example, infrastructure offerings. **(iii)** To derive the tenant-specific configuration by considering the variability of the devices with which each tenant needs to access the implemented functionality.

For example, SaaS applications allow users to customize the captions used in the application and modifying business processes implemented in the systems. Such tenant-specific adaptations of a SaaS application affect all layers of the application: from functional requirements to business processes and even database schemas. Tenants do not only have various requirements with respect to functional features, but also require different non-functional requirements. While some tenants want an application to be highly available, other tenants are not so much interested in high-availability, but care more about performance. Traditionally, this was handled through different pre-configured software packages with different prices. However, cloud allows a more robust delivery models in which software is licensed on a subscription basis and is hosted on cloud platforms by independent vendors. Therefore, cloud service providers face the following challenges for the configuration and customizations of their products:

Challenge1. *Tenant-specific configuration and customizations.* Cloud applications are typically multi-tenant and each tenant require its own specific functional and non-functional requirements.

Challenge2. *Multi-cloud configuration.* The main difficulty is to deal with the wide range of deployment options at different layers on different cloud platforms. Such dimensions are certainly orthogonal to the application architecture and make a large solution space for the deployment architecture.

Challenge3. *Multi-device and cross-platform configuration.* With the rise of smartphones and devices on the one hand and heterogeneity in the platforms that they support, tenants are required to access to the cloud-based services on specific devices.

We highlight these challenges through a case study in the next section.

3 Running Example

To highlight the challenges and to exemplify our approach, we introduce a video-processing application [10], which is a cloud-enabled system deployed on a multi-cloud environment. In this example, the video processing software is offered as a service, which has the capability to be customized for different tenants based on their required functions, quality and end-point devices. The application comprises a number of components as depicted in Fig. 1. The system is illustrated in three different architectural views, i.e., application architecture, deployment architecture and accessibility devices.

Tenants can choose different subsets of the components, considering that the architectural constraints are not violated. One of the constraint is that the configuration must include Player (VP), Decoder (Dec) and Data-Provider (DP) components, which form the core of the video processing (this represents the commonalities among the derived products). The functional variability of the video-processing application is: Video-Manager (VM), which offers a graphical UI to add and remove videos. Icon component, which injects a tenant-specific logo into the videos before they are played. Subtitle (Sub) component, which introduces subtitles as overlays on videos.

The StreamProcessor (SP) is the parent of the Decoder, Icon and Subtitle components. This abstraction enables the tenant to choose a combination of the three inheriting components. Note that in this setting different sub-architecture of the system can potentially be deployed on different cloud platforms. This is because all deployment of the same parts provide the same functionality, but differ in their non-functional properties. For example, the VideoPlayer-StreamProcessor binding is realized by the pipes and filters style on Windows Azure and Amazon AWS. Both deployments facilitate playing a video, but Azure deployment offers a different rendering resolution and performance than AWS does. Furthermore, the accessibility on the two deployments is different. For example, AWS deployment does not support refrigerator device.

Table 1. Tenants configuration and requirements.

Tenants	Components	NFRs	Accessibility
T1	VP, Dec, DP	Bandwidth: 1000 MB/s Availability: Standard, Latency: 1 s	PC, Mobile (Android), Mobile (iOS), Refrigerator
T2	VP, Dec, Sub, DP	Bandwidth: 1000 MB/s Availability: Standard, Latency: 0.1 s	All
T3	VP, Dec, Sub, Icon, DP, VM	Bandwidth: 10 MB/s Availability: Super, Latency: 0.01 s	PC (Mac OS), Car

For each tenant an own configuration/deployment of the application can be created. For our example, we assume three tenants: the first tenant (T1) does not use any optional component, whereas the second tenant (T2) has decided to use the Subtitle component to enhance the application. The third tenant (T3) has decided to have all the functionalities. Besides the functionality that each tenant is required, they require their own specific non-functional requirements (NFRs) (cf. Fig. 2), which characterize how the provided functionality can be fulfilled. Besides, each tenant requires to access the functions in different devices, see Table 1.

The architectural style of the video-processing application is pipes and filters. Such architectural style when realized on cloud platforms allows for the on-demand provisioning of multi-part job processing. It can be used for instantaneous or delayed deployment of a heterogeneous, scalable "grid" of worker nodes that can quickly crunch through large batch processing tasks in parallel [6, 14–16]. Numerous batch-oriented applications are in place that can leverage such on-demand processing including video transcoding. The video-processing application behaves as follows:

1. Users interact with the end-points, which is deployed on a cloud platform. This component controls the process of video management and playing.
2. Raw video data is transformed to a cloud storage, a highly available and persistent data store. The transcoding tasks are inserted by an elastic queue.
3. Worker nodes are cloud instances that can be scaled. Worker nodes pick up tasks from the input queue and perform single tasks that are part of the list of batch processing steps. Interim results from worker nodes can be stored in a storage.
4. Progress information and statistics are stored on the storage as well. This component can be either a cloud storage or a relational database.

The video-processing application is a multi-tenant SaaS application and as we indicated in Table 1, each tenant requires its own specific functional and non-functional

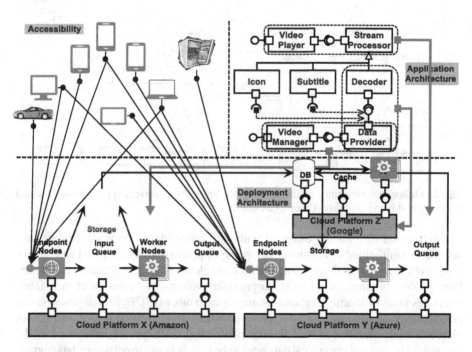

Fig. 1. Application and deployment architecture of video processing system.

features accessible on specific platform. The main challenge here is how to deal with the wide range of deployment options and this situation becomes more challenging when we consider multi-cloud. In this work, we address the complexity of multi-cloud application configuration through a model that we introduce in the next section.

4   Approach

In order to build highly scalable applications, *multi-cloud deployment* is appropriate [11, 17]. The objective of this work is to provide a model-based approach that facilitates tenant-specific configuration and customizations for applications that run on multiple independent clouds.

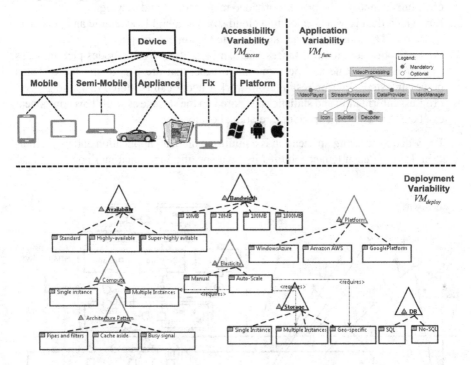

Fig. 2. Orthogonal variability model showing the accessibility-driven, application-driven and deployment-driven variability (Color figure online).

Multi-cloud denotes the usage of multiple, independent clouds by a client or a service. A multi-cloud environment is capable of processing user demand and distributing work to resources deployed across multiple clouds [18]. A multi-cloud is different from *federation* where, a set of cloud providers voluntarily interconnect their infrastructures to allow sharing of resources among each other [18]. *Hybrid deployment* can be considered as a special case of multi-cloud where an application is deployed in both on premise infrastructure as well as cloud platform(s). Such type of deployment model is essential in cases where critical data need to be kept in house in corporate data centers.

We have reviewed different application types and specific requirements that necessitate multi-cloud deployment – see the supplementary materials [15].

In a multi-cloud configuration perspective, parts of the application can be deployed at either PaaS, IaaS or both levels [17, 19], see Fig. 1. The wide range of cloud providers likely to host the application makes the choice difficult. To fit these requirements and dimensions, we find 15 possibilities in terms of patterns, reported in [15]. The key reasons behind such multi-cloud migration are as follows:

- Users are widely distributed where they are located around multiple data centers.
- Country regulations limit options for storing data in specific data centers, e.g., EU.
- Circumstances where public clouds are used jointly with on-premises resources.
- Cloud-based application must be resilient to the loss of a single data center.

To address the challenges identified in this paper, we define an orthogonal variability model used to (i) capture cloud providers visible options for tenants-specific deployment and (ii) enable tenants to configure functional and non-functional aspects of the application, (iii) enable tenants to choose their preferences of accessibility options.

In this work, we combine three different variability models at different levels of abstractions regarding the three above-mentioned concerns into a single model (i.e., $3OVM$) that gives strong support to all tenants involved in cloud deployment. As illustrated in Fig. 2, the approach allows users to (i) define a functional specification of the system through choosing the options in the application variability model (VM_{func}). Also, it allows users (ii) to select alternatives for realizing and deploying the application on a (multi-)cloud environment as well as selecting the non-functional preferences of the system in the deployment variability model (VM_{deploy}). Such aspects themselves affect some internal non-visible aspects of the system (red triangles in Fig. 2), which are only visible for the development team of the cloud-based application. This will be realized by combining several valid cloud configurations to fit the requirements. (iii) To choose the accessibility options that are required by the users comprising multi-device and multi-platform capabilities in the accessibility variability model (VM_{access}).

Therefore, $3OVM$ consists of three variability models at different levels regarding different concerns of multi-cloud application deployments. VM_{func} is a fully fledged variability model that represents both functional commonalities and variabilities of the cloud-based software products. However, VM_{deploy} and VM_{access} represent only variabilities that determines the non-functional aspects of the cloud-based products. They represent, in other words, a reference point to where different variants regarding the deployment options or accessibility can be attached. The variants manifest a concrete variability in terms of deployment or accessibility. In this model, all variation points in VM_{deploy} and VM_{access} are related to at least one functional variant in VM_{func}, and all variations in VM_{func} are related to at least one variation point in either VM_{deploy} or VM_{access}. This reduces the complexity of the variability model and therefore enhances the readability of the model facilitating a robust application customization.

For defining VM_{func} and VM_{access}, we use feature model defined in [20], while for specifying VM_{deploy}, we employ the OVM (Orthogonal Variability Model) introduced in [3]. The reason behind such choice for VM_{deploy} is that the OVMs are smaller and less complex since they only model variability and not the commonalities. This is useful in the context of multi-cloud environments since for modeling the deployment space we only need to consider different variability that each platform may offer and not thinking about their commonalities.

The $3OVM$ model distinguishes between different roles: application developers (Dev), cloud experts (Ops) and the tenants (Ten). Application developers provides the functional variability and commonality points of the system, resulting in the corresponding variability model (i.e., VM_{func}). Cloud experts are involved in the platform specific descriptions. They describe cloud platform variability and commonality points, thus providing the corresponding variability model (i.e., VM_{deploy}) to the architecture. Cloud experts are also responsible for providing the accessibility variability model (i.e., VM_{access}). Tenants are all user groups involved in externally visible option (bold triangles in Fig. 2) selection through such orthogonal variability models. Using such an approach only requires having necessary knowledge to properly configure the cloud application and to properly cooperate to develop such knowledge to the system. We will describe the usage process of our approach in detail in the next section.

5   Multi-cloud Deployment Support

Having specified the variability of cloud applications, the three variability models can be used to further support the customization and deployment lifecycle. In this section, we describe a process to perform such deployment by utilizing $3OVM$ via the example.

In order to customize a cloud-based application, (i) *tenants need to decide which variants*, whether they are functional or non-functional or accessibility aspects, *should become part of their application*. Therefore, tenants need to have the capability to choose among the potential configuration options in order to bind the variability of the cloud application. In the product line engineering, several approaches are existed to realize such a customization support [7].

After binding the tenant-specific variability of a cloud-based application, (ii) *the deployment actions should be accomplished* in order to prepare the application for users belonging to that tenant. The deployment actions depend on the binding of the deployment variability, which itself depends on the cloud platform and the information about already bounded variability, i.e. deployed features of the application. Therefore, to bind the deployment variability, the cloud platform needs to consider the tenant-specific variability as well as the binding information about the parts of the application that have already been deployed for other tenants.

Some variation points must be bound because of dependencies to variants that have been chosen by the binding of the tenant-specific variability. For each open variation point, the cloud service provider is aware of the possible variants because it already knows the variability model via $3OVM$. Now the most appropriate variant for the provider must be chosen. This can be done through (iii) *annotating individual variants* with, for example, a cost parameter and using optimization algorithms to find the least expensive variant combination. This, however, is beyond the scope of this paper.

The deployment actions do not only depend on the status but also on the services that are used for a particular tenant. For the services that are used in a single instance mode, the cloud service provider must make sure that enough resources are available to run the new tenant on the instance of the service that is already deployed. In multi-cloud setting, this however can manage through live migration from one platform to another one if the resources are not sufficient in one particular platform. For the services in multiple instances mode, the appropriate infrastructure must be provisioned. In sum, the purpose of this step is **(iv)** *to perform the required reconfiguration* to adjust the platform for proper deployment of the application.

We now describe the above–mentioned customization and deployment process through our running example. Table 2 shows three possible configurations for the video processing application. The table shows the bounded alternatives for each variation point (here we only concentrated on VM_{deploy}). Config. 1 and Config. 2 are the same in terms of external variability points, since every variation point is bound with the same variant. Note that they differ in the platform variation point; however, platform variation point is internal and is not visible to the tenants. Therefore, these two configurations are externally equivalent and the same in the view of tenants. The result of such situation is that two tenants that bind all external variability points in a similar way can end up with two different solutions, as one solution for example is deployed on a cloud platform while the other is deployed on another platform. Such configuration, although might have the same functional behaviour, they may show different non-functional behaviour due to heterogeneous cloud platforms.

Table 2. Exemplary configurations of the video processing system.

Variation point		Config. 1	Config. 2	Config. 3
External	Availability	Standard	Standard	Super available
	Bandwidth	1000	1000	10
	Storage	Multiple-instance	Multiple-instance	Geo-specific, single instance
	DB	SQL	SQL	No-SQL
Internal	Platform	Azure	AWS	Azure/AWS/Google
	Compute	Multiple-instance	Multiple-instance	Multiple-instance
	Elasticity	Auto-scale	Auto-scale	Auto-scale
	Pattern	Pipes and filters	Pipes and filters	Cache-aside, Pipes and filters

The deployment for tenant 3 (Config. 3) must provision resources for the storage service as this tenant chose to store the data in specific location and cannot share its data with the other tenants due to security concerns. Therefore, the service must also be deployed in single instances mode, as privacy is important to that tenant. As the tenant also selected the option of super availability, the application is deployed on multiple cloud platforms. Now a situation arises where tenant 3 requires the resources on Google cloud platform in which the functionality of the video processing application is not deployed since the other two tenants are on Azure and AWS platforms (cf. Fig. 1).

Once a tenant decides to unsubscribe from a cloud application, it must be undeployed from the system [7]. This might be as simple as removing a line in a configuration setting.

However, in case a tenant has used services that are deployed on multiple cloud platforms, these services must be undeployed from each specific platform by issuing platform specific undeployment commands. Nevertheless, it is important to know which combination of functionality, accessibility and deployment has been used by a tenant to perform the necessary steps to undeploy the services.

In addition to provisioning and de-provisioning scripts, "tenant transfer" scripts can be generated that describe how a tenant is transferred from one configuration to another one or from one specific platform to another platform or hybrid or even multiple platforms.

6   Related Work

Multi-cloud application configuration. Quinton et al. [21] present a model-driven approach based on feature models and ontology to handle heterogeneity in cloud variability and managing cloud configurations. The approach considers technical as well as non-functional requirements to provide a set of valid configurations. Their focus is mostly on managing the heterogeneity in multi-cloud environments via a mapping from an ontology model to platform specific feature models. This work is the closest existing work to our approach. However, our main concern is to manage functional and accessibility aspects in accordance with multi-cloud deployment aspects in a homogenous variability model that different roles in developments and operations (known as DevOps) can cooperate to build up the model and provide a unified model that tenants can choose their preferences through it without requiring specific technical knowledge.

Sampaio et al. [22] propose an approach that facilitates modeling, deployment and configuration of software applications over multiple heterogeneous IaaS clouds. In this approach, the application to be deployed is specified using open standards to be run in VMs while our approach is based on the variability model that enable tenants to choose from three different aspects of the system considering its tenant-specific requirements.

Brandtzæg et al. [23] propose a component-based approach that leverages the existing deployment descriptors into a domain-specific language (DSL). The DSL is used to model the deployment and an interpreter is provided to identify which resources have to be used in the platform to fulfill requirements. Although this work facilitates a semi-automated deployment, they do not consider the cloud offer heterogeneity.

Paraiso et al. [24] present a multi-cloud PaaS infrastructure deployed on existing IaaS/PaaS. This infrastructure is based on an open service model. Contrarily to our approach, they do not need to consider the capability to configure the multi-cloud platform since they use the same service model for both SaaS and PaaS.

Multi-tenant application configuration. Mietzner et al. [7] show how variability modeling techniques from software product line can support cloud service providers to manage the variability of cloud-based applications and tenant specific configurations. They propose using explicit variability models to systematically derive customization and deployment information for individual tenants. Gaddar et al. [9] introduce the new concept of Variability as a Service (VaaS) model to relieve cloud providers from developing expensive variability models by decreasing the variability management complexity.

More recently, Quinton et al. [8] propose an automated approach to face the configuration of cloud-based applications. Their approach automates the deployment of such configurations through the generation of executable scripts. Schroeter et al. [10] identify requirements for runtime architecture addressing the individual interests of tenants in multi-tenant architectures. They show how dynamic architectures can be extended for the development of multi-tenant applications. This work, as opposed to the other approaches, concentrates on the variability at the architecture level.

These above mentioned work although inspiring, they are only applicable for single platform SaaS based applications as opposed to our approach, which targeted multi-cloud environments. In fact, in terms of technical contribution, all of the multi-cloud configuration management approaches, are an extension of [7].

7 Conclusion and Outlook

We presented how orthogonal variability models that we borrowed from software product line engineering, can be used to model variability in 3 different yet important aspects of cloud applications in the multi-cloud environments. We have applied the concepts of configuration management from software product line engineering to the problem of deployment support for multi-cloud applications and have demonstrated the benefits of our approach by means of a case study. The key benefit of the proposed model is to manage different interrelated deployment aspects through a unified model consists of models at different levels of abstractions.

In our future work, we plan to automate this approach by developing a tool that enables the creation of the $3OVM$ variability models facilitating the automated deployment of multi-cloud application at runtime. We plan to employ the approach in the context of a multi-cloud runtime adaptation mechanism, a similar approach as have been pursued in projects like MODAClouds [19], CloudMF [25], mOSAIC [26] and OPTIMIS [27], however, targeting different concerns: (i) uncertainty handling in elastic systems, (ii) multi-cloud auto-scaling, (iii) auto-scaling in data-intensive applications and (iv) the application of control theory in auto-scaling [28].

Acknowledgments. The research work described in this paper was supported by the Irish Centre for Cloud Computing and Commerce (IC4), an Irish national Technology Centre funded by Enterprise Ireland and the Irish Industrial Development Authority.

References

1. Jamshidi, P., Ahmad, A., Pahl, C.: Cloud migration research: a systematic review. IEEE Trans. Cloud Comput. **1**, 142–157 (2013)
2. Sun, W., Zhang, X., Guo, C.J., Sun, P., Su, H.: Software as a service: configuration and customization perspectives. In: 2008 IEEE Congress on Services Part II (Services-2 2008), pp. 18–25. IEEE (2008)
3. Pohl, K., Böckle, G., Van Der Linden, F.: Software Product Line Engineering. Springer, Heidelberg (2005)

4. Svahnberg, M., van Gurp, J., Bosch, J.: A taxonomy of variability realization techniques. Softw. Pract. Exp. **35**, 705–754 (2005)
5. Kabbedijk, J., Jansen, S.: Variability in multi-tenant environments: architectural design patterns from industry. Adv. Concept. Model. Recent Dev. New Dir. **6999**, 151–160 (2011)
6. Wilder, B.: Cloud Architecture Patterns: Using Microsoft Azure. O'Reilly Media, Sebastopol (2012)
7. Mietzner, R., Metzger, A., Leymann, F., Pohl, K.: Variability modeling to support customization and deployment of multi-tenant-aware software as a service applications. In: 2009 ICSE Workshop on Principles of Engineering Service Oriented Systems. IEEE (2009)
8. Quinton, C., Romero, D., Duchien, L.: Automated selection and configuration of cloud environments using software product lines principles. In: IEEE CLOUD 2014 (2014)
9. Ghaddar, A., Tamzalit, D., Assaf, A., Bitar, A.: Variability as a service: outsourcing variability management in multi-tenant saas applications. Adv. Inf. Syst. Eng. **7328**, 175–189 (2012)
10. Schroeter, J., Cech, S., Götz, S., Wilke, C., Aßmann, U.: Towards modeling a variable architecture for multi-tenant SaaS-applications. In: Proceedings of the Sixth International Workshop on Variability Modeling of Software-Intensive Systems - VaMoS 2012, pp. 111–120. ACM Press, New York (2012)
11. Petcu, D.: Multi-cloud. In: Proceedings of the 2013 International Workshop on Multi-cloud Applications and Federated Clouds - MultiCloud 2013, p. 1. ACM Press, New York (2013)
12. Koetter, F., Kochanowski, M., Renner, T., Fehling, C., Leymann, F.: Unifying compliance management in adaptive environments through variability descriptors. In: 2013 IEEE 6th International Conference on Service-Oriented Computing and Applications. IEEE (2013)
13. Jrad, F., Tao, J., Streit, A.: A broker-based framework for multi-cloud workflows. In: Proceedings of the 2013 International Workshop on Multi-cloud Applications and Federated Clouds - MultiCloud 2013, p. 61. ACM Press, New York (2013)
14. Homer, A., Sharp, J., Brader, L., Narumoto, M., Swanson, T.: Cloud Design Patterns: Prescriptive Architecture Guidance for Cloud Applications. Microsoft, New York (2014)
15. Jamshidi, P., Pahl, C.: Cloud Migration Patterns - Supplementary Materials. http://www.computing.dcu.ie/~pjamshidi/Materials/CMP.html
16. Fehling, C., Leymann, F., Retter, R., Schupeck, W., Arbitter, P.: Cloud Computing Patterns. Springer Vienna, Vienna (2014)
17. Petcu, D., et al.: Experiences in building a mOSAIC of clouds. J. Cloud Comput. Adv. Syst. Appl. **2**, 12 (2013)
18. Grozev, N., Buyya, R.: Inter-Cloud architectures and application brokering: taxonomy and survey. Softw. Pract. Exp. **44**, 369–390 (2014)
19. Di Nitto, E., da Silva, M.A.A., Ardagna, D., Casale, G., Craciun, C.D., Ferry, N., Muntes, V., Solberg, A.: Supporting the development and operation of multi-cloud applications: the MODAClouds approach. In: 2013 15th International Symposium on Symbolic and Numeric Algorithms for Scientific Computing, pp. 417–423. IEEE (2013)
20. Kang, K., Lee, J., Donohoe, P.: Feature-oriented product line engineering. IEEE Softw. **19**, 58–65 (2002)
21. Quinton, C., Haderer, N., Rouvoy, R., Duchien, L.: Towards multi-cloud configurations using feature models and ontologies. In: Proceedings of the 2013 International Workshop on Multi-cloud Applications and Federated Clouds - MultiCloud 2013, p. 21. ACM Press, New York (2013)

22. Sampaio, A., Mendonça, N.: Uni4Cloud: an approach based on open standards for deployment and management of multi-cloud applications. In: Proceeding of the 2nd International Workshop on Software Engineering for Cloud Computing - SECLOUD 2011, p. 15. ACM Press, New York (2011)

23. Brandtzæg, E., Mohagheghi, P., Mosser, S.: Towards a domain-specific language to deploy applications in the clouds. In: CLOUD Computing (2012)

24. Paraiso, F., et al.: A federated multi-cloud PaaS infrastructure. In: 2012 IEEE Fifth International Conference on Cloud Computing, pp. 392–399. IEEE (2012)

25. Ferry, N., Chauvel, F., Rossini, A., Morin, B., Solberg, A.: Managing multi-cloud systems with CloudMF. In: Proceedings of the Second Nordic Symposium on Cloud Computing & Internet Technologies - NordiCloud 2013. ACM Press, New York (2013)

26. mOSAIC EU project. http://www.mosaic-project.eu/

27. Ferrer, A.J., et al.: OPTIMIS: a holistic approach to cloud service provisioning. Futur. Gener. Comput. Syst. **28**, 66–77 (2012)

28. Jamshidi, P., Ahmad, A., Pahl, C.: Autonomic resource provisioning for cloud-based software. In: Proceedings of the 9th International Symposium on Software Engineering for Adaptive and Self-Managing Systems - SEAMS 2014, pp. 95–104. ACM Press, New York (2014)

A Marketplace Broker for Platform-as-a-Service Portability

Bholanathsingh Surajbali[1](✉) and Adrián Juan-Verdejo[1,2](✉)

[1] Smart Research Development Centre, CAS Software AG, Karlsruhe, Germany
{b.surajbali,adrian.juan}@cas.de
[2] Information Systems Chair, Stuttgart University, Stuttgart, Germany

Abstract. Platform as a Service (PaaS) has become a strong techno-
logical solution in particular for small medium enterprises (SMEs) to
achieve cost savings and rapid time to market of their software solutions.
However, for SMEs how to choose the PaaS provider becomes a bottleneck due to the number of offerings each PaaS vendor offers. Another
challenge often faced by enterprises is how to match their software system requirements to PaaS offerings. Furthermore, searching for the best
PaaS offering is even more difficult when enterprises need to migrate
their existing software solutions from one PaaS vendor to another. In
such cases, the portability of the enterprises data and application components becomes cumbersome. If their software solutions are bound to a
specific PaaS provider, enterprises suffer from vendor lock-in. This paper
addresses these portability challenges by proposing a high-level architecture to ease the portability of software solutions over PaaS vendors
taking into consideration the various life-cycle stages, such as identifying and analysing Paas offerings in the market; selecting the best PaaS
offering according to organisation's requirements; and the deployment,
management, and monitoring of the software solutions.

1 Introduction

Platform as Service (PaaS) has established itself as the lynchpin for organisations to take advantage of the decreased information technology (IT) costs and
increasing application development performance. PaaS offerings offer a higher-
level development platform which hides low-level details from the developer, such
as the operating system, the load balancing, and the data storage and access.
This developing platform enables programmers to write code and create applications without worrying about software versioning or limited infrastructure
resources. A PaaS vendor provides a runtime framework which enables developers to program the application's code and execute it. For example, libraries and
application programming interfaces (APIs) which give access to the computational and storage resources.

In particular, organisations can take advantage of productivity gains which
allow them to develop and deploy their applications. By leveraging PaaS faster
application testing and deployment, development teams can easily try different

G. Ortiz and C. Tran (Eds.): ESOCC 2014, CCIS 508, pp. 262–270, 2015.
DOI: 10.1007/978-3-319-14886-1_24

configuration, assess application's performance, and identify compatibility issues. From a business perspective, PaaS allows enterprises to focus on their core business interests.

However, PaaS are becoming increasingly *complex* due to offerings heterogeneity, such as the number of runtime or services supported making it harder for enterprises to choose among PaaS vendors. These include, but are not limited to efficient deployment, security of PaaS provider—e.g. secure protocols, QoS guarantees, trust issues, and cost sharing models. In addition, enterprises may face the vendor lock-in problem when they want to migrate their system from one PaaS provider to another one. These are due to lack of PaaS vendors compliance to standards which makes the portability of data, application, and infrastructure difficult. But even if portability is supported in theory, the *high complexity* and the switching costs still discourage organisations from porting their applications [1]. Furthermore, new PaaS vendors face tough competition to make their offerings available to enterprises with giant vendors having suitable marketing and financial backing to publicise their offerings and cope with losses.

Enterprises developing applications should be able to choose between different Cloud PaaS offerings by selecting the most reliable, well-reputed, or cost-efficient offering; or simply the one that meets their technical requirements. Organisations should also be able to switch easily and transparently between PaaS providers whenever needed—for example, when a Service-Level Agreement (SLA) is breached or when the cost is too high—without setting data and applications at risk—for example, loss of data or inability to run the application on a different platform. Moreover, they should be able to compare PaaS offerings with different characteristics—such as resource, pricing or Quality of Service (QoS) model—and to choose the one that best matches the computing needs of their services and applications [2].

In this paper, we propose a *PaaS Marketplace* to allow PaaS provider selection according to the organisation's offerings, and to assess the application's portability to increase the level of service and minimise the potential occurrence of any vendor lock-in problem.

The rest of the paper is structured as follows. In Sect. 2, we describe the main motivation to build the broker marketplace using a use-case scenario. Next, in Sect. 3, we describe the PaaS offerings taxonomy. Next, in Sect. 4, we provide a discussion on the related work. Finally, in Sect. 5, we provide the conclusion and future work.

2   Marketplace Use Cases

A myriad of PaaS service offerings exist today and it is difficult for organisations to select the most adequate PaaS environment for them. Organisations choose depending on the PaaS environment capabilities and requirements. At the same time, they consider potential compatibility issues with their software components, the services offered by the PaaS environment, and potential interoperability and portability issues. To illustrate the complexity around PaaS selection and application adaptation we use the Business Intelligence (BI) portability scenario [3] as an explanatory example.

1. **Portability of a BI application from a legacy information system to a PaaS offering.** Organisations have different interdependent constraints to port their BI applications from one PaaS environment to another one; and want to achieve specific objectives in different dimensions. Nevertheless, when they improve the system in a dimension, as increased data storage, they could damage the system in another one, for example cost reduction. These dimensions are not always equally important to all organisations and they can trade one for another one. An organisation cannot overcome some of the constraints. As an example, one organisation might not be allowed to move its BI data to a public PaaS environment. The nature of the application components to be ported, the application's users, and the offering gained by porting the BI application to PaaS environments and how to choose the best offerings are crucial decisions for organisations.

2. **Partial portability of BI business logic or data layers.** An organisation can choose to move only part of the BI layers to the PaaS offering. For instance, for security reasons, an organisation may choose to keep the data layer on its premises while using BI tools in cloud environments to extract information from those data. At the same time, the organisation needs to make sure the system's performance is not affected by such a portability.

3. **Portability of a PaaS BI application from one PaaS platform to another.** The BI software engineer must evaluate each PaaS offering to reduce the effort to adapt its BI application to the new PaaS environment. The selection of the PaaS offering which requires less adaptation of the ported application reduces costs. The adaptation effort depends on the levels of portability transparently. That is, the portability achieved without using any additional software, changing the application settings, or putting the application and data at risk.

4. **Portability of a BI application to a PaaS offering provided by a new cloud provider within the marketplace.** This scenario is related to how a new PaaS provider joins the marketplace—Manage User Profile use case. The marketplace offers a graphical user interface with credential access to let PaaS providers seamlessly join the marketplace and transparently exchange data and applications with other PaaS providers—Manage Semantic Profile of Application use case. From a business perspective, PaaS providers access a large pool of potential customers to form alliances or build their competitive advantage.

3   PaaS Offerings Taxonomy

Based on the use cases presented and the BI example, we show in Fig. 1 the six PaaS offerings dimensions in which PaaS offerings differentiate from one another:

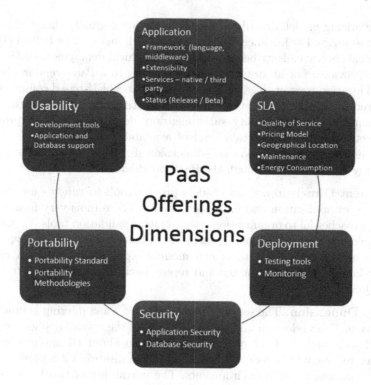

Fig. 1. PaaS offerings dimensions

Application Dimension. It is an essential dimension related to the application under migration and consists of four sub-dimensions (i) Application Framework; (ii) Extensibility; (iii) Services; and (iv) Status. The framework represents the underlying framework used to build the application, which can be for instance the language framework such as Java, .Net Framework, Spring; or computing framework such that Java EE, JBoss. The Extensibility sub-dimension represents application extensibility capability once it has been deployed and these can be in terms of *built-in* application monitoring, logging, and message queuing technologies. The services sub-dimension describe the application services by which can be *native* or *add-on* services. A native service is typically part of the PaaS application—such as the data storage service; while an add-on service is a third-party service integrated with the application—for example a search engine. The status of the application describe the deployed application in terms of beta or final release version.

SLA Dimension. The SLA specifies the PaaS offering service contract in terms of the quality of service (QoS), pricing model, geographical coverage, maintenance, and energy consumption of the applications/data. The QoS describes the response and resolution times the application service requests, providing the minimal, acceptable and maximal level of QoS supplied by the PaaS provider.

Next, the pricing model, describe what PaaS providers usually charge according to resources usage. For instance, billing can be fixed, metered, or hybrid [4]. The geographical coverage, describes the multi-geographical deployments offerings of the PaaS provider. For an organisation subscribing to a PaaS vendor, the geographical location presents legal concerns. For instance, EU-based companies are not allowed to transfer any of their customer-related data outside of the European Union [5]. The availability sub-dimension, describes the PaaS providers commitment to provide a certain level of availability for their PaaS offering. Finally, the energy-consumption sub-dimension describes, the application and data energy consumption through the PaaS provider.

Deployment Dimension. PaaS vendors provide tools to *validate* and *test* the deployment of application and data components. These tools vary from model-driven approaches [6] to organisations requirements validation tools [7], and software development life-cycle tooling facilities. Additionally, once deployed PaaS providers offer a number of tools can monitor application and data components performance based on usage and report back to organisations to ensure proper QoS.

Security Dimension. The security dimension of a PaaS offering is crucial for organisations PaaS selection and to let them assess the overall application security levels achieved. As from our use case scenario about BI applications, the data layer represents the asset of the BI user organisation interested on porting the BI system to PaaS environments. The portability of this layer to PaaS environments poses important security concerns for the organisation related to the trustworthiness of the PaaS provider in charge of storing the data layer. The portability process itself has to keep data integrity and let users access them effectively. For example some users work with the data from different geographical locations. We consider three BI portability models: (i) private PaaS model whereby the organisation wants to ensure total data ownership through self data security enforcement; (ii) public PaaS model whereby the organisation trust cloud provider offerings; and (iii) a hybrid PaaS model whereby the system can use more computational resources on demand while keeping sensitive data in the organisation premises.

Portability Dimension. PaaS offerings provide information on the different standards they comply to in order to ensure application and data portability or recommend portability methodologies. Standards range from cloud standards such as Open Cloud Computing Interface (OCCI) [8], The Topology and Orchestration Specification for Cloud Applications (TOSCA) [9], or Cloud Infrastructure Management Interface (CIMI) [10]; to PaaS standards such as OASIS Cloud Application Management for Platforms (CAMP) which help avoiding vendor lock-in.

Usability Offering. PaaS providers support application development with a set of rapid PaaS application development tools. PaaS vendors offer offerings with different levels of support. Furthermore, PaaS offerings application and database usability varies as well as the training and documentation they offer.

The usability dimension determines the application and database knowledge needed to maintain and extend an application deployed to a PaaS offering.

4 PaaS MarketPlace Broker Architecture

The PaaS marketplace broker architecture in Fig. 2 consists of three tiers: (i) the PaaS Front-End Tier; (ii) the PaaS Selection and Assessment Tier; and (iii) the PaaS Portability Tier.

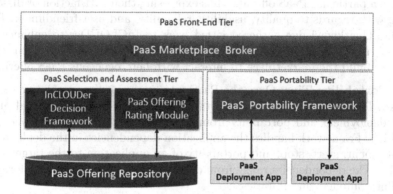

Fig. 2. PaaS marketplace architecture

PaaS Front-End Tier. The PaaS front-end tier comprises the Paas Marketplace Broker allowing end users to track PaaS offerings, services, interdependencies, and offers. The main goal of the marketplace broker is to make it easier, safer, and more productive for PaaS adopters to navigate, integrate, consume, extend, and maintain cloud services. In this respect, the broker offers a range of added-value services to both PaaS vendors and consumers. It supports seamless interaction between the PaaS consumer and the PaaS offering. Paas consumers interact with the PaaS marketplace broker to find available PaaS offerings which comply to their application's requirements and their criteria for porting their application. Additionally, the broker supports the actual application porting to PaaS environments.

PaaS Selection and Assessment Tier. The PaaS Selection and Assessment tier selects and assesses the existing PaaS offerings and contains three modules: *The InCLOUDer Decision Framework* [7] supports the PaaS offering selection and application porting. InCLOUDer discards PaaS offerings which cannot support the application to be ported. Further, InCLOUDer follows the Analytical Hierarchy Process [11] to recommend strategies to port an application to a different PaaS offering and rank all these porting alternatives. This module implements core functionalities such as PaaS offering discovery, PaaS Offering Analysis, and PaaS recommendation. InCLOUDers reasons according to the application's architecture, requirements, and constraints. It finds suitable PaaS offerings to port the application and maximises the criteria a particular organisation wants to achieve by porting that application to candidate PaaS offerings. InCLOUDer calculates the local rankings for every alternative based on the portability criteria. These criteria depend on the PaaS offerings dimensions described in Sect. 3. Finally, InCLOUDer produces a final rating incorporating the knowledge about the application, the portability criteria, and the PaaS offerings information. *The Paas Offering Rating Module* lets a Software SMEs Engineer rate a particular PaaS offering. Each engineer can leave a comment and rate a particular PaaS offering, thus expressing their satisfaction or dissatisfaction with regards to quality, usability, reliability, and user-friendliness of the offering. This knowledge gathered is fed back to InCLOUDer to enhance the PaaS offering description and selection. *The PaaS Offering Repository*, on top of which we build the marketplace to interact with heterogeneous PaaS offerings.

PaaS Portability Tier. Once the PaaS selection and assessment tier recommends a PaaS offering, the PaaS portability tier helps with the actual application deployment and portability from one PaaS vendor to another one. Our Portability Framework handles the application dependencies in the deployment, undeployment, start, stop, and portability of an application to the target PaaS provider. The dependencies range from operating system to executable formats, including compilers and libraries.

5   Discussion and Related Work

Selecting the PaaS offerings which best matches organisations' criteria to move applications to PaaS offerings is a current and interesting research topic [12]. In this respect, organisations interested in moving their applications to a PaaS environment need to identify PaaS vendors offerings and access a classification of them. Several research works address the multi-criteria cloud selection. In [4,13], the authors discuss a methodology for multi-criteria cloud selection as Maiya [14] proposes the use of cloud ontologies to be able to do so. Cloud4SOA [15] proposes the use of semantics to identify the best PaaS offerings and similar to our approach Cloud4SOA proposes a PaaS API for portability from one PaaS provider to another. However, Cloud4SOA differs from our approach in that it requires the annotation of each PaaS Provider offerings, and the annotation process of each offering is only feasible if there are established benchmark of PaaS offerings so that all PaaS vendors offerings can be taken into consideration. The mOSAIC project [16] focuses on application portability at both IaaS and PaaS using a Cloud ontology to analyse the offerings of the cloud and using similar to our approach uses a brokering mechanism, to search offerings requirements.

There are numerous efforts from Cloud API standardisation to unify incompatible APIs from PaaS providers CAMP [17], OCCI [8], CIMI [10]. However, the standard on portability is a concern when applications need to be migrated from one PaaS provider making use of one standard and another PaaS provider using a different standard. Porting from one provider to another one brings in these cases portability and standard lock-in issues. To address standard lock-in we use our middleware layer and port applications by leveraging an approach to allow cross-standard to interoperate with each other [18].

6   Conclusion and Futurework

In this paper we propose a PaaS Marketplace broker to allow PaaS vendors (in particular SMEs) to roll out PaaS offerings leveraging their competitive advantage and the quality of service delivered to their customers, making their offerings more attractive and improving their outreach to potential customers in the software industry. Our approach will facilitate the identification and deployment of business applications on the best-matching PaaS offerings using our InCLOUDer framework. InCLOUDer uses the hierarchy of PaaS offerings making it easier for organisations to weight different PaaS offerings to one another and ranks the best PaaS offerings in accordance with how determinant it is for the success of the application portability.

As future work we plan to address the challenges with respect to standard lock-in and security concerns as discussed in Sect. 5.

Acknowledgement. This work is part of the RELATE project supported by the European Commission under the 7th Framework Programme FP7 with Grant Agreement No. 264840 ITN and the PaasPort European Commision project under the 7th Framework Programme FP7-SME-2013-605193.

References

1. Joe, M.: Does platform as a service have interoperability issues (2010)
2. Borenstein, N., Blake, J.: Cloud computing standards: Where's the beef? IEEE Internet Comput. **15**, 74–78 (2011)
3. Juan-Verdejo, A., Surajbali, B., Baars, H., Kemper, H.G.: Moving business intelligence to cloud environments. In: Proceedings IEEE INFOCOMM, Cross Cloud 2014, Toronto (2014)
4. Kolb, S., Wirtz, G.: Towards application portability in platform as a service. In: Proceedings of the 8th IEEE International Symposium on Service-Oriented System Engineering (SOSE), IEEE, Oxford 7–10 April 2014
5. Strobl, J., Cave, E., Walley, T.: Data protection legislation: interpretation and barriers to research. Br. Med. J. (BMJ) **321**, 890–892 (2000)
6. Fleurey, F., Steel, J., Baudry, B.: Validation in model-driven engineering: testing model transformations. In: Proceedings - 2004 First International Workshop on Model, Design and Validation, pp. 29–40. IEEE (2004)
7. Juan-Verdejo, A., Zschaler, S., Surajbali, B., Baars, H., Kemper, H.G.: Inclouder: effective partial migration of pre-existing applications to the appropriate cloud environment. In: Proceedings 40th Euromicro Conference on Software Engineering and Advanced Applications (SEAA 2014) (2014)
8. Edmonds, O.W.A.: Open cloud computing interface-infrastructure. Deliverable GFD **184**, 06 (2011)

9. Binz, T., Breitenbücher, U., Haupt, F., Kopp, O., Leymann, F., Nowak, A., Wagner, S.: OpenTOSCA – a runtime for TOSCA-based cloud applications. In: Basu, S., Pautasso, C., Zhang, L., Fu, X. (eds.) ICSOC 2013. LNCS, vol. 8274, pp. 692–695. Springer, Heidelberg (2013)
10. Initiative, C.M.: Cloud infrastructure management interface (2014)
11. Saaty, T.L., Vargas, L.G.: Models, Methods, Concepts & Applications of the Analytic Hierarchy Process. International Series in Operations Research & Management Science, vol. 175. Springer, Heidelberg (2001)
12. Petcu, D.: Portability and interoperability between clouds: challenges and case study. In: Abramowicz, W., Llorente, I.M., Surridge, M., Zisman, A., Vayssière, J. (eds.) ServiceWave 2011. LNCS, vol. 6994, pp. 62–74. Springer, Heidelberg (2011)
13. Hussain, F.K., Hussain, O.K., et al.: Towards multi-criteria cloud service selection. In: 2011 Fifth International Conference on Innovative Mobile and Internet Services in Ubiquitous Computing (IMIS), pp. 44–48. IEEE (2011)
14. Maiya, M., Dasari, S., Yadav, R., Shivaprasad, S., Milojicic, D.: Quantifying manageability of cloud platforms. In: 2012 IEEE 5th International Conference on Cloud Computing (CLOUD), pp. 993–995. IEEE (2012)
15. D'Andria, F., Bocconi, S., Cruz, J.G., Ahtes, J., Zeginis, D.: Cloud4soa: multi-cloud application management across PaaS offerings. In: Proceedings of the 2012 14th International Symposium on Symbolic and Numeric Algorithms for Scientific Computing, pp. 407–414. IEEE Computer Society (2012)
16. Petcu, D., Di Martino, B., Venticinque, S., Rak, M., Máhr, T., Lopez, G.E., Brito, F., Cossu, R., Stopar, M., Šperka, S., et al.: Experiences in building a mosaic of clouds. J. Cloud Comput. **2**, 1–22 (2013)
17. OASIS: Cloud application management for platforms version 1.1 draft 03 (2014)
18. Bromberg, Y.D., Grace, P., Réveillère, L.: Starlink: runtime interoperability between heterogeneous middleware protocols. In: 2011 31st International Conference on Distributed Computing Systems (ICDCS), pp. 446–455. IEEE (2011)

Towards a Classification of Multiple-Cloud Computing Concepts and Terms

Hassan Saad Alqahtani[✉] and Ghita Kouadri-Mostefaoui

UCMK, University of Bedfordshire, Milton Keynes, UK
{hassan.alqahtani,Ghita.Kouadri-Mostefaoui}
@beds.ac.uk

Abstract. In order to enhance the quality of the delivered services, dependency avoidance, and operational costs optimization, the *multiple-cloud* computing emerged. The complexity of *multiple-clouds* causes a lot of opacity in the definitions and classifications. This paper attempts to provide an accurate definition of the *multiple-clouds* and, a classification of the available types based on a set of pre-defined criteria. It also outlines the differences between the terms that have been used to refer to the *multiple-cloud* computing concept.

Keywords: Multiple-clouds · Ontology definition · Multi-cloud · Federated cloud

1 Introduction

Cloud computing has become the optimum solution for many businesses and private users. The advantages of cloud computing such as; pay as use, elasticity, on-demand, remote access, and resource pooling [13] make it the best choice for storing data and providing functionality. In order to optimize the operational costs, improve the delivered quality of services and promote independency, businesses and private users need to use more than one cloud as their service providers [16]. This infrastructure is known as the *multiple-clouds*. It refers to the ability of two or more distributed cloud services to collaborate and work together to be consumed in serial or simultaneously [8]. The literature on cloud computing highlights a number of terms referring to the cloud-computing collaboration [8]; these terms include; cloud of the clouds [1], sky computing [10], aggregated cloud [14], and so on. It is worth mentioning that *multiple-clouds* computing is a newly founded area and it is still suffering from a lot of opacity; there are various concepts and forms of multiple clouding; for that reason, the majority of presented definitions are too generic and do not provide accurate specifications. This paper aims to clarify the concept of multiple clouding and provide a clear classification of *multiple-clouds* types based on a set of selected criteria.

Section 2 discusses our motivation for this research. In the following sections, we review existing literature on multiple-clouds computing focusing on the definitions of the new concepts related to the field. Based on that, we devise a set of criteria (Sect. 3)

© Springer International Publishing Switzerland 2015
G. Ortiz and C. Tran (Eds.): ESOCC 2014, CCIS 508, pp. 271–277, 2015.
DOI: 10.1007/978-3-319-14886-1_25

that will be used to provide a first classification of multiple-clouds concepts (Sect. 4). Section 5 concludes the paper with a discussion of future work.

2   Motivation

Shifting from a single cloud to the *multiple-clouds* becomes necessary for many businesses and customers. The *multiple-clouds* is, however, a relatively new field and therefore, no standard definitions neither classifications that state the features, advantages, disadvantages, and requirements of the existing multiple-clouds models exist. In other words, a potential user of the multi-clouds will be confronted with a wideband of terms that are used for referring to the different *multiple-clouds* models. Many of the used terms do not properly highlight the key features of a specific multi-clouds model. The problem is not limited to the absence of clarity in models definitions; a user will also find out that more than one term are used to represent exactly the same model.

3   Criteria

Many criteria might be used to develop a *multiple-clouds* classification; for instance, ownership, management, charge, control, migration, and so on. In this paper, we focus on harmony and inter-operability between the different instances of the multiple-clouds, as we believe it's the added-value of the latter upon the single cloud. This brings forth three main aspects:

(1) Agreement [5]
(2) Collaboration types [5], and
(3) Migration methods [11, 15].

In regards to 'agreement' categorization, two criteria emerge:

1. *Prior-agreement:* the cloud service providers have a formal agreement between them, and that agreement identifies all the collaboration aspects, responsibilities and privileges. The end-user will consume these clouds resources/capabilities as a single cloud.
2. *No prior-agreement:* the cloud service providers are not bound by an a priori agreement, and the third party (generally the end-user) negotiates with the providers independently in order to build the multi-clouds and use it.

The collaboration aspect brings out the following three criteria.

1. *Loosely coupled*, which usually occurs between independent clouds. For example, a private and a public one. The best example for this is the hybrid cloud. In this case, the private cloud manager has complete control over the private cloud; but has very limited control over the public one. In some cases, there is no control over the remote cloud at all. This type of collaboration is needed when the resources have to be expanded – even temporarily – to deal with the private cloud's overload. It is also used by small organizations in order to reduce the operational costs.

2. **Partially coupled** that occurs when two or more independent clouds have an official agreement to establish pre-defined collaboration framework. Regardless of the collaboration level, this agreement should define all the collaborative resources, terms, conditions, and control privileges. In this level, the control and monitor information will be exchanged between the clouds, and some clouds will have a defined level of control over the other clouds. The partially-coupled model is suitable for organizations that require some control over the different remote clouds/resources.
3. **Tightly coupled**, which applies to clouds that belong to the same organization, which allows advanced control over the collaborating clouds, which means that the cloud manager has all the privileges for monitoring, auditing, managing, creating images, and configuring the clouds. This model is optimum for systems that need a sort of centralized management.

   "Cloud migration is the process of moving data, applications or other business elements from an organization's onsite computers to the cloud, or moving them from one cloud environment to another" [17].

In regards to the migration aspect, and depending on (a) what is being migrated: service or application, and also on (b) how migration is being performed: one time or real time, four criteria have been identified:

1. **Service migration,** this is when the user consumes the remote cloud service using one of the following stacks: Software as a Service (SaaS), Platform as a Service (PaaS) and/or Infrastructure as a Service (IaaS).
2. **Application migration,** when only applications migrate to the remote cloud.
3. **One time migration;** refers to the migration process done only once, by redeploying/ rewriting the data/applications. Also, there is a sort of limited synchronization process that takes place.
4. **Real time migration;** in this case, a synchronization process between all the involved clouds takes place as the applications/data is being moved to the cloud in real-time.

4   Classification

The following classification is developed according to the previous criteria. The terms that define generic concepts and the ones that lack definitions are not included in the current classification. In order to enhance and facilitate comparing between the different cloud models, Table 1 summarizes the developed classification based on the used criteria.

4.1   Intra Cloud (Clouds of Clouds)

The intra-cloud computing happens when there are two different cloud services or more, that belong to the same cloud service provider and that collaborate together [18]. Some literature [3] defines the intra-cloud as a cloud-networking method rather than *multiple-clouds* model. The intra-cloud is a type of internal collaboration to deliver the required services.

4.2 Hybrid Cloud

The hybrid-cloud has been defined by NIST as deployment method other than the public and private cloud [8]. The hybrid-cloud model is used when the private cloud cannot deal with the processing and/or data load. In this case, the private cloud needs to expand the resources/capabilities to achieve the agreed service level, and that can be done by using public cloud resources/capabilities for a specific period of time [1, 4, 12]. The problem with the hybrid-cloud model is the absence of security, because being public will threaten the private cloud directly and exposes its resources/capabilities and data to danger [4]. In this model, there is no need for prior-agreement, and the clouds will be loosely coupled. Technically, the remote resources will not be associated all the time for the same private cloud, and the private cloud must release these resources after a period of time; in order to associate with other customers. For that, it is suitable for one-time application migration.

4.3 Federated Cloud

The federated-cloud is a form of inter-operability cloud computing, when two or more independent cloud-service providers agreed to share their infrastructure and collaborate together for sharing these resources/capabilities and deliver the required services with the agreed Quality of Service (QoS) [5]. Technically, the federated-cloud is preferred for governmental uses for several reasons, such as the high cost of the required infra-structure and operation and the ownership problems [2]. The federated-cloud could be categorized into two categories based on the communication (interact) methods. Namely, centralized and peer-to-peer methods [14]. In this model, there is a prior-agreement between the cloud service providers; and the clouds collaborative level and migration will vary between the centralized and peer-to-peer.

Centralized federated-cloud. In this case, the federated-cloud uses a central entity as a connection/control node between the clouds. The central entity will be responsible of resource allocation, resource optimization, load balancing, cloud interconnecting, moni-toring, and management [6]. This type provides more control over the federated-cloud because of the central entity; also, the operational cost will be less than the operational cost of the peer-to-peer model. The centralized federated-cloud model provides only a single communication channel between each independent cloud and the central entity. This implies losing the availability of the federated-cloud if the central entity is down; or, isolating the cloud that losses its connection channel to the central entity.

Peer-to-peer federated-cloud. In the peer-to-peer model, each cloud will be connected to the other directly, and all the management, load balancing, communication, charging, and monitoring processes will be embedded in each independent cloud [19]. This model will provide the user the highest availability and performance levels because of the redundancy and dynamicity in the communication channels between the clouds [7, 9]. On the other hand, the operational cost will be very high, and it is caused by:

- The number of commutation channels that each cloud uses.
- The need to keep the status of each cloud synchronised.
- The number of operational processes that used to ensure load balancing.
- The exchange of data needed in order to calculate the optimum resources/capabilities.

As a result, this model might not be an efficient solution for a large number of clouds, because as much as the cloud number increases, the operational cost will increase as well. In case of losing the direct connectivity between two independent clouds, there are additional channels that could be used, and the user request could be handled easily. Also, losing the availability of an independent cloud will not impact on the system availability, because all the requests that were assigned to the unavailable cloud will be directed to an available one.

4.4 Multi-Cloud

In the multi-cloud computing model, there are more than one independent cloud that will be used to execute the requested tasks through consuming the provided resources/ capabilities; and here the customers will take the onuses of resources/capabilities managing, task scheduling, and load balancing [5]. The multi-cloud can be applied through the private cloud, regardless of the ownership identity (governmental/private). Similar to the federated-cloud, the multi-cloud could be categorized into services and libraries. In this model, there is a prior-agreement, which will vary between the services and libraries models. In addition, the collaboration level varies between loosely and partially.

Multi-cloud services. In the multi-cloud service model, the cloud-service providers have to define and agree on the rules for the execution and delivery processes. After that, the developers will develop a service, which will be used to deliver the multi-cloud services [4, 6]. The developed service will work more like a mediator between the users and the multi-cloud. The problem with this model is that in the case of the absence of a multi-cloud service, this may lead to losing the multi-cloud availability completely.

Multi-cloud libraries. In this model, the users develop their own service broker through a unified Application Programming Interface (API) [11]. The developed broker will be in the form of libraries and be embedded in the users' access point (host) [15]. This model offers an availability level higher than the previous model, and that is caused by associating the multi-cloud library with the user's machine. However, the users must be qualified to develop their multi-cloud libraries.

In the following, Table 1 provides a comparison between the different *multiple-clouds* models based on the criteria discussed earlier.

Table 1. *Multiple-clouds* models compasion

Criteria\Model	Intra	Hybrid	Centralized	Peer-to-Peer	Services	Libraries
Prior-Agreement	√		√	√		
No prior-Agreement		√			√	√
Loosely coupled		√				√
Partially coupled				√	√	
Tightly coupled	√		√			
Service Migration	√		√	√	√	
App Migration		√				√
Real-time Migration	√		√			
One-time Migration		√		√	√	√

5 Conclusion and Future Work

Being an emerging and new field, *multiple-clouds* suffers from a lack of standard terminology and concise ontology. There is no clear, or agreed definition nor are there clear
classifications criteria for the different multiple-clouds types. The wide diversity of the
developed frameworks and lack of standardization encourages the proliferation of new
terms leading to more confusion. This paper attempts to provide a first classification of
multiple-clouds aspects based on a set of identified criteria including *agreement, collaboration* and *migration*. This effort aims at providing a framework for existing multiple-
clouds models. In addition, there are a number of definitions that have been explained
and discussed, in order to provide a clear understanding of these concepts and to help
distinguish between them. As future work, we intend to include more aspects in order
to widen the classification. For example, the portability aspect need to be explored and
investigated. Finally, it is worth mentioning that the proposed classification and selected
criteria are not definitive and require more development in order to enhance the classification accuracy and cover future multi-clouds models.

References

1. Bessani, A., Correia, M., Quaresma, B., André, F., Sousa, P.: DepSky: Dependable and secure
storage in a cloud-of-clouds. ACM Trans. Storage (TOS) **9**(4), 12 (2013)
2. Buyya, R., Ranjan, R., Calheiros, R.N.: InterCloud: utility-oriented federation of cloud
computing environments for scaling of application services. In: Hsu, C.-H., Yang, L.T., Park,
J.H., Yeo, S.-S. (eds.) Algorithms and architectures for parallel processing. LNCS, vol. 6081.
Springer, Heidelberg (2010)
3. Cisco. Cisco InterCloud: Enable a Hybrid Cloud (2014). http://www.cisco.com/c/en/us/td/
docs/solutions/Hybrid_Cloud/InterCloud/InterCloud.pdf

4. Elmroth, E., Tordsson, J., Hernández, F., Ali-Eldin, A., Svärd, P., Sedaghat, M., et al.: Self-management challenges for multi-cloud architectures. In: Hsu, C.-H., Yang, L.T., Park, J.H., Yeo, S.-S. (eds.) Towards a Service-Based Internet. LNCS, vol. 6994. Springer, Heidelberg (2011)

5. Ferrer, A.J., Hernández, F., Tordsson, J., Elmroth, E., Ali-Eldin, A., Zsigri, C., et al.: OPTIMIS: a holistic approach to cloud service provisioning. Future Gener. Comput. Syst. **28**(1), 66–77 (2012)

6. Grozev, N., Buyya, R.: Inter-cloud architectures and application brokering: Taxonomy and survey. Softw. Pract. Experience **44**(3), 369–390 (2014)

7. Hassan, M.M., Hossain, M.S., Sarkar, A.J., Huh, E.: Cooperative game-based distributed resource allocation in horizontal dynamic cloud federation platform. Inf. Syst. Frontiers 1–20 (2012)

8. Hogan, M., Liu, F., Sokol, A., Tong, J.: Nist cloud computing standards roadmap, p. 35. NIST Special Publication, New York (2011)

9. Li, J., Li, B., Du, Z., Meng, L.: CloudVO: Building a secure virtual organization for multiple clouds collaboration. In: 2010 11th ACIS International Conference on Software Engineering Artificial Intelligence Networking and Parallel/Distributed Computing (SNPD), pp. 181–186 (2010)

10. Keahey, K., Tsugawa, M., Matsunaga, A., Fortes, J.A.B.: Sky computing. Internet Comput. IEEE **13**(5), 43–51 (2009)

11. Kecskemeti, G., Kertesz, A., Marosi, A., Kacsuk, P.: Interoperable resource management for establishing federated clouds, Theory and Practice, pp. 18–35. IGI Global, Hershey (2012)

12. Leavitt, N.: Hybrid clouds move to the forefront. Computer **46**(5), 15–18 (2013)

13. Mell, P., Grance, T.: The NIST definition of cloud computing. Nat. Inst. Stand. Technol. **53**(6), 50 (2009)

14. Moreno-Vozmediano, R., Montero, R.S., Llorente, I.M.: IaaS cloud architecture: From virtualized datacenters to federated cloud infrastructures. Computer **45**(12), 65–72 (2012)

15. Ostermann, S., Plankensteiner, K., Bodner, D., Kraler, G., Prodan, R.: Integration of an event-based simulation framework into a scientific workflow execution environment for grids and clouds. In: Abramowicz, W., Llorente, I.M., Surridge, M., Zisman, A., Vayssière, J. (eds.) ServiceWave 2011. LNCS, vol. 6994, pp. 1–13. Springer, Heidelberg (2011)

16. Riteau, P.: Building dynamic computing infrastructures over distributed clouds. In: 2011 First International Symposium on Network Cloud Computing and Applications (NCCA), pp. 127–130 (2011)

17. SearchCLousApplications (2014). Cloud migration definition (2014). http://searchcloudapplications.techtarget.com/definition/cloud-migration. Accessed 13 July 2014

18. Chen, S., Nepal, S., Liu, R.: Secure connectivity for intra-cloud and inter-cloud communication. In: 2011 40th International Conference on Parallel Processing Workshops (ICPPW), pp. 154–159 (2011)

19. Villari, M., Tusa, F., Celesti, A., Puliafito, A.: How to federate vision clouds through saml/shibboleth authentication. Service-oriented and cloud computing, pp. 259–274. Springer (2012)

Towards a Flexible Deployment of Multi-cloud Applications Based on TOSCA and CAMP

Jose Carrasco$^{(\boxtimes)}$, Javier Cubo, and Ernesto Pimentel

Departamento Lenguajes Y Ciencias de la Computación,
Universidad de Málaga, Málaga, Spain
{josec,cubo,ernesto}@lcc.uma.es

Abstract. Cloud Computing platforms offer diverse services and capabilities with own features. Hence, the provider services could be used by end users to compose a heterogeneous context of multiple cloud platforms in order to deploy their cloud applications made up of a set of modules, according to the best capabilities of the cloud providers. However, this is an ideal scenario, since the cloud platforms are being conducted in an isolated way by presenting many interoperability and portability restrictions, which complicate the integration of diverse provider services to achieve an heterogeneous deployment of multi-cloud applications. In this ongoing work, we present an approach based on model transformation to deploy multi-cloud applications by reusing standardization efforts related to the management and deployment of cloud applications. Specifically, using mechanisms specified by both standards, TOSCA and CAMP, we propose a methodology to describe the topology and distribution of modules of a cloud application and to deploy the interconnected modules over heterogeneous clouds. We illustrate our idea using a running example.

Keywords: Heterogeneous cloud · Cloud application · Multi-deployment · Model transformation · TOSCA · CAMP

1 Introduction

Cloud Computing is a new paradigm which has become increasingly popular in the last years. It defines a model for enabling convenient and on-demand network access to a shared pool of configurable computing resources that can be rapidly provisioned [1]. In this model the providers expose these resources as several services through a cloud platform classified in various levels (IaaS, PaaS, SaaS). They can develop, deploy, and sell cloud applications globally without the need of significant investments in IT infrastructure. The provided services are used by the clients to deploy their applications and systems on concrete provides. Hence, the users could select the services from several providers whose properties

Work partially supported by projects TIN2012-35669, funded by Spanish Ministry MINECO, FEDER; P11-TIC-7659 funded by Andalusian Gov; FP7-610531 SeaClouds funded by EU; and Univ. Málaga, Campus Excelencia Int. Andalucía Tech.

G. Ortiz and C. Tran (Eds.): ESOCC 2014, CCIS 508, pp. 278–286, 2015.
DOI: 10.1007/978-3-319-14886-1_26

and capabilities fit with the requirements of the multi-module cloud application, achieving a flexible deployment context that fully adapts the deployment and execution of the application. However, this is a complex task, since the cloud platforms are being conducted in an isolated way by presenting many interoperability and portability restrictions and offering similar resources in a different manner. Each provider defines its own API to the exposed services, its non-functional requirements, QoS, add-ons and so on. As a result, cloud developers are often locked in a specific set of services from a concrete cloud environment. Thus, it is complicated to integrate heterogeneous provider services to achieve a multi-deployment of a cloud application [2]. Currently, several organizations propose different approaches to mitigate these issues through the homogenization and normalization of the cloud application descriptions and management. Specifically, there exist two OASIS standards which pretend to solve some of the problems related with portability, automated deployment, interoperability and management of cloud applications: TOSCA (Topology and Orchestration Specification for Cloud Applications) [3] and CAMP (Cloud Application Management for Platforms) [4]. Both standards specify a particular methodology to describe and wrap the cloud application structure (components and relationships), and how they must be orchestrated (by means of a plan) in a portable way to increase a vendor-neutral ecosystem. Moreover, they describe the mechanisms which must be implemented by the clouds to support standard-based application deployment and management. Nevertheless, the standard efforts do not focus on getting an heterogeneous multi-cloud solution, so distributing a complex application over multiple cloud service providers is still a challenging task [5]. TOSCA and CAMP are emergent standards and they do not have official implementations yet. We can consider available approaches that support a large set of characteristics defined by these standards, i.e., OpenTOSCA Environment [6] (for TOSCA) and Brooklyn [7] (for CAMP).

However, these approaches have some disadvantages. On the one hand, although TOSCA is a good option to represent the application topology and the orchestration, the management of a possible TOSCA-compliant deployment (for example, using OpenTOSCA) would be a complex task, since the topology and the orchestration plan should be modified when some module of the application is migrated to a different target provider. On the other hand, although the CAMP-compliant solutions are not mainly focused on obtaining a multi-deployment, they present an appropriate set of properties to obtain this goal following a unified API which wraps the interface of the cloud providers (for example, Brooklyn which uses jClouds [8]). Nevertheless, CAMP lacks of a topology specification, which is crucial to maintain application model in case of monitoring and reconfiguration actions need to be performed over the distribution of the application. In this ongoing work, we discuss our proposal for combining the advantages of both TOSCA and CAMP specifications and their respective approaches. The main contributions of our idea are: (i) to define a flexible methodology to perform heterogeneous deployment of multi-cloud applications, (ii) to analyse the architectural and technical concepts needed to combine both TOSCA and CAMP specifications, (iii) to address vendor lock-in and portability issues, and (iv) to comply with (and contribute to) major standards for cloud interoperability.

The rest of this paper is structured as follows. Section 2 exposes the motivation and challenges of our approach. In Sect. 3, we present our proposal based on the combination of TOSCA- and CAMP-compliant solutions to provide a flexible multi-cloud deployment. In Sect. 4, we briefly discuss the advantages of our work with respect to current cloud initiatives, and we present some future work.

2   Motivation and Challenges

In this section, we motivate our proposal presenting the challenges to be tackle to deploy cloud applications over heterogenous cloud providers.

2.1   Motivating Example

To illustrate our work, we introduce an example related to an *Online Retailing Application*, composed of four modules: a main Webpage to access the application, two databases (one for the users and another one for the products' stock), and a payment module.

This application could be deployed as a whole on a provider in IaaS or PaaS level, Google (https://cloud.google.com), Amazon (http://aws.amazon.com), HP Cloud (http://www.hpcloud.com), etc. These Cloud providers offer a range of different technologies each appropriate for particular types of applications. So, users can access computing resources in a dynamic, flexible and scalable manner to deploy the mentioned cloud-based application, where each computing resources has its own capabilities, constraints, life cycle and specification (*e.g.* pricing policies, Service Level Agreement (SLAs)). Also, the modules of the application possess own features and requirement. In this sense, it would be interesting to develop a methodology capable of selecting the provider services whose specification fit with the application's requirements and features in order to compose the best heterogeneous deployment context for the distribution of the modules. A large number of companies are trying to simplify the speed and adoption of their products and services to the cloud. The main issue is the lack of interoperability among different vendor approaches, which complicate the deployment over several providers simultaneously.

2.2   Challenges

To perform the multi-deployment, our approach addresses these main challenges:

- **Topology specification.** An application is composed by several modules and relationships, which is essential to maintain the knowledge about the application structure, dependencies among modules and how they are related. We pretend to specify the topology and distribution using a TOSCA-compliant methodology, which allows the maintenance of the application model if some redistribution is required.

- **Unified interface of cloud providers.** Currently, the application developers need to know the interface of the final cloud providers where their applications will be deployed. Our approach proposes to solve this necessity by unifying the features of the heterogeneous platforms by means of a CAMP-compliant approach.
- **Interoperability and portability issues.** In an heterogeneous distribution context, interoperability and portability problems occur. Using our proposal based on the unified interface, the deployment will be in charge of solving these issues related to the heterogeneity of cloud providers, managing the services needed by the application's modules in an homogeneous manner.
- **Scalability and elasticity resources.** Our deployment process allows the users to consider the scalability and elasticity advantages of cloud provider in order to the best deployment scenario.

3 Proposal in a Nutshell

We present our proposal for the TOSCA- and CAMP-compliant multi-cloud deployment.

3.1 Heterogeneous Deployment Using TOSCA and CAMP

As shown in Fig. 1, our methodology consists of two phases well-defined. Initially, in the first step, we propose to specify the full application topology using TOSCA methodology through the OpenTOSCA environment, specifically the Winery tool (TOSCA-compliant), which allows the description of the applications structure in an exhaustive and user-friendly graphic way. Moreover, we also propose to enrich the TOSCA specification by including information about the final providers where each component of the application will be deployed, with the purpose of facilitating the orchestration according to the expected multi-cloud distribution. In the second step, the application will be distributed over the target clouds through the deployment mechanisms used by Brooklyn (CAMP-compliant). In order to solve the connection between both specification,

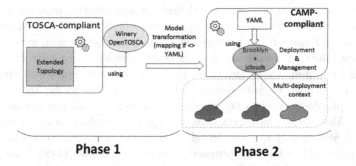

Fig. 1. Overview of our TOSCA- and CAMP-compliant multi-deployment.

we propose a transformation methodology to adapt the TOSCA-compliant specification defined to the CAMP-compliant specification expected by Brooklyn.

3.2 Phase 1: Topology Description and Orchestration

TOSCA allows the specification of a detailed application topology using an XML-based file. We use TOSCA to obtain a full description of the application modeling its components (application's modules) and dependencies. Then, TOSCA description is composed by several components which present types, properties, requirements, capabilities, and relationships among them. Thus, modifying, deleting or adding some components could provoke an error-prone task due to the need of maintaining the consistency of the initial topology description. In order to solve this problem, we propose to use the Winery tool [9], developed by the OpenTOSCA Team. This tool allows the representation of the application's modules through forms and the composition of the topology in a graphical way by means of the drag-and-drop technique. In Fig. 2 is presented the topology for our running example using Winery.

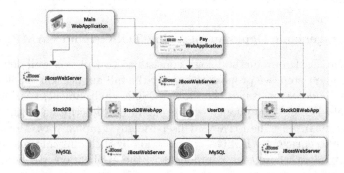

Fig. 2. TOSCA topology for the Online Retailing Application using Winery.

Although we have mentioned the TOSCA expressiveness, this standard does not define in the topology any property to specify the target provider to deploy the application's modules. Instead, it defines an orchestration plan and the implementation artifacts to specify the deployment operations. However, this information does not appear into the topology description, so we need a methodology which allows the clear specification of the final providers. Also, currently, the definition and maintenance of an orchestration plan is a complex and error-prone task.The plans have to fully define each necessary step to deploy and configure the application taking into account all properties and requirements of the providers. Morever, if the target cloud changes, the definition of the mentioned steps must also change in order to reference to the services exposed by the new selected cloud. Therefore, we propose an extension of the TOSCA topology to allow the inclusion of the final providers which are needed to perform the multi-deployment orchestration. In the following text we can see as the NodeTemplate defines a new item to define the **location** where the node (representing the application's module) has to be deployed. To exemplify this extension, the next text models the **UserDBWebApp** by specifying the cloud provider 'AWS' as location.

```
1  <NodeTemplate id="xs:ID" name="xs:string"? type="xs:QName"
2    ...
3    <Properties>
4            XML fragment
5    </Properties>
6    <location provider= "xs:string">
7    ...
8  </NodeTemplate>
```

```
1  <NodeTemplate id="UserDBWebApp" name="User Web App"
2    type="ns3:UserDBWebApplication">
3    <Properties>
4        <ns3:UserDBWebApplicationProperties
5        ...
6        </ns3:UserDBWebApplicationProperties>
7    </Properties>
8    <location>aws-ec2:us-west-2</location>
9  </NodeTemplate>
```

Note that the location denition could be modeled like a property in the Node Templates. This could be very usefull to avoid a large negotation of the consortium to approve the standard extension and the providers could feel free to support this feature implementing the necessary mechanisms in their platforms. However, although the mentioned approach has several advantages, our goal goes beyond, by defining an extension of the standard to ensure the performance of the multi-deployment and allow the correct denition of the used providers.

3.3 Phase 2: Transformation Model and Deployment

The second phase of our proposal is in charge of distributing the application's modules over the different target providers. To tackle these issues, we build this process using a CAMP-compliant environment to take advantage of the homogeneity features aimed by the standard. Then, we use Brooklyn, which (in the latest releases) allows the description of a YAML-based multi-deployment plan. We have defined the topology using TOSCA in the first phase, since CAMP lacks of a topology specification. Therefore, we need to unify the TOSCA-compliant topology definition and the CAMP-compliant deployment mechanism. We propose a model transformation to obtain a Brooklyn YAML plan from TOSCA topology description, by means of two possible transformation processes. The first one is

Table 1. Transformation pattern between TOSCA and Brooklyn (CAMP)

TOSCA	YAML CAMP
JBoss	brooklyn.entity.webapp.jboss.JBoss7Server
Apache Tomcat	brooklyn.entity.webapp.tomcat.TomcatServer
Jetty Server	brooklyn.entity.webapp.jetty.Jetty6Server
MongoDB Server	brooklyn.entity.nosql.mongodb.MongoDB
Cassandra Data Base	brooklyn.entity.nosql.cassandra.CassandraNode
MySQL Data Base	brooklyn.entity.database.mysql.MySqlNode
Postgre	brooklyn.entity.database.postgresql.PostgreSqlNode
Cluster	brooklyn.entity.webapp.ControlledDynamicWebAppCluster

based on an agnostic graph, as depicted in Fig. 3. Taking advantage of TOSCA
topology definition (similar to a graph structure) we can generate an intermediate graph containing all the details of the application's modules and their
relationships. From this agnostic graph we can generate the final (orchestration)
plan deployment expected by several technologies, *e.g.*, the CAMP-compliant
used in this work, Brooklyn. This task is performed following a set of transformation patterns from the TOSCA-compliant to CAMP-compliant elements
(see Table 1). The second proposal is based in meta-model transformations to
expose a formal methodology, as shown in Fig. 4. In this context, it is necessary
to define the meta-model of TOSCA-extended and the Brooklyn plan, together
with the ATL rules required to transform a concrete (topology) TOSCA model
into a Brooklyn YAML concrete plan.

4   Discussion and Conclusions

In this section, we mention some projects, initiatives and standards in the same
scope of our proposal, with the intention of briefly discussing about the contributions of our approach, and finally, we present the future work.

There are several initiatives and standards that target services deployed on
the cloud using different approaches, with the consequence that software developers need to either use special APIs or programming models to code their applications, or to model them using project-specific domain languages. The Broker@
Cloud project (http://www.broker-cloud.eu/) aims at helping enterprises to
move to the cloud while enforcing quality control on the developed services.
The PaaSage project (http://www.paasage.eu/) also intends to match application requirements against platform characteristics and make deployment recom-
mendations and dynamic mapping of components to the platform(s) selected.
The aim of the Cloud4SOA project (http://www.cloud4soa.eu/) is to solve
the semantic interoperability issues that exist in current cloud platforms and
infrastructures. The mOSAIC project (http://www.mosaic-cloud.eu/) allows
applications can be deployed on different IaaS using a sort of mOSAIC virtual

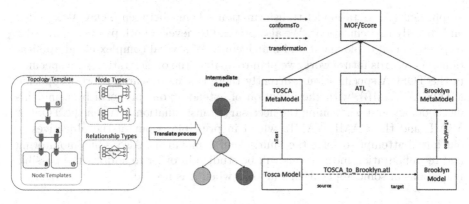

Fig. 3. Abstraction of the TOSCA topology using an agnostic graph.

Fig. 4. Meta-model transformation between TOSCA and Brooklyn.

machine. The REMICS project (http://www.remics.eu/) focuses its work on developing advanced model-driven methodology and tools for the reuse and migration of legacy applications to interoperable Cloud services. Cloud standardisation is one of the most active lines in Cloud research. Relevant associations like IEEE or OASIS are working on standards in order to tackle the interoperability and portability between Cloud platforms. The Guide for Cloud Portability and Interoperability Profiles is among the active IEEE projects. TOSCA and CAMP are two OASIS standard concentrating efforts in reducing the deployment and management of cloud applications. These and other Cloud standards, such as DMTF Cloud Infrastructure Management Interface, can be found in the Cloud Standards Wiki (http://cloud-standards.org/). In the scope of commercial solutions, we can find some new platforms and open source initiatives that are working on providing flexibility to users allowing the IaaS selection, and in some cases the migration over some specific PaaSes, such as the Cloud Foundry Core (http://core.cloudfoundry.org/), which defines a baseline of common capabilities to promote Cloud portability across instances of Cloud Foundry.

A distinguish aspect of our approach is that we propose a flexible multi-cloud deployment and management via orchestration and therefore it does not require code modifications to existing services. Thus, we base on the two OASIS standards TOSCA and CAMP to represent the application topology and orchestrate the distribution, and to deploy the modules of the application in multiple and heterogeneous platforms, respectively. Indeed, TOSCA provides a powerful modelling language to describe the structure of an application as a typed topology graph, in a portable and vendor-agnostic way. Also, the use of TOSCA topology templates (and of TOSCA node types) to represent an application topology simplifies its management and fosters the reusability of cloud services. Moreover, CAMP offers a unification in the interfaces of the cloud platforms which allows the management of heterogeneous providers's features in an homogeneous way.

Currently, we are formalising the two proposed model transformation options presented in Sect. 3: (i) Abstraction of the TOSCA topology using an agnostic graph, and (ii) Meta-model transformation schema between TOSCA-extended and Brooklyn specifications. We also pretend to develop both processes, in order to perform real deployment and management of several complex cloud applications. As regards future work, we plan to analyse the orchestration plan specified in the TOSCA specification (currently there is some research efforts proposing a TOSCA YAML), with the intention of extending our proposal by using this methodology and performing the necessary transformation between the TOSCA YAML and the CAMP YAML, which in principle is out of the objectives of our initial attempt to solve the multi-cloud deployment. Also, some monitoring and reconfiguration mechanisms will be studied in order to address the possible migrations of some application's module when it is needed.

References

1. Mell, P., Grance, T.: The NIST Definition of Cloud Computing. NIST, Gaithersburg (2011). http://csrc.nist.gov/publications/nistpubs/800-145/SP800-145.pdf
2. Petcu, D., Macariu, G., Panica, S., Craciun, C.: Portable cloud applications: from theory to practice. Future Gener. Comput. Syst. **29**, 1417–1430 (2013)
3. OASIS: TOSCA 1.0 (Topology and Orchestration Spec for Cloud Applications), V1.0 (2012). http://docs.oasis-open.org/tosca/TOSCA/v1.0/TOSCA-v1.0.pdf
4. OASIS: CAMP 1.0 (Cloud Application Management for Platforms), V1.0 (2012). http://docs.oasis-open.org/camp/camp-spec/v1.1/camp-spec-v1.1.html/
5. Leymann, F., Fehling, C., Mietzner, R., Nowak, A., Dustdar, S.: Moving applications to the cloud: an approach based on application model enrichment. Int. J. Coop. Inf. Syst. **20**, 307–356 (2011)
6. IAAS: OpenTOSCA (2012). http://www.opentosca.org
7. CloudSoft: Brooklyn project (2012). http://brooklyncentral.github.io/
8. Apache: jClouds Project page (2014). http://jclouds.apache.org/
9. Kopp, O., Binz, T., Breitenbücher, U., Leymann, F.: Winery – a modeling tool for TOSCA-Based cloud applications. In: Basu, S., Pautasso, C., Zhang, L., Fu, X. (eds.) ICSOC 2013. LNCS, vol. 8274, pp. 700–704. Springer, Heidelberg (2013)

Author Index